Communications
in Computer and Information Science 1959

Editorial Board Members

Rationale

The CCIS series is devoted to the publication of proceedings of computer science conferences. Its aim is to efficiently disseminate original research results in informatics in printed and electronic form. While the focus is on publication of peer-reviewed full papers presenting mature work, inclusion of reviewed short papers reporting on work in progress is welcome, too. Besides globally relevant meetings with internationally representative program committees guaranteeing a strict peer-reviewing and paper selection process, conferences run by societies or of high regional or national relevance are also considered for publication.

Topics

The topical scope of CCIS spans the entire spectrum of informatics ranging from foundational topics in the theory of computing to information and communications science and technology and a broad variety of interdisciplinary application fields.

Information for Volume Editors and Authors

Publication in CCIS is free of charge. No royalties are paid, however, we offer registered conference participants temporary free access to the online version of the conference proceedings on SpringerLink (http://link.springer.com) by means of an http referrer from the conference website and/or a number of complimentary printed copies, as specified in the official acceptance email of the event.

CCIS proceedings can be published in time for distribution at conferences or as post-proceedings, and delivered in the form of printed books and/or electronically as USBs and/or e-content licenses for accessing proceedings at SpringerLink. Furthermore, CCIS proceedings are included in the CCIS electronic book series hosted in the SpringerLink digital library at http://link.springer.com/bookseries/7899. Conferences publishing in CCIS are allowed to use Online Conference Service (OCS) for managing the whole proceedings lifecycle (from submission and reviewing to preparing for publication) free of charge.

Publication process

The language of publication is exclusively English. Authors publishing in CCIS have to sign the Springer CCIS copyright transfer form, however, they are free to use their material published in CCIS for substantially changed, more elaborate subsequent publications elsewhere. For the preparation of the camera-ready papers/files, authors have to strictly adhere to the Springer CCIS Authors' Instructions and are strongly encouraged to use the CCIS LaTeX style files or templates.

Abstracting/Indexing

CCIS is abstracted/indexed in DBLP, Google Scholar, EI-Compendex, Mathematical Reviews, SCImago, Scopus. CCIS volumes are also submitted for the inclusion in ISI Proceedings.

How to start

To start the evaluation of your proposal for inclusion in the CCIS series, please send an e-mail to ccis@springer.com.

Min Zhang · Bin Xu · Fuyuan Hu · Junyu Lin ·
Xianhua Song · Zeguang Lu

Editors

Computer Applications

38th CCF Conference of Computer Applications, CCF NCCA 2023
Suzhou, China, July 16–20, 2023
Proceedings, Part I

 Springer

Editors
Min Zhang
Suzhou University
Suzhou, China

Fuyuan Hu
Suzhou University of Science
and Technology
Suzhou, China

Xianhua Song
Harbin University of Science and Technology
Harbin, China

Bin Xu
Tsinghua University
Beijing, China

Junyu Lin
Institute of Information Engineering, CAS
Beijing, China

Zeguang Lu
National Academy of Guo Ding Institute
of Data Science
Beijing, China

ISSN 1865-0929   ISSN 1865-0937 (electronic)
Communications in Computer and Information Science
ISBN 978-981-99-8763-4   ISBN 978-981-99-8764-1 (eBook)
https://doi.org/10.1007/978-981-99-8764-1

This Springer imprint is published by the registered company Springer Nature Singapore Pte Ltd.
The registered company address is: 152 Beach Road, #21-01/04 Gateway East, Singapore 189721, Singapore

Paper in this product is recyclable.

Preface

As the chairs of the 38th CCF National Conference of Computer Applications (CCF NCCA 2023), it is our great pleasure to welcome you to the conference proceedings. NCCA 2023 was held in Suzhou, China, during July 16–20, 2023, and hosted by the China Computer Federation (CCF), organized by the CCF Computer Applications Professional Committee, and co-organized by Suzhou University, Suzhou University of Science and Technology, Jiangnan University, Nanjing University, Nanjing University of Science and Technology, Wuxi University, Nanjing University of Aeronautics and Astronautics, Nanjing University of Posts and Telecommunications, etc., supported by Jiangsu Computer Society, Guangdong Computer Society, Heilongjiang Computer Society, Jilin Computer Society, Shenzhen Computer Society, Shenyang Computer Society, Dalian Computer Society, CCF Suzhou Member Activity Center, CCF Wuxi Member Activity Center, and other academic associations.

This year's conference attracted 197 paper submissions. After the hard work of the Program Committee, 39 papers were accepted to appear in the conference proceedings, with an acceptance rate of 19.8%. The major topic of this conference was artificial intelligence and its applications. The accepted papers cover a wide range of areas related to basic theory and techniques for artificial intelligence and its applications including artificial intelligence and its applications, pattern recognition and machine learning, data science and technology, network communication and security, and frontier and comprehensive applications.

We would like to thank all the Program Committee members, a total of 267 people from 46 different institutes or companies, for their hard work in completing the review tasks. There were at least 3 reviewers for each article, and each reviewer reviewed no more than 5 articles. Their collective efforts made it possible to attain quality reviews for all the submissions within a few weeks. Their diverse expertise in each research area helped us to create an exciting program for the conference. Their comments and advice helped the authors to improve the quality of their papers and gain deeper insights.

We thank the team at Springer, whose professional assistance was invaluable in the production of the proceedings. A big thank you also goes to the authors and participants for their tremendous support in making the conference a success.

Besides the technical program, this year NCCA offered different experiences to the participants. We hope you enjoyed the conference.

July 2023

Min Zhang
Bin Xu
Fuyuan Hu
Junyu Lin

Organization

Honorary Chair

Weimin Zheng   Tsinghua University, China

General Chairs

Min Zhang   Suzhou University, China
Bin Xu   Tsinghua University, China

General Vice Co-chairs

Xuebin Chen   North China University of Science and
                               Technology, China
Junhui Zhao   Beijing Jiaotong University, China
Shaoliang Peng   Hunan University, China

Secretary General

Zeguang Lu   National Academy of Guo Ding Institute of Data
                               Science, China

Vice Secretary General

Jing Liu   Hebei University of Technology, China

Program Chairs

Fuyuan Hu   Suzhou University of Science and Technology,
                               China
Junyu Lin   Chinese Academy of Sciences, China

Secretary General of the Steering Committee

Peng Liu   Changchun University of Science and
                                   Technology, China

Domain Chairs of Procedural Committee

Guanghui Yan   Lanzhou Jiaotong University, China
Biqing Zeng   South China Normal University, China
Weipeng Jing   Northeast Forestry University, China
Jing Liu   Hebei University of Technology, China
Zhaowen Qiu   Northeast Forestry University, China
Xuebin Chen   North China University of Science and
                                   Technology, China
Bing Xia   Zhongyuan University of Technology, China
Jianquan Ouyang   Xiangtan University, China
Youxi Wu   Hebei University of Technology, China

Organization Chair

Lan Huang   Jilin University, China

Secretary General of the Organizational Committee

Tian Bai   Jilin University, China

Award Committee Chair

Zumin Wang   Dalian University, China

Secretary General of the Award Committee

Bing Xia   Zhongyuan University of Technology, China

Award Committee Members

Jing Liu	Hebei University of Technology, China
Lan Huang	Jilin University, China
Mei Li	China University of Geosciences, China
Guanghui Yan	Lanzhou Jiaotong University, China
Biqing Zeng	South China Normal University, China

Competition Committee Chair

Bin Xu	Tsinghua University, China

Competition Committee Vice Chairs

Bo Lin	Weiye Xuanran Education Technology (Beijing) Co., Ltd., China
Xinbo Wang	Chengxiang Training School Co., Ltd., China

Propaganda Committee Chairs

Aibin Chen	Central South University of Forestry and Technology, China
Zhongchan Sun	National Academy of Guo Ding Institute of Data Science, China

Industrial Applications and Exhibition Chairs

Jing Liu	Hebei University of Technology, China
Zhaowen Qiu	Northeast Forestry University, China

Contents – Part I

Artificial Intelligence and Applications

Contents – Part II

Network Communication and Security

Frontier and Comprehensive Applications

Artificial Intelligence and Applications

PRiskLoc: An Enhanced Multi-dimensional Root Cause Localization Algorithm Aided by a Fine-Grained Evaluation System

Tian Ding[1,2]([✉]) and Yanli Wang[1,2]

[1] Intelligence Service Lab, Samsung Electronics (China) R&D Center, Yuhuatai District, Nanjing, Jiangsu, China
tian123.ding@samsung.com
[2] R&D Center, Yuhuatai District, Nanjing, Jiangsu, China

Abstract. Root cause localization within multi-dimensions is a challenging task due to its large search space within a limited time. There are a series of algorithms to handle this task, but to our knowledge, there is no evaluation system to help users analyse or optimize them according to their specific data and needs. In this paper, there are two main contributions: first, we provide a multi-dimensional evaluation system to evaluate the performance of algorithms in full aspects, which can help us comprehensively and finely analyse, compare, and choose the applicable scenario of algorithms or optimize targeted algorithms; second, we analyse and find the weakness of the SoTA algorithm RiskLoc based on our contributed evaluation system, aiming at its weakness. To tackle the issue of RiskLoc found by our evaluation system, we present PRiskLoc, an efficient and effective multi-dimensional root cause localization algorithm. We demonstrate that PRiskLoc consistently outperforms state-of-the-art baselines, especially in more challenging root cause scenarios, with the F1 improved from 0.635049 to 0.724687.

Keywords: Multi-dimensional Root Cause · Potential Score · Anomaly Detection

1 Introduction

In the process of system operation and maintenance, abnormal changes in key indicators often mean service abnormalities, system failures and so on. Therefore, we need to check key indicators frequently [1–3]. In practice, anomaly detection models are applied to these collected time series and quickly positioning abnormalities.

However, various measures with many attributes are accompanied by a huge search space, which means that this is a very challenging task. Table 1 shows an example with two attributes where the aggregated measure (total) is abnormal with the root cause being $\{(BE, *)\}$, where $*$ indicates an aggregated attribute. Due to the nature of the problem, the root cause is a set of elements with different levels of aggregation. The main challenge is the huge search space since we need to consider all possible combinations of any number of attribute values. For a measure with dimensions each with n values, the number of valid elements is $\sum_{i=1}^{d} \binom{d}{i} n^i = (n+1)^d - 1$, which gives $2^{(n+1)^d - 1} - 1$ number of possible combinations.

Recent works have made great efforts to rapidly search for multi-dimensional root causes [4–7]. However, most of them only work for specific application scenarios. Adtributor [4] is limited to identifying root causes in one dimension. Squeeze [5] and AutoRoot [6] are only applicable in a scenario with a relatively large difference in abnormal amplitude and are sensitive to the clustering outcome. RiskLoc [7] has almost no restrictions on the applicable scenario and is significantly better than the previous algorithm in terms of effectivity and efficiency.

The evaluation of these algorithms is based on individual datasets, so the results presented are not sufficiently convincing, and there is a lack of uniform standards for the evaluation of algorithms. To address this problem, we proposed an algorithm evaluation system that can assist us with algorithm evaluation, selection and optimization. With the help of our evaluation system, we analysed how the algorithms perform in various scenarios and found that RiskLoc performs best in complex scenarios but not well when the magnitude of the anomaly is not obvious. To address this issue, we propose PRiskLoc, which can significantly improve the performance of RiskLoc when the abnormality is not significant, which is a universally difficult topic in current SOTA algorithms. For the improved PRickLoc, we also use the evaluation system to demonstrate its effectiveness.

Table 1. Example of a multi-d measure with two attributes.

Country	Device Series	Actual	Forecast
BE	G71	1500	50
BE	G72	900	100
BR	G70	2000	1990
BR	G72	1005	1000
BR	G71	2005	2000
Total		7410	5140

Our main contributions are as follows:

- We propose an evaluation system that allows for a comprehensive and efficient comparison of algorithms.
- Based on the evaluation system we constructed, we propose PRiskLoc, which can compensate for the lack of RiskLoc. We propose an augmented density-based partitioning approach that compensates for the inadequacy of RiskLoc in cases where the magnitude of the anomaly is not obvious.
- We design the experiment and complete the effectiveness validation of PRiskLoc based on the evaluation system we constructed.

2 Background

In this section, we begin by defining the problem, the related notation, and terminology. Then, we briefly introduce the ripple effect [9] and grounded theory of root cause algorithms.

2.1 Definition

Many time-series indicators can be broken down into a number of dimensions, each with a different value domain, and when anomalies occur, each dimension can be a potential root cause.

More formally, for a measure, we assume that it has n dimensions of attributes $(A_1, A_2, \ldots, A_n)$, and each dimension has values $(V_1, V_2, \ldots, V_n)$. We can obtain different subsequences depending on the degree of decomposition, which form sets of elements called cuboids. For the most fine-grained scenarios $(A_{1,2,\ldots,n})$, we can obtain $V_1 * V_2 * \cdots * V_n$ measures, which we call leaf elements, and for the coarsest-grained decomposition $(A_1, *) \cup (A_2, *) \cup \cdots \cup (A_n, *)$, we can obtain $V_1 + V_2 + \cdots + V_n$ sub measures. For example, the scene of selling cell phones has the following dimensions: country, device and quarter. Each dimension has its own attributes, for example, {Country1, Country2, Country3}, {Device1, Device2, Device3}, {Quarter1, Quarter2, Quarter3, Quarter4}. We can analyse sales from country, device, quarter, respectively, or combine their attributes, such as (Country, Device), or more fine-grained (Country, Device, Quarter) (Fig. 1).

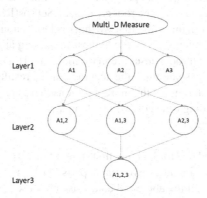

Fig. 1. Cuboid relation graph with n = 3

2.2 Deviation Score

The deviation score is presented by Li [5], and is derived from the ripple effect [9]. The deviation score of element e is defined as:

$$ds(e) = 2 \cdot \frac{f(e) - v(e)}{f(e) + v(e)} \tag{1}$$

$f(e)$ is the predicted value, and $v(e)$ is the true value. It shows the quantitative relationship between elements caused by the same cause. If A_1 is a root cause, leaf elements that are inherited from A_1 necessarily contribute together to the anomalous change, and the proportion of the change in the root cause at this time will be assigned to all its leaf elements in proportion to the predicted value, which means that leaf elements in the same root cause have similar deviation scores. Generally, if the prediction algorithm is accurate enough, their forecast residuals are small, which means that leaf elements with small deviation scores can be considered normal. In the case of abnormalities, the difference between the predicted and true values is relatively large, and the deviation score will be far from zero. Then, at this point, the problem is how to find combinations inside the huge search space to satisfy leaf elements with similar ds values, and these combinations are the root cause of the anomaly. It is noteworthy that the targeted combinations should satisfy two requirements: 1) the leaf elements of the targeted combination satisfy the ripple effect, and 2) most of the elements in the targeted combination are anomalous.

2.3   Related Work

In the following, we will present some algorithms based on the ripple effect.

- HotSpot

HotSpot [9] proposes a metric called PS (Potential Score) to measure how well all leaf elements of a given combination follow the ripple effect. PS is actually a combined attribute, which means that it can be compared between all element combinations. Facing such a huge search space, HotSpot adopts MCTS to optimize the search. From layer 1 to layer L (L is the number of layers), the root cause set RSet (ps(RSet) > PT) is obtained, where PT (ps Threshold) is a threshold that we think is large enough to be regarded, and finally, we obtain the combination with the highest PS among all cuboids.

HotSpot assumes that all root causes are in a cuboid and HotSpot is not available for the derived measure. At the same time, the accuracy of the results is greatly influenced by the number of MCTS iterations; the more iterations there are, the more accurate the results, but the corresponding time cost will be longer.

- Squeeze

Unlike the MCTS used by HotSpot, the first step of Squeeze [5] is filtering to reduce the search space. Squeeze includes two major parts: 1) from bottom to top, filtering most of the normal data, and the abnormal data clustered based on ds values; 2) cluster internal location from top to bottom. Similar to HotSpot's PS, Squeeze proposes GPS as a quantitative criterion for root cause.

Squeeze extends the theory based on HotSpot to increase the generality and robustness of the algorithm. However, actual business scenarios may have some impact on the accuracy of the algorithm: 1) for different data distributions, the filtering algorithm is not always effective, which could lead to errors in the later analysis; 2) it is highly dependent on the accuracy of the cluster; and 3) it cannot be used when there are multiple anomalies with similar ds.

- AutoRoot

Similar to Squeeze, AutoRoot [6] can be divided into filtering, aggregation, and root cause search within the cluster, and the different points from Squeeze are mainly as follows: 1) empirical values are used when filtering normal data; 2) the measurement of root cause search within the cluster is no longer GPS but RS instead, which is more comprehensive.

AutoRoot has a large improvement over Squeeze in terms of performance and efficiency, but it is still unable to avoid the drawbacks of clustering: 1) reliance on accurate clustering and 2) inability to be used when there are multiple anomalies with similar ds.

- RiskLoc

Abandoning the idea of cluster, RiskLoc [7] presents a new idea that employs three main components in its search for the root cause set: 1) leaf element partitioning and weighting; 2) risk score; and 3) element search and iteration. Specifically, RiskLoc separates leaf elements into a normal and an abnormal set with a simple 2-way partitioning scheme at the first step, and each leaf element is given a weight corresponding to the distance from the partitioning point. In this way, RiskLoc believes that it can mitigate the effects of incorrect partitioning. Then, RiskLoc proposes a risk score to identify potential root cause elements in each cuboid. Finally, RiskLoc searches from the lower layer to the higher layer, and when a combination satisfies the condition, its leaf elements are deleted, and the iteration is repeated until none of the remaining elements can satisfy the condition. Since iterations rather than ds-based clustering are used, RiskLoc can handle multiple anomalies with ds-like conditions very well.

RiskLoc [7] has almost no restrictions on the applicable scenario and is significantly better than the previous algorithm in terms of effectivity and efficiency. However, the accuracy of the partitioning in the first step has a large impact on the results, which leads to limitations in use.

3 Evaluation

3.1 Evaluation System

Multi-dimensional root cause localization is a complex problem, and there are various algorithms. However, algorithms are often validated on specific datasets, and these datasets lack specific descriptions, which presents a huge challenge to choose according to your needs or targeted optimization. Therefore, a comprehensive evaluation system is necessary.

As stated earlier, the deviation score (ds) is the cornerstone of multi-dimensional root cause localization algorithms. By analysing the false cases of various algorithms, we propose an evaluation system with four main factors that affect ds:

- The abnormal amplitude (the smaller the amplitude, the harder to locate);
- The layer of anomalies (the higher the layer, the harder to locate);
- The amplitude between different anomalies (the more similar, the harder to locate);
- The anomaly number (the more, the harder to locate).

We construct fine-grained datasets considering these factors. Meanwhile, we verify that the evaluation system is effective.

3.2 Dataset Generation

The existing public datasets have insufficient information about anomaly injection, and a single anomaly case cannot provide a comprehensive algorithm performance comparison. To generate datasets for different scenarios, we employ an approach to generate datasets [7]. Each element has only a single actual value $v(e)$ and a single forecast value $f(e)$. Actual values $v(e)$ are sampled from a one-parameter Weibull distribution with $\alpha \sim U [0.5, 1.0]$, where U is a uniform distribution. Actually, the accuracy of the prediction algorithm has a relatively large impact on the results. To reduce the interference term, we assume that the prediction is accurate and simulate it by adding prediction residuals to the true value:

$$f(e) = v(e) \times N(1, \sigma) \tag{2}$$

When anomaly injection occurs, there are several steps: 1) select the anomaly layer; 2) select the anomaly combinations; 3) set the anomaly magnitude; and 4) change the actual value of the target combination according to the set anomaly magnitude. To better simulate reality, we make the magnitude change obey $N(s, d)$, where s means anomaly severity and d means anomaly deviation. All elements in a single anomaly are scaled the same (i.e., following the ripple effect [9]) with:

$$x = max(x * (1 - N(s, d)), 0) \tag{3}$$

where $x = v (e)$, if $\sum v(e) > \sum f(e)$; otherwise, $x = f (e)$, which ensures the balance of the anomaly direction. We can generate datasets with different magnitudes by changing the value of s, and a smaller s means that the anomaly magnitude is less obvious and hard to locate.

Based on our evaluation system, combined with the data synthesis approach described above, we construct multi-dimensional datasets. Dataset S is provided by RiskLoc, while S1 and S2 are the comprehensive datasets constructed by us. Dataset L is a combination of different anomaly layers. The difference between datasets F and L is that F has only one anomaly, while L has 1–3 anomalies. Dataset D is a set of datasets with different anomaly magnitudes. The details of each generated dataset can be found in Appendix A.

3.3 Evaluation Metrics

We assess the effectiveness of the methods using the F1-score. TP means true positive, FP means false positive and FN means false negative.

$$F1 = \frac{2 \cdot TP}{2 \cdot TP + FP + FN} \tag{4}$$

3.4 Results and Discussion

Based on our evaluation system and the corresponding fine-grained datasets, we performed the following experiments. Due to the long execution time of HotSpot, we only compare Squeeze, AutoRoot and RiskLoc in this paper. The comprehensive comparison of algorithms is displayed in Fig. 2.RiskLoc and AutoRoot perform far better than Squeeze, and RiskLoc is undoubtedly the best. In the following, we will compare each algorithm in terms of each dimension of the evaluation system.

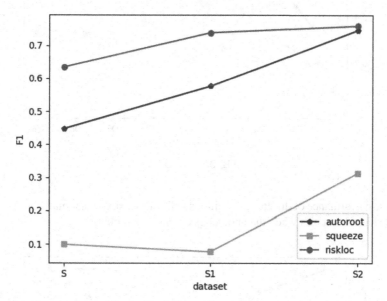

Fig. 2. F1 of Comprehensive datasets

Anomaly Amplitude. Dataset D is employed to complete this task, and D1 to D9 indicate that the anomaly severity in Eq. (3) changes from 0.1 to 0.9, which indicates that the anomaly is becoming increasingly obvious. When the abnormal amplitude is small, RiskLoc does not perform as well as AutoRoot (Fig. 3).

Anomaly Layer. Datasets F and L are both for layer level comparison, F1 or L1 means the anomaly is in the first layer, while F2 or L2 means the anomaly is in the second layer. From Fig. 4 and Fig. 5, we found that the deeper layer the anomaly in, the worse the performance.

Amplitude Between Different Anomalies. In this dimension, we can see the different performances of S1 and S2 (Fig. 2), while the only difference between S1 and S2 is that S1 has similar anomaly magnitudes and S2 has different anomaly magnitudes. The results show that RiskLoc performs better when the magnitudes of the anomalies are similar.

Anomaly Number. The difference between datasets L and F is that there are multiple anomalies in L, while there is only one anomaly in F. A comparison of Fig. 4 and Fig. 5

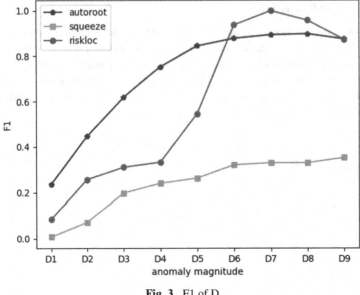

Fig. 3. F1 of D

shows the performance of different algorithms in the dimension of anomaly number, and RiskLoc has advantages when the anomalies are more complex.

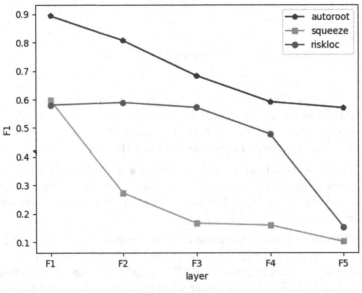

Fig. 4. F1 of D

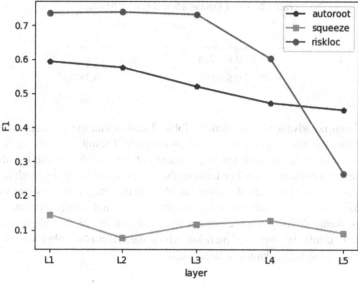

Fig. 5. F1 of D

From the results, the performance of algorithms is influenced by abnormal amplitude and abnormal layer, and there is no doubt that the less obvious the abnormal magnitude is, the more difficult it is to locate, and the higher the abnormal layer is, the harder it is to locate. RiskLoc and AutoRoot are actually complementary, and RiskLoc is good at handling scenarios with multiple anomalies of similar magnitude, while AutoRoot is skilled in handling cases where the anomaly magnitude is not obvious or there is only one anomaly. However, on the comprehensive datasets, RiskLoc consistently outperforms other algorithms, which also shows that further optimization of RiskLoc is necessary. It is worth noting that Squeeze performs poorly and is very sensitive to changes in the number of anomalies.

4 PRiskloc

RiskLoc is significantly better than the other algorithms but not well when the magnitude of the anomaly is not obvious. In this section, we will analyse the inefficiency of RiskLoc and propose an optimization plan to obtain PRiskLoc, and our evaluation system verifies the effectiveness of PRiskLoc.

4.1 Inefficiency of 2-Way Partitioning Scheme

In the following, we have performed an experiment on the datasets S and L presented by RiskLoc, where we partitioned the data according to the actual situation before the root cause search, i.e., the partitioning accuracy was 100%, and then the results were

Table 2. F1 of Datasets S and L with RiskLoc

Dataset	S	L
No partitioned	0.676724	0.6767
Partitioned	0.808694	0.757839

compared with no advanced partitioning. Table 2 shows that the accuracy of the first step of partitioning has a significant impact on the overall result.

With the help of self-constructed fine-grained datasets, we found that the abnormal amplitude is an important factor. The basis of the 2-way partitioning approach is that the normal element ds is smaller and the abnormal element ds is larger. When some abnormal elements have $|ds|$ < cutpoint (meaning the abnormal is not significant), these points will be mistakenly divided into the normal set, as shown in Fig. 6. Although RiskLoc uses weight to dilute the impact of partition errors, the effect is not obvious, which will also influence subsequent abnormal localization.

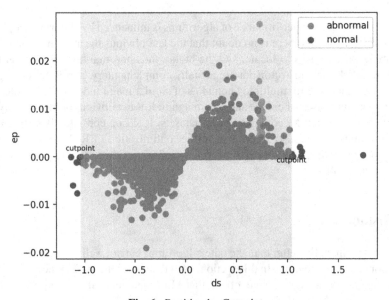

Fig. 6. Partition by Cutpoint

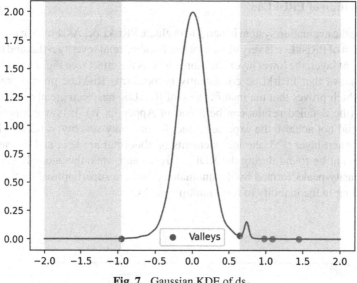

Fig. 7. Gaussian KDE of ds

4.2 Partition by KDE

We apply simple but effective kernel density estimation (KDE) [10] with a Gaussian kernel to obtain the distribution density of the deviation score of the normal part partitioned by RiskLoc, and Fig. 7 shows the KDE plot. After clustering, the relative maximum values are the centers of each cluster, and the nearby relative minimum values are the clusters' boundaries. Thus, we can obtain different clusters. Based on the heuristics that anomalies always hold a small part, except for the data in the largest cluster, we put the other data to the abnormal part. The overall framework refers to Fig. 8.

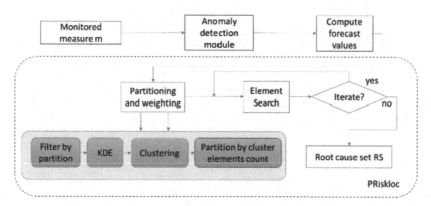

Fig. 8. System framework of PRiskLoc

4.3   Evaluation of PRiskLoc

We also use the evaluation system in part 3 to evaluate PRiskLoc. As shown in Fig. 10, the improvement of PRiskLoc is very obvious when the abnormal severity >0.2, and from the perspective of layer, the lower layer, the more obvious the effect (see Fig. 11 and Fig. 12). Figure 9 shows that PRiskLoc consistently outperforms RiskLoc on comprehensive datasets, which proves that the insufficiency of RiskLoc has been greatly improved by PRiskLoc (the detailed results can be found in Appendix B). It is worth noting that PRiskLoc did not achieve the expected effect for anomaly severity < 0.2 and layer > 3 because when layer > 3, the leaf elements of abnormal are less, and the abnormal element cannot be found during the KDE analysis, and when the anomaly severity < 0.2, the density peaks formed by the anomalous data are superimposed on the normal data, resulting in the inability to form multiple peaks.

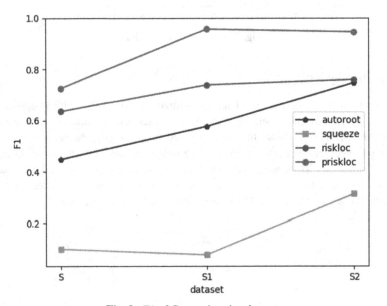

Fig. 9. F1 of Comprehensive dataset

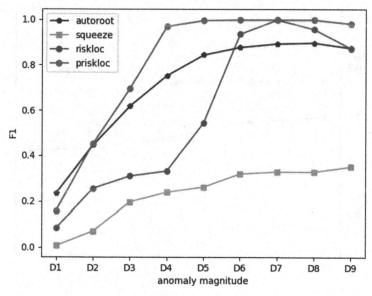

Fig. 10. F1 of D

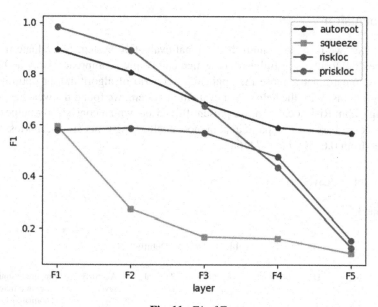

Fig. 11. F1 of F

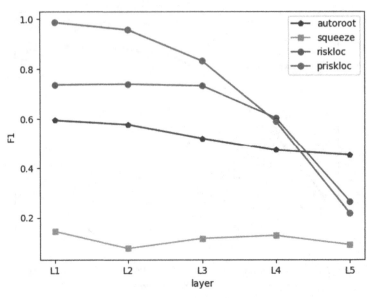

Fig. 12. F1 of L

5 Conclusion

In this paper, we provide a multi-dimensional evaluation system to evaluate the performance of algorithms in full aspects, which can help us comprehensively and finely analyse, compare, and choose the applicable scenario of algorithms or optimize targeted algorithms. With the help of our evaluation system, we found the weakness of the SoTA algorithm RiskLoc. Then, we present PRiskLoc, which consistently outperforms state-of-the-art baselines. In particular, in more challenging root cause scenarios, the F1 improved from 0.635049 to 0.724687.

A Dataset Details

See Table 3.

Table 3. Dataset Details

Dataset	N	D	Elements	Anomaly num	Anomaly layer	Anomaly severity	Amplitude similar between different abnormalities
S	1000	5	480000	[1, 9]	[1, 5]	[0.2,1.0]	Both
S1	1000	5	480000	[1, 3]	2	[0.2,0.9]	Yes
S2							No
L	1000	4	36000	[1, 5]	4	[0.5,1.0]	No

(continued)

Table 3. (*continued*)

Dataset	N	D	Elements	Anomaly num	Anomaly layer	Anomaly severity	Amplitude similar between different abnormalities
L1	1000	5	480000	[1, 3]	1	[0.2,0.9]	Yes
L2					2		
L3					3		
L4					4		
L5					5		
F1	1000	5	480000	1	1	[0.2,0.9]	-
F2					2		
F3					3		
F4					4		
F5					5		
D1	200	5	480000	[1, 3]	2	0.1	Yes
D2						0.2	
D3						0.3	
D4						0.4	
D5						0.5	
D6						0.6	
D7						0.7	
D8						0.8	
D9						0.9	

B Result Details

See Tables 4, 5 and 6.

Table 4. F1-score of L and F

Algorithm	L1	L2	L3	L4	L5	F1	F2	F3	F4	F5
Squeeze	0.145608	0.076923	0.116894	0.128627	0.09173	0.597074	0.273303	0.166527	0.159615	0.101911
AutoRoot	0.594142	0.576687	0.52037	0.472305	**0.452158**	0.89377	0.807187	**0.68316**	**0.591513**	**0.569174**
RiskLoc	0.736708	0.738944	0.732294	**0.603129**	0.265487	0.579802	0.589247	0.570931	0.477546	0.15288
PRiskLoc	**0.986328**	**0.957026**	**0.832447**	0.589744	0.218144	**0.983202**	**0.893358**	0.675841	0.436701	0.124502

Table 5. F1-score of D

Algorithm	D1	D2	D3	D4	D5	D6	D7	D8	D9
Squeeze	0.00641	0.07028	0.197647	0.239829	0.262366	0.320346	0.32906	0.32906	0.351893
AutoRoot	**0.234667**	0.446009	0.618026	0.752066	0.843882	0.877193	0.892857	0.896861	0.873874
RiskLoc	0.083333	0.256158	0.310395	0.332121	0.545455	0.935867	**0.997506**	0.956311	0.87156
PRiskLoc	0.159259	**0.45283**	**0.694949**	**0.96837**	**0.995025**	**0.997506**	**0.997506**	**0.997506**	**0.980392**

Table 6. F1-score of S

Algorithm	S	S1	S2
Squeeze	0.099115	0.076923	0.313357
AutoRoot	0.447842	0.576687	0.747053
RiskLoc	0.635049	0.738944	0.759644
PRiskLoc	**0.74687**	**0.957026**	**0.945873**

References

1. Meng, W., et al.: LogAnomaly: Unsupervised detection of sequential and quantitative anomalies in unstructured logs. In: IJCAI, vol. 19, pp. 4739–4745 (2019)
2. Zhang, S., et al.: Rapid and robust impact assessment of software changes in large internet-based services. In: Proceedings of the 11th ACM Conference on Emerging Networking Experiments and Technologies, pp. 1–13 (2015)
3. Zhang, S., et al.: Funnel: assessing software changes in web-based services. IEEE Trans. Serv. Comput. **11**(1), 34–48 (2016)
4. Bhagwan, R., et al.: Adtributor: revenue debugging in advertising systems. In: Proceedings of the 11th USENIX Conference on Networked Systems Design and Implementation, NSDI 2014, Seattle, WA, pp. 43–55. USENIX Association, USA (2014)
5. Li, Z., et al.: Generic and robust localization of multi-dimensional root causes. In: 2019 IEEE 30th International Symposium on Software Reliability Engineering (ISSRE), pp. 47–57. IEEE (2019)
6. Jing, P., Han, Y., Sun, J., Lin, T., Hu, Y.: AutoRoot: a novel fault localization schema of multi-dimensional root causes. In: 2021 IEEE Wireless Communications and Networking Conference (WCNC), pp. 1–7. IEEE (2021)
7. Kalander, M.: RiskLoc: localization of multi-dimensional root causes by weighted risk. arXiv preprint arXiv:2205.10004 (2022)
8. Silverman, B.W.: Density Estimation for Statistics and Data Analysis, vol. 26. CRC Press (1986)
9. Sun, Y., et al.: HotSpot: anomaly localization for additive KPIs with multi-dimensional attributes. IEEE Access **6**, 10909–10923 (2018)
10. Davis, R.A., Lii, KS., Politis, D.N.: Remarks on some nonparametric estimates of a density function. In: Davis, R., Lii, KS., Politis, D. (eds.) Selected Works of Murray Rosenblatt. Selected Works in Probability and Statistics. Springer, New York (2011). https://doi.org/10.1007/978-1-4419-8339-8_13

Blockchain Enhanced Whole-Life-Cycle Engineering Cost Management

Peiyu Tang[1] (iD), Jiaxun Wang[1,2], Li Li[3], Haifan Hua[1], and Guohui Yuan[1(✉)]

[1] Shenzhen Key Lab for Content-Centric Networking and Blockchain Technologies (ICNLAB),
Shenzhen Graduate School, Peking University, Beijing 518055, China
yuangh@pku.edu.cn
[2] Inner Mongolia University, Hohhot 010021, China
[3] Tencent Group, Inc., Shenzhen, China

Abstract. Digital transformation refers to the systematic and holistic transformation and upgrading of enterprises to adapt to the digital economy environment. This paper explores the whole-life-cycle engineering cost management scheme for subway projects in the context of digital transformation. The paper adopts blockchain and BIM technology as the main supporting tools for the scheme. The paper discusses the theoretical basis, application exploration, and empirical analysis of the scheme and summarizes the main conclusions, innovation points, shortcomings, and future research directions. The paper has theoretical significance and practical value for promoting the digital transformation of the construction engineering industry, exploring how blockchain enhances whole-life-cycle engineering cost management, improving the level of engineering cost management, and facilitating the energy savings, emission reduction and sustainable development of subway projects.

Keywords: Digital Transformation · Blockchain · Whole-Life-Cycle Engineering Cost Management · Subway Projects · BIM · Big Data

1 Introduction

With the continuous development and application of the new generation of digital technologies, digital transformation has become an inevitable trend and an important option for the construction engineering industry. Digital transformation is the proactive, systematic and holistic transformation and upgrading of enterprises in the context of global digital transformation, in order to adapt to the needs of enterprise survival and development and market changes in the digital economy environment.

In January 2023, the National Housing and Urban–Rural Construction Work Conference was held in Beijing, which proposed to "strictly implement dynamic supervision throughout the project construction process and make good use of digital means", emphasizing the importance of emerging information technologies in the application

Supported by Key-Area Research and Development Program of Guangdong Province (Grant 2020B0101090003) Shenzhen Key Research Project (JCYJ20220818100810023).

of the construction industry. Engineering cost management, an essential part of the construction engineering industry, also faces opportunities and challenges from digital transformation. The traditional whole-process engineering cost model can no longer adapt to the current social and economic conditions and market demand, and there are problems such as untimely information transmission, inaccurate engineering quantity evaluation, and failure to update price fluctuations in time, which may lead to project investment out of control or engineering quality not guaranteed, or even trigger local debt risks, affecting the economic order and development of the national engineering cost field. Therefore, there is a strong need to explore scientifically sound cost management schemes for engineering over the life of the project.

In this paper, based on the context of digital transformation, we focus on cost management over the whole-life-cycle of an engineering project supported by blockchain and BIM and technologies, focusing on the metro project as the subject of theoretical discussion and empirical analysis. The main body of the paper is divided into five parts (see Fig. 1).

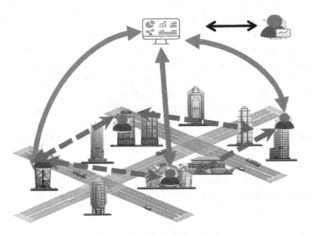

Fig. 1. The idea of the paper

- Section 1 is the introduction, which presents the research background, implications, domestic and foreign research status, main contents and innovative points of the paper.
- Section 2 is the theoretical basis of whole-life-cycle engineering cost management under the background of digital transformation, which expounds the theoretical basis of this paper from three aspects: the concept and characteristics of digital transformation, the connotation and principles of whole-life-cycle engineering cost management, and the definition and functions of BIM technology.
- Section 3 is an application exploration of engineering cost management across the life cycle in the context of digital transformation, which builds an information database and uses data mining and analytics techniques to analyse and forecast engineering costs to provide data support for cost control. We propose a blockchain-based framework for engineering cost management that covers the four stages of project initiation, planning, execution, and closure.

- Section 4 presents the construction and empirical analysis of a whole-life-cycle cost engineering model for subway projects based on BIM technology. Based on the characteristics and needs of emerging cities, a cost–benefit model is proposed for the whole-life-cycle of a metro project, and an empirical analysis is performed using a metro project as an example to validate the effectiveness and feasibility of the model.
- Section 5 is devoted to conclusions and outlook, which summarize the main conclusions and innovative points of the paper and point out its shortcomings and future research directions.

2   Review of the Research

2.1   Current Situation of Applying Blockchain Technology to the Engineering Cost Management Field

In the area of engineering cost management, data can enhance the transparency of material costs in the construction process, which is beneficial to standardize price competition among construction enterprises. However, most of the current data suffer from improper storage, poor data analysis efficiency, and outdated market price information. Although blockchain technology has been applied in the field of engineering cost management, its application is still limited to the descriptive and predictive levels, and it is challenging to play a guiding role. In addition, there are problems such as narrow application scope, difficult implementation, low return on investment, and difficult transition outcomes. To explore how blockchain technology can be applied to whole-life-cycle project cost management to solve the problems of difficult multiparty collaboration, difficult timely cost synchronization and inefficient management processes. Facing massive, multidimensional, and multisource data, mining the hidden "underwater iceberg" in the data requires us to scientifically analyse sufficient data to sort out and refine more instructive and valuable information. At present, the most widely used application is electronic bidding, which can effectively screen out dishonesty, violation, illegal and other behaviors and further standardize the bidding process in engineering cost management. Most of the current applications of big data technology are to mine and analyse massive data. There are still limits. Due to the limited and restricted amount of data owned by a single institution, if the data source channels are also relatively single and the data dimension levels are thin, due to unreasonable allocation of information resources and difficulty in sharing, it leads to lack of transparency and authority of information [1]. At the construction stage, the data of multiple parties are very complex, and the standardization is low.

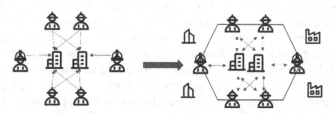

Fig. 2. Applying blockchain technology to the engineering cost management field

This leads to multiplicity due to the singularity of the construction project. In particular, the coding of human resources and machinery has not improved. It is difficult to achieve structured standardized collection for its collection and scientific data processing [6] (see Fig. 2).

2.2 Whole-Life-Cycle Cost Management and BIM Technology

Whole process engineering cost management refers to the cost control of the project itself based on basic quantity management, which can end management after project completion [12]. This management mode has difficulty meeting the actual needs of engineering cost management, and it is difficult to achieve information exchange among different construction stages and participants. The organizational management mode is relatively backwards, and the risk avoidance ability is poor [13]. Different from the whole process engineering cost management mode, the whole-life-cycle engineering cost management mode considers the whole-life-cycle of the project, including decision-making, design, construction, use, maintenance, demolition and other stages. It applies cost engineering and cost management principles, proven methodologies, and the latest technology to problems of business and program planning, cost estimating, economic and financial analysis, cost control, program and project management, planning and scheduling, cost and schedule performance measurement, and change control. It not only avoids the disadvantages of the whole process cost mode but also makes the budgeting and maintenance of engineering costs in a series of processes convenient and fast [14, 15].

3 New Trends of Blockchain Technology in Engineering Cost Management

What is the mechanism by which existing cost information management platforms update costs in a timely manner through blockchain technology? Blockchain technology employs time stamps and full life cycles to accomplish this objective. A time stamp is complete and verifiable data that can attest to the existence of the data prior to a certain time. Blockchain technology generates a chain of blocks that are chronologically ordered and affixed with time stamps. Each block encompasses cost information. A full life cycle denotes various stages from project planning, design, construction, and operation to abandonment. Blockchain technology gathers and examines cost information from the whole-life-cycle of a project and updates the costs accordingly. Therefore, by utilizing blockchain technology, existing cost information management platforms can update costs in a timely manner. Therefore, it is necessary to propose a blockchain-based construction cost management framework for the whole-lifecycle, which includes elements such as participation roles, data flow, consensus mechanisms and smart contracts, to build an engineering cost database based on data mining techniques to fully utilize the data, prevent the loss of data value, and provide the driving force for the digital transformation of cost enterprises. The digital transformation and upgrading of engineering cost management should be advanced from four aspects: collaborative construction, risk sharing, benefit sharing and new infrastructure innovation (see Fig. 3).

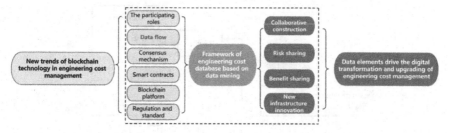

Fig. 3. A blockchain-based framework for the whole-life-cycle engineering cost management

3.1 Data Elements Drive the Digital Transformation and Upgrading of Engineering Cost Management

Data elements, as a new type of production factor, are leading the digital transformation and upgrading of engineering cost management. Many provinces have developed their own digital cost management platforms, which have achieved the deep integration of data elements and engineering cost data, offering new opportunities and challenges for the construction industry. In every stage of cost management, digital technologies have been widely applied, such as CAD drawing, BIM technology, cloud computing, and the Internet of Things, to realize the digital intelligence of engineering construction. In the market-oriented environment of data elements, the demand for big data in engineering cost management is growing rapidly. In the preliminary stage of design, the collected data are used to predict and analyse the project; in the design stage, the concept of data elements is widely accepted. Common CAD drawing and BIM technology are continuously empowering this. BIM technology provides computer-aided design models for architectural design. The digital transformation and upgrading of engineering cost management is the requirement of the times. In this unprecedented process of digital transformation and upgrading, there are many issues that need our deep reflection, such as how to promote its development, how to enhance data sharing, and how to liberate digital productivity while protecting data security to form a well-ordered and sustainable system. Common big data technologies such as Hadoop and Spark can improve efficiency, reduce cost and optimize decision-making in engineering cost management.

3.2 The Whole Process of Engineering Cost Database Design Based on Data Mining

Framework

The enterprise cost database can provide services such as investment estimation, design estimation, bid price analysis, preliminary design optimization and cost dynamic control for projects. Based on the above practical functional requirements, the whole engineering cost database system consists of three parts, namely, the database entity, analysis module and prediction module (see Fig. 4).

The database entity is mainly established according to the original engineering cost data. The data indicators refer to the Classification and Calculation Standard of Construction Engineering Cost Index GB/T 51290-2018 [18], and the detailed indicator classification is excerpted as follows in Table 1.

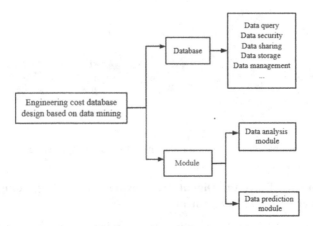

Fig. 4. Framework of Engineering cost database based on data mining.

Historical engineering data have some issues, such as missing data, redundancy, inconsistency, and nonstandardization. Therefore, directly using these data for analysis and prediction cannot ensure the accuracy of the results and may even lead to erroneous or misleading conclusions. For this reason, data preprocessing must be performed before data analysis and prediction. Data preprocessing is the foundation for mining valuable information, including cleaning, correction, transformation, normalization and other methods, to make the data reach a standardized and orderly state and provide reliable data support for subsequent data mining and analysis [20]. Natural language processing (NLP), a common technique in machine learning, is used to reduce nonstandard phenomena such as data omission and error caused by human factors during input.

Module Design

After completing the creation of the database entity, the engineering cost data are input into the data analysis module for technical change statistical analysis, cost–benefit regression analysis, design scheme classification analysis, engineering price clustering analysis, cost association rule mining and cost data visualization analysis. The process data generated are imported into the data prediction module, combined with neural networks, case-based reasoning, fuzzy mathematics and other prediction methods and techniques, to achieve data-driven project case similarity analysis, project cost trend prediction and project cost rule prediction.

In the context of big data, relying on scientific and advanced technology to process and analyse a large amount of data in the database, data mining technology is compatible with the requirements of this study for big data processing. Database and data mining tools are complementary to each other. The database is responsible for storing and managing data, while data mining tools are responsible for extracting data from the database for analysis. Data mining technology meets the requirements of the deep-level design of the database.

Table 1. Extract of basic project information data indicators

	Project name	-
The basic information of projects	Construct properties	-
	Investment type	-
	Construction location	-
	Site type	-
	Seismic fortification intensity	-
	Floor area ratio	-
	Fire protection requirements	-
	Greening rate	-
	Land area	-
	Total construction area	-
	Above-ground construction area	-
	Underground construction area	-
	Auxiliary construction area	-
	Number of project buildings	-
	Total number of households	-
	Construction area	-
	Housing area	-
	Commercial area	-
	Building height	-
	Floor height	-
	Standard floor area	-
	Number of units	-

4 Application of BIM Technology in the Whole-Life-Cycle Cost Management of Emerging Urban Subway Engineering

With the rapid growth of the social economy, emerging cities have different development paths from developed cities in the construction of subway systems. The construction of subway systems requires a large amount of capital investment, which can easily lead to financial pressure. In addition, due to the small population size, subway systems in emerging cities may not be economically efficient, and most of the time, trains are underutilized, resulting in low subway operation efficiency, high maintenance costs, and long payback periods.

In view of the above problems, integrating BIM technology with the development process of emerging urban subway engineering projects can greatly enhance the management level, reduce resource waste, save construction duration, and lower labor and maintenance costs.

Preliminary Stage

By creating a BIM model of the proposed subway engineering project, preliminary information integration of the project can be achieved, and the feasibility and potential risks of the project can be analysed and evaluated using the model information. Using the cost database based on BIM, combined with the engineering characteristics of the proposed project, the construction project information of similar projects in the past can be compared, different construction schemes can be designed and quantified, and the project price data can be determined by using the cost software to quickly calculate the investment cost of different schemes. On the other hand, based on the BIM model and value management techniques, passenger flow simulation and forecasting can be realized. Based on meeting the functional requirements of key stakeholders, scientific plans for subway station size and interstation distance can be formulated.

Design and Bidding Stage

Through the three-dimensional visualization function of the BIM model, collaborative design can be realized, which can enable all parties, especially the technical personnel of the construction unit, to participate in the scheme formulation and optimization with the design and other departments in the early stage of scheme design, communicate efficiently for different needs, ensure that the construction feasibility and actual needs are fully considered in the engineering design stage, and reduce the probability of design change in the later stage. In addition, in the design stage, value management techniques should be used to clarify the functional requirements of subway projects, delete unnecessary functions and lower investment costs, and optimize the actual functional design to enhance the overall value of subway engineering.

Combining the complete engineering quantity information provided by the BIM model in the decision-making and design stages, the owner can quickly and accurately compile the engineering quantity list of the subway project, and the bidder can also quickly check the engineering quantity list according to the BIM model, combined with the relevant clauses of the bidding documents, prevent the problems of insufficient information such as omission and miscalculation, and prepare effective and competitive bidding schemes.

Construction Stage

With the help of the BIM model, functions such as automatic collision detection and virtual construction can be realized to evaluate the rationality and feasibility of construction schemes at each stage in advance and optimize the construction plan to make the process connection more compact, strengthen schedule management, and effectively avoid idle work phenomena. For the economic losses caused by construction errors or unreasonable planning in the construction process, strict management is needed to minimize the increase in project construction cost. By comparing the time-space data and process data generated in the construction process with the design target data contained in the BIM database, check the cost, actual cost and planned budget of the completed project, complete the deviation analysis and correction work of progress and cost. Embed the market information interface in the BIM model to provide real-time market information such as machinery and materials, rationally plan resource procurement and payment schedules by using a 5D dynamic cost control model, and realize fine-grained cost control at the construction stage.

Completion Acceptance, Operation and Maintenance Stage
BIM technology plays an important role in the process of project construction and operation. On the one hand, project cost information in BIM can dynamically record and reflect the actual situation of engineering. Project information is stored in the BIM cost model database of subway engineering projects, which provides rich engineering data assets for project investment benefit evaluation, cost database improvement and further development of subway engineering projects in the future, which helps to lower development costs and improve development efficiency. On the other hand, BIM technology can also manage the daily operation and maintenance of subway systems. The operation and maintenance unit can quickly grasp the overall situation of the project, including the design and construction scheme, concealed work record and other related parameter information, which provides a reliable basis for equipment operation and maintenance and uses this information to improve subway system utilization efficiency, achieve subway system operation and maintenance cost reduction and efficiency increase.

5 Conclusion

Through a literature review, this paper analyses the current research status, issues and trends in big data technology and BIM in the context of digital transformation. At the same time, it summarizes successful experiences and shortcomings, explores cost management schemes across the lifecycle of projects, and attempts to apply them in metro projects in emerging cities. The following conclusions have been drawn in this paper:

Issues to be addressed in project cost management schemes across the life cycle in the context of digital transformation include data acquisition, data storage, data standardization and data sharing. Taking the whole-life-cycle cost management of metro projects in emerging cities based on BIM technology proposed in this paper as an example, in the implementation process, enterprises need to choose appropriate and targeted digital technologies and take corresponding implementation plans and management measures according to their own business needs and actual situation.

In the process of digital transformation and construction of engineering cost information databases, enterprises need to cooperate with technology suppliers, architects, engineering contractors and other relevant parties to jointly promote the construction of digital transformation and engineering cost information databases. Bolstered by this idea, the application of blockchain technology can also provide a new approach to the construction of databases of engineering cost information. Through the combination of blockchain technology and other digital technologies such as BIM, cloud computing, and big data, data standardization and data privacy issues have been overcome, and application modes and management mechanisms have been continuously innovated.

Therefore, managers should plan for the overall situation, have clear insight and take the initiative in the rapidly changing and complex structure of the environment. The ability of big data, blockchain and other technologies to be applied can be actively improved, and pain points that have long existed in the cost sector can be effectively addressed through active interaction between various sectors, mutual coordination and overall government planning.

This paper provides some guidance and references for the digital transformation of construction engineering enterprises, but it also has certain limitations. Future research can further explore the technology of digital transformation and construction of engineering cost information databases and the whole-life-cycle management and policy of smart city projects to further explore the whole picture and development trend of the whole-life-cycle engineering cost management scheme under the background of digital transformation.

Bibliography

1. Zhai, H.: Research on the Application of Blockchain Technology in Engineering Bidding. Zhengzhou University, MA thesis (2021)
2. Zhang, Y.: Research and design of highway engineering cost database. J. China Foreign Highw. **22**(6), 3 (2002)
3. Li, Z.: On the information management of construction cost. China Econ. **04**, 273–275 (2004)
4. Wang, C.: Construction project construction cost management information system construction and application. Enterp. Econ. **32**(02), 73–75 (2013). https://doi.org/10.13529/j.carolc arrollnkienterprise.Pa. Accessed 06 Feb 2013
5. Huang, W.: The application and development of information technology in construction project cost. Manage. Technol. SME (in the Ten-day Issue) **04**, 305–306 (2012)
6. Zhang, Y.: Establishment of database of project cost management and its application. Eng. Constr. **32**(6), 22–25 (2000)
7. Zhou, S.Q., Zhou, B.J.: Thinking on the development trend of engineering cost management. Eng. Cost Manage. **06**, 34–42 (2020). https://doi.org/10.19730/j.cnki.1008-2166.2020-06-034
8. Zhang Y., Tan, X.: Consideration on the development of cost consulting enterprises under the background of engineering cost industry reform. Eng. Cost Manage. **02**, 14–19 (2021). https://doi.org/10.19730/j.cnki.1008-2166.2021-02-014
9. Li, R., Qin, Y., Wang, C., Li, M., Chu, X.: A blockchain-enabled framework for enhancing scalability and security in IIoT. IEEE Trans. Ind. Inf. **19**, 7389–7400 (2022)
10. Guo, Y.: The determination and control strategy of the whole-life-cycle cost of subway engineering. Constr. Mach. Maint. **06**, 163–165 (2022)
11. Xu, D.: Comparative analysis of whole process and whole-life-cycle engineering cost management. Ju She **22**, 186 (2018)
12. Li, Y., et al.: Research on life cycle cost management of power transmission and transformation projects based on BIM technology under the background of smart infrastructure. Constr. Econ. **43**(10), 58–65 (2022). https://doi.org/10.14181/j.cnki.1002-851x.202210058
13. Lei, K., Huang, S., Huang, J., Liu, H., Liu, J.: Intelligent eco networking (IEN) II: a knowledge-driven future internet infrastructure for value-oriented ecosystem. In: 2019 2nd International Conference on Hot Information-Centric Networking (HotICN) (2019)
14. Fang, G.Y., Liu, Z.M.: Using Big Data to build database. Eng. Cost Manage. **04**, 82–87 (2020). https://doi.org/10.19730/j.cnki.1008-2166.2020-04-082

15. Sun, Y.: Research on project cost management based on Big Data and BIM technology. Bulk Cem. **06**, 46–48 (2021)
16. Wang, Q.: Research on construction of artificial intelligence engineering cost information management platform. Constr. Econ. **41**(10), 69–72 (2020). https://doi.org/10.14181/j.cnki. 1002-851x.202010069
17. Ministry of Housing and Urban–RuralUrban-Rural Development of the People's Republic of China: Index Classification and Measurement Standard of Construction project cost Index. GB/T 51290-2018.2018-03-07
18. Hu, X.: Comparative analysis of whole process project cost management and whole-life-cycle project cost management. Hous. Real Estate **15**, 40–41 (2021)
19. Zhang, W.S.: Analysis on construction technology and quality management method of building mechanical and electrical equipment installation engineering. Res. Eng. Technol. **6**(06), 162–163 (2021). https://doi.org/10.19537/j.cnki.2096-2789.2021.06.074
20. Liu, T.: Data Mining Technology and Its Application. National Defense Industry Press (2001)
21. Kou, X.: Research on the Whole-life-cycle Cost Management of Engineering Projects based on BIM Technology. MA Thesis, Northeast Forestry University (2016)
22. Huang, S., Chen, R., Li, Y., Zhang, M., Yu, X.: Intelligent Eco Networking (IEN) III: a shared in-network computing infrastructure towards future internet. In: 2020 3rd International Conference on Hot Information-Centric Networking (HotICN) (2020)
23. Samad, M.E., et al.: BIM and Digital tools for state-of-the-art construction cost management. Buildings **12**(4), 396 (2022)
24. Parsamehr, M., et al.: A review of construction management challenges and BIM-based solutions: perspectives from the schedule, cost, quality, and safety management. Asian J. Civ. Eng. **24**(1), 353–389 (2023)

A Review of Point Cloud 3D Object Detection Methods Based on Deep Learning

Xiyuan Wang⬛, Jie Lin(✉)⬛, Longrui Yang⬛, and Sicong Wang⬛

College of Electrical Engineering and Information Engineering, Lanzhou University of
Technology, Lanzhou 730050, China
449066528@qq.com

Abstract. Based on introducing the coupling relationship between deep learning and three-dimensional point clouds, this paper reviews the three characteristics and research problems of point clouds, randomness, sparsity, and unstructuredness, and discusses three-dimensional point cloud target detection based on deep neural networks, including point cloud detection techniques following graph convolution, detection techniques following the original point cloud, and detection algorithms based on fusion processing of graph convolution and the original point cloud. Focusing on future research direction and development, the field of point cloud analysis is currently undergoing further development through the application of deep learning techniques.

Keywords: 3D Point Cloud · Deep Leaning · Semantic Segmentation · Target Detection

1 Introduction

Three-dimensional target detection [1–3] is a complex process of interpreting environmental information and the spatial location of the target based on the geometric model and mathematical information obtained by three-dimensional intelligent sensors. In this way, we could obtain profitable data such as the type, location, and direction of motion of the desired target. In recent years, with the increasing requirement for the diagnostic accuracy and stabilization of the detection of objects in three-dimensional space, traditional two-dimensional object detection methods have difficulty meeting the needs of researchers. At present, three-dimensional object detection technology based on deep neural frameworks features the advantages of economical acquisition, fast recognition speed, and exact measurements, which provide great help for feature extraction and accurate classification of point clouds [4–8]. Due to the swift progress of three-dimensional innovation in recent years, three-dimensional object detection has gradually become an important research field and hot industry for researchers [9, 10].

The perceptual images and 3D point clouds obtained based on lidar have difficulties such as sparsity, disorder, and unstructured, which makes it difficult for researchers to further decompose and process the original point clouds. Over the past few years, the combination of deep learning and 3D laser point clouds has been continuously

M. Zhang et al. (Eds.): CCF NCCA 2023, CCIS 1959, pp. 30–39, 2024.
https://doi.org/10.1007/978-981-99-8764-1_3

valued and supported by researchers [11–13]. Through its rich, diverse, and nonstructural characteristics, point cloud data have been efficiently used in feature processing and feature classification and have achieved rapid development in 3D data processing based on point clouds. Concurrently, due to its excellent classification accuracy index and real-time performance, it has attracted the attention of scholars in many fields, such as autonomous driving [14, 15], model reconstruction [16], and ground inspection [17].

2 Relationship Between Deep Learning and Point Cloud

The process of recognizing and categorizing different semantic regions within a point cloud is known as three-dimensional point cloud object recognition. In the research of traditional point cloud classification methods, most of the features used by researchers are based on the three-dimensional structure of the local areas of the point cloud, such as lattice constant, curvature, normal vector, and spatial distribution. For this reason, researchers have developed many point descriptors and selected the appropriate point cloud classifier for predicting the semantic labels of the point cloud, such as support vector machine [18], random forest [19], AddBoost [20], Gaussian mixture model [21], and JointBoost [22]. However, this kind of artificial extraction method mainly depends on the judgment of the experimenter and does not fully consider the objectivity and stability of the adjacent point cloud. Alterations to this aspect can significantly impact the classification outcomes of the point cloud. Later, researchers developed methods to correlate data information before and after, such as the Markov random field [23–25] and discriminative random field [26, 27]. These methods effectively improve the classification effect and reduce the cost of task completion. These methods also show different levels of constraint effects under different scenarios and constraints, and the universality and accuracy in complex environments are not strong, which is also a major difficulty in research classification and model design [28]. Over the past few years, advancements in iterative updates for computer arithmetic processing, as well as the creation and expansion of a large three-dimensional scene database, have accelerated the development and implementation of deep learning tools within three-dimensional point cloud areas. As a result, traditional feature classifiers and classification techniques are becoming outdated and are being replaced by newer, more advanced skills. Initially, researchers usually use the method of projecting the original point cloud data onto a two-dimensional image when preprocessing the point cloud. This method [29–33] of three-dimensional projection to two-dimensional projection often loses critical information in the process of processing, which eventually leads to incomplete model training and decision-making errors, which greatly limits the performance of the model. For this reason, researchers decided to start from the source of the three-dimensional point cloud and directly input the original point cloud to avoid losing key information. In 2017, Reference [34] first proposed a new network architecture called PointNet, which was introduced in the field of point cloud analysis. This network is unique in that it can directly process raw point clouds and has since gained widespread attention and usage in various applications, such as point cloud categorization, semantic segmentation, and object detection.

Deep learning has emerged as a powerful technique for point cloud 3D object detection, enabling impressive advancements in various domains such as scene classification and object detection. Aiming at the method of point cloud 3D object detection based on deep learning, this paper uses a knowledge graph to collect data, process information and summarize conclusions and expounds the structural characteristics and research contents of this hot field to study and reveal the development trend and prospect of this direction in the field over the last couple of years. Based on data from the Web of Science (WoS), this paper summarizes and plans the papers from 2016 to 2023. The keywords are 'Three-dimensional Point Cloud', 'Point Cloud Based on Deep Learning', 'Object Recognition from Point Cloud', and 'Semantic Labelling of Point Cloud'. A total of 1067 Chinese literature and 1193 English literature records (SCI source journals, EI source journals, CCSCI WoS core set) were obtained, including many articles and reviews. Through literature collation, refinement, and filtering, 366 closely related Chinese studies and 535 closely related English studies were finally obtained.

By analysing the search results and refining the keyword content, the research hotspots are visually displayed. Figure 1 shows the research hotspots of papers obtained from WoS. In Fig. 1, the size of the circle and the density between the associated lines directly represent the degree of the close correlation between research hotspots. In this way, the links between hot research fields are effectively clustered together.

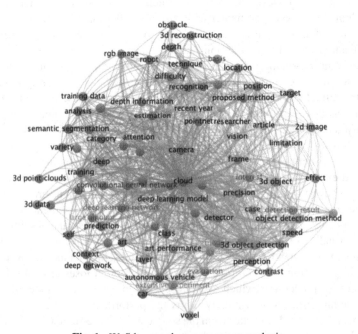

Fig. 1. WoS keyword co-occurrence analysis

Through visual analysis, it can be seen that the exploration in this branch mainly includes 3D laser point clouds, deep neural networks, 3D target detection, and point cloud processing. At present, some review articles have discussed and summarized point cloud target detection based on deep learning [35]. Based on previous work and existing research, this paper enriches and improves the content summary of the deep learning method for 3D target detection in the point cloud field.

3 Point Cloud Processing Method

In recent years, the training and information processing of 3D laser point clouds [36–39] has become a research hotspot at home and abroad. The algorithms for detecting three-dimensional objects from point clouds based on deep learning can be divided into three categories: classification processing methods based on graph convolution, object detection methods based on the original point cloud, and detection methods based on fusion graph features and original point cloud information.

3.1 Based on Graph Convolution

The early VoxNet algorithm has many problems, such as high computational and memory costs and large model capacity constraints. The processing effect of the depth map has not been improved. In 2018, Reference [40] improved and proposed a VoxelNet with end-to-end results on this basis, which not only improves the connection between the front and back features of the point cloud in the environment but also expands the learning range of the broader visual features, as shown in Fig. 2. In the same year, Zhang proposed graph convolutional neural networks, Graph-CNN (Point-VGG), by using graph convolution and point cloud downsampling. The network combines the comparison of the features of convolutional kernels, max-pooling layers, and densely connected layers. Reference [2] proposed Point-GNN, which connects and aggregates the feature relationship between adjacent regions and point cloud center points, to perform point cloud target detection quickly and effectively.

In addition, DGCNN [41], MVCNN [42], and other algorithms are similar to the methods of traditional convolutional neural network models, convolution operations

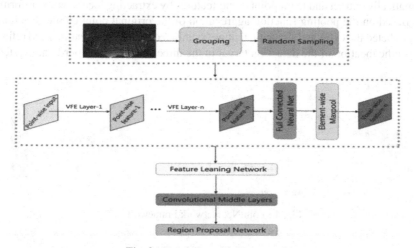

Fig. 2. Voxel Network Framework

are performed directly on point cloud images, and good experimental results are also obtained. Figure 3 displays the flow chart for the MVCNN model.

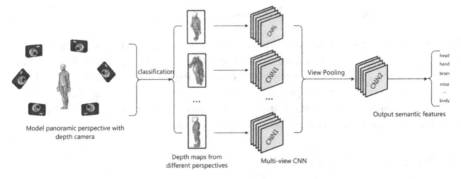

Fig. 3. MVCNN Network Framework

3.2 Based on Original Point Cloud

Based on the point cloud data of image processing, there are always problems such as information loss. Therefore, researchers decided to process the original point cloud data directly. In the early stage, Reference [36] pioneered the point cloud feature learning network PointNet, which used the spatial transformation network to solve the problem of point cloud rotation invariance. This contributed significantly to the establishment of fundamental principles for the study of original point cloud manipulation. Therefore, researchers have proposed more feature classification networks based on PointNet++, such as PointConv, PointWeb, and PointRCNN [43, 44]. The algorithm flow is shown in Fig. 4 and Fig. 5. Reference [35] proposes an adaptive feature learning mechanism to automatically extract and learn point cloud features by extracting local context information. Based on the pooling function aggregation of the original point cloud, Reference [45] predicted the extracted semantic features combined with spatial features and refined the specific location of the detection target in the three-dimensional coordinate system.

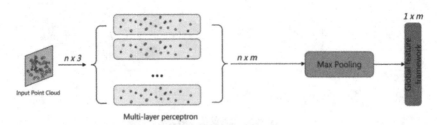

Fig. 4. PointNet Network Framework

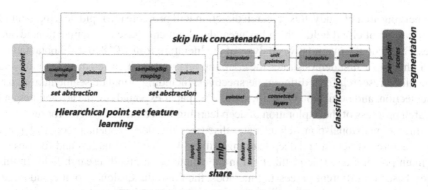

Fig. 5. PointNet++ Network Framework

3.3 Fusion Processing Algorithm

It can be seen from the above methods that both graph convolution-based and original point cloud processing-based methods can obtain rich semantic features and obtain extraction effects at different speeds according to the semantic resolution. Therefore, researchers have proposed a fusion algorithm that combines the advantages of graph convolution and original point clouds and uses image processing as an auxiliary to fuse the results of image data and point cloud detection on the existing 3D object detection technology.

The MV3D model proposed by Reference [46] in the early stage is one of the main-stream methods of early fusion processing. The convolution layer is used to analyse both the top-down and forward-facing views of the bird's perspective, fuse with the depth RGB image through the pooling function, predict the target category and return the detection box. Due to the low accuracy of the early MV3D model and the loss of key information, reference [23] proposed the AVOD neural network structure model. The algorithm flow is shown in Fig. 6. More underlying information and semantic information are restored, and the model accuracy is further improved. Inspired by graph convolution and semantic segmentation, Reference [48] proposed a multitask multisensor detection model in 2019. This method fuses the ROI pooling region with the features detected by the sensor system and uses the deep convolution network to complete the image information to obtain better point cloud feature fusion information. In 2020, Reference [47] unified the image of the deep learning network with the three-dimensional target data of the point cloud. Based on a new decision function Hough, the upsampling points and downsampling points of the point cloud are distinguished, and the geometric characteristics of the red-green-blue (RGB) visual data and the point cloud are combined or merged.

4 Generalize

Utilizing deep learning techniques for the identification of three-dimensional point clouds not only improves the operation ability of the system to process point cloud information and strengthens the flexibility and expansibility of a detection system but also improves the participation ability of the original point cloud data information. As an emerging area of study, this research direction will promote the rapid development of the future point cloud field, which has great development space and application advantages. Based on the quantitative analysis of the literature from 2018 to 2023 obtained by WoS, this paper first demonstrates the coupling relationship between deep learning and point cloud research from different perspectives, including semantic segmentation, target detection, and point cloud classification. This paper expounds on the advantages and research progress of the exploration of deep learning-based methodologies for researching three-dimensional point cloud data, discusses the development process of point cloud feature extraction and deep learning utilized for detecting targets and focuses on the main position and role of this field in the whole point cloud research field. In this paper, based on different processing methods, the three-dimensional point cloud target detection method based on deep learning atmosphere based on graph convolution processing method, based on the original point cloud processing approach and based on graph convolution and original point cloud data fusion processing method in different categories show their respective advantages and disadvantages.

In the future, including larger and more complex environmental point cloud data technology, how to support the rapid development of point cloud research with more efficient, more accurate, and more intelligent methods and technologies and realize the full mining of point cloud value through the coupling of deep learning technology is a research topic with broad scientific research prospects and major national needs in the future.

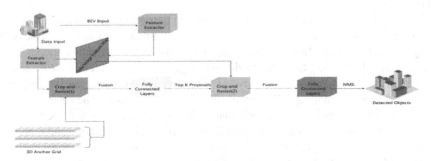

Fig. 6. AVOD Network Framework

5 Prospect

In general, the current methods based on graph convolution, original point cloud, or fusion processing have achieved different advantages. The method based on graph convolution has high detection efficiency and fast recognition. Converting a three-dimensional point cloud into a two-dimensional image can significantly reduce the time required for processing but also loses much key information. The method based on the original point cloud retains all key information well, increases the operation cost and is difficult to calculate. The method based on fusion processing is currently a relatively safe and efficient method. It uses image information as an aid to retain the original information of the point cloud while ensuring high efficiency. Based on the current research progress and problems, this paper proposes the following suggestions for future research:

- The input of the original point cloud is preprocessed to retain key information while removing redundant scene information. To enhance both the accuracy and efficiency of detection…
- The filter and recognition framework is redesigned for the point cloud effect of image processing, and the accuracy of the two-dimensional converter is optimized to achieve higher precision levels for the model.
- Because the hardware computing cost is too high and the image auxiliary function of fusion processing makes up for this shortcoming well, the fusion processing method will be a main development trend and the current research trend in target detection using three-dimensional point clouds.

References

1. Li, B., Ouyang, W., Sheng, L., et al.: Gs3D: an efficient 3D object detection framework for autonomous driving. In: Proceedings of the IEEE/CVF Conference on Computer Vision and Pattern Recognition, pp. 1019–1028 (2019)
2. Zhou, Y., Tuzel, O.: VoxelNet: end-to-end learning for point cloud based 3D object detection. In: Proceedings of the IEEE Conference on Computer Vision and Pattern Recognition, pp. 4490–4499 (2018)
3. Ku, J., Mozifian, M., Lee, J., et al.: Joint 3D proposal generation and object detection from view aggregation. In: 2018 IEEE/RSJ International Conference on Intelligent Robots and Systems (IROS), pp. 1–8. IEEE (2018)
4. Girshick, R.: Fast R-CNN. In: IEEE International Conference on Computer Vision (ICCV), pp. 1440–1448 (2015)
5. Ren, S., He, K., Girshick, R., et al.: Faster R-CNN: towards real-time object detection with region proposal networks. IEEE Trans. Pattern Anal. Mach. Intell. **39**(6), 1137–1149 (2015)
6. Redmon, J., Divvala, S., Girshick, R., et al.: You only look once: unified, real-time object detection. In: IEEE Conference on Computer Vision and Pattern Recognition (CVPR), pp. 779–788 (2015)
7. Liu, W., et al.: SSD: single shot multibox detector. In: Leibe, B., Matas, J., Sebe, N., Welling, M. (eds.) ECCV 2016. LNCS, vol. 9905, pp. 21–37. Springer, Cham (2016). https://doi.org/10.1007/978-3-319-46448-0_2
8. Redmon, J., Farhadi, A.: YOLO9000: better, faster, stronger. In: 30th IEEE Conference on Computer Vision and Pattern Recognition (CVPR), pp. 6517–6525 (2017)
9. Ma, X., Hovy, E.: End-to-end sequence labelling via bi-directional LSTM-CNNs-CRF. In: 54th Annual Meeting of the Association for Computational Linguistics (ACL), pp. 1064–1074 (2016)
10. Yoon, S., Kim, E.: Temporal classification error compensation of convolutional neural network for traffic sign recognition. In: International Conference on Control Engineering and Artificial Intelligence (CCEAI) (2017)
11. Zhou, Y., Tuzel, O.: VoxelNet: end-to-end learning for point cloud based 3D object detection. In: IEEE/CVF Conference on Computer Vision and Pattern Recognition (CVPR), pp. 4490–4499 (2018)
12. Chen, X., Ma, H., Wan, J., Li, B., Xia, T.: Multi-view 3D object detection network for autonomous driving. In: 30th IEEE Conference on Computer Vision and Pattern Recognition (CVPR), pp. 6526–6534 (2017)

13. Qi, C.R., Su, H., Mo, K., Guibas, L.J.: PointNet: deep learning on point sets for 3D classification and segmentation. In: 30th IEEE Conference on Computer Vision and Pattern Recognition (CVPR), pp. 77–85 (2017)

14. Kim, K., Kim, C., Jang, C., Kim, J., Kim, H.: Deep learning-based dynamic object classification using LiDAR point cloud augmented by layer-based accumulation for intelligent vehicles. Exp. Syst. Appl. **167**, 113861 (2020)

15. Zermas, D., Izzat, I., Papanikolopoulos, N.: Fast segmentation of 3D point clouds: a paradigm on LiDAR data for autonomous vehicle applications. In: 2017 IEEE International Conference on Robotics and Automation (ICRA), pp. 5067–5073 (2017)

16. Bisheng, Y., Ronggang, H., Jianping, L., Jian, Y., Jiayuan, L.: Automated reconstruction of building LoDs from airborne LiDAR point clouds using an improved morphological scale space. Remote Sens. **9**(1), 14 (2016)

17. Ene, L.T., Næsset, E., Gobakken, T., Gregoire, T.G.: Large-scale estimation of change in aboveground biomass in miombo woodlands using airborne laser scanning and national forest inventory data. Remote Sens. Environ. **188**, 106–117 (2017)

18. Chen, C., Li, X., Belkacem, A.N., Zhang, H., Xiang, S.: The mixed kernel function SVM-based point cloud classification. Int. J. Precis. Eng. Manuf. **20**(5), 737–747 (2019)

19. Ni, H., Lin, X., Zhang, J.: Classification of ALS point cloud with improved point cloud segmentation and random forests. Remote Sens. **9**(3), 288 (2017)

20. Weinmann, M., Jutzi, B., Hinz, S., Mallet, C.: Semantic point cloud interpretation based on optimal neighborhoods, relevant features and efficient classifiers. ISPRS J. Photogramm. Remote Sens. **105**(7), 286–304 (2015)

21. Chan, C.W., Paelinckx, D.: Evaluation of Random Forest and Adaboost tree-based ensemble classification and spectral band selection for ecotope mapping using airborne hyperspectral imagery. Remote Sens. Environ. **112**(6), 2999–3011 (2008)

22. Lalonde, J.F., Unnikrishnan, R., Vandapel, N., Hebert, M.: Scale selection for classification of point-sampled 3D surfaces. In: The Fifth International Conference on 3D Digital Imaging and Modelling, 3DIM 2005, pp. 285–292. IEEE (2005)

23. Han, Y., Sun, H., Lu, Y., Zhong, R., Ji, C., Xie, S.: 3D point cloud generation based on multi-sensor fusion. Appl. Sci. **12**(19), 9433 (2022)

24. Niemeyer, J., Rottensteiner, F., Soergel, U.: Contextual classification of LiDAR data and building object detection in urban areas. ISPRS J. Photogramm. Remote Sens. **87**, 152–165 (2014)

25. Munoz, D., Bagnell, J.A., Vandapel, N., Hebert, M.: Contextual classification with functional maxmargin Markov networks. In: 2009 IEEE Conference on Computer Vision and Pattern Recognition, pp. 975–982 (2009)

26. Shapovalov, R., Velizhev, E., Barinova, O.: Nonassociative Markov networks for 3D point cloud classification. In: International Archives of the Photogrammetry, Remote Sensing and Spatial Information Sciences (2010)

27. Munoz, D., Bagnell, J.A., Vandapel, N., Hebert, M.: Contextual classification with functional max-margin Markov networks. In: 2009 IEEE Conference on Computer Vision and Pattern Recognition, pp. 975–982 (2009)

28. Niemeyer, J., Rottensteiner, F., Soergel, U.: Contextual classification of LiDAR data and building object detection in urban areas. ISPRS J. Photogramm. Remote Sens. **87**(1), 152–165 (2014)

29. Maturana, D., Scherer, S.: Voxnet: A 3D convolutional neural network for real-time object recognition. In: 2015 IEEE/RSJ International Conference on Intelligent Robots and Systems (IROS), pp. 922–928 (2015)

30. Wu, Z., Song, S., Khosla, A., et al.: 3D ShapeNets: a deep representation for volumetric shapes. In: Proceedings of the IEEE Conference on Computer Vision and Pattern Recognition, pp. 1912–1920 (2015)

31. Cohen, T.S., Geiger, M., Köhler, J., et al.: Spherical CNNs. arXiv preprint arXiv:1801.10130 (2018)
32. You, Y., Lou, Y., Liu, Q., et al.: Pointwise rotation-invariant network with adaptive sampling and 3D spherical voxel convolution. In: Proceedings of the AAAI Conference on Artificial Intelligence, pp. 12717–12724 (2020)
33. Riegler, G., Osman Ulusoy, A., Geiger, A.: OctNet: learning deep 3D representations at high resolutions. In: Proceedings of the IEEE Conference on Computer Vision and Pattern Recognition, pp. 3577–3586 (2017)
34. Wang, Y., Tian, Y., Li, G., et al.: A review of 3D object detection based on convolutional neural network. Pattern Recogn. Artif. Intell. **34**(12), 1103–1119 (2011)
35. Guo, Y. L., Wang, H., Hu, Q., et al.: Deep learning for 3D point clouds: a survey. arXiv preprint arXiv:1912.12033 (2019)
36. Qi, C. R., Su, H., Mo, K., et al.: PointNet: deep learning on point sets for 3D classification and segmentation. In: 2017 IEEE CVPR, pp. 652–660 (2017)
37. Blanco, L., Sellés, D.G., Guinau, M., et al.: Machine learning-based Rockfalls detection with 3D point clouds, example in the Montserrat Massif (Spain). Remote Sens. **14**(17), 4306 (2022)
38. Dabetwar, S., Kulkarni, N. N., Angelosanti, M., Niezrecki, C., Sabato, A.: Sensitivity analysis of unmanned aerial vehicle-borne 3D point cloud reconstruction from infrared images. J. Build. Eng. **58**, 105070 (2022)
39. Li, T., et al.: Gait recognition using spatio-temporal information of 3D point cloud via Millimeter Wave Radar. Wirel. Commun. Mob. Comput. **2022**, 1–16 (2022)
40. Maturana, D., Scherer, S.: VoxNet: a 3D convolutional neural network for real-time object recognition. In: 2015 IEEE/RSJ International Conference on Intelligent Robots and Systems (IROS), pp. 922–928. IEEE (2015)
41. Kalogerakis, E., Averkiou, M., Maji, S., et al.: 3D shape segmentation with projective convolutional networks. In: Proceedings of the IEEE Conference on Computer Vision and Pattern Recognition, pp. 3779–3788 (2017)
42. Qi, C.R., Su, H., Niessner, M., et al.: Volumetric and multi-view CNNs for object classification on 3D data. In: IEEE Conference on Computer Vision and Pattern Recognition (CVPR), pp. 5648–5656 (2016)
43. Duc-Phong, N., et al.: Automatic part segmentation of facial anatomies using geometric deep learning toward a computer-aided facial rehabilitation. Eng. Appl. Artif. Intell. **119**, 105832 (2023)
44. Hao, H., Yu, J., Yin, L., Cai, G., Zhang, S., Zhang, H.: An improved PointNet++ point cloud segmentation model applied to automatic measurement method of pig body size. Comput. Electron. Agric. **205**, 107560 (2023)
45. Shi, S., Wang, X., Li, H.: PointRCNN: 3D object proposal generation and detection from point cloud. In: Proceedings of the 32nd IEEE/CVF Conference on Computer Vision and Pattern Recognition, pp. 770–779. IEEE, Piscataway (2019)
46. Chen, Y., Liu, S., Shen, X., et al.: Fast point R-CNN. In: Proceedings of the IEEE/CVF International Conference on Computer Vision, pp. 9775–9784 (2019)
47. Yan, Y., Mao, Y., Li, B.: Second: sparsely embedded convolutional detection. Sensors **18**(10), 3337 (2018)
48. Mac, G., Guoy, Y., Yang, J., et al.: Learning multiview representation with LSTM for 3D shape recognition and retrieval. IEEE Trans. Multimedia **21**(5), 1169–1182 (2018)

A Review of Intelligent Opponent Modelling Research for Air Combat Simulation Training

Yanan Guo[1,2], Xiaoqun Cao[2(✉)], Yeping Li[3], Xiaoguang Zhou[1], Guohui Huang[1], and Kecheng Peng[2]

[1] Simulation and Training Center, Naval Aviation University, Huludao 125001, Liaoning, China
[2] College of Meteorology and Oceanography, National University of Defense Technology, Changsha 410073, Hunan, China
guoyn18@163.com
[3] The No. 91658 Troop of PLA, Huludao 125001, Liaoning, China

Abstract. Air combat simulation is an important way to improve the combat capability of pilots, and virtual intelligent opponents have become an important part of the fighter simulation training system. In recent years, the rapid development of artificial intelligence technology has greatly promoted the development of air combat intelligent opponent modelling technology. With powerful self-learning and decision-making capabilities, intelligent virtual opponents are able to help pilots complete complex tactical training. At the same time, the large amount of training data in the virtual environment provides for the iterative optimization of intelligent opponent modelling technology. To promote the development of intelligent opponent modelling technology in air combat simulation training systems, this paper analyses the situational awareness, autonomous decision making, self-confrontation optimization methods and anti-interference technology of intelligent agents from key technologies such as deep learning and reinforcement learning to provide support for the development of air combat simulation training systems.

Keywords: Air Combat Simulation · Intelligent Opponent Modelling · Reinforcement Learning

1 Introduction

Air combat confrontation is an important part of modern warfare, and to win air battles, not only advanced fighters but also highly qualified fighter pilots are needed [1, 2]. In realistic training, relying on real aircraft to conduct countermeasure training to develop pilots' combat skills is close to real combat, but it takes up more resources and is more difficult to organize, and the realism of the hypothetical enemy is limited. Therefore, the cost of training fighter pilots through real-world countermeasures is very high, and relying solely on real-world flight training often makes it difficult to achieve the desired results. In contrast, simulation training in a virtual environment generates digital virtual opponents through computers, which can significantly reduce training costs. By

M. Zhang et al. (Eds.): CCF NCCA 2023, CCIS 1959, pp. 40–48, 2024.
https://doi.org/10.1007/978-981-99-8764-1_4

simulating the enemy and its weaponry through advanced virtual reality technology, various engagement scenarios can be generated according to training needs, thus effectively improving the relevance of air combat training, expanding training coverage, and improving training efficiency [3–6]. In addition, virtual simulation training can provide a more comprehensive and complex training scenario. As the performance of fighter aircraft continues to improve and as the form of warfare evolves, with joint operations and system operations becoming the dominant form, it is almost imperative to develop a high-fidelity flight training simulator. Only a more comprehensive and realistic simulation of the combat environment of advanced warplanes or aircraft groups can provide pilots with a training experience almost as good as real flight, as well as more complex and realistic training content, speeding up the pilot training process and improving training efficiency.

In recent years, with the improvement of computing power and the emergence of big data, the rise of deep learning has triggered a new round of artificial intelligence (AI) research [7–10]. The construction of intelligent virtual opponents based on AI technology to assist pilots in confrontation training can greatly reduce training costs, avoid the problems caused by the lack of pilot coaches, and enrich the simulation of confrontation scenarios, greatly promoting the study of air combat simulation training systems [11–14]. To test the feasibility of AI virtual opponents, DARPA conducted research on an AI-based air combat program in which human pilots were engaged in air combat against virtual opponents, with the AI virtual pilots eventually winning, demonstrating the great potential of AI in the field of air combat simulation training. Although significant progress has been made in the application of AI in air combat, there are still many challenges. First, most previous AI-based air combat research has been limited to ideal environments, while the actual air combat environment is characterized by a high degree of uncertainty and various deceptive interferences, and there is a large gap between simulated scenarios and reality. In addition, although AI methods have obvious advantages in information mining and optimal decision-making, they are still a long way from practical engineering implementation and still need to overcome many challenges, especially bottlenecks such as uncertainty, interpretability, transferability, and deception resistance.

To deeply understand the opportunities and challenges of intelligent virtual opponent modelling technology in air combat simulation training, this paper analyses the related technologies according to the needs and problems in air combat simulation training and proposes the research direction of intelligent opponent modelling technology for future air combat simulation training.

2 Background and Requirements

In air combat confrontations, situational awareness capability is an important factor that can affect the success or failure of warfare. With the rapid development of artificial intelligence technology and high-performance computing, a large number of situational assessment methods have emerged. Intelligent virtual opponents perform situational calculations, which must take into account the combat weapons, sensor performance, and the number of personnel of both belligerents. In the future, how to combine information fusion technology, comprehensive use of multisource information, and establishment of expert knowledge-based and data-driven situational assessment models are the primary issues for intelligent decision-making of virtual opponents.

In air combat simulation confrontation, the virtual opponent needs to have autonomous decision-making capability. After acquiring information from both sides, the virtual opponent needs to make tactical decisions. The traditional decision-making method is search-based decision-making. The decision model simulates the tactical response of both sides, performs multistep projection, and makes tactical choices based on the results of the projection. With the rise of deep neural networks, functional decision making has been rapidly developed, i.e., the decision model is a direct mapping of input information to output decisions, and the decision computation is completed in one step. In short, the deep neural network-based decision model is a function of battlefield information for the best tactical decision-making. In the context of intelligent air warfare, the development of advanced artificial intelligence-driven decision models is an important research topic.

Finally, the virtual opponent needs to have the ability to self-improve and be able to continuously improve its strategy during the confrontation. A virtual opponent based on deep reinforcement learning needs to automatically adapt to the dynamic battlefield environment, making it highly flexible. By leveraging self-training algorithms, intelligent virtual opponents should be able to exploit existing tactical skills and even develop new air combat strategies that may not currently exist, thereby continuously improving their air combat proficiency.

3   Key Technologies for Virtual Opponent Modelling

3.1   High-Performance Computing Technology

In flight simulation training, the flight simulator is a critical component that consists of several key parts. These include the simulation cockpit, motion system, vision system, computer system, and instructor console. While the hardware elements of the training simulator are important, the flight simulation software plays a crucial role, as it significantly impacts the simulator's performance. The advanced level of the simulation software directly determines the capabilities and effectiveness of the flight training simulator. The simulation software must accurately simulate aerodynamic parameters to replicate the flight characteristics of real aircraft. This requires precise simulation models and fast calculation speeds. The flight simulation model encompasses various modules, such as aerodynamics, equations of motion, moments, atmospheric turbulence, mass characteristics, destruction conditions, and repositioning. These modules work together to provide a comprehensive representation of the flight training simulator's behavior. Executing these simulation calculations requires substantial computational resources. Hence, it is necessary to consider the hardware limitations of the onboard embedded environment when performing flight simulation calculations. To ensure efficient execution of the flight simulation program, advanced high-performance computing technologies are utilized. These include advanced parallel algorithms, distributed computing, and cloud computing. Implementing these technologies improves the efficiency of flight simulation and enhances the fidelity of simulation scenarios.

Figure 1 depicts the schematic diagram of virtual opponent modelling for air combat based on high-performance computing technology. This diagram illustrates the integration of advanced computing resources and techniques to enhance the realism and effectiveness of modelling virtual opponents in air combat scenarios within the flight simulation environment.

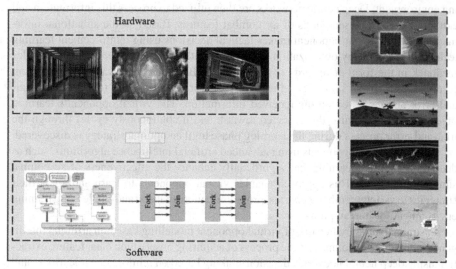

Fig. 1. Schematic diagram of virtual opponent modelling for air combat based on high-performance computing technology

3.2 Virtual Opponent Modelling Based on Artificial Intelligence Technology

In recent years, there has been remarkable progress in artificial intelligence (AI) technology, particularly in the fields of deep learning (DL) and deep reinforcement learning (DRL). These approaches have achieved significant success in solving various decision problems, including Atari games and chess, leading to the advancement of intelligent decision-making systems. In the military domain, deep learning technology has found applications in rapidly processing battlefield intelligence information to support decision-making and situational analysis. Deep neural networks, known for their powerful fitting capability, enable virtual opponents to understand and master fundamental tactical manoeuvres. This understanding allows them to make correct decision-making actions in different air combat scenarios. During simulated confrontations, virtual opponents receive real-time situational information as input and make decisions through nonlinear mapping. Reinforcement learning (RL) is a key method for solving sequential decision-making tasks. It involves learning strategies by interacting with the environment through trial and error. RL aligns well with human empirical learning and decision-making processes, allowing it to effectively tackle problems where access to sample data is challenging. Deep reinforcement learning combines the strengths of deep learning and reinforcement learning. It overcomes the limitations of traditional tabular reinforcement learning methods, which can only handle low-dimensional inputs. DRL possesses superior feature extraction capabilities, making it a crucial research direction in the field of artificial intelligence.

When applying deep reinforcement learning to air combat training, the agent (the virtual opponent) acquires high-dimensional observation data from the simulated training environment. Deep neural networks are then utilized to process this information and extract abstract representations of air combat features. Based on the situational information, the intelligent opponent makes tactical decisions using reinforcement learning techniques for strategy optimization. It interacts with the environment, which provides feedback in the form of rewards or punishments. By receiving reward or punishment feedback, the virtual opponent adjusts its behavior and continues to engage in trial-and-error actions based on the received information. The virtual opponent's learning objective is to maximize the expected reward, and it continuously cycles through the trial-and-error process during the learning phase until an optimal strategy is discovered.

Building virtual opponents using advanced artificial intelligence algorithms, such as deep reinforcement learning, can significantly enhance the effectiveness of air combat simulation training. This approach enables virtual opponents to learn and adapt their strategies to various combat scenarios, providing a more realistic and challenging training environment for human pilots.

In summary, the framework of virtual opponent modelling based on artificial intelligence technology encompasses the process of acquiring observation data, feature extraction using deep neural networks, decision-making based on reinforcement learning, and iterative learning cycles. This framework improves the overall realism and effectiveness of air combat simulation training. The different levels of virtual opponents built based on artificial intelligence technology are shown in Fig. 2.

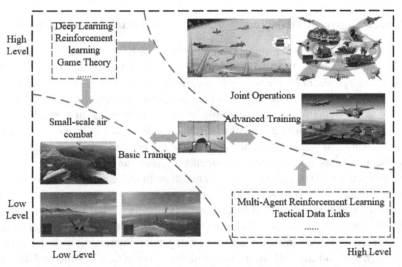

Fig. 2. Schematic diagram of different levels of virtual opponents built based on artificial intelligence technology.

3.3 Virtual Opponent Modelling Technology for Live-Virtual-Constructive (LVC) Training

Future warfare will gradually evolve towards system-level confrontation and joint operations. Therefore, simulated training scenarios need to encompass multidomain joint operations. Emerging forms of combat, such as swarm drone operations and manned-unmanned teaming, will become the main styles of future air warfare. Flight training simulation systems must adapt to this characteristic and fully leverage technologies such as interconnectedness and virtual-physical interaction.

In the air combat simulation training system, virtual opponents with matched combat capabilities need to be generated based on the performance of target fighter aircraft and the manoeuvrability and decision-making characteristics of pilots. Additionally, by utilizing distributed simulation technology, elements such as fighter aircraft, simulation training platforms, and natural environments are integrated to construct comprehensive battlefield scenarios, facilitating multidomain joint training and tactical research. This integration will become a new trend in future flight training simulators. Figure 3 illustrates a simplified Live-Virtual-Constructive (LVC) training scenario, providing trainees with a highly realistic training experience and enhancing the effectiveness of simulation training. As training scenarios become increasingly complex, the integration of flight simulators and digitized forces with live ammunition training has already become the mainstream trend in air combat simulation training. Applying advanced technologies such as expert systems and deep reinforcement learning to the LVC constructive simulation of aerial combat will greatly enrich simulation training scenarios, improve the effectiveness of air combat simulation training, and enhance the operational capabilities of fighter pilots.

Fig. 3. Schematic diagram of "Live-Virtual-Construction" simulation training system

3.4 Virtual Opponent Anti-deception Technology

To date, research on virtual opponent modelling for air combat simulation training has been limited to simple scenarios, resulting in a certain gap between simulations and real combat environments. Additionally, supervised learning models often struggle to handle untrained scenarios, especially when faced with deceptive input information. This results in poor transferability and susceptibility to interference for air combat virtual opponents. To address the security challenges faced by air combat virtual opponents, ensuring their robustness against deceptive attacks and guaranteeing the effectiveness of air combat simulation training, it is necessary to develop virtual opponent systems capable of effectively defending against enemy deception intentions, including both specific and planned attacks as well as unexpected situations.

Current research indicates that explainable reinforcement learning will progressively drive artificial intelligence systems toward general intelligence, promoting breakthrough innovations in autonomous decision-making. Therefore, this technology will become a vital research direction for constructing explainable air combat virtual opponents. In the next steps, researchers will further integrate prior knowledge, data, models, and algorithms to enhance the robustness and security of virtual opponents. In the future, new intelligent opponents will be developed based on distributed reinforcement learning, joint learning, and cryptography technologies to achieve robustness and security. Through in-depth research on causality-driven robust decision-making methods, it is expected to build safe and reliable virtual opponents for air warfare.

3.5 Intelligent Evaluation Technology

Efficient utilization of big data resources and in-depth analysis of simulation training data hold significant value for future air warfare research. Traditional information processing and data evaluation methods are no longer adequate for the demands of air combat simulation training data analysis. Artificial intelligence algorithms possess inherent advantages in processing large volumes of simulation training data. For instance, deep neural networks can effectively analyse vast amounts of flight parameter data, enabling the identification of complex flight manoeuvres when combined with expert systems for evaluation. Constructing an intelligent evaluation system for virtual opponents and real pilots can significantly enhance training efficiency. The ongoing development of artificial intelligence, big data, and other technologies has paved the way for collecting data from virtual opponents and pilots during flight training. This enables accurate evaluation of their operational capabilities, thereby improving training effectiveness. Furthermore, providing tailored advice and suggestions based on individual pilots' strengths and weaknesses, utilizing advanced recommendation technology, customizing personalized training content, and creating virtual opponents at varying difficulty levels have emerged as new trends in flight training simulation.

In some countries, flight schools have already begun enhancing simulators to act as judges in assessing trainees' fitness to fly and their potential to become combat pilots. By establishing pilot growth profiles and flight training databases and leveraging data-driven evaluation systems, intelligent assessment methods can be employed to evaluate virtual opponents and human pilots. This approach facilitates the provision of intelligent training programs, significantly enhancing the effectiveness and progress of training.

4   Conclusion

Simulation training is a crucial section of flight training, offering numerous benefits such as improved training efficiency, cost savings, and reduced flight risks. As technology rapidly evolves, the application of virtual environments to augment simulation training has become increasingly popular globally. Artificial intelligence technology, in particular, has played a significant role in enhancing the capabilities of virtual simulation training platforms, bringing them closer to real combat scenarios. In this paper, we aim to analyse the capability requirements of virtual adversaries and delve into the key technologies linked to virtual opponent modelling research. Additionally, we explore the potential of artificial intelligence applications in air combat simulation training and provide an outlook on the challenges and progress of virtual opponent modelling. Specifically, it delves into virtual opponent modelling for live, virtual and constructive (LVC) training, as well as intelligent assessment based on simulated training big data and safety studies of virtual opponents. LVC training combines real, virtual and constructive elements that can create a comprehensive training experience. Intelligent assessment techniques allow for the evaluation of pilot performance and the identification of issues that need improvement. While there are still numerous challenges to be addressed in the field of air combat simulation, ongoing research efforts will continue to advance virtual opponent modelling technology. This progress holds great promise for the future of air combat simulation training, leading to more realistic and effective training scenarios. As virtual opponents become increasingly sophisticated, they will contribute significantly to training outcomes and enrich the overall training experience for aspiring pilots.

References

1. Berkowitz, B.D.: The New Face of War: How War Will be Fought in the 21st Century. Simon and Schuster (2003)
2. Joseph, C.: An overview of psychological factors and interventions in air combat operations. Indian J. Aerosp. Med. **51**(2), 1–16 (2007)
3. Ma, S., Zhang, H., Yang, G.: Target threat level assessment based on cloud model under fuzzy and uncertain conditions in air combat simulation. Aerosp. Sci. Technol. **67**, 49–53 (2017)
4. Toubman, A., Roessingh, J.J., Spronck, P., et al.: Rewarding air combat behavior in training simulations. In: 2015 IEEE international conference on systems, man, and cybernetics, pp. 1397–1402. IEEE (2015)
5. Houck, M.R., Thomas, G.S., Bell, H.H.: Training potential of multiplayer air combat simulation. In: Proceedings of the Human Factors Society Annual Meeting. Sage CA: Los Angeles, CA: SAGE Publications, vol. 33, no. 19, pp. 1300-1304 (1989)
6. Gheorghiu, A.: Flight simulation in air force training. a knowledge transfer eficiency perspective. J. Defense Resour. Manag. (JoDRM), **4**(2), 153–158 (2013)
7. Bengio, Y., Goodfellow, I., Courville, A.: Deep Learning. MIT press, Cambridge, MA, USA (2017)
8. Guo, Y., Cao, X., Liu, B., et al.: Cloud detection for satellite imagery using attention-based U-Net convolutional neural network. Symmetry **12**(6), 1056 (2020)
9. Wang, R., Ma, Y., Sun, W., et al.: Multilevel nested pyramid network for mass segmentation in mammograms. Neurocomputing **363**, 313–320 (2019)

10. Guo, Y., Cao, X., Liu, B., et al.: Solving partial differential equations using deep learning and physical constraints. Appl. Sci. **10**(17), 5917 (2020)
11. Pope, A.P., Ide, J.S., Mićović, D., et al.: Hierarchical reinforcement learning for air-to-air combat. In: 2021 International Conference on Unmanned Aircraft Systems (ICUAS), pp. 275–284. IEEE (2021)
12. Yoo, J., Kim, D., Shim, D.H.: Deep reinforcement learning based autonomous air-to-air combat using target trajectory prediction. In: 2021 21st International Conference on Control, Automation and Systems (ICCAS), pp. 2172–2176. IEEE (2021)
13. Kurniawan, B., Vamplew, P., Papasimeon, M., Dazeley, R., Foale, C.: An empirical study of reward structures for actor-critic reinforcement learning in air combat manoeuvring simulation. In: Liu, J., Bailey, J. (eds.) AI 2019: Advances in Artificial Intelligence. AI 2019. Lecture Notes in Computer Science, vol. 11919, pp. 54–65. Springer, Cham (2019). https://doi.org/10.1007/978-3-030-35288-2_5
14. Roessingh, J.J., Toubman, A., van Oijen, J., et al.: Machine learning techniques for autonomous agents in military simulations—Multum in Parvo. In: 2017 IEEE International Conference on Systems, Man, and Cybernetics (SMC), pp. 3445–3450. IEEE (2017)

Design of a Blind Guidance System Based on RealSense and the Improved YOLOv5 Algorithm

Zhao Zhang[1] , Xiaobin Shen[1] , Jing Ge[1] , Yingying Zha[1] , Lisai Liu[1] ,
and Sheng Liu[1,2(✉)]

[1] College of Computer Science and Technology, Huaibei Normal University, Huaibei 235000, China
Liurise@139.com

[2] Anui Engineering Research Center for Intelligent Computing and Application on Cognitive Behavior, Huaibei 235000, China

Abstract. To assist blind people in travelling and solve the problems of high hardware costs, insufficient portability of blind assistance devices, and vulnerability to environmental impacts, a modified YOLOv5 algorithm (YOLOv5-CM) based on ground plane segmentation and Euclidean clustering algorithms is proposed and applied to a blind guidance system based on RealSense D435. This proposed algorithm adds coordinate attention and uses MobileNetv3 as the backbone network for YOLOv5s to extract the main features. Compared with those of the YOLOv5 model, the mAP was improved by 0.7%, the model size was decreased by 79.1%, and the number of parameters was reduced by 80.3%. In this study, the YOLOv5-CM algorithm was applied to design a blind guidance system. When the system detects a traffic light, the RealSense D435 is used to obtain depth images to detect and measure the distance from the pedestrian traffic light. The system provides warnings based on the measured distance. When the system does not detect a traffic light, it utilizes the ground plane segmentation and Euclidean clustering algorithms to obtain the location and distance of obstacles. This information is conveyed to the blind through voice guidance, which aids navigation.

Keywords: Machine Vision · Blind Guidance System · RealSense · YOLOv5 · MobileNetv3 · Coordinate

1 Introduction

According to statistics from the World Health Organization, over 2.2 billion people worldwide were visually impaired in a 2022 survey [1]. Visually impaired people face great difficulties and dangers in daily travel due to the unavailability of proper visual information support. Therefore, the development of assistive technology facilitating safe travel has attracted much research attention. Correspondingly, we have designed a blind guide system to provide better support while travelling.

Among the numerous challenges faced by blind people, some are unemployment, reading, writing, daily activities, and travel [2–4]. In particular, blind people face several travel-related difficulties. Accordingly, guide dogs, guide poles, and GPS-enabled devices are widely used to assist in travel. Although guide dogs possess the advantages of speed, flexibility, and good affinity, there are some problems, such as scarcity and long training times [5]. Likewise, guide poles offer the advantages of convenience and low cost; however, they cannot provide remote warnings and guidance. GPS-enabled devices have benefits such as high positioning accuracy and real-time performance; however, they cannot cope with indoor environments. Perception systems based on artificial intelligence (AI) are considered the best means to assist blind people in travelling. Recently, various AI-based blind-assistance systems have been introduced and applied. For instance, Tapu et al. [6] used a multi-scale Lucas Kanade feature tracking algorithm combined with a smartphone camera to detect obstacles. However, the system lacks three-dimensional (3D) information and cannot determine the distance between obstacles. Rodriguez et al. [7]put forward a system depended on stereo vision, which first conducted plane segmentation to detect pixels on the ground and then used polar grid symbols to detect obstacles in depth images. Although these systems have reliable obstacle detection capabilities, they cannot understand scenes of traffic roads and sidewalks or possess advanced perceptual capabilities depended on deep learning, such as semantic image segmentation and object detection.

This paper introduces a guide system based on RealSense and the YOLOv5-CM object detection algorithm. The system can not only judge the location and distance of obstacles according to 3D information but also obtain the status and distance information of traffic lights on sidewalks and transmit the results to a blind person through voice prompts to improve their perception and cognitive ability of the surrounding environment and reduce their risk of encountering dangers during travel.

2 Methodology

In the system operation process, when a traffic light is detected, the system performs recognition and distance measurements. When a visually impaired person walks at a pedestrian crossing, the system announces the traffic light status every 5 s. When a visually impaired person is less than 2 m from a traffic light, the system prompts them to cross the pedestrian crossing. If traffic lights are not detected, the system detects the positions and distances of obstacles. The camera field of view is divided into five directions: front, front-left, front-right, left, and right. The system first performs ground plane segmentation, followed by obstacle clustering and distance measurements. Every 3 s, the system announces the direction and distance of the nearest obstacle within 2 m. The visually impaired person receives relevant detection information through headphones. Fig. 1 illustrates a schematic of the system design.

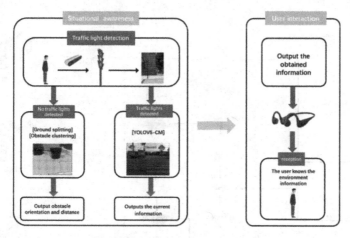

Fig. 1. The guide system diagram.

2.1 The YOLOv5-CM Improved Algorithm

Introduction to the YOLOv5 Algorithm. Target detection algorithms for deep learning can be categorized into two-stage algorithms, such as faster region-based convolutional neural network (R-CNN) [8], and one-stage algorithms, such as solid-state drive (SSD) [9] and you only look once (YOLO) [10–13]. These algorithms are widely used in computer vision applications. These two types of algorithms exhibit unique characteristics. One-stage algorithms have advantages in speed, while two-stage algorithms have advantages in accuracy. Considering both model precision and timeliness, this study used the improved version 5 of YOLOv5s as a pretrained model to implement pedestrian traffic light detection. The structure comprises the input, backbone, neck, and head, as shown in Fig. 2. The input is used to preprocess image; the backbone ex-tracts features from the preprocessed image; the neck module blends or combines the feature maps to form more complex features; and the head module generates bounding boxes, predicts the features of the image, and predicts the classes.

Embedded Coordinate Attention Mechanism. During the convolution process in the YOLOv5 algorithm, the iterations of the algorithm can accumulate a large amount of redundant background information, which can easily cause the loss of features related to traffic lights, resulting in low precision. Therefore, we added a coordinate attention mechanism (CA) [14]. To ease the previous attention mechanisms (such as squeeze and excitation networks (SENets) [15] and convolutional block attention module (CBAM) [16]) and address the two-dimensional global pooling location information loss problem, the CA mechanism module improves the expression ability of feature learning in mobile networks. As shown in Fig. 3, there are two steps in this process. The first step is the embedding of coordinate information. For the input feature graph X with dimensions of $C \times H \times W$, global average pooling is performed using the pooling kernels of size $(H, 1)$ and $(1, W)$ in the horizontal and vertical coordinate directions, respectively. The second step is to generate the coordinate information feature map. Both generated feature graphs are first concatenated, and the dimensionality is subsequently reduced using a

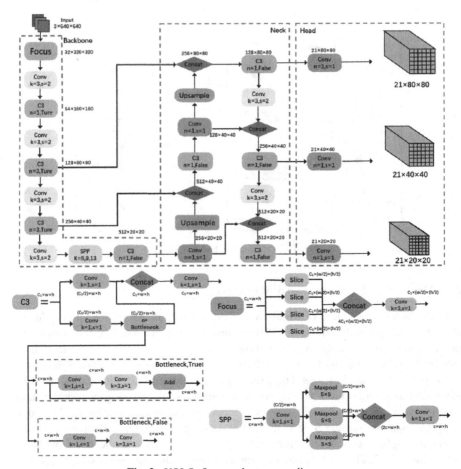

Fig. 2. YOLOv5 network structure diagram.

1×1 convolutional kernel. After processing with a BN and an activation function, they were divided into two independent tensors. The resulting tensors undergo two convolutional transformations to produce tensors with the same channel number and are then expanded and output as attention weight allocation values. To identify and locate pedestrian traffic lights more accurately, this paper embedded the CA attention module in the C3 module after the 13th layer. Experiments demonstrate that the improvement can effectively enhance the feature-extraction capability of the network.

Improvement of Backbone Network. If the trained YOLOv5 is directly applied to real-world scenarios, issues such as memory and latency must be considered. Lightweight networks have the advantages of low computational costs, few parameters, and short inference time. The MobileNet series of lightweight networks has received considerable attention. As shown in Fig. 4, where the overall structures of the "large" and "small" versions are the same, except for the number of basic units "bneck" and their internal parameters. In this paper, the "small" version of MobileNetv3 is used.

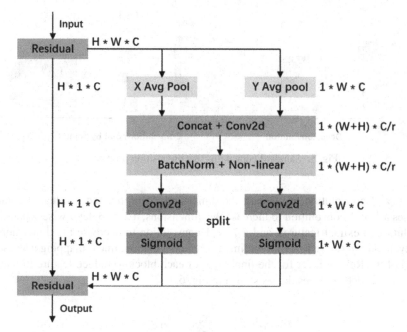

Fig. 3. CA structure.

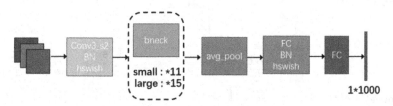

Fig. 4. MobileNetv3 Network structure diagram.

In the MobileNet series of networks, MobileNetv3 [17] is the latest version and has the following four features. First, depthwise separable convolutions are introduced. The depthwise separable convolutions comprise two parts: depthwise and pointwise convolutions for filtering and merging, respectively. The depthwise convolution is performed in the 2D plane, with each kernel corresponding to one channel, which reduces the computation of the network. The pointwise convolution is combined with the output of the depthwise convolution to generate new feature maps. Fig. 5 shows the decomposition of a standard convolution into depthwise and pointwise convolutions. Using depthwise separable convolutions, the computation of the network can be significantly reduced while maintaining good accuracy [18].

MobileNetv3, similar to MobileNetv2 [19], introduces linear bottlenecks and inverted residual structures. The inverted residual structure was significantly different from the original residual structure. The original residual structure first uses a 1 × 1 convolution to reduce the dimensions, a 3 × 3 convolution to achieve feature extraction,

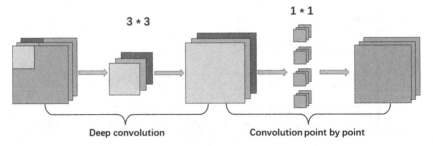

Fig. 5. Standard convolution decomposition process.

and a 1 × 1 convolution to increase the dimensions. The inverted residual structure first uses a 1 × 1 convolution to increase the dimensions, a 3 × 3 depthwise separable convolution to extract features, and a 1 × 1 convolution to decrease the dimensions. To prevent the excessive loss of low-dimensional information, linear mapping was used instead of the ReLU6 layer for the final layer of each block to reduce feature loss and achieve better detection results, as shown in Fig. 6.

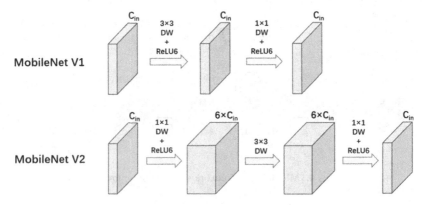

Fig. 6. Reverse residual module structure.

The lightweight attention mechanism of the SENet network is introduced, which is a typical channel attention mechanism, as shown in Fig. 7, Here, Ftr represents the traditional convolution operation; X and U are the input and output of Ftr, respectively; and (H′ × W′ × C′) and (H × W × C) are the dimensions of the original feature map and convolutional feature layer obtained after Ftr convolution, respectively. H′, W′, C′ and H, W, C represent the height, width, and channel number, respectively, of the original feature map and the feature layer obtained after Ftr convolution, respectively. The network structure following Ftr is the part added by SENet. SENet can be divided into two parts: squeeze (Fsq(.) in the figure), which primarily uses global average pooling along the height and width directions to get a (1 × 1 × C) feature vector. The excitation (Fex(., W) in the figure) primarily performs two different fully connected operations on the feature vector obtained by the squeeze part, one for dimension reduction and the other for dimension expansion, to obtain the importance of the different channels. Fscale(.,.) represents a weighting operation that applies the learned importance of different channels to the corresponding channels of the previous feature map to obtain an (H × W × C) output feature map. This structure enhances the directionality of the extracted features by changing the scale of the attention mechanism.

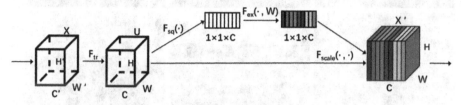

Fig. 7. SENet attention mechanism structure.

Because of the high computational cost, complex derivation, and difficult quantization process of the swish activation function, an h-swish activation function was proposed [20]. The h-swish uses the ReLU6 approximation of the sigmoid function σ(X) to approximate swish, thereby significantly reducing mobile computational resource consumption. The formulas for the swish and h-swish functions are given by Eqs. (1) and (2), respectively.

$$\text{swish} = x \times \sigma(x) \tag{1}$$

$$\text{h - swish} = x \times \frac{\text{RELU6}\,(x + 3)}{6} \tag{2}$$

To further apply the model to real-world scenarios, the backbone network of YOLOv5s was replaced with a MobileNetv3 backbone network to extract features. Experiments demonstrated that this improvement could significantly reduce hardware requirements and the number of parameters.

Pedestrian Crosswalk Traffic Light Detection and Range Experiment. As shown in Fig. 8, after the depth camera captures the video stream, the traffic lights are recognized, and the current traffic light status can be effectively distinguished. In addition, using RealSense's infrared range, the distance from the location to the traffic light can be obtained. Through numerous experiments, it is proven that the trained model had high accuracy and stability for real-time detection.

2.2 Ground Plane Segmentation

Methods for Acquiring Point Clouds. There are many techniques for acquiring point clouds, such as light detection and ranging (LiDAR) [21], structured light [22], stereo cameras [23], and red-green-blue-depth (RGB-D) cameras [24]. LiDAR is expensive, requires contact-based acquisition, and has a slow data processing speed. Structured light is sensitive to lighting and is suitable only for indoor environments. Stereo cameras

Fig. 8. Ranging of traffic lights in different scenes.

typically capture relatively coarse depth information. Compared with other point cloud acquisition methods, RGB-D cameras have the advantages of fast data processing, adaptation to lighting changes, and acquisition of more accurate depth information. These advantages make RGB-D cameras more suitable as point-cloud acquisition devices in many application scenarios.

Real-Time Ground Plane Segmentation. The point cloud obtained by the sensor contained two categories: obstacles and ground. To obtain accurate obstacle information and avoid introducing additional errors, the ground point cloud needs to be extracted in advance.

The coordinates of each point in the original image were obtained before obtaining the data of the point cloud. From the RGB and depth images obtained by Real D435, the x and y coordinates in the pixel coordinate system and the z coordinate in the camera coordinate system are obtained. The depth image obtained from the RealSense D435 was converted into a point cloud by transforming the coordinate system. Equation (3) is used to transform the pixel coordinate system P' into the camera coordinate system P.

$$Z_cP' = Z_c \begin{bmatrix} X_P \\ Y_P \\ 1 \end{bmatrix} = \begin{bmatrix} f_x & 0 & c_x \\ 0 & f_y & c_y \\ 0 & 0 & 1 \end{bmatrix} \begin{bmatrix} X_c \\ Y_c \\ Z_c \end{bmatrix} = KP \tag{3}$$

In the equation, (X_c, Y_c, Z_c) and (X_P, Y_P) represent the coordinates in the camera and the pixel coordinate systems, respectively, and K represents the camera intrinsic matrix.

The transformation between the world coordinate system and camera coordinate system requires only rotation and translation. The rotation matrices were obtained by rotating around different coordinate axes at different angles. First, rotate around the z-axis by α degrees as in Eq. (4), then rotate around the y-axis by β degrees as in Eq. (5), and finally rotate around the x-axis by φ degrees as in Eq. (6):

$$\begin{bmatrix} x \\ y \\ z \end{bmatrix} = \begin{bmatrix} \cos a & -\sin a & 0 \\ \sin a & \cos a & 0 \\ 0 & 0 & 1 \end{bmatrix} \begin{bmatrix} x' \\ y' \\ z' \end{bmatrix} = R_1 \begin{bmatrix} x' \\ y' \\ z' \end{bmatrix} \tag{4}$$

Similarly, rotating around the y-axis and x-axis yields

$$\begin{bmatrix} x \\ y \\ z \end{bmatrix} = \begin{bmatrix} \cos b & 0 & \sin b \\ 0 & 1 & 0 \\ -\sin b & 0 & \cos \beta \end{bmatrix} \begin{bmatrix} x' \\ y' \\ 1 \end{bmatrix} = R_2 \begin{bmatrix} x' \\ y' \\ z' \end{bmatrix} \tag{5}$$

$$\begin{bmatrix} x \\ y \\ z \end{bmatrix} = \begin{bmatrix} 1 & 0 & 0 \\ 0 & \cos\# & -\sin\# \\ 0 & \sin\# & \cos\# \end{bmatrix} \begin{bmatrix} x' \\ y' \\ 1 \end{bmatrix} = R_3 \begin{bmatrix} x' \\ y' \\ z' \end{bmatrix} \tag{6}$$

From this, the rotation matrix R can be obtained as shown in Eq. (7).

$$R = R_1 R_2 R_3 \tag{7}$$

Multiplying the rotation matrix by the camera coordinate system coordinates and adding the offset vector yields the coordinates in the world coordinate system, as expressed in Eq. (8)

$$\begin{bmatrix} X_w \\ Y_w \\ Z_w \end{bmatrix} = R \begin{bmatrix} X_c \\ Y_c \\ Z_c \end{bmatrix} + T \tag{8}$$

As the sensor maintains a certain posture with respect to the ground after it is worn, fitting a plane [25] using the random sample consensus (RANSAC) algorithm can yield a ground point cloud. The key of the RANSAC algorithm is to select three points randomly and repeatedly to construct a plane equation, as shown in Eq. (9). If this plane contained sufficient points, it was considered the ground. Using the RANSAC algorithm for robust estimation and random search on the ground point cloud, points are determined to be ground based on Eq. (10). After K iterations, the ground can be preliminarily segmented [26], as shown in Eq. (11).

$$AX_c + BY_c + CZ_c + D = 0 \tag{9}$$

$$d = \frac{|AX_c + BY_c + CZ_c + D|}{\sqrt{A^2 + B^2 + C^2}} < T \tag{10}$$

$$K = \frac{\log(1 - P)}{\log(1 - W^n)} \tag{11}$$

A drawback of the RANSAC algorithm is that the calculation time for fitting a plane using the RANSAC algorithm is too long, resulting in a loss of real-time performance. Therefore, a method of rotating the ground point cloud was adopted. In general, the coordinate system of the original point cloud obtained by the depth camera is z moving forward along the optical center, x to the right, and y downward. For ease of processing, the point cloud coordinates are transformed into z moving forward in the direction of the optical center, x to the left, and y upward. For real-time processing, the same rotation was loaded. In order to reduce the operation time after the conversion, the VoxelGrid voxel filter in the Point Cloud Library is used to downsample the point cloud. Generally, the ground is located at the bottom of the image point cloud and is concentrated near the smallest coordinates in the point cloud. Therefore, the ground point cloud plane can be obtained by calculating the minimum value of the coordinates and setting a threshold. This eliminates the need for extensive calculations using the RANSAC algorithm, thereby improving the computational efficiency.

In point cloud rotation, let vector n_0 be the original normal vector and n_1 be the target vector. The goal is to rotate n_0 to direction n_1. The coordinate of n_0 is (x_0, y_0, z_0), that of n_1 is (x_1, y_1, z_1), and that of the origin is $O(0, 0, 0)$. These three coordinates form a plane. From the cross-product of the coordinates, it is concluded that the normal vector of the plane is perpendicular to the plane and passes through the origin of the coordinates, namely the axis of rotation. Using these three points, the equation of the plane can be calculated as shown in Eq. (12).

$$\frac{z_1 y_0 - z_0 y_1}{x_0 y_1 - x_1 y_0} \cdot x - \frac{z_1 x_0 - z_0 x_1}{x_0 y_1 - x_1 y_0} \cdot y + z = 0 \tag{12}$$

A normal vector of the plane, which is also the vector of the axis of rotation, can be calculated as shown in Eq. (13).

$$\left(z_1 y_0 - z_0 y_1\right)x - (z_1 x_0 - z_0 x_1)y + \left(x_0 y_1 - x_1 y_0\right)z = 0 \tag{13}$$

The rotation angle θ between vector n_0 and vector n_1 can be calculated as the angle between these two vectors, as shown in Eq. (14):

$$\theta = \frac{\overrightarrow{n}_0 * \overrightarrow{n}_1}{|\overrightarrow{n}_0||\overrightarrow{n}_1|} \tag{14}$$

Obstacle Clustering. After obtaining the ground point cloud, clustering was performed on the point clouds of the obstacles to obtain more information. After clustering, each point cloud cluster can be regarded as an obstacle, and the distance and azimuth from the sensor to the center point are then obtained.

The clustering of obstacles has three steps:

Step 1: Filtering and denoising. Filtering serves many purposes, such as removing noise points and outliers [27], smoothing point clouds [28], filling holes, and compressing data. Subsequent processing can be conducted more effectively only by filtering out noise and outliers during preprocessing. In this study, a statistical outlier removal (SOR) filter was used for filtering and denoising.

The implementation principle of the SOR filter is as follows: The average distance between a point and its k nearest neighboring points is calculated, and the shape of the Gaussian distribution depends on the mean distance value μ and the standard deviation σ. The distance threshold is then calculated using Eq. (15).

$$d = \mu + A \times \sigma, \tag{15}$$

where A is a proportionality constant that is determined by the number of neighboring points k. Finally, points with an average distance greater than d from their k-nearest neighbors are removed.

Step 2: Obtain the obstacle point clusters using Euclidean clustering [29]. Obstacles can be separated by performing Euclidean clustering on point clouds, and invalid points can be removed. This algorithm comprises the following steps:

1. Starting from an arbitrary point P (seed point), search the KD-Tree for its k-nearest neighbors. If the distance between these neighboring points is less than the set threshold, these points are considered to belong to the same class and are marked.
2. Use the neighboring points as new seed points and repeat the process in (1) until no neighboring points can be found, at which point the points are considered to belong to the same cluster.
3. Find the next unmarked point and repeat processes (1) and (2) until all points have been searched for and marked, at which point the algorithm ends. After performing Euclidean clustering, the original point cloud was divided into multiple clusters, and each cluster was regarded as an obstacle that appeared in front.

Step 3: Determination of the azimuth angle. After performing Euclidean clustering, multiple sets of obstacle point clouds were obtained, and it was necessary to determine their positions in sight. In this study, the horizontal field of view was divided into five directions: left, left front, front, right front, and right. The median method, which uses the midpoint to represent the entire set of point clouds, was employed to accelerate the computation when determining the direction to which the obstacle belongs.

As seen in Fig. 9, the orange obstacle is located in the left direction. Although the purple obstacle occupies the left, left-front, and front directions, it is mainly distributed in the left-front direction and is therefore considered to be in the left-front direction.

At this point, we can obtain the distance and azimuth from the sensor to the obstacle and then output the information to the visually impaired person through the voice system.

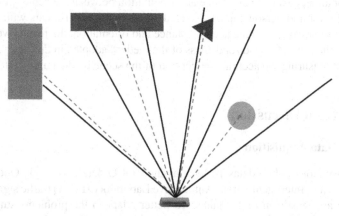

Fig. 9. Schematic diagram of the obstacle clustering principle.

Clustering Experiment on Obstacles. The proposed method was incorporated into an auxiliary system. As seen in Fig. 10, the system comprises a RealSense sensor, computer (NVIDIA GeForce GTX 1650, Ubuntu system), and bone-conduction headset that feeds nonsemantic stereo sound back to the ear. RealSense uses a USB 3.0 interface and computer to transmit data. The computer communicated with the headset using Bluetooth 4.0. A computer was placed in a backpack, a RealSense sensor was placed on the chest, and bone-conducting headphones were attached to each ear. The bone conduction headphones do not clog the user's ears. Therefore, an auxiliary prototype allows blind people to hear ambient sounds simultaneously. This is very important for assisting the blind in travelling, as they need to maintain awareness of their surroundings to ensure safety.

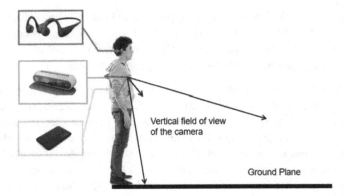

Fig. 10. Schematic diagram of blind wearing

As shown in Fig. 11, this method could effectively segment flat ground in complex environments. The obstacle point cloud is then clustered, and the center point of the obstacle is obtained. Thus, the distance and orientation between the center point of the obstacle and the blind person can be detected. After many experiments with different scenes and comparisons with the actual distance and orientation, the results were accurate, proving the reliability and robustness of the method adopted in this study, and to a certain extent, ensuring the accurate perception of the scene by the guide system.

3 Results and Discussion

3.1 Image Data Acquisition

Presently, in various public datasets, such as the COCO dataset, Google Open Image (GOI) dataset, and Intelligent Safety Automotive Laboratory (LISA) traffic sign dataset, traffic lights are mostly in motor lanes. To better adapt to the problems studied, we selected a self-built dataset. To enhance the ability to generalize of the learned model, environmental factors such as sunny, cloudy, and rainy days, days, and nights were also considered in the image acquisition, and different scenes, environments, shooting

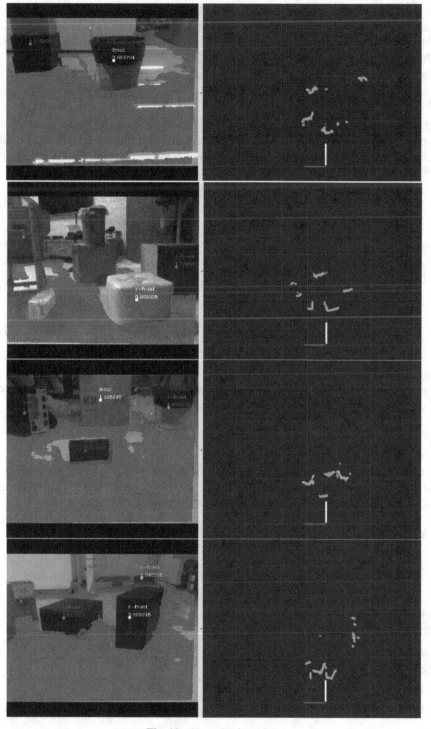

Fig. 11. Obstacle clustering.

distances, backgrounds, and angles were adopted to shoot the sidewalk traffic lights. After manual screening and labelling using Labellmg dataset software, the dataset included 3401 images. The dataset was divided into a test set and a training set in the ratio of 2:8, including two kinds of targets: "green" and "red."

3.2 Model Evaluation Index

In this experiment, an RTX 3060 graphics card was used to train and test the server. Set the number of iterations to 300. The recall, precision, mAP, and model size were used to compare the performance of each model, which was calculated using the following formula.

$$P = \frac{TP}{FP + TP} \tag{16}$$

$$R = \frac{TP}{FN + TP} \tag{17}$$

$$AP = \int_0^1 P(R)dR \tag{18}$$

$$mAP = \frac{1}{m} \sum_{i=1}^{m} AP_i, \tag{19}$$

where TP is the number of samples correctly predicted as the true class, FN is the number of samples incorrectly predicted as the other class, and FP is the number of samples of the other class incorrectly predicted as the true class.

3.3 Comparative Experiment

To better demonstrate the advantages, an experiment was conducted to compare YOLOv5-CM with the faster R-CNN, SSD, YOLOv6 [30], YOLOv7 [30], and YOLOv5s. The models used the same dataset for training and verification.

Table 1. Experimental comparison results

	P (%)	R (%)	mAP (%)	Size of Model 1. (MB)	Parameters (MB)
Faster R-CNN	57.83	88.7	86.2	110.8	28.5
SSD	98.1	67.6	90.9	93.3	26.3
YOLOv5s	98.6	93.0	95.6	14.4	7.1
YOLOv6s	97.4	93.0	94.8	36.3	17.2
YOLOv7	98.8	91.7	95.4	74.8	36.5
YOLOv5-CM	98.5	92.5	96.3	3.0	1.4

As seen in Table 1, in the YOLOv5 detection algorithm, the YOLOv5s model is a lightweight network model for Faster R-CNN and SSD. Compared with those of the YOLOv5 model, the mAP of the YOLOV5-CM was improved by 0.7%, the size of the model was decreased by 79.1%, and the number of parameters was decreased by 80.3%. The YOLOv5-CM model is better than YOLOv6s and YOLOv7 in terms of the mAP, model size, and parameters, which may also be the reason for the dataset. This shows that, compared with current mainstream detection algorithms, YOLOv5-CM maintains a higher mAP while reducing the size and number of parameters.

3.4 Ablation Experiment

An ablation experiment was conducted to verify the optimization of the individual improvement modules. As shown in Table 2, mAP improved by 0.4% when the backbone network was replaced with MobileNetV3. After adding coordinate attention, the mAP improved by 0.7%. The ablation results show that YOLOv5-CM has good performance, achieving the goal of reducing the parameters and the size of the model on the premise of maintaining a good mAP.

Table 2. Ablation experimental results

	P (%)	R (%)	mAP (%)	Size of Model (MB)	Parameters (MB)
YOLOv5s	98.6	93.0	95.6	14.4	7.1
YOLOv5-M	97.4	93.3	96.0	3.0	1.4
YOLOv5-CM	98.5	92.5	96.3	3.0	1.4

4   Conclusion

This study proposes an improved YOLOv5 algorithm combined with RealSense, ground plane segmentation, and Euclidean clustering algorithms to assist visually impaired individuals in travel.

1. Improved the network structure of YOLOv5. MobileNetv3 was used to replace the main network of YOLOv5s, and coordinate attention was added. Compared with the traditional YOLOv5 target detection algorithm, the mAP was improved by 0.7%, the size of the model was decreased by 79.1%, and the number of parameters was decreased by 80.3%.
2. Based on RealSense and YOLOv5-CM, a comprehensive visual guide system was developed that can identify and measure the distance of sidewalk traffic lights, as well as detect the location and distance of obstacles. We believe that this study has great practical significance for assisting blind people with their travel.

Our future work will accelerate the implementation of the algorithm and deepen the study of guide systems with attitude sensors and GPS positioning systems.

Acknowledgement. This work was supported in part by the National University Student Innovation and Entrepreneurship in Training Program of China, the Provincial University Student Innovation and Entrepreneurship in Training Program of China, the Laboratory Opening Project Fund of Huaibei Normal University (No. 2022sykf022), and the Special Needs Project of Huaibei Normal University (No. 2021zlgc147).

References

1. World Health Organization. https://www.who.int/zh/news-room/fact-sheets/detail/blindness-and-visual-impairment. Accessed 13 Oct 2022
2. Munemo, E., Tom, T.: Problems of unemployment faced by visually impaired people. Greener J. Soc. Sci. **3**(4) (2013). https://doi.org/10.15580/GJSS.2013.4.020713437
3. Daily Life Problems Faced by Blind People, In Daily Life Problems Faced by Blind People. https://wecapable.com/problems-faced-by-blind-people/. Accessed 25 Feb 2021
4. Challenges blind people face when living life. In Challenges blind people face when living life. https://www.letsenvision.com/blog/challenges-blindpeople-face-when-living-life. Accessed 25 Feb 2021
5. Guide Dogs of America, Frequently Asked Questions, Guide Dogs of America, https://guidedogsofamerica.org/about-gda/frequently-asked-questions/. Accessed 28 Sept 2022
6. Tapu, R., Mocanu, B., Zaharia, T.: A computer vision system that ensure the autonomous navigation of blind people. In: E-Health and Bioengineering Conference 2013, pp. 1–4 (2013). https://doi.org/10.1109/EHB.2013.6707267
7. Rodríguez, A., Yebes, J.J., Alcantarilla, P.F., Bergasa, L.M., Almazán, J., Cela, A.: Assisting the visually impaired: obstacle detection and warning system by acoustic feedback. Sensors **12**(12) (2012). https://doi.org/10.3390/s121217476
8. Ren, S., He, K., Girshick, R., Sun, J.: Faster R-CNN: Towards real-time object detection with region proposal networks. Adv. Neural Inf. Process. Syst. **28** (2015)
9. Liu, W., Anguelov, D., Erhan, D., Szegedy, C., Reed, S., Fu, C.-Y., Berg, A.C.: Ssd: Single shot multibox detector. In: Leibe, B., Matas, J., Sebe, N., Welling, M. (eds.) ECCV 2016. LNCS, vol. 9905, pp. 21–37. Springer, Cham (2016). https://doi.org/10.1007/978-3-319-46448-0_2
10. Redmon, J., Divvala, S., Girshick, R., Farhadi, A.: You only look once: unified, real-time object detection. In: Proceedings of the IEEE Conference on Computer Vision and Pattern Recognition, pp. 779–788 (2016). https://doi.org/10.1109/CVPR.2016.91
11. Redmon, J., Farhadi, A.: YOLO9000: better, faster, stronger. In: Proceedings of the IEEE Conference on Computer Vision and Pattern Recognition, pp. 7263–7271, (2017). https://doi.org/10.1109/CVPR.2017.690
12. Redmon, J., Farhadi, A.: YOLOv3: An incremental improvement, arXiv preprint arXiv:1804.02767 (2018)
13. Bochkovskiy, A., Wang, C.Y., Liao, H.: YOLOv4: Optimal speed and accuracy of object detection, arXiv preprint arXiv:2004.10934 (2020)
14. Hou, Q., Zhou, D., Feng, J.: Coordinate attention for efficient mobile network design. In: Proceedings of the IEEE/CVF Conference on Computer Vision and Pattern Recognition, pp. 13713–13722, (2021). https://doi.org/10.1109/CVPR46437.2021.01350

15. Hu, J., Shen, L., Sun, G.: Squeeze-and-excitation networks. In: Proceedings of the IEEE Conference on Computer Vision and Pattern Recognition, pp. 7132–7141, (2018). https://doi.org/10.1109/CVPR.2018.00745

16. Woo, S., Park, J., Lee, J.Y., Kweon, I.S.: CBAM: convolutional block attention module. In: Proceedings of the European conference on computer vision (ECCV), pp. 3–19, (2018). https://doi.org/10.1007/978-3-030-01234-2_1

17. Howard, A., et al.: Searching for MobileNetV3. In: IEEE/CVF International Conference on Computer Vision (ICCV) 2019, pp. 1314–1324 (2019). https://doi.org/10.1109/ICCV.2019.00140

18. Wang, W., Li, Y.T., Zou, T., et al.: A novel image classification approach via dense- mobilenet models. Mob. Inf. Syst. 1–8 (2020). https://doi.org/10.1155/2020/7602384

19. Sandler, M., Howard, A., Zhu, M., Zhmoginov, A., Chen, L.C.: Mobilenetv2: inverted residuals and linear bottlenecks. In: Proceedings of the IEEE Conference on Computer Vision and Pattern Recognition, pp. 4510–4520, (2018). https://doi.org/10.1109/CVPR.2018.00474

20. Ramachandran, P., Zoph, B., Le, Q.V.: Searching for activation functions, ArXiv. preprint (2017)

21. Kumar, S.S., Likhachev, S., Kaess, M.F.: PointNetLK: Robust & efficient point cloud registration using PointNet, arXiv:1908.09852 [cs] (2019)

22. Dai, Q., Lee, Y., Liao, H.: Deformation analysis of shape memory alloys using structured light and 3D point cloud registration. Int. J. Adv. Manufact. Technol. 106(5–6), 1697–1713 (2020)

23. Zhang, Z.: A flexible new technique for camera calibration. IEEE Trans. Pattern Anal. Mach. Intell. 22(11), 1330–1334 (2000). https://doi.org/10.1109/34.888718

24. Song, S., Xiao, J.: Deep sliding shapes for a modal 3D object detection in RGB-D images. In: Proceedings of the IEEE Conference on Computer Vision and Pattern Recognition, pp. 808–816, (2016). https://doi.org/10.1109/CVPR.2016.94

25. Derpanis, K.G.: Overview of the RANSAC algorithm. Image Rochester NY 4(1), 2–3 (2010)

26. Yang, K., Wang, K., Hu, W., Bai, J.: Expanding the detection of traversable area with RealSense for the visually impaired. Sensors 16(11), 1954 (2016). https://doi.org/10.3390/s16111954

27. de Cheveigné, A., Simon, J.Z.: Denoising based on spatial filtering. J. Neurosci. Methods 171(2), 331–339 (2008). https://doi.org/10.1016/j.jneumeth.2008.03.015

28. Mederos, B., Velho, L., de Figueiredo, L.H.: Robust smoothing of noisy point clouds. In: Proceeding SIAM Conference on Geometric Design and Computing, vol. 2004, no. 1, p. 2, Philadelphia, PA, USA: SIAM (2003)

29. Sun, Z., Li, Z., Liu, Y.: An improved lidar data segmentation algorithm based on Euclidean clustering. In: Wang, R., Chen, Z., Zhang, W., Zhu, Q. (eds.) Proceedings of the 11th International Conference on Modelling, Identification and Control (ICMIC2019). LNEE, vol. 582, pp. 1119–1130. Springer, Singapore (2020). https://doi.org/10.1007/978-981-15-0474-7_105

30. Li, C., et al.: YOLOv6: A single-stage object detection framework for industrial applications. arXiv preprint arXiv:2209.02976 (2022)

31. Wang, C.Y., Bochkovskiy, A., Liao, H.Y.M.: YOLOv7: Trainable bag-of-freebies sets new state-of-the-art for real-time object detectors, 7464–7475. arXiv preprint arXiv:2207.02696 (2022)

AHM: A Novel Model for Mining Academic Hot Spots Based on a Scientific Knowledge Graph

Xin Liu[1], Xiujuan Xu[1,2(✉)], Xiaowei Zhao[1,2], Yu Liu[1,2], and Lin Yao[1,2]

[1] School of Software, Dalian University of Technology, Dalian 116620, China
xjxu@dlut.edu.cn
[2] Key Laboratory for Ubiquitous Network and Service Software of Liaoning Province, Dalian 116620, China

Abstract. Academic hot spots refer to a group of words that are widely considered in a specific period. Academic hot-spot mining is an essential task in the bibliometrics field, and the purpose is to mine academic hot-spots in a large number of studies. The common methods at present are bibliometrics, based analysis tools and machine learning methods, and these methods cannot fully apply deep semantic features. With the increase in academic papers, extracting hot spots is difficult through bibliometrics and machine learning methods. Combining deep learning technology to extract deep features and mine hot spots more efficiently and accurately is a challenge in the field of academic hot spot research. This paper proposed a novel model called AHM to compensate for the current shortcomings, which improves the feature representation of k-means++, obtains deep semantic and contextual features by applying deep learning technology, and fuses the two features as feature inputs for k-means++. The experimental results of a comparison of AHM with four baselines (i.e., k-means++, TF-IDF+k-means++, Word2vector+k-means++, and Node2vector+k-means++) on the literature datasets in the artificial intelligence field show that the AHM model has a better effect in academic hot-spot mining tasks. In addition, this paper presents an overall framework for evolution analysis and analyses the evolution path of academic hot spots during 2010−2020.

Keywords: Knowledge Graph · Academic Hot Spots · Data Mining · Evolution Analysis

1 Introduction

An influential domain vocabulary may affect the future development direction of the domain, and people usually use bibliometrics to analyse the domain topics and the evolution of the theme over time. Academic hot spots are often closely related to applications in reality, and they are related to theoretical achievements, practical applications, and future development. The purpose of mining hot spots is to find important research topics, which is very useful for scientific research and helps evaluate a discipline.

With the development of science and technology, the literature reflecting academic research discoveries is also increasing [1]. Facing unstructured data in the context of

M. Zhang et al. (Eds.): CCF NCCA 2023, CCIS 1959, pp. 66–77, 2024.
https://doi.org/10.1007/978-981-99-8764-1_6

big data, it is not easy to objectively extract the hot spots only by traditional methods. To more accurately mine the primary information in the text from a large scale of data, researchers have made many attempts at topic extraction, and the existing research in topic extraction also provides an important reference for the analysis of academic hot spots. Blei et al. presented the latent Dirichlet allocation (LDA) topic model based on unsupervised learning [2]. The model can extract similar words in documents on the same topic and obtain the distribution of each topic word. Yau et al. [3] used four different topic modelling methods to model and cluster documents.

However, the process based on the topic model requires more labor costs and cannot capture the context semantic information of documents. With the constant maturity of artificial intelligence (AI) technology, especially the development of deep learning technology, new feasible solutions have been brought to computing tasks based on big data. Zhang et al. [1] proposed a topic-mining method based on deep learning combined with the word embedding model. They conducted a comparative study with the traditional topic-mining method, fully utilizing the structural information in the graph to mine hot topics, proving the progressiveness based on the deep learning method.

In summary, the disadvantage of these methods is that deep semantic information and structural information need to be fully applied. With the application of the deep learning model in the natural language processing (NLP) field, this paper presented a novel model called AHM for hot-spot mining tasks to improve these shortcomings. This model combines deep semantic and structural information to achieve hot-spot mining. The specific process of the model is as follows: first, high-quality structured data with domain characteristics are represented by vectors through word embedding technology in the NLP domain. Second, graph neural network (GNN) technology is used to obtain the structural information contained in the domain graph. Through the fusion of semantic and structural information, the characteristics of hot spots can be more accurately found. This model improves the feature vector representation of k-means++, replacing the traditional feature vector with the feature vector of structural features and semantic features. The model structure is clear and easy to understand, reducing the complex cost of extracting meteorological features, improving the accuracy of hot-spot extraction, and providing a good reference value for researchers to choose research directions in the future and analyse future development.

The main contributions of this paper are as follows. (1) We develop a novel AHM model for extracting academic hot spots based on knowledge graphs (KGs) and deep learning techniques. (2) We construct datasets of hot-spot mining tasks with labels in the field of AI. (3) We develop a framework for hot-spot evolution analysis based on the AHM model, which skips the cost of manual annotation in domain keyword extraction and applies this method to the task of evolution analysis.

This paper is organized as follows: Sect. 2 discusses previous work related to our research. Section 3 introduces the overall framework of hot-spot evolution analysis and the AHM model in detail. Section 4 introduces the measurement metrics, comparison model and analysis of experimental results. Section 5 summarizes the paper and describes further research.

2 Related Work

Academic hot spot mining is the core research in the field of knowledge discovery. Its result is based on a group of words with high concern in existing data mining, which is mainly used based on literature metrology, software tools and algorithms for analysis. Academic hot-spot mining based on bibliometrics mainly includes word frequency statistical analysis, co-word analysis and other quantifiable indicators for analysis. For example, based on knowledge networks to evaluate influence, a new potential indicator was proposed to measure hot spots [4]. Based on software analysis tools, Citespace provides methods such as keyword co-occurrence analysis, co-citation analysis, co-word analysis, clustering analysis, and cooperative network analysis. In terms of topic research using machine learning methods, a novel kernel k-means clustering method [1] was proposed and incorporated with a word embedding model to create a solution that effectively extracts topics from bibliometric data [3]. This study was designed to enhance the ability of four different topic modelling algorithms, named LDA, CTM, hierarchical LDA, and HDP, to differentiate and automatically cluster documents and to evaluate the performance of different algorithms through experiments. It can be seen that improving based on classical methods is a relatively novel research approach in hot-spot mining.

3 Methodology

This section introduces the topic mining model AHM based on KG and analyses the overall process of hot-spot evolution. The overall method of this paper includes five stages: data collection, data preprocessing, keyword extraction, academic hot-spot extraction, and evolution analysis. Fig. 1 shows the overall framework of this study.

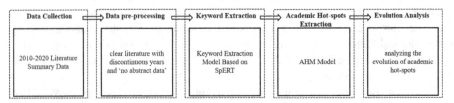

Fig. 1. Research Framework.

3.1 Data Collection

This study is based on 25 A-class and B-class journals in the field of AI in the China Computer Federation and crawled data from 31394 literature abstracts published in Scopus [5] during 2010−2020.

3.2 Data Preprocessing

The data preprocessing stage includes data cleaning and data format conversion. Data cleaning was used to remove the literature data with "[no abstract data]" as the abstract content and the literature sources with discontinuous literature during 2010–2020. The specific process is to judge through a Python program. If the content does not meet the conditions, the literature data will not be placed in the datasets. Data format conversion divides the text into sentences based on four types of characters: ". ", ". ", "?", "!", and then divide each sentence into words based on the characters "", ";".

3.3 Keyword Extraction

The purpose of modelling based on scientific knowledge graphs is to filter out domain-independent information and provide data with domain characteristics for the model. Meanwhile, the contextual relation between keywords in the graph can be preserved. After investigating the existing methods of entity and relation extraction [6–9], the SpERT model has advantages in extracting structured data from the literature abstract datasets [6], so this study can refer to this method to obtain structured data. This stage work is to convert the abstract data into triplet sets. Eberts et al. [6] showed that Sci-bert has better performance on SciERC datasets, so we first finetune Sci-bert on SciERC and then extract structured data. The implementation of the model is shown in Fig. 2, and the specific process is as follows.

(1) **Embedding**: First, the preprocessed text sequence is used as input, where sci-bert randomly masks the input based on probability. By fine-tuning the sci-bert encoding, obtain the feature vectors of the text sequence and capture contextual information tokens.

(2) **Span classification**: The span represents the length of the subsequence. First, obtain the embedding of all spans in the sequence: combine each word vector contained in the span using the maximum pooling fusion function; then, find the corresponding span embedding vector matrix from the weight matrix and splice it to obtain the span representation; concatenate the context features token to eliminate ambiguity; input the embedding of subsequence into the softmax classifier for classification, and select the category with the highest score as the final classification result.

(3) **Span filtering**: Since the span is too long to be an entity, priority has been given to filtering out spans longer than 10. Based on the results of span classification, the words with the classification result of "None" category were filtered out.

(4) **Relation classification**: This part of the work extracts relations based on entities. First, the filtered span is combined in pairs, and then, we study whether there is a relation between these two entities through relation classification. The specific process is as follows: For the two candidate entities, the maximum pooling of the content contained in the span between them is used as a context representation. Since the relation is generally asymmetric, we need to enter both "entity1 ⊚context represents ⊚entity2" and "entity2 ⊚context represents ⊚entity1" into the sigmoid binary classification model, where ⊚denotes concatenation. If the sigmoid value of a relation category in the output result is greater than the threshold value, it indicates that there is a relation; otherwise, it indicates that there is no relation.

(5) **Output**: Finally, extract the results from the model into a dataset composed of (Entity1, Relation Category, Entity2) forms.

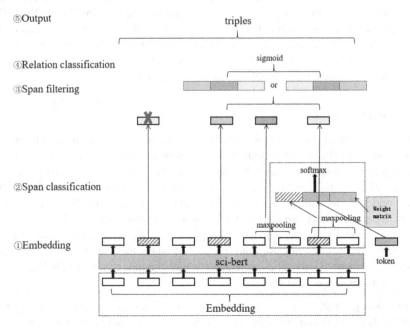

Fig. 2. Data formatting conversion diagram.

3.4   AHM Model

This study comprehensively considers semantic features and graph structure features for embedding. Sun et al. [10] proposed that the pretraining language model (PLM) has a positive effect on grad2text. PLM has brought amazing performance improvement in various tasks [11]. Wu et al. [12] mentioned the successful application of GNN technology in NLP. GNN can effectively aggregate neighborhood context information, so structured data are embedded based on PLM and GNN technology. In terms of PLM selection, this study chose Bart [13]. Bart can use bidirectional information of sequences for encoding, rather than using only the last hidden state of the sequence as the representation. Therefore, the Bart encoder has stronger structured semantic representation capabilities, which can provide better potential semantic representation. Relations in triples are useful [14]; thus, we mine relation type features and graph context features based on the RGCN [15] method. Finally, the two types of features are aligned and fused. Fig. 3 shows the AHM model structure diagram, with the specific process as follows.

PLM Embedding: Bart is a standard sequence-to-sequence architecture with encoding and decoding layers consisting of 6 or 12 layers each. The encoding layer performs bidirectional feature representation. Since the task of this article is not to generate sequences,

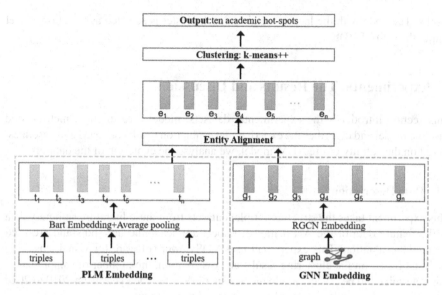

Fig. 3. Data formatting conversion diagram.

only the Bart encoding layer is used to obtain the feature vectors in the hidden state. Given the triplet sequence datasets, input each triplet sequence into Bart. Each word in the sequence is serialized using BartTokenizer, and the encoding result is a hidden vector represented by serialization. Each entity may consist of multiple sequences, so the sequence representations contained in each entity are averaged and pooled as vectors of each entity. Finally, the eigenvector matrix of all nodes is obtained.

GNN Embedding: RGCN enables nodes to aggregate contextual features of neighboring nodes, resulting in representations with graph structure features. This study constructed a two-layer graph neural network based on RGCN to aggregate neighbor features of two skips. Given the input of the original graph, including node sets, edge sets, and relation type sets, the feature vector of the node is obtained by embedding it into the first layer of the RGCN model, filtering redundant features and using an activation function to enable the model to have learning ability, and the activated results are transferred to the second layer of the RGCN network to obtain the topological feature matrix.

Entity Alignment: The matrices obtained by PLM embedding and GNN embedding are two matrices with the same dimension size. The purpose of entity alignment is to align the feature matrices one by one through the corresponding entity ID. Afterwards, the two corresponding features of each entity are fused by adding them together, and the aligned feature matrix is finally output.

Clustering: Through analysis, this study uses the k-means++ [16] method for clustering, which is an improvement on the classic partition based on the clustering algorithm k-means and improves the shortcomings of k-means. The specific implementation is to specify the number of clusters and use the representation of all entities in the feature fusion matrix as the input of k-means++. The algorithm will ultimately output the cluster results. The node with the largest weight in each cluster is selected as the cluster label output through TF-IDF.

4 Experimenta. The Results and Discussion

This section introduces the experimental datasets, model measurement metrics, and baseline model and describes the experimental evaluation results of AHM and baselines. Based on the validity of the AHM model, we analyse the evolution of the datasets.

4.1 Data Description

This experiment takes the structured triplet datasets from these literature summary data as the feature data of the AHM model. Labels are academic hot spots and are used for model evaluation. This experiment uses VOSviewer software for visual clustering analysis. Based on the clustering results and distribution, the number of sample labels was determined to be 10, and academic hot-spot labels for each year from 2010 to 2020 were obtained by combining word frequency and peer review.

4.2 Model Measurement Metrics

This study determined three indicators based on similarity: cosine similarity (CS), Euclidean distance similarity (ES), and average similarity (AS).

CS can evaluate the similarity between two vectors, which is commonly used to calculate the similarity between texts, calculated by Eq. 1. Euclidean distance can measure the absolute distance between points in multidimensional space, and standardized Euclidean distance is often used for measurement, as shown in Eq. 2. AS is used to evaluate the average similarity between all predicted results and actual labels. $AS(y_i, y_i\prime)$ is given by Eq. 错误!未找到引用源。. X1 and X2 represent two vectors. k represents the vector of the k-th dimension, and dim represents the dimension of the feature vector. Meanwhile, n represents the number of hot spots. i denotes the i-th hot spot. y_i represents the prediction vector of the i-th hot spot, and $y_i\prime$ represents the feature vector with the largest similarity to y_i.

$$CS(X1, X2) = \left| \frac{\sum_{k=1}^{dim} X1_k \times X2_k}{\sqrt{\sum_{k=1}^{dim} X2_k^2} \sqrt{\sum_{k=1}^{dim} X1_k^2}} \right| \tag{1}$$

$$ES(X1, X2) = \frac{1}{n} \sum_i^n \frac{1}{1 + Distance(X1, X2)} \tag{2}$$

$$AS(y_i, y_i') = \frac{1}{n} \sum_i^n \cos(y_i, y_i') \tag{3}$$

4.3 Baselines

TF-IDF+k-means++: TF-IDF [17] can model a text as a word frequency vector and use it as the input of k-means++.

Word2vec+k-means++: Word2vec [18] obtains the vector representation of words by using the vectors in the authoritative pretraining word vector library and inputs the vector representation into k-means++.

Node2vec+k-means++: Node2vec [19] is a graph-based embedding method to obtain the feature vectors of nodes in the graph and input the vectors into k-means++.

k-means++: K-means [20] uses one-hot for feature representation, and k-means++ is consistent with k-means.

4.4 Extraction of Academic Hot Spots

Obtain triplet datasets through the Keyword extraction model. Contains 6 entity types: Task, Method, Material, OtherScientificTerm, Metric, and Generic, as well as 7 relation types: Used for, Feature of, Hyponym of, Evaluate for, Part of, Compare, and Junction. Each node in the graph represents a domain academic keyword. After obtaining the triples and entities, the NLTK toolkit is applied to align the capitalization, abbreviations, and different etymologies of entities, and aligned structured triples are used as inputs to the AHM model.

Table 1. Assessment of Experimental.

Method	CS	ES	AS
k-means++	0.086	0.512	0.097
TF-IDF+k-means++	0.218	0.576	0.226
Word2vec+k-means++	0.13	0.566	0.143
Node2vec+k-means++	0.247	0.597	0.25
AHM (Our Method)	**0.278**	**0.622**	**0.283**

Through the evaluation of three indicators, the evaluation results are shown in Table 1. AHM is superior to k-means++, which proves that the improvement of k-means++ is successful in the artificial intelligence literature datasets. The effect of k-means++ is the worst, indicating that compared to the original embedding of the k-means++ model, GNN and PLM can extract more feature information related to hot spots. The indicators of word2vec + k-means++are slightly lower than those of TF-IDF+k-means++, node2vec + k-means++, and AHM, which further indicates that word frequency-based and structure-based features cannot be ignored. The AHM model has higher results on three indicators than other baseline models, indicating that AHM can effectively extract deep features. In summary, semantic and structural features play a positive role in mining academic hot spots.

4.5   Evolutionary Analysis

An analysis of the evolution of literature quantity annually during 2010–2020 is shown in Fig. 4, indicating an upwards trend in the number of papers during 2010–2020. Figure 5 shows the evolution of academic hot spots based on cosine similarity analysis, which can intuitively observe the emergence, transformation, or extinction process of academic hot spots over time. From left to right, each column represents academic hot spots of one year, each rectangle represents academic hot spots, and the edges between two years represent the transformation based on the similarity between two nodes. The wider the edge is, the more similar the two hot spots connected by the edge are, and the greater the weight of the transformation is. Not every year there are ten hot-spots evolving. For example, there are only six hot spots in 2014, indicating that the appearance of the remaining four hot spots does not depend on the past hot spots or play a significant role in promoting the emergence of future hot spots; they appear one year and then disappear. For the emergence of hot spots, the emergence of new hot spots each year will depend on some hot spots of the previous year, and different hot spots will play a positive role in the emergence of future hot spots to varying degrees. On the whole, there is a process of emergence, transformation, and extinction of academic hot spots in the field of AI, which is also consistent with the evolution law of the life cycle of things.

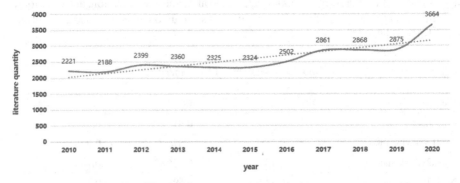

Fig. 4. Literature quantity evolution.

Efficiently obtaining academic hot spots and researching the evolution of academic fields is still a challenging problem. Effective use of the information in literature data is a breakthrough to solve this problem. To solve this challenge, this paper proposes a new research framework based on a KG to mine the semantic features and structural features contained in texts to solve this problem. We use empirical research based on the abstract data of 25 journals in the field of AI retrieved from Scopus from 2010 to 2020. The experimental results show that the overall framework of this paper makes more effective use of domain features than the baseline model. At the same time, the article conducts evolutionary analysis based on effective AHM. In the past 11 years, we can see the cumulative growth of scientific research achievements in the field of AI, indicating that the field is in the development stage. According to the above analysis, academic hot-spot evolution has different evolution patterns in different periods, and different evolutions have different reasons. In the process of evolution, the emergence, transformation, and demise of academic hot spots have unpredictable regular patterns, which need to be considered according to actual data.

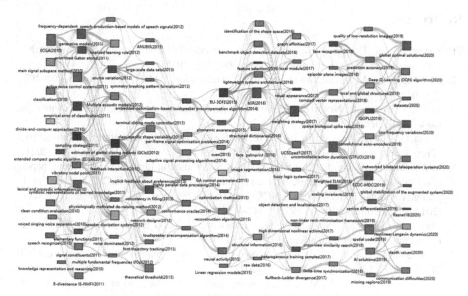

Fig. 5. 2010–2020 Evolution path of academic hot spots.

5 Conclusion

Modern scientific metrology and bibliometrics can be applied to the multivariate and diachronic dynamic analysis of massive literature data. The scientific KG is a representative method of literature analysis and visualization. In this paper, we deployed a hot-spot mining model called AHM based on the scientific KG, which is reliable and concise. Based on this model, we proposed an overall framework for evolution analysis. The framework tried to mine hot spots and visualize the evolution of hot spots by fusing high-level semantic features and topological features. Experiments show that our proposed method effectively combines structural and semantic features and is a promising research task.

This study has some limitations. In the exploration of the evolution of the field of AI, the model ignores the influence of time series. In future research, we will try to integrate time series features to improve the performance of the proposed model, such as applying LSTM and Transformer methods to the overall framework to obtain time series features to more comprehensively study hot-spot evolution. This research will guide future research in the field of AI. In the future, we can make reasonable attempts to improve the current limitations and provide more valuable information for future research.

Acknowledgment. This work was supported in part by the Natural Science Foundation of China under Grant 62272084.

References

1. Zhang, Y., et al.: Does deep learning help topic extraction? a kernel k-means clustering method with word embedding. J. Informet. **12**(4), 1099–1117 (2018)
2. Blei, D.M., Ng, A., Jordan, M.I.: Latent dirichlet allocation. J. Mach. Learn. Res. **3**, 993–1022 (2003)
3. Yau, C.K., Porter, A., Newman, N., Suominen, A.: Clustering scientific documents with topic modelling. Scientometrics **100**(3), 767–786 (2014)
4. Qiang, G., Zla, B., Ping, W., Jh, B., Xc, B., Ml, B.: Potential index: revealing the future impact of research topics based on current knowledge networks. J. Informet. **15**(3), 101165 (2021)
5. McNamara, D., Wong, P., Christen, P., Ng, K.S.: Predicting high impact academic papers using citation network features. In: Li, J., Cao, L., Wang, C., Tan, K.C., Liu, Bo., Pei, J., Tseng, V.S. (eds.) PAKDD 2013. LNCS (LNAI), vol. 7867, pp. 14–25. Springer, Heidelberg (2013). https://doi.org/10.1007/978-3-642-40319-4_2
6. Eberts, M., Ulges, A.: Span-based Joint Entity and Relation Extraction with Transformer Pretraining. arXiv preprint arXiv:1909.07755 (2019)
7. Li, J., Sun, A., Han, J., Li, C.: A survey on deep learning for named entity recognition. IEEE Trans. Knowl. Data Eng. **34**(1), 50–70 (2022)
8. Shang, Y.M., Huang, H., Mao, X.L.: Onerel: joint entity and relation extraction with one module in one step. arXiv preprint arXiv:2203.05412v2 (2022)
9. Raza, S., Schwartz, B.: Entity and relation extraction from clinical case reports of COVID-19: a natural language processing approach. BMC Med. Inform. Decis. Mak. **23**(1), 20 (2023)
10. Sun, Y., Qiu, H., Zheng, Y., Wang, Z., Zhang, C.: Sifrank: a new baseline for unsupervised keyphrase extraction based on pretrained language model. IEEE Access **8**, 10896–10906 (2020)
11. Meng, Y., Zhang, Y., Huang, J., Zhang, Y., Han, J.: Topic Discovery via Latent Space Clustering of Pretrained Language Model Representations. arXiv preprint arXiv: 2202.04582 (2022)
12. Wu, L., Chen, Y., Shen, K., Guo, X., Long, B.: Graph neural networks for natural language processing: a survey. arXiv preprint arXiv:2106.06090 (2021)
13. Lewis, M., et al.: Bart: Denoising Sequence-to-Sequence Pretraining for Natural Language Generation, Translation, and Comprehension. arXiv preprint arXiv:1910.13461 (2019)
14. Koncel-Kedziorski, R., Bekal, D., Luan, Y., Lapata, M., Hajishirzi, H.: Text Generation from Knowledge Graphs with Graph Transformers. arXiv preprint arXiv:1904.02342 (2019)
15. Li, J., Tang, T., Zhao, W.X., Wei, Z., Yuan, N.J., Wen, J.R.: Few-shot Knowledge Graph-to-Text Generation with Pretrained Language Models. arXiv preprint arXiv:2106.01623 (2021)
16. Arthur, D., Vassilvitskii, S.: K-Means++: the advantages of careful seeding. In: Proceedings of the Eighteenth Annual ACM-SIAM Symposium on Discrete Algorithms, pp. 1027–1035. ACM, New Orleans (2007)
17. Bafna, P., Pramod, D., Vaidya, A.: Document clustering: TF-IDF approach. In: 2016 International Conference on Electrical, Electronics, and Optimization Techniques (ICEEOT). pp. 61–66. IEEE, Chennai (2016)
18. Mikolov, T., Chen, K., Corrado, G., Dean, J.: Efficient estimation of word representations in vector space. arXiv preprint arXiv:1301.3781 (2013)

19. Shen, Z., Chen, F., Yang, L., Wu, J.: Node2vec representation for clustering journals and as a possible measure of diversity. J. Data Inf. Sci. **4**(2), 81–94 (2019)
20. Macqueen, J.: Some methods for classification and analysis of multivariate observations. In: Proceedings of the Fifth Berkeley Symposium on Mathematical Statistics and Probability, vol. 1, pp. 281–297 (1967)

How to Define a Multi-modal Knowledge Graph?

Nan Wang[1], Hankiz Yilahun[2(✉)], Askar Hamdulla[3], and ZhenXuan Qiu[1]

[1] Xinjiang University, Urumqi 830017, Xinjiang, China
[2] School of Information Science and Engineering, Urumqi 830017, Xinjiang, China
hansumuruh@xju.edu.cn
[3] Xinjiang Key Laboratory of Multilingual Information Technology, Urumqi 830017, Xinjiang, China
askar@xju.edu.cn

Abstract. As a form of structured human knowledge, knowledge graphs (KG) have attracted great attention from both the academic and industrial communities since their emergence. It is widely used in the field of artificial intelligence for applications such as information retrieval, data analysis, intelligent question-answering and recommendation systems. In recent years, various types of information on the internet have exploded in growth. In response, multimodal knowledge graphs (MMKGs) have emerged to serve the management and applications of different types of data. However, since the proposal of KG in 2012, there has not been a unified and standardized definition to describe KG, let alone MMKG. Based on previous research and experience, this paper has summarized the definition of KG through extensive investigation and explores the concept of MMKG. To provide a better illustration, this paper constructed a sample MMKG in the medical field based on an ontology and resource description framework (RDF). We use Neo4j for visualization and design a UI to extract node information. Finally, the shortcomings of the work were summarized, and future research directions were proposed.

Keywords: Multimodal Knowledge Graph · Ontology · Neo4j

1   Introduction

Knowledge is the crystallization of human understanding of the objective world in practice. As a form of structured knowledge, knowledge graphs (KGs) can be traced back to semantic nets proposed by Richens in 1956 [1,2]. Later, expert systems such as MYCIN were proposed and became a research hotspot [3]. Expert systems were also considered the precursor of KG. As the builder of a search engine, Google is committed to understanding the words that users use. In other words, when users search, the words they enter refer to things that actually exist in the world, rather than just their surface meanings. Based on this idea, Google

This work was supported by the provincial and ministerial key project of the 14th Five-Year Scientific Research Plan of the State Language Commission in 2022 (ZDI145-58), and Xinjiang University PhD Start-up Fund Project (620320015).

attempted to establish relationships between real-world entities by building the KG. In 2012, it was integrated into the Google search engine, making it easier for users to access knowledge related to their search queries.

KG is a collection of information about real-world entities, including people, books, movies and many other types of things. For example, for a celebrity, relevant data such as their birthday and height are collected, and the person is linked to other closely related entities in the KG. More specifically, if a user wants to learn about astronomers, they may search for Galileo, as shown in Fig. 1. Based on the knowledge graph, the search result will directly display relevant information and show Galileo's scientific contributions. It can also help users discover other famous astronomers, such as Copernicus and Kepler. The goal of the KG is to move from an information engine to a knowledge engine.

The proposal of knowledge graphs has attracted widespread attention from academia and industry. As the knowledge graph continues to develop, it will become larger in scale and more content-rich. An increasing number of knowledge graphs are being created to support downstream applications such as knowledge management, search engines, intelligent question answering and recommendation systems. The research fields include: medical, archeology, e-commerce, catering, and economics [4–9].

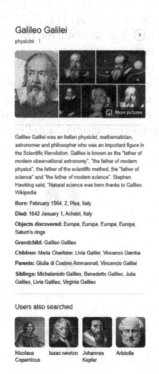

Fig. 1. Google search for Galileo

The concept of modal, similar to the concept of neural networks, was initially a biological concept. Humans have visual, auditory, tactile, and olfactory senses. Each different form of information can be referred to as a modal. In machine learning, it generally refers to different media of information, such as text, images, speech and videos. Multimodal refers to the combination of multiple different types of data. With the rapid development of the Internet, the explosive growth of information in different modalities has become a critical and challenging problem in terms of how to efficiently utilize these diverse types of information [24]. On the other hand, to overcome the limitations of a single mode in practical applications, the demand for machines to learn multimodal knowledge has also been increasing. For example, the image captioning task is one of the first tasks involving the combination of multimodal images and text. Machines need to automatically generate natural language descriptions of images, which requires more than the image understanding level provided by typical image recognition and object detection methods [12,13]. Visual question answering is often seen as a visual Turing test, where the system needs to understand any form of natural language question (usually related to visual information in the image) and answer it in a natural way [17,18].

However, as shown in Fig. 2(a), KGs mostly use pure symbolic text as objects, constructing a semantic network using triples. This approach limits the machines' understanding and expression capabilities [11,12]. If we only tell the machine about the description of "*dogs*", it is difficult for the machine to understand the concept of "*dogs*", which makes the application of KGs difficult. However, if we combine different modalities of information about dogs, such as pictures of dogs and the sound of barking, the image of "*dogs*" becomes vivid. In other words, if we want machines to truly gain intelligence, single-modal information alone is far from sufficient. Therefore, multimodal knowledge graph (MMKG), as shown in Fig. 2(b), has great help in achieving artificial intelligence. KGs are also urgently in need of multimodality.

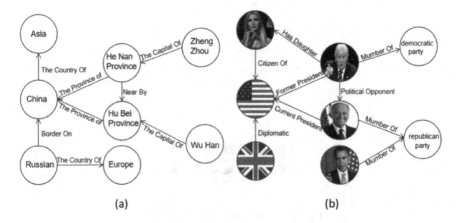

(a)   (b)

Fig. 2. (a) An example of unimodal KG (b) An example of a MMKG

In this context, the construction and application of MMKGs have become a research hotspot. However, there has been a thorny issue that has not been resolved, which is the definition of MMKG. Starting from the KG itself, this paper summarizes the definition of KG, explores the definition of MMKG, and provides an example MMKG in the medical field. The rest of this paper is organized as follows: Section 2 summarizes the definition of KG, and Sect. 3 explores the concept of MMKG. To illustrate the concept, Sect. 4 constructs an example MMKG in the medical field, and Sect. 5 provides a summary of the entire paper.

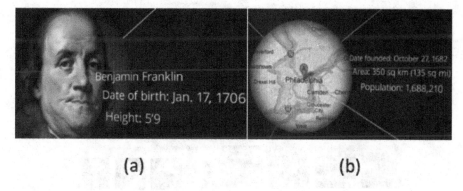

Fig. 3. (a) The introduction of Franklin (b) The introduction of Benjamin

2   Definition of KG

2.1   Description of the Problem

The definition of KG has been a longstanding topic of discussion among experts and scholars, but a consensus has not yet been reached [10–12,19–23]. The root cause of this problem is that Google's introduction to its KG blog did not mention the definition and related technical issues of KG, which has led to conflicting definitions and descriptions of KG in its development [1,20]. For example, Paulheim et al. defined KG as a graph-based organization used to describe entities and their relationships in the real world [21]. This definition is too abstract and not sufficiently detailed to KG. Ehrlinger et al. defined KG as the acquisition of knowledge and integration into ontology, using a reasoning engine to deduce new knowledge [20]. The implication is that KG consists of two parts, knowledge and reasoning engine, which is also biased. Zheng et al. simply defined KG as representing entities with nodes and relationships with edges [4]. Most other papers mention the representation of KG, rather than its definition. For example, Ji et al. defined a knowledge graph as $\mathcal{G} = \{\mathcal{E}, \mathcal{R}, \mathcal{F}\}$, where $\mathcal{E}$, $\mathcal{R}$ and $\mathcal{F}$ are sets of entities, relationships, and facts, respectively. Facts are represented as triples $\{h, r, t\} \in \mathcal{F}$ [23]. However, there is no distinction made between relationships and attributes and no discussion of directivity between triples. As seen, even the representation of KG is difficult to have a unified standard [11]. This is very unfriendly for research in this field. Therefore, a unified and standard definition of KG is needed.

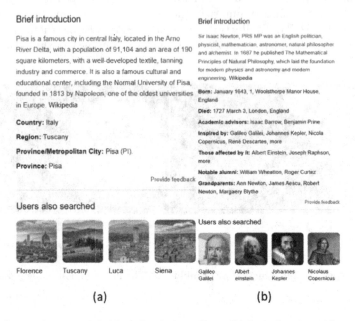

Fig. 4. (a) Introduction of Galileo's birthplace, Pisa. (b) Introduction of Isaac Newton, a figure related to Galileo.

2.2   Inquiry into the Problem

To solve this thorny problem, must go back to the source and start with Google's blog on KG. The blog provides a case of how KG is used for search, as shown in Fig. 1. We can see that the search result for Galileo consists of the following parts:

- The first part is Galileo's name and classification: Galileo belongs to the category of physicists. We can view this classification as a part of the framework of ontology, and Galileo is an instance under this class.
- Then, are his images, which come from different sources such as BaiduPedia, StarWalk, Wikipedia [1].
- After the images, there is a section on Galileo's personal information, including his life events, and contributions. The users could click the blue text and will have a page jump. The black text could not be clicked.

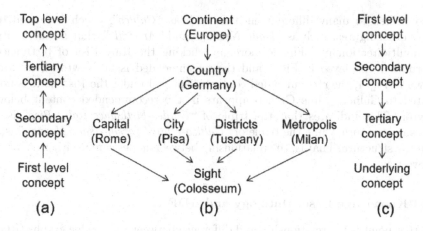

Fig. 5. (a) Inductive method for ontology construction (b) Ontology diagram (c) Taxonomic method for ontology construction

- At the bottom, there are related figures such as Copernicus, Newton. The text and images are integrated as a whole, and clicking on them can lead to their corresponding pages.

Therefore, we can see that the data in KG should include two types: resources and literals. Resources refer to resource links from different data sources. Literals can be understood as strings in programming languages, which do not have meaning in themselves. With the concept of *"trees"* in data structures, literals are similar to *"leaves"* with a degree of 0. Combined with another instance in the introduction, as shown in Fig. 3, resources exist in the form of entity nodes, and different entity nodes are connected through relationships, represented by white lines in the graph. Literals are usually considered internal information of entity nodes and are not connected to other nodes, which is called the property value. These two types of information can be described by triples. For example, *"Galileo - birth place - Pisa, Italy"*, *"Galileo - died in - January 8, 1642"*. The first triple was defined as entity-relationship-entity, and the other was defined as entity-property-property value. These two together form the basic components of a KG. One important point to note is the directivity of the entities in KG. Some literature mentions this issue, suggesting that KG should be defined as a directed graph structure [10,11]. However, these studies has not provided a clear explanation on this issue: whether it is the directivity of the relationship between entities or the directivity between entities and property values, and whether this directivity refers to one-way or two-way, or multidirectional? This paper explains this issue: using the previous example, *"Galileo - died in - January 8, 1642"* is a reasonable expression, rather than *"January 8, 1642 - died in - Galileo"*. That is, in the triple of entity-property-property value, the node points to the property value, and the node's property is only connected to that node, which is unidirectional. This matches the representation in Fig. 3. For the triple of entity-relationship-entity, such as *"Galileo - birth place - Pisa, Italy"*. An entity is connected to many different entities, such as "*Galileo*", which is related to many other figures, such as "*Isaac Newton*" and "*Aristotle*"; that is, the entity has multidirectionality. Furthermore, by clicking the Italy Pisa of birthplace information displayed in Fig. 1 and the recommended Isaac Newton below, as shown in Fig. 4, the recommended content displayed under the Pisa node is not related to Galileo, while Galileo appears in the recommended content below Newton. This indicates that the triple of "*Galileo-birthplace-Italy, Pisa*" is a one-way structure, while the triple of "*Galileo-related person-Isaac Newton*" is a two-way structure. That is, the relationship between nodes can be either one-way or two-way.

2.3 Knowledge Base, Ontology and RDF

Another point is the relationship and difference between knowledge graphs (KG) and knowledge bases. Many recent papers do not distinguish between these two concepts and treat KG and knowledge bases as equivalent [10,11]. They consider semantic networks, graph databases, and knowledge bases such as WordNet (1995), BabelNet (2010), Freebase (2008), DBpedia (2007), YAGO (2007), and WikiData (2014) as KG without explanation, which is obviously unreasonable [28–33]. One piece of evidence is that Johanna Wright, the product management director, mentioned in her introduction of KG that Google uses search engines to understand user search content and add some of this content to the knowledge base. This indicates that KG is a kind of knowledge base. However, other descriptions from Google employees suggest that these two concepts are not identical [1]. To this end, this paper explains that a knowledge base is a special database used for knowledge management. It is a collection of heterogeneous knowledge from multiple sources in a required field, including basic facts, rules, and other related information. A KG is a processed knowledge base that has a graph structure and contains structured and semistructured data. In addition to KG, two other frequently mentioned concepts are ontology and Resource Description Framework (RDF) [25,26]. RDF is a data model developed by W3C, which provides a uni-

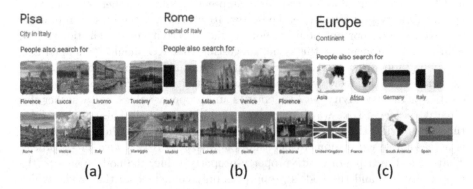

Fig. 6. (a) Search result of Pisa (b) Search result of Rome (c) Search result of Europe

fied standard for describing things and their relationships. RDF is composed
of nodes and edges, where nodes represent specific entity resources or property
values and edges represent relationships between entities or between entities and
property values. RDF has constraints on each part of the SPO triple: "*s*" should
be Internationalized Resource Identifiers (IRI) or blank node, "*p*" should be IRI
and "*o*" could be IRI, resource or literals. However, RDF has a serious limitation
in that it cannot distinguish between classes and objects. It also cannot define
and describe class relationships and properties. In other words, RDF is mainly
used to describe concrete things and lacks the ability to abstractly categorize
and define groups of similar things. This clearly limits the expressive power of
the model. Therefore, the assistance of an ontology is needed.

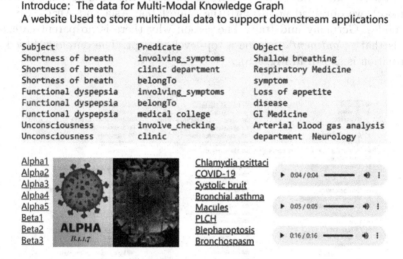

Fig. 7. Part of data of COMMKG-19

Ontology is a philosophical concept that involves dividing entities into basic
categories and hierarchies. Ontology has a classification system and basic reasoning principles. The classification system defines the relationship between categories, providing the basis for reasoning. Some ontologies are widely used in
the medical field, such as CIDO, GO, UberOn and DOID [34–37]. There are two
main ways to build ontologies: the bottom-up inductive approach as shown in
Fig. 5(a), and the top-down classification approach as shown in Fig. 5(c). Generally, the construction of open-domain KGs often uses the inductive method to
classify features from underlying data due to the large amount of data involved.
In contrary, domain-specific KGs often define classification categories before filling in the data. Google's KG is full of the shadows of category in ontology. As
previously mentioned, Galileo belongs to the category of physicists. As shown
in Fig. 6(a), there is a comment line: "*Pisa: The City of Italy*", which can be

viewed as a category label. In the recommended content below, we can see four recommended places, Florence, Lucca, Livorno and Tuscany. The category label of Florence, Lucca and Livorno is "*City in Italy*", and the category label of Tuscany is "*Administrative districts of Italy*". All of this recommended content belongs to places (cities or administrative regions) in Italy. In the additional recommendations, there are two items worth noting: one is "*Rome, the capital of Italy*", and the other is "*Italy, Countries in Europe*". When searching for Rome, as shown in Fig. 6(b), the related content includes Italy, Milan, Venice, and Florence. The corresponding category tags are countries in Europe and cities in Italy. In the additional recommendations, there are also Madrid (the capital of Spain) and London (the capital of the United Kingdom). It could be speculate that the recommended entities in the KG come from three categories: entities with the same label in the same category, with subcategory labels, and with parent category labels. Search for "*Europe*" to verify this assumption. As shown in Fig. 6(c), we obtained nodes with the same label: Asia and Africa. Subcategory nodes: Germany and Italy. The reason why there is no parent category entity is that "*Continent*" may be a top-level concept. The ontology based on this situation is shown in Fig. 5(b).

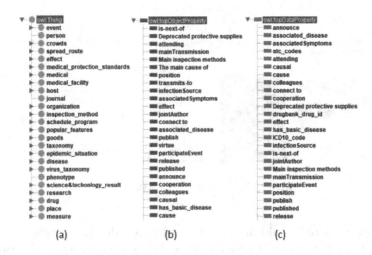

(a)   (b)   (c)

Fig. 8. (a) Some top-level concepts in the ontology (b) Some relationships in the ontology (c) Some properties in the ontology (c) Some properties in the ontology

2.4   Conclusion

In summary, this paper provides the definition of KG: KG is a kind of knowledge base composed of ontology and resource description framework, which can serve downstream applications. Its symbolic language is $\mathcal{G} = \{\mathcal{E}, \mathcal{R}, \mathcal{P}, \mathcal{V}, \mathcal{T_R}, \mathcal{T_P}\}$, which is a set of elements and knowledge, where $\mathcal{E}, \mathcal{R}, \mathcal{P}, \mathcal{V}$ is a set of entities, relationships, properties, property values. Knowledge $\mathcal{T_R}$ is a set of triples of entity-relationship-entity, and $\mathcal{T_P}$ is a set of triples of entity-property-property value. One piece of knowledge can be represented as $\mathcal{T_R} = \{\mathcal{E}, \mathcal{R}, \mathcal{E}\}$ or $\mathcal{T_P} = \{\mathcal{E}, \mathcal{P}, \mathcal{V}\}$. where $\mathcal{R}$ and $\mathcal{P}$ are directional, pointing from the head entity to the tail entity or property value. For example, *"Zhengzhou belongs to Henan Province"* can be expressed as $\mathcal{T_R} = (Zhengzhou, belongs to, Henan Province)$, and *"Biden is 81 years old this year"* can be expressed as $\mathcal{T_P} = (Biden, age, 81)$.

3   Exploring the Concept of MMKG

Most literature researching MMKG does not mention the definition, and the definitions in some literature are too abstract [41, 44]. Wang et al. directly introduced the RDF model into Richpedia and regarded it as a finite set of RDF triples [43]. Zhu et al. mentions that MMKG is a multimodal representation of part of the knowledge in KG [11]. In view of this phenomenon, it is necessary to summarize a unified and complete definition of MMKG.

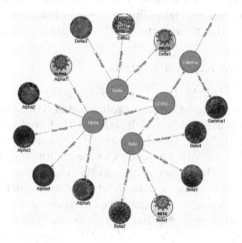

Fig. 9. COMMKG-19 visualization by Neo4j

3.1   Multimodality of Knowledge Graphs

Some literature uses *"CKG"* to refer to knowledge graphs based solely on text modal [10]. This statement is unreasonable. The reason is that relevant researchers have ignored such a problem: Has the KG been multimodal since its inception? The answer is affirmative. The root cause of this problem is that Google does not mention the multimodal problem about KG in the relevant introduction. Although the concept of *"multimodal"* has been proposed for a long time, it was not until approximately 2015 that it received widespread attention in the field of artificial intelligence, and most of the research was based on text and images [46]. As the key to Google's search engine, the KG improves the performance of search engines in three ways: find the right thing, get the best summary and go deeper and broader. As the view in the blog, *"Language can be ambiguous-do you mean Taj Mahal the monument, or Taj Mahal the musician?"*, in order to provide better recommendations, KG has added image elements to relevant recommendations, such as Fig. 1 and Fig. 4. However, research based on KG, including construction and application, initially focused on text modal [47–52]. For example, Sören Auer built a KG for the exchange of academic information [49]. In the field of natural language processing (NLP), named entity recognition (NER) and relationship extraction(RE) work based on text modal has been greatly developed [50,51]. With the proposal of the TransE model, knowledge representation learning(KRL) based on text information has become a major research hotspot [52,53]. It is only in recent years that research on multimodality of KG has progressed. Examples include Liu et al.'s proposal of MMKG in 2019 and Wang et al.'s proposal of Richpedia in 2020 [43,44].

It can be seen that the development of knowledge graphs is from multimodal to unimodal and then to multimodal. One of the main reasons for this is that: there is a lack of a unified understanding of the knowledge graph in academia and industry. This is why this paper explores the definition of a knowledge graph.

3.2   Comparison of KG and MMKG

Contrary to existing beliefs, based on the foregoing, this paper argues that MMKG should not be regarded as a generalization of KG; rather, KG is a special case of MMKG. In other words, KG is MMKG that contains only text modal information. Therefore, in terms of definition, MMKG and KG should conform to the same definition framework. Compared to the definition of KG, the definition of MMKG is broader. This paper defines MMKG as follows: MMKG is a kind of knowledge base that contains data in at least two different modals forms: text, voice, images, videos, etc. Follow the ontology and resource description framework, which can serve downstream applications. The symbolic language of MMKG is $\mathcal{G} = \{\mathcal{E}^M, \mathcal{R}^M, \mathcal{P}^M, \mathcal{V}^M, \mathcal{T}_{\mathcal{R}}^M, \mathcal{T}_{\mathcal{P}}^M\}$, where $\mathcal{E}^M$, $\mathcal{R}^M$, $\mathcal{P}^M$, and $\mathcal{V}^M$ are a set of entities, relationships, properties, and property values and could be different modes. Knowledge $\mathcal{T}_{\mathcal{R}}^M$ is a set of triples of entity-relationship-entity with different modal, and $\mathcal{T}_{\mathcal{P}}^M$ is a set of triples of entity-property-property value with different modal. One piece of knowledge can be represented as $\mathcal{T}_{\mathcal{R}}^M = \{\mathcal{E}^M, \mathcal{R}^M, \mathcal{E}^M\}$ or $\mathcal{T}_{\mathcal{P}}^M = \{\mathcal{E}^M, \mathcal{P}^M, \mathcal{V}^M\}$, where $\mathcal{R}^M$ and $\mathcal{P}^M$ are directional, pointing from the head entity to the tail entity or property value.

The difference between KG and MMKG is mainly reflected in the application level, which is also the core issue of extensive research in academia. A major difficulty in researching MMKG is how to fuse the features of different modal data in a reasonable way to support downstream applications. Compared with the interaction between text modals in KG, MMKG needs to consider the features of different modal data. Current research focuses on supplementing text information with image information to improve the accuracy of downstream tasks. Sun et al. designed a recommendation system based on the MMKG, which effectively alleviated the problems of cold start and data sparseness in the recommendation system [27]. Zheng et al. used doctor-patient dialogue and related examination pictures (CT, X-ray and ultrasound) to improve the accuracy of the diagnostic system for COVID-19 [39]. For KRL, the semantic information of unimodal limits the performance of the model. The introduction of modal data makes the performance of such models have more room for improvement. Wang et al. fused text and image modal features through the multihead self-attention mechanism to improve the accuracy of link prediction [55]. One thing to note is that image information should be as important as text information.

Table 1. Comparison of data between COKG-19 and COMMKG-19.

Model	Volume of Data						
	Concept	Property	Relationship	Entity	Triple	Speech	Image
COKG-19	505	393	82	26,282	32,352	/	/
COMMKG-19	512	397	84	26,432	60,039	268	2,700

4 Construction of MMKG

4.1 Two Different Ways to Build MMKG

At present, academia and industry generally use two different ways to construct MMKGs. One is to build MMKG using images as entity nodes. After that, the node information is enriched through the properties of the node, such as the size of the picture and the content of the image. This paper refers to this build as E-MMKG for short. Wang et al. built Richpedia following RDF. The text entity comes from Wikidata's IRI. For image entities, collect images from Wikipedia and create corresponding IRIs in Richpedia. The result was a collection of 30,638 entities about cities, attractions, and celebrities. On average, a total of 99.2 images were retained for each entity. However, in Richpedia, the number of relationships between images is smaller and the ontology is simpler [43].

The other way is to build MMKG using the image as a property of the node, which this paper refers to as P-MMKG for short. Daniel et al. created ImageGraph, which contains 14,860 entities and 829,931 images. Its relationship structure is based on FB15K. For image data, more than 462 GB of image data was downloaded from different search engines. Corrupted, duplicate, and low-quality images are removed. In addition, triples in the header or tail entities that cannot be linked to the image data are filtered [54].

Compared with the construction method of E-MMKG, the construction of P-MMKG is simpler because the current attributes in the knowledge graph are not connected to other nodes, and there is no need to consider the relationship between images. The construction of E-MMKG often needs to consider the relationship between images, such as similar or different. Although it enriches the amount of data in MMKG, it also increases the complexity of the build. In some fields where the relationship between images is not in high demand, the P-MMKG construction method is recommended. However, in some specific fields, such as in the Encyclopedia Knowledge Graph, illustrating the relationships between different species of animals through images (tigers and lions share a common ancestor), E-MMKG must be considered. These two different MMKG construction methods follow the ontology and RDF structure, which is consistent with the definition of MMKG in this paper.

4.2 Building Sample MMKG in the Medical Field

The potential of KG in the medical field is enormous and is considered the cornerstone for achieving smart healthcare. Some work based on KG in the medical field has made good progress [4,39]. The outbreak of the COVID-19 virus in 2019 has had a profound impact on human life. Research based on the COVID-19 virus has been a hot topic in recent years. However, the shortcomings of these KGs are also very obvious: most medical KGs are based on textual data. A few MMKGs have limited types of image data, and these MMKGs do not consider speech data [39]. To provide a better illustration and facilitate better research by experts and scholars, this paper constructed a sample MMKG based on the COVID-19 virus, including textual, image and speech data.

Since there is no need to consider the relationship between images, this paper uses P-MMKG to construct the sample MMKG. The ontology and some of the textual data were referenced from COKG-19[1]. COKG-19 is an opensource KG on COVID-19 primarily based on textual information jointly released by the AMiner team of the Department of Computer Science and Technology at Tsinghua University and the ZhikuAI team. The KG collected data from 8 COVID- 19-related KGs that are open-source on OPENKG[2]. Through various algorithms such as entity recognition, semantic matching and disambiguation, and knowledge fusion, the KG merged concepts with the same meaning, differentiated polysemous concepts, and supplemented and corrected them based on the opinions of relevant experts. In recent years, there have been some new variants of the COVID-19 virus. Therefore, this paper added some concepts, attributes, relationships, and instances to COKG.

For image data, a web crawler system is built to retrieve images related to entities from different search engines, which collect URL links to the topranking images of different search engines. Taking into account the cost of manual construction, the sample size is selected as 10% of the number of entities. To ensure the quality of the picture, we manually adjusted the size of some pictures and deleted low-quality pictures considering factors such as image size, clarity, and reliability. Filter out the most representative pictures as the property store of the node. It is worth mentioning that figurative pictures are chosen to convey

---

[1] https://covid-19.aminer.cn/kg/class/neurology_disease.
[2] http://www.openkg.cn/.

some non-visual concepts such as delirium. In the end, a total of 2700 pictures passed the screening, and some important nodes were assigned multiple images.

For speech data, the content of the dataset is mainly the clinical manifestations of partial symptoms. Through Text-To-Speech (TTS) technology, 268 audio files were generated using the open-source API of iFlytek[3]. We refer to the sample MMKG as COMMKG-19, in addition, COMMKG-19 additionally extracted English triples. The data pairs for COKG-19 and COMMKG-19 are shown in Table 1.

To store the above information and provide URL links, as shown in Fig. 7, this paper has established an open source website[4]. Protégé is an ontology editor developed by Stanford University, that is used to create and maintain ontologies and knowledge graphs. In this paper, Protégé was used to add, modify and supplement the ontology data of COKG-19, such as concepts, relationships and properties, as shown in Fig. 8.

The MMKG visualization was achieved by importing data into a Neo4j graph database by generating Turtle files, as shown in Fig. 9. In addition, to facilitate the extraction and utilization of MMKG data, a user interface was designed to retrieve node information, as shown in Fig. 10.

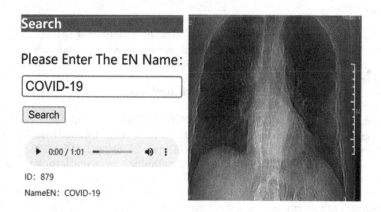

Fig. 10. User interface

5 Summary

In recent years, KG has made significant progress, and many MMKG-based studies have achieved remarkable advances. To promote a unified understanding of KG in the academic and industrial communities and to use the term "*KG*" more rigorously, this paper starts from the KG itself, conducts investigations

---

[3] https://www.xfyun.cn/.
[4] https://xiangrui521.github.io/KnowledgeGraphData/.

and research, summarizes previous work, proposes a definition of KG, explores the concept of MMKG, and provides a sample MMKG in the medical field.

The work presented in this paper has some limitations. First, the proposed definition of KG needs to be widely recognized and further refined by relevant researchers. Second, the MMKG sample constructed in the medical field has relatively few image and speech data, partly due to the high cost of manual work. Therefore, in future work, we will consider automated processing of speech and image data. In addition, video data have not been considered because there is currently limited research on video modal data, but video data often contain more information, which is an important aspect to consider. Due to article constraints, some of the content cannot be described in detail. We will focus on outlining the MMKG technical system to establish connections between different research fields and promote the development of the KG field in the future.

Acknowledgements. This work was supported by the provincial and ministerial key project of the 14th Five-Year Scientific Research Plan of the State Language Commission in 2022 (ZDI145-58), and this work was supported by the National Social Science Foundation of China (No. 22XYY048).

References

1. Singhal, A.: Introducing the Knowledge Graph: Things, not Strings, May 2012. https://blog.google/products/search/introducing-knowledge-graph-things-not/
2. Richens, R.H.: Preprogramming for mechanical translation. Mech. Transl. Comput. Linguist. **3**(1), 20–25 (1956)
3. Shortliffe, E. (ed.): Computer-Based Medical Consultations: MYCIN. Elsevier (2012)
4. Zheng, X., Xiao, Y., Song, W., et al.: COVID19-OBKG: an ontology-based knowledge graph and web service for COVID-19. In: 2021 IEEE International Conference on Bioinformatics and Biomedicine (BIBM), pp. 2456–2462. IEEE (2021)
5. Haase, P., Herzig, D.M., Kozlov, A., et al.: metaphactory: a platform for knowledge graph management. Semantic Web **10**(6), 1109–1125 (2019)
6. Do, P., Phan, T.H.V.: Developing a BERT based triple classification model using knowledge graph embedding for question answering system. Appl. Intell. **52**(1), 636–651 (2022)
7. Jiang, Z., Chi, C., Zhan, Y.: Research on medical question answering system based on knowledge graph. IEEE Access **9**, 21094–21101 (2021)
8. Fan, H., Zhong, Y., Zeng, G., et al.: Improving recommender system via knowledge graph based exploring user preference. Appl. Intell., 1–13 (2022)
9. Gogleva, A., Polychronopoulos, D., Pfeifer, M., et al.: Knowledge graph-based recommendation framework identifies drivers of resistance in EGFR mutant non-small cell lung cancer. Nat. Commun. **13**(1), 1667 (2022)
10. Peng, J., Hu, X., Huang, W., et al.: What is a multi-modal knowledge graph: a survey. Big Data Res., 100380 (2023)
11. Zhu, X., Li, Z., Wang, X., et al.: Multimodal knowledge graph construction and application: a survey. IEEE Trans. Knowl. Data Eng. (2022)
12. Zhang, C., Yang, Z., He, X., et al.: Multimodal intelligence: representation learning, information fusion, and applications. IEEE J. Sel. Top. Sig. Process. **14**(3), 478–493 (2020)

13. He, X., Deng, L.: Deep learning for image-to-text generation: a technical overview. IEEE Signal Process. Mag. **34**(6), 109–116 (2017)
14. Zhang, Z., Xie, Y., Yang, L.: Photographic text-to-image synthesis with a hierarchically nested adversarial network. In: Proceedings of the IEEE Conference on Computer Vision and Pattern Recognition, pp. 6199–6208 (2018)
15. Zhou, R., Jiang, C., Xu, Q.: A survey on generative adversarial network-based text-to-image synthesis. Neurocomputing **451**, 316–336 (2021)
16. Tan, H., Liu, X., Liu, M., et al.: KT-GAN: knowledge-transfer generative adversarial network for text-to-image synthesis. IEEE Trans. Image Process. **30**, 1275–1290 (2020)
17. Wu, Q., Teney, D., Wang, P., et al.: Visual question answering: a survey of methods and datasets. Comput. Vis. Image Underst. **163**, 21–40 (2017)
18. Wang, P., Wu, Q., Shen, C., et al.: FVQA: fact-based visual question answering. IEEE Trans. Pattern Anal. Mach. Intell. **40**(10), 2413–2427 (2017)
19. Wang, Q., Mao, Z., Wang, B., et al.: Knowledge graph embedding: a survey of approaches and applications. IEEE Trans. Knowl. Data Eng. **29**(12), 2724–2743 (2017)
20. Ehrlinger, L., Wöß, W.: Towards a definition of knowledge graphs. SEMANTiCS (Posters, Demos, SuCCESS) **48**(1–4), 2 (2016)
21. Paulheim, H.: Knowledge graph refinement: a survey of approaches and evaluation methods. Semantic Web **8**(3), 489–508 (2017)
22. Alani, H., et al. (eds.): ISWC 2013. LNCS, vol. 8219. Springer, Heidelberg (2013). https://doi.org/10.1007/978-3-642-41338-4
23. Ji, S., Pan, S., Cambria, E., et al.: A survey on knowledge graphs: representation, acquisition, and applications. IEEE Trans. Neural Netw. Learn. Syst. **33**(2), 494–514 (2021)
24. Ye, C., Zhou, G., Lu, J.: Survey on construction and application research for multimodal knowledge graphs. Appl. Res. Comput. **38**(12), 3535–3543 (2021)
25. Bunge, M.: Treatise on Basic Philosophy: Ontology I: The Furniture of the World. Springer, Dordrecht (1977). https://doi.org/10.1007/978-94-010-9924-0
26. Klyne, G.: Resource description framework (RDF): concepts and abstract syntax (2004). http://www.w3.org/TR/rdf-concepts/
27. Sun, R., Cao, X., Zhao, Y., et al.: Multi-modal knowledge graphs for recommender systems. In: Proceedings of the 29th ACM International Conference on Information & Knowledge Management, pp. 1405–1414 (2020)
28. Miller, G.A.: WordNet: a lexical database for English. Commun. ACM **38**(11), 39–41 (1995)
29. Navigli, R., Ponzetto, S.P.: BabelNet: building a very large multilingual semantic network. In: Proceedings of the 48th Annual Meeting of the Association for Computational Linguistics, pp. 216–225 (2010)
30. Bollacker, K., Evans, C., Paritosh, P., et al.: Freebase: a collaboratively created graph database for structuring human knowledge. In: Proceedings of the ACM SIGMOD International Conference on Management of Data, pp. 1247–1250 (2008)
31. Auer, S., Bizer, C., Kobilarov, G., Lehmann, J., Cyganiak, R., Ives, Z.: DBpedia: a nucleus for a web of open data. In: Aberer, K., et al. (eds.) ASWC/ISWC - 2007. LNCS, vol. 4825, pp. 722–735. Springer, Heidelberg (2007). https://doi.org/10.1007/978-3-540-76298-0_52
32. Suchanek, F.M., Kasneci, G., Weikum, G.: YAGO: a core of semantic knowledge. In: Proceedings of the 16th International Conference on World Wide Web, pp. 697–706 (2007)

33. Vrandečić, D., Krötzsch, M.: Wikidata: a free collaborative knowledgebase. Commun. ACM **57**(10), 78–85 (2014)
34. He, Y., Yu, H., Ong, E., et al.: CIDO, a community-based ontology for coronavirus disease knowledge and data integration, sharing, and analysis. Sci. Data **7**(1), 181 (2020)
35. Ashburner, M., Ball, C.A., Blake, J.A., et al.: Gene ontology: tool for the unification of biology. Nat. Genet. **25**(1), 25–29 (2000)
36. Mungall, C.J., Torniai, C., Gkoutos, G.V., et al.: Uberon, an integrative multi-species anatomy ontology. Genome Biol. **13**(1), 1–20 (2012)
37. Schriml, L.M., Arze, C., Nadendla, S., et al.: Disease ontology: a backbone for disease semantic integration. Nucleic Acids Res. **40**(D1), D940–D946 (2012)
38. Bordes, A., Usunier, N., Garcia-Duran, A., et al.: Translating embeddings for modeling multi-relational data. In: Advances in Neural Information Processing Systems, vol. 26 (2013)
39. Zheng, W., Yan, L., Gou, C., et al.: Pay attention to doctor-patient dialogues: multimodal knowledge graph attention image-text embedding for COVID-19 diagnosis. Inf. Fusion **75**, 168–185 (2021)
40. Xiong, J., Liu, G., Liu, Y., et al.: Oracle bone inscriptions information processing based on multimodal knowledge graph. Comput. Electric. Eng. **92**, 107173 (2021)
41. Xu, G., Chen, H., Li, F.L., et al.: AliMe MKG: a multimodal knowledge graph for live-streaming e-commerce. In: Proceedings of the 30th ACM International Conference on Information & Knowledge Management, pp. 4808–4812 (2021)
42. Lei, Z., Haq, A.U., Zeb, A., et al.: Is the suggested food your desired?: Multimodal recipe recommendation with demand-based knowledge graph. Expert Syst. Appl. **186**, 115708 (2021)
43. Wang, M., Wang, H., Qi, G., et al.: Richpedia: a large-scale, comprehensive multimodal knowledge graph. Big Data Res. **22**, 100159 (2020)
44. Liu, Y., Li, H., Garcia-Duran, A., Niepert, M., Onoro-Rubio, D., Rosenblum, D.S.: MMKG: multi-modal knowledge graphs. In: Hitzler, P., et al. (eds.) ESWC 2019. LNCS, vol. 11503, pp. 459–474. Springer, Cham (2019). https://doi.org/10.1007/978-3-030-21348-0_30
45. Alberts, H., Huang, T., Deshpande, Y., et al.: VisualSem: a high-quality knowledge graph for vision and language. arXiv preprint arXiv:2008.09150 (2020)
46. Baltrušaitis, T., Ahuja, C., Morency, L.-P.: Multimodal machine learning: a survey and taxonomy. IEEE Trans. Pattern Anal. Mach. Intell. **41**(2), 423–443 (2018)
47. Wang, Z., et al.: XLore: a large-scale English-Chinese bilingual knowledge graph. In: ISWC (Posters & Demos) (2013)
48. Wu, T., et al.: A survey of techniques for constructing Chinese knowledge graphs and their applications. Sustainability **10**(9), 3245 (2018)
49. Auer, S., et al.: Towards a knowledge graph for science. In: Proceedings of the 8th International Conference on Web Intelligence, Mining and Semantics (2018)
50. Chiu, J.P.C., Nichols, E.: Named entity recognition with bidirectional LSTM-CNNs. Trans. Assoc. Comput. Linguist. **4**, 357–370 (2016)
51. Mintz, M., et al.: Distant supervision for relation extraction without labelled data. In: Proceedings of the Joint Conference of the 47th Annual Meeting of the ACL and the 4th International Joint Conference on Natural Language Processing of the AFNLP (2009)
52. Bordes, A., et al.: Translating embeddings for modelling multi-relational data. In: Advances in Neural Information Processing Systems, vol. 26 (2013)
53. Lin, Y., et al.: Knowledge representation learning: a quantitative review. arXiv preprint arXiv:1812.10901 (2018)

54. Oñoro-Rubio, D., et al.: Answering visual-relational queries in web-extracted knowledge graphs. arXiv preprint arXiv:1709.02314 (2017)
55. Wang, E., et al.: Multimodal knowledge graphs representation learning via multi-headed self-attention. Inf. Fusion **88**, 78–85 (2022)

Research on Feature Fusion Methods for Multimodal Medical Data

Zhaogang Xu, Xi Yang, Yu Jin, and Shuyu Chen$^{(\boxtimes)}$

Chongqing University, Chongqing 400044, China
610922554@qq.com

Abstract. With the rapid development of artificial intelligence, knowledge graph, image processing, etc. have been widely used, and smart medical care, as a major application scenario of artificial intelligence, has received a lot of attention. Traditional diagnostic methods have problems such as low accuracy and low efficiency, and the research and application of knowledge graph and image classification in the field of dermatology are also in the initial stage, but text-based knowledge graph technology and image-based image classification technology have developed very maturely. Considering that various current image classification algorithms extract features, feature calculation, and model matching from images, they do not consider obtaining information such as features or relationships that are not in images from text data to participate in image classification tasks. In this paper, the optimized hierarchical perception model H-HAKE based on hierarchical perception model KGE-HAKE calculates selector parameters by improving the hierarchical perception model to add category dimension to the TransE coordinate system, divide more image features and entities with the same attribute into the same level, increase the number of links between image and map entities, and produce better data coverage effect. Aiming at the image classification task, this paper proposes a game tree model to optimize the classification results, including calculating the confidence degree based on the map, the aggregation degree of the classification results, the inference value of the entities in the domain, etc., and comprehensively designing the fusion mode of knowledge graph and image classification algorithm KG-based CNN in scenarios such as multi-map input and feature pre-extraction. The mode is effective enough to enable the image classification task to utilize multimodal data, and the effectiveness is verified by multi-scenario and data ablation experiments on the public data collection.

Keywords: KEG-HAKE · Entity Extraction · Knowledge Reasoning · Image Classification

1 Introduction

1.1 A Subsection Sample

At present, the number of skin disease patients worldwide has reached about 420 million, of which the number of skin disease patients in China alone has exceeded 150 million, and the incidence rate has reached 40%−70%. Traditional diagnostic methods often rely

M. Zhang et al. (Eds.): CCF NCCA 2023, CCIS 1959, pp. 96–114, 2024.
https://doi.org/10.1007/978-981-99-8764-1_8

on the experience of doctors and visual observation, which has problems such as low diagnostic accuracy and susceptibility to subjective factors. Computer assisted diagnosis (CAD) technology has made significant progress in this social context. However, current image classification methods have some limitations, such as the lack of background features in some images, difficulty in extracting fuzzy features from images, and the fact that patients often lack professional medical terminology, they may omit or provide incomplete symptom descriptions, increasing the difficulty of disease diagnosis. Therefore, the key to handling the preliminary diagnosis of skin diseases is to confirm the disease range of patients according to the description of less symptom information, use the domain knowledge atlas to carry out and complete the missing information, and combine the text information with the patient's disease image to identify.

In China, research on disease knowledge maps and skin image diagnosis is also gradually emerging. In recent years, more and more research teams have begun to explore the use of artificial intelligence technologies such as deep learning for automated diagnosis of diseases. For example, Professor Gong Lejun's team of Southeast University uses knowledge maps to model long non coding RNA (LncRNA), describes data and corresponding relationships through Resource Description Framework and Web Ontology Language, and studies the relationship between genes and diseases [1]. Li Guojing, Xia Qiuting, and others used attention mechanism and multi model fusion based on ResNet for fundus retinal image assisted diagnosis [2]. Liu Zhaorui, Zhang Yi, and others from Peking University Union Medical College conducted a convolutional neural network (CNN) binary classification model based on dermatoscopy images for the differential diagnosis of mycosis fungoides (MF) and inflammatory skin diseases under dermatoscopy, with an accuracy of 75.02% [3].

Internationally, there has been some relevant research and practice on the construction of skin image diagnosis systems based on the knowledge graph of skin diseases. For example, Tao Meng and Lin Lin proposed a subspace projection model (C-RSPM) at the IEEE multimedia seminar to divide cell images into 25 blocks to reduce computational spatial complexity, and to use multimodal data for voting on image blocks to improve accuracy [4]. At the ACM International Multimedia Conference, A Znaidia and A Shabou proposed the concept hierarchy and the data collected from the photo sharing platform and images to complete the photo multi label marking work. Through the integration of two text and one image classification mode, computational complexity was reduced [3]. At the 2020 IEEE/CFF Symposium on Computer Vision and Pattern Recognition, E Raisi and SH Bach proposed conducting neural network training to improve model generalization ability while simultaneously training two related tasks. One is the original task (target), and the other is the auxiliary task (source). The auxiliary task is completed using a knowledge graph, reducing the error rate by 2.1% [5].

Overall, with the continuous development and application of artificial intelligence technology, skin image diagnosis systems have been widely studied and applied internationally and domestically. There is a trend towards multimodal data fusion. However, the image diagnosis system based on dermatology knowledge map has not been formally developed due to the lack of domain knowledge base and the construction model of multimodal data in image classification. However, the research on this system is expected to further improve the diagnostic accuracy of skin diseases and promote the true digitization and intelligence of clinical practice. Therefore, it is necessary to explore new ways to integrate knowledge graphs into image classification modes.

2 Background Knowledge

2.1 TransR

The knowledge graph completion technology is an important technology for constructing knowledge graphs. The methods for inferring new entities and relationships based on the entity relationships of knowledge graphs can be summarized as follows: translation models, bilinear models, and neural network models.

Knowledge representation is the projection of the real world into the virtual world, just like computer compilation, transforming human knowledge into a form that computers can understand and easily calculate. This form can be used to simulate human reasoning about the world and then handle difficult problems in the field of artificial intelligence. Knowledge representation learning: The process of low-level embedded knowledge representation of entities and relationships in a knowledge graph.

Common Translation Distance Model Knowledge Representation Learning Methods:

2.2 TransE

(Fig. 1)

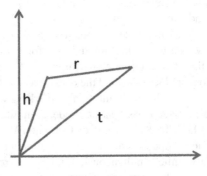

Fig. 1. TransE.

TransE proposed a translation based knowledge graph embedding model that can capture the phenomenon of translation variance invariance in multiple relationship graphs [6]. The facts in the knowledge graph are represented by triples, and the idea of TransE algorithm is very simple, which has the same translation invariance characteristics as another text computing model, Word2vec.

TransE's loss function:

L\left(y,y^\prime\right) = \max\{\left(0,margin-y + y^\prime\right)\}

The construction process is to minimize the value of the loss function. Due to having only one entity space, the disadvantage of the model is that when dealing with multi entity problems, the calculation of the distance function may result in incorrect relationship links due to the fact that the entities are the same. For example, there are two types of knowledge, (Ogawa, get, girlfriend) and (Ogawa, get, dermatosis). After training, in a one-to-many situation, the "girlfriend" entity vector will be very close to the "psoriasis" entity vector. But in reality, they do not have such similarity.

The TransE model defines vectors in semantic space as entities and relationships, but this method can cause problems when conducting relationship inference. The calculation distances of the same entity in space are very close, but the relationships can be very different because there are more than one type of entity relationship, and distance based calculations cannot obtain such a distinction. For example, the relationship between (anti-inflammatory drugs, including, cephalosporins) is inclusive, while the relationship between (Ogawa, Allergy, cephalosporins) is allergic. These two relationships are very different (Fig. 2).

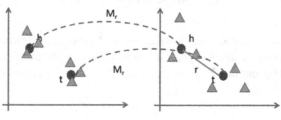

Fig. 2. TransR.

Due to the extremely close distance relationship calculated by the same entity in the entity space, TransR technology allows the same entity to be projected into two different spaces, that is, the entity space and multiple relationship spaces (relationship specific entity spaces) to model entities and relationships, and then perform transformation operations to solve the proposed problem. In this way, all entity relationship transformations become transformations in the corresponding space. Therefore, this method is named TransR [7]. It can be understood that the entity relationship in the original space is close because the entities are the same, and the relationships between adjacent entities are also close. However, if we switch to different spaces, the relationships between adjacent entities are different, and differences can be reflected.

ResNet

ResNet was the champion of the 2015 ImageNet competition, reducing the error rate of image classification recognition to 3.6%, which even exceeded the accuracy of normal human eye recognition.

The model also follows the development direction of the VGG model by adding more network layers. Theoretically, the more layers the model has, the more parameters the original layer can learn. The new layer can learn more parameters, which increases the solution space. However, in reality, the network error will become larger. ResNet proposed a solution here, based on its basic idea.

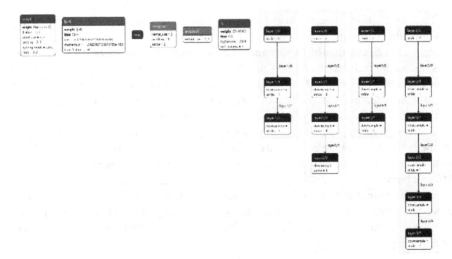

Fig. 3. ResNet network structure.

Not learning complete data, only learning residual terms means learning the Y sample residual space, not the X sample space. If you want to learn the same network, you can make X = Y, and by learning Y-X, you can deepen the training layers of the model and reduce model error [8].

3   Knowledge Graph Construction

Construction of a knowledge map of skin diseases At present, there are no researchers building a specialized Chinese knowledge map of skin diseases. Therefore, we use crawler technology to collect data on publicly available skin disease descriptions, diagnosis, and treatment information on internet medical websites. This article first evaluates internet medical websites based on the World Health Organization's disease classification standard documents, and selects data sources with rich disease symptom descriptions and hierarchical classification information, The selected data sources are the Medical Search and Medicine Website (www.XYWY.com) and the 99 Health Website (www. 99.com.cn).

The following is the collected text data of skin diseases. Currently, there are about 1000 known types of skin diseases in the world, with over 200 common diseases. The two atlas datasets used in this article are 271 common diseases and 789 universal diseases. This article will store the collected text data in JSON format, classify and label it according to name, symptoms, drugs, food, etc. Then, use Re to clean the data and delete the segmented text parts, such as numbers and symbols. Use Jieba to segment and label the text data, and use Word2vec for feature processing. The following figure shows the collected text information .

Then we construct the text information into a knowledge graph of dermatology, where we use Eno4j for storage and representation to facilitate observation of changes in entity relationships during subsequent operations. Neo4j is a high-performance NoSQL

Fig. 4. Crawled Text Information.

graphical database, which stores structured data on the network (called graph from a mathematical point of view) rather than in tables. Neo4j can also be seen as a high-performance graph engine that has all the characteristics of a mature database. The construction process is to define the Eno4j connection; Define entity nodes, such as disease symptom overview drugs, etc.; Define entity relationships such as disease examination items, disease symptoms, disease complications, disease departments, and then create other nodes with the disease as the center node, and finally create relationships. The following figure shows the constructed knowledge graph.

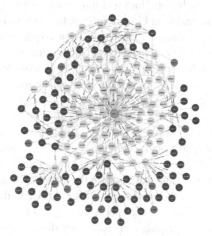

Fig. 5. Eno4j Knowledge Map.

In the practical application process of knowledge graph, we found that there are many hidden entities and entity relationships that have not been created. In this section, after comparing the characteristics of translation models, bilinear models, and neural network models, we selected a translation model, also known as the translation vector model. Because the goal of this study is to enable image classification algorithms to use textual information from patients, whose expressions are often fuzzy and incomplete, and the output of image classification generally corresponds to disease entities in the knowledge graph (the use of links between image classification and symptom information will be mentioned later), this article hopes to extract information from patients that can limit the scope of image classification, Referring to the selection of departments during the hospital consultation process and the consultation process, traditional Chinese medicine students first determine the approximate range and then determine the type of disease based on specific medical examination data. The process of constructing a domain limited knowledge graph is equivalent to the process of consultation, while image classification is a simulation of the analysis of physical and chemical test results [10] (Fig. 6).

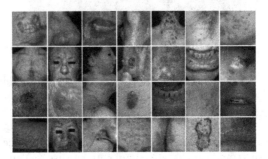

Fig. 6. Skin diseases of different parts and forms.

The research in this article combines text information such as entity shape features, part features, symptom features, and image information as a multimodal data source to assist in disease image classification. Even based on the construction of entity recognition within the field, it is supported by medical theory. According to the analysis of the content of the commonly used teaching materials of Peking University Medical Department and Medical College, the classification of skin diseases in the medical diagnosis textbooks of skin diseases starts from the naming of morphology, such as psoriasis, and the gradual transition from erythema multiforme to the classification of etiology and pathogenesis, such as infectious diseases, viral fungal dermatitis, autoimmune diseases, eczema, drug rash, genetic skin diseases and other ichthyosis keratosis [9]. The diagnosis of the disease as shown in Figs. 3, 4 and Figs. 3, 5 can be based on the morphology of the skin lesion, site of infection, pathogen, dietary habits, drug reactions, etc., and there is a diagnostic sequence that gradually narrows the scope from the surface to the inside [10].

Combining computer knowledge graph technology to model medical information, the translation vector model TransE constructed by disease entities has modulus and phase information. Since the output of image classification generally corresponds to disease entities of knowledge graph types, this article hopes to find disease entities with similar positions at the same level, and modulus and phase information can help construct knowledge graphs with hierarchical relationships. Therefore, this article adopts Hierarchical Perceived Knowledge Graph Embedding (HAKE) as the basic model for model completion. Two parameters, modulus and phase information, are constructed to construct a polar coordinate system, mapping entities to the polar coordinate system.

The concentric circles in the polar coordinate system can naturally reflect the hierarchical characteristics. The angular coordinates in the coordinate system can distinguish different entities at the same level (Fig. 7).

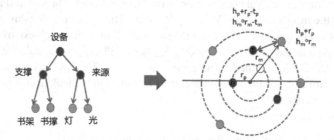

Fig. 7. KEG-HAKE Schematic Diagram.

The above figure is a schematic diagram of KEG-HAKE. The modulus parameter m in the figure represents the modeling of entities with the same hierarchical structure, while the phase information p represents the modeling of entities with different hierarchical structures. m and p can be used to represent all entities in the entity space [11].

When performing entity completion, calculate the distance between two entities, represented by the following formula.

The research purpose of this article in terms of knowledge graph is to provide domain limited knowledge graphs for image classification, and to appropriately extend knowledge in the graph when there are keywords related to entity relationships input by patient knowledge Q&A. As most of the entities obtained from Q&A activities are located at the edge of the graph, in order to extend to more entities that can be utilized by image classification, the KEG-HAKE knowledge embedding method needs to be used for entity embedding, Construct a hierarchical perceptual knowledge graph, so that we can control the scope of knowledge extension according to the hierarchy. If we can further control the direction of knowledge extension, we can solve the problem of knowledge boundaries that are not interconnected. For example, in knowledge Q&A tasks such as (Ogawa, infection, tinea manus), (Ogawa, infection, tinea cruris), (dermatosis, including, tinea manus), and (dermatosis, including, tinea cruris), we can expand knowledge to the center and draw the conclusion that Ogawa has dermatosis. In addition, for image classification tasks optimization, Since the classifier rating in the following text needs to be based on whether it is within the domain as a parameter, centripetal expansion can reduce errors. However, KEG-HAKE cannot divide entities with the same attribute into the same level. Therefore, we optimize based on the KEG-HAKE model to add hierarchical features to the graph [12]. Through the analysis of the HAKE model paper, it was found that the key to the hierarchical perception characteristics of the model lies in the fact that it is based on the TransE model as the basic model, and then adds the concepts of modulus and phase information. Analyzing the specific code of the model, it was found that the HAKE model and the reference model, Mode, take KEGmodel as input, and there is not much difference in input attributes. Both models contain knowledge graph entities (Num

Entity, Num Correlation, Hidden Dim, Gamma), Relationship hidden layer, etc. Therefore, in the HAKE model, two additional parameters are introduced for comparison with modulus. In addition, in terms of filter introduction rating and type selection after rating, weighting and phase related calculations are performed. The Func function is the key code location for hierarchical construction of the HAKE model. Through test analysis, it is found that the model calculates Mod by_ Relation, Bias_ The relationship calculation score control model generates entities at the same level. In order to achieve more entities of the same type at the same level, modify R_ Score, Phase_ Score calculation, based on HEAD_ BATCH header node, relationship with AIL_ The BATCH tail node, with a relationship similarity count as a parameter, is added to the calculation, and then filter parameters are generated.

The details are as follows:

a) Add Batch to the input parameters of the function body_ Sigle,
b) Calculate Dr. Dm distance parameter
c) Calculate Dr. Dp distance parameter
d) Import HEAD_ BATCH: (?, r, t), TAIL_ BATCH: (h, r, ?)
e) Batch_ Sigle calculates the similarity between head and tail entities and r
f) Calculate R_ Score, Phase_ Score
g) Generate Filter Filter Parameters
h) Entity attribute annotation, entity type comparison with Filter return value, weighted calculation
i) Data entity generation call

After the above steps, the probability of data generation for similar entities can be enhanced.

4   Image Classification and Fusion Mode Based on Knowledge Atlas

4.1   Comparison of Optimization Plans

Model optimization is often involved in image classification tasks, and there are several main aspects for optimizing convolutional neural networks, including accuracy optimization, memory optimization, and training time optimization. The main purpose of this paper is to improve the accuracy of the model. Therefore, the image fusion mode will be compared with other convolutional neural network optimization schemes to analyze the advantages of the fusion mode.

Common model optimization methods include optimizing data and optimizing the structure of convolutional neural networks. The optimization of data includes data cleaning and data enhancement, which essentially improve the quality of the dataset. Data cleaning can reduce erroneous and invalid data. Incorrect data can help data learn incorrect parameters and reduce classification accuracy. Increasing data can fully train model parameters, Especially in large models, where there are many layers of the network and the amount of data is too small, it can lead to underfitting during model training. Therefore, data augmentation techniques can be used to rotate, clip, invert, scale, shift, and reduce Gaussian noise on data, such as image data. Even generate adversarial network GANs. For the problem of data as a whole, for example, if the data volume is small, you can use the oversampling method to repeatedly sample the insufficient categories, or SMOT can generate less category data based on similarity to increase the weight of less sample data. For a large amount of data, we can use undersampling to prevent model overfitting, cluster first, then randomly sample the large class, or randomly sample first, and then use Boosting algorithm to integrate weak classifiers to generate strong classifiers. However, there is a problem with optimizing the data aspect, which is through data optimization. There are always limitations to the model itself, and the degree of data optimization improvement is not infinite.

The network optimization of convolutional neural networks is relatively rich, and the development history of convolutional neural networks mainly revolves around the optimization of network structure. The optimization of network structure includes convolutional kernel optimization. Generally, the larger the convolutional kernel, the higher the accuracy, but it will consume memory. Moreover, due to the complex connection between features of convolutional kernels, the generalization performance of the model will deteriorate, with ResNet and VGGNet being representatives. Optimizing network size and increasing network width will enable each layer of the network to learn more features, and increasing depth will also improve accuracy, but the training process will become slower. Activation function optimization. ReLU, Sigmaid, ELU, PReLU, Sigmaid, or LeakyReLU activation function can be used to improve the effect. Optimizer optimization, including SGD, Adam, etc., requires repeated attempts.

Through analyzing data optimization and network structure optimization, we have found that any optimization to the extreme cannot exceed the limitations of the model itself. For example, processors, memory, and even faster processors have operational limitations, requiring memory coordination when the calculation data is too large. The development of models is parallel to the development of knowledge graphs. Returning to the knowledge graph and comparing image classification algorithms, knowledge graphs are like external storage that stores a large amount of resource information. Image classification algorithms cannot obtain information such as pain, lifestyle habits, past illnesses, etc. They need to be mutually verified in the knowledge graph. The results of image classification are scoped on a knowledge graph, which disassociates certain results of image classification and ultimately reduces the classification range to 1, resulting in correct results. Therefore, there is no doubt that the combination of the two will bring better results. As a whole, the key to the fusion mode is to put the part of the image classification results with low accuracy into the knowledge map for clustering analysis, and then calculate the overall probability, that is, the samples that were judged correctly by the convolutional neural network continue to remain, and the uncertain samples are handed over to the knowledge map for judgment, so as to improve the classification accuracy.

Usually, image classification tasks, especially multi classification tasks, use probability distributions to represent the calculation results of each category, while binary classification outputs as 01. Multi classification adds a SoftMax() function at the end of the network to obtain probability values. The commonly used indicators for binary evaluation include accuracy, recall, and F1. Multi classification evaluation indicators include Micro F1 and Macro F1. In addition to binary classification and multi classification, there is also multi label classification, where each sample can be predicted as one or more categories.

From previous research, it can be seen that the solution to any problem is a gradual decomposition of the problem, breaking it into smaller parts. The solution to the multi classification problem is also the same. Multi classification can be converted into an OvO pairwise combination and converted into N (N-1)/2 binary classification tasks, and the results can be voted out; Train N classifiers with OvRn combinations, with the highest confidence in the selection; Multiple labels and multiple classifications can also be decomposed into N binary classification problems. However, if such decomposition is done directly, when the total category is greater than the number of labels to be selected, there will be category imbalance, as there are too many categories, leading to imbalance between positive and negative samples. So a second idea emerged, whether it is possible to transform the multi label problem into a multi classification problem and then into a binary classification problem. Based on the previous understanding of the problem of knowledge map construction, we are very familiar with the concept of mapping. The idea of fusion mode in this chapter is to reduce the dimension of multi label problem to multi classification problem, and then map the problem to the knowledge map for solution, and gradually solve it in the knowledge map.

Returning to the multi classification problem to see if there are specific solutions, the solution of the multi classification problem

In image classification, there are two types of tasks: multi classification tasks and binary classification tasks. However, overall, multi classification tasks are decomposed into binary classification tasks for processing. The decomposition from multi classification tasks to binary classification tasks involves dividing them into scatter points for voting, direct N classification with the highest confidence, and constructing a binary classification classifier with a graph to calculate distance. Another method is based on hierarchical classification, which calculates confidence through tree structure.

Overall, this article believes that although image classification, especially disease classification, usually adopts multi classification methods, in fact, disease image classification should be considered as multi label classification from the perspective of images, because some diseases and diseases cover the symptoms of another disease, which are similar or subclasses themselves. Therefore, multi classification, a single-layer classification result, is not very suitable for disease classification diagnosis, Therefore, introducing hierarchical attributes into the classification results can better determine the level of the disease and thus determine its name.

4.2 Gambling Tree

Based on the concept of hierarchical two classifiers mentioned and the domain limited knowledge map built based on the improved hierarchical awareness knowledge map in this paper, we can naturally think about whether we can use the knowledge map with hierarchical characteristics to optimize classification and generate computing strategies based on the classification results of hierarchical two classifiers. Because nodes are tree structure and hierarchical structure, computing strategies are generated by computing trees [13–15].

Therefore, this article proposes the concept of game tree, including credit parameter Cre (Credict), power parameter Mig (Migt), and inference parameter Ill (Illation). Cre represents the degree of trustworthiness of the preliminary results of image classification within domain limitations. The Silhouette Coefficent Si and the probability Pi $\{1,2,3\ldots i\}$ of entities in multiple classification domains are used to calculate the aggregation degree formula based on the entities in the domain.

The formula for Cre is expressed as:

$$Cre(i) = \frac{O(i) - I(i)}{max(I(i), O(i))}$$

$$Cre(i) = \begin{cases} 1 - \dfrac{I(i)}{O(i)} & I(i) < O(i) \\ 0 & I(i) = O(i) \\ \dfrac{O(i)}{I(i)} - 1 & I(i) > O(i) \end{cases}$$

In addition, the formulas for I (i) and O (i) are expressed as:

$$I(i) = \frac{1}{n-1} \sum_{\substack{j \neq i}}^{n} distance(i,j) / PiPj$$

$$O(m) = \frac{1}{n-1} \sum_{\substack{j \neq i}}^{n} distance(i,j) / PiPj$$

$$O(i) = Min\{O_1(i)O_2(i)O_3(i)\ldots O_m(i)\}$$

I represents other sample points within the same class as sample j, and Distance represents the distance between i and j. So the more novel I (i) is, the closer it becomes.

The calculation method of O (i) is similar to that of I (i). Just need to traverse other class clusters to obtain multiple values and select the smallest one from them.

The strength parameter Mig represents the degree of possible difference between the classification result with the highest probability among multiple classification results and other classification results. When the strength parameter is greater than the threshold, domain restrictions can be ignored. The setting concept of referring to the real world is that regardless of the difference in symptoms described by patients, the results of physical and chemical tests still prevail.

$$Mig(i) = \frac{1}{n-1} \sum_{\substack{j \neq i}}^{n} ((Pi - Pj))$$

The inference parameter Ill correctly represents the score obtained by combining knowledge inference with multiple classification probabilities when the strong parameters outside the domain fail and the strong parameters within the domain also fail. In cases where the probability of multi classification is generally low for inference parameters, more reliable data information comes from the knowledge graph, which selects the optimal classification result based on the number of knowledge inference question answering entities and edge links.

$$Ill(i) = Max\{(M(i)+N(i)), M(i+1)+N(i+1)),\ldots M(n)+N(n),\}$$

Calculate Path

Game trees can generate image classification models that utilize information from knowledge graphs. The input stack of the game tree is the classifier probability of all classification results, as well as the entity nodes and relationships represented in the domain restricted knowledge graph. Firstly, the strength parameters of all classification results are calculated from the root node, and if they are greater than the threshold, the results are output. Otherwise, match the domain restricted knowledge graph. If the maximum probability is not within the domain, delete the maximum classification result in the stack, and then calculate the domain strong parameter. If it is greater than the threshold, output the result. Otherwise, calculate the maximum possible result in the domain through knowledge reasoning. Calculate the game value when the input is a multi graph input:

Gambling = Mig\ast Ill + Cre\funcapply(i)-\beta

Output the results with large values.

KG based CNN image classification fusion model based on domain limited knowledge map

There are several task scenarios for the fusion of knowledge graph and image classification:

① Only image classification data is input. When only image classification data is input in the fusion model, it is impossible to generate a domain limited knowledge map, but there is still a hierarchical perception knowledge map that can be used to calculate the map. The principle of the fusion mode is to project the uncertain classification of image recognition into the map for calculation. When the map range is large and not accurate enough, it can control to reduce the threshold value of the powerful parameter Mig, Enable probability selection conditions to take effect through threshold control.

② Image input and low confidence/high confidence Q&A knowledge input, when there is image input and low confidence Q&A knowledge input, it means that there will be domain restrictions on knowledge graph generation with low confidence. However, due to probability threshold control, the overall classification accuracy will not change much, as the graph only affects data with uncertain image classification algorithms. When high confidence Q&A knowledge is input, the aggregation of entities projected into the knowledge graph will be very high, and the overall game value will change to make it the output classification result. In theory, when the knowledge graph is detailed enough and the threshold is lowered, the classification result will approach complete accuracy.

③ Multi graph input and question answering knowledge input. When there are multiple graph data inputs, the real multi graph data may belong to different categories or the same category. If all the multiple graphs are input into the model, multiple results will be calculated in the game tree, and the strength parameters will be calculated on the results. If it is greater than the threshold, one result will be output, and if it is less than the threshold, multiple results will be output.

In disease image classification tasks, the usual decision tree input is the corresponding disease entity, but symptom entity parts such as hands, feet, red, purple, rules, blur, and other information can also be inputted [16–18]. Target detection can be used for recognition, and sometimes there may be no input from the question answering system.

Therefore, this paper expands the game tree to an image classification fusion mode KG based CNN that is more suitable for various situations to deal with various use scenarios.

Image input can use object detection algorithms for entity extraction, followed by knowledge graph comparison, game tree calculation, and finally output the best classification result [19]. The specific fusion mode has the following levels: the first is the input layer, which is image data and knowledge question and answer data (knowledge question and answer data can be empty). The question and answer data is entities and entity attributes filled with a value of 0/1. Connected with the input layer is the convolutional neural network model layer. The model layer pre trains the classification data to output the classification probability value softmaxt, and then the knowledge map layer, Project the entities onto the knowledge map (when there is no question and answer data input, cluster the entities and calculate the entity distance) (when there is question and answer data input, knowledge extraction is conducted according to the input entities to form a domain limited knowledge map, and the entities and probability obtained by classification are projected onto this map), carry out the calculation path of the game tree, when multiple maps are input, carry out the calculation of multiple game trees, and finally output the classification results.

5 Experiment and Analysis

5.1 Evaluating Indicator

The evaluation index used in this paper is Accuracy, true positive (TP): melanoma is diagnosed, but actually there is also melanoma. False positive (FP): diagnosed as melanoma, but not actually. True negative (TN): there is no melanoma diagnosed, and there is no melanoma in fact. False negative (FN): there is no melanoma, but there is. Due to the unreliable accuracy evaluation when data is abnormally imbalanced, several other indicators are introduced for comprehensive evaluation. Precision focuses on evaluating how much of the data predicted to be positive is actually positive? Recall focuses on evaluating how much of all Positive data has been successfully predicted as Positive

Calculation formula:

Accuracy = TP + FN/TP + FP + TN + FN

Precision = TP/TP + FP

Recall = FN / TN + FN

F1 score = 2 Precision* Recall / Precision + Recall

The confusion matrix is usually used as the evaluation standard of model performance in multi classification, and the confusion matrix can describe the gap between the predicted value and the real value. Specifically, it is to calculate the prediction of each category in a certain category. It is represented by a matrix representation. The horizontal and vertical coordinates are multi category categories. Each horizontal row represents the prediction value of each category in the corresponding vertical coordinate category. Observing the performance of the model in various categories can calculate the accuracy and recall of the model corresponding to each category. Through the confusion matrix, we can observe which categories are not easy to distinguish directly, such as how many of category A are classified into category B, which can be targeted to design features, making categories more differentiated. Simply put, it's about seeing how many misjudgments there are.

HAM10000 has 10000 image data, with 6000 as model training data and 1500 as test data. From the remaining 2500, 1400 samples of seven balanced classifications (with the same number of samples for each classification) were extracted as validation data. As shown in Fig. 5.2, a confidence level of about 95% for sample size calculation is more appropriate (Fig. 8).

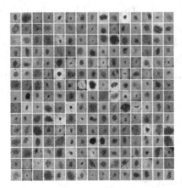

Fig. 8. Skin dataset HAM10000.

5.2   Performance Comparison Experiment of Fusion Pattern Classification Model

The experimental control model is ResNet, and the accuracy rate of the model is 68%. According to the reasoning in the previous summary, overfitting phenomenon should have occurred. To ensure the balance of samples, a lot of training set data has been sampled, generally 7000 training data. In addition, the training model in this paper does not use the pre training model for transfer learning, which may also lead to the reduction of classification accuracy, but the fusion model can still improve the accuracy of the low performance model. Compared to other situations, as shown in Fig. 5.5. It can be seen that the classification calculation strategy of fusion mode is applied without input, NAN_ Compared with ResNet, the accuracy rate of INPUT has increased to 104%. When the text data with confidence is input, the accuracy rate of INPUT is slightly improved compared with the method of directly applying knowledge map clustering without input. However, when the confidence is increased, the accuracy rate of single map input is improved to 108%. In addition, when conducting multi graph input data experiments, the accuracy significantly increased. Specifically, the multi graph experiment conditions were to input a total of 140 sets of test sample graphs, 420 images, and obtain a single graph conclusion through game tree analysis. The results were compared with other graph classification results for election voting. The minority followed the majority and then compared based on the Gambling value (Fig. 9).

Based on the decrease in accuracy of the experimental model mentioned earlier, this section obtained the model ResNet++ by retraining the model parameters. As shown in

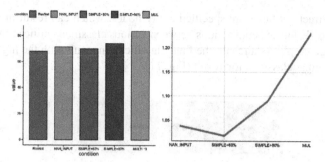

Fig. 9. Comparison of High and Low Confidence Multiple Input Performance

the figure, it can be seen from the data that the high-performance classification model has a higher accuracy improvement after applying the knowledge graph. In the SIMPLE and 80% confidence knowledge Q&A text input scenario, compared to the ResNet model, it has improved to 113%, with a classification accuracy of 77.21%. The confusion matrix of ResNet++ model is shown on the right side of the figure above. It can be seen that the accuracy of the model in BCC, NV and VASC is high, while other items are still scattered, but there is a general trend of bias towards a certain category. At the same time, it can be seen that the high probability part still maintains the same distribution as before using the fusion mode. Analyzing the reasons, the probability distribution of failure data in high-performance classification model testing may be difficult to disperse, and correction may be possible after game tree calculation. The low performance classification model is easy to keep the wrong classification unchanged when calculating the game tree due to the comparative calculation of overfitting probability distribution (Fig. 10).

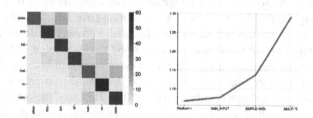

Fig. 10. High performance model ResNet + + confusion matrix and ratio curve with ResNet

5.3 Ablation Experiment

As shown in the figure, the accuracy comparison between ResNet and improved Res'net++ is shown. By analyzing the accuracy changes of ResNet and optimized ResNet++ without domain restricted knowledge graph conditions, and comparing the knowledge graph based on ordinary data extraction methods, it can be seen that the accuracy of domain restricted knowledge graph in the figure has been improved. Analyze the reasons, The main method for extracting non domain restricted knowledge graphs is to iteratively extract entities from specified entity nodes, which can result in excessively dispersed knowledge and connections between various classified entities projected onto the knowledge graph. As a result, the final classification result with the highest weight is still the original classification result (Fig. 11).

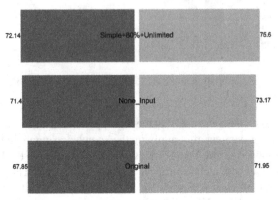

Fig. 11. ResNet and ResNet + + Domain Restricted Knowledge Graph Ablation Experiment SAMPLE ANALYSIS

As shown in the figure, the horizontal axis represents the classification of seven skin diseases, and the vertical axis represents the sample label, which is the case of single image input. The above figure shows a heat map, of which thirty samples were extracted from the HAM10000 dataset, and all the intercepted samples belong to Akiec. By observing the color depth, it can be determined that the probability values obtained by multiple classifiers Softmax in the image are still distributed among other categories. It is obvious that sample 19 is in a state of classification error, which is relatively evenly distributed among four categories. Generally, data with a probability distribution similar to this can be repositioned to the correct category by the knowledge graph in multiple sample data, but samples like sample 23 cannot be repositioned because the threshold of the strength parameter Mig is generally set to 0.4, and the difference between the maximum probability and other probabilities is 40%, This way, the calculation results will be returned at the first level of the game tree. However, setting the threshold too high may lead to classification errors in sample 13, as the distance between mel and Nv on the graph is very close, and the corresponding trusted values in the graph are also relatively large. Comparing the Gambling parameter will exclude the Akiec class from the computational space.

In general, the fusion mode can relocate some wrong samples to the correct position, and will only classify the original correctly classified samples into the wrong category with a very small probability. For example, the probability gap between the sample needs and other samples is less than the threshold, and then the probability sum of other classifications is greater than it, and the gap is further increased after the calculation of aggregation, execution, and reasoning values, This is a small probability because the calculation of these values is biased towards the correct classification (Fig. 12).

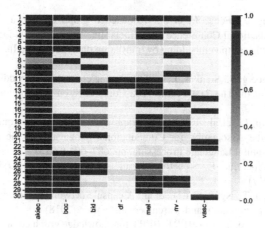

Fig. 12. Sample Thermogram

6 Conclusion and Future Work

In future research work, further exploration can be conducted on the construction of knowledge maps and diagnostic reasoning for skin diseases. Firstly, the application of knowledge graphs can help doctors better understand the causes, symptoms, treatment methods, and other aspects of skin diseases. We can consider introducing more multimodal data sources, such as videos, text, etc., to expand the breadth and depth of the knowledge graph and explore new medical knowledge from it. For example, by structuring, linking and representing the existing literature, cases, drugs, pathological images and other data, a more complete and systematic knowledge system of skin diseases can be built. You can try to deeply explore the correlation and regularity between medical data based on more complex and complete data, combined with medical images and laboratory test results. This knowledge map can be applied to natural language processing, image analysis, intelligent question and answer and other aspects to help doctors diagnose and treat more quickly and accurately.

References

1. Ridell, P., Spett, H.: Training Set Size for Skin Cancer Classification Using Google's Inception v3 (2017)
2. Alabduljabbar, R., Alshamlan, H.: Intelligent multiclass skin cancer detection using convolution neural networks. (010):000 (2021)
3. Meng, T., Lin, L., Shyu, M.L., Chen, S.C.: Histology image classification using supervised classification and multimodal fusion. In: 2010 IEEE International Symposium on Multimedia, Taichung, Taiwan, pp. 145–152 (2010).https://doi.org/10.1109/ISM.2010.29
4. Znaidia, A., Shabou, A., Popescu, A., et al.: Multimodal feature generation framework for semantic image classification. In: ACM International Conference on Multimedia Retrieval, pp. 1–8. ACM (2012)
5. Ji, S., Pan, S., Cambria, E., et al.: A survey on knowledge graphs: representation, acquisition, and applications. IEEE Trans. Neural Netw. Learn. Syst. (99) (2021)

6. Zhen, W., Zhang, J., Feng, J., et al.: Knowledge graph embedding by translating on hyperplanes. In: National Conference on Artificial Intelligence. AAAI Press (2014)

7. Feng, J.: Knowledge graph embedding by translating on hyperplanes. In: AAAI, vol. 28, no. 1 (2014)

8. Moon, C., Harenberg, S., Slankas, J., et al.: Learning contextual embeddings for knowledge graph completion. In: The 21st Pacific Asia Conference on Information Systems, vol. 10 (2017)

9. Ji, G., He, S., Xu, L., et al.: Knowledge graph embedding via dynamic mapping matrix. In: Meeting of the Association for Computational Linguistics & the International Joint Conference on Natural Language Processing, pp. 687–696 (2015)

10. Dettmers, T., Minervini, P., Stenetorp, P., et al.: Convolutional 2D Knowledge Graph Embeddings (2017)

11. Nguyen, D.Q., Vu, T., Nguyen, T.D., et al.: A capsule network-based embedding model for knowledge graph completion and search personalization (2018)

12. Yao, L., Mao, C., Luo, Y.: KG-BERT: BERT for knowledge graph completion (2019)

13. Nordhausen, K.: An introduction to statistical learning—with applications in R by Gareth James, Daniela Witten, Trevor Hastie & Robert Tibshirani. Int. Stat. Rev. **82**(1), 156–157 (2014)

14. Wang, H., Zhang, F., Xie, X., et al.: DKN: deep knowledgeaware network for news recommendation. In: Proceedings of the 2018 World Wide Web Conference on World Wide Web, pp. 1835–1844 (2018)

15. Wang, Q., Mao, Z., Wang, B., et al.: Knowledge graph embedding: a survey of approaches and applications. IEEE Trans. Knowl. Data Eng. **29**(12), 2724–2743 (2017)

16. Liu, Y., Li, H., GarciaDuran, A., et al.: MMKG: multimodal knowledge graphs. In: European Se mantic Web Conference, pp. 459–474 (2019)

17. MoussellySergieh, H., Botschen, T., Gurevych, I., et al.: A multimodal translationbased approach for knowledge graph representation learning. In: Proceedings of the Seventh Joint Conference on Lexical and Computational Semantics, New Orleans, Louisiana, pp. 225–234 (2018)

18. Cun, Y.L., Boser, B., Denker, J.S., et al.: Handwritten digit recognition with a back-propagation network. Adv. Neural. Inf. Process. Syst. **2**(2), 396–404 (1990)

19. Krizhevsky, A., Sutskever, I., Hinton, G.: ImageNet classification with deep convolutional neural networks. Adv. Neural Inf. Process. Syst. **25**(2) (2012)

Incorporating Syntactic Knowledge and Position Information for Aspect-Based Sentiment Analysis

Hongsong Wang⬤, Jiazhan Li$^{(\boxtimes)}$⬤, and Haoxian Ye⬤

School of Software, South China Normal University, Foshan 528225, China
957794003@qq.com

Abstract. Aspect-based sentiment analysis (ABSA) is a subtask of fine-grained sentiment analysis that focuses on analysing the sentiment polarity of aspect terms in a given sentence. Previous studies have extracted sentiment interaction information between aspect and target sentiment words with a dependency syntax parse tree (DSPT). However, those models relied excessively on DSPT and thus did not perform well in identifying local context information. Moreover, modelling syntactic information equivalently with complex dependency information may introduce noise and degrade the model's performance. Therefore, we incorporate sentence constituent information into DSPT such that the model can learn the association information not only within a sentence but also between remote words. Furthermore, we also capture the sentiment interaction information between aspect terms based on their distance in the context to reduce internal noise and the effect of irrelevant words.

Keywords: Natural Language Processing · ABSA · Context Information · Syntactic Information

1 Introduction

ABSA stands for aspect-based sentiment analysis, which focuses on analysing the sentiment polarity of aspect terms within a given text. ABSA aims to analyse the sentiment polarity of an aspect term in a given text. As shown in Fig. 1, in the sentence "the battery life is also relatively excellent.", the target sentiment word "excellent" for the aspect term "battery life" expresses positive sentiment. ABSA is a method used for fine-grained sentiment classification to extract sentiment information related to aspect terms.

Earlier research approaches focused on manually designing or extracting sentiment information related to the target word. However, the proposed approach focused solely on the target information and neglected the contextual information, thus overlooking the importance of the attention mechanism in establishing

Supported by the National Natural Science Foundation of China (No. 62076103).

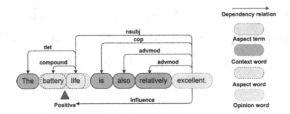

Fig. 1. Structure of dependency parse tree.

an implicit link between the target and context. Therefore, self-attention was introduced to implicitly connect the target and context.

Chen et al. [1] introduced a memory neural network model that incorporates multiple attention mechanisms for capturing the sentiment polarity of aspect-specific words in lengthy texts by utilizing memory storage units. However, the attention-based approach lacked syntax constraints and long-range word dependencies. To address this issue, several researchers [2,3] have incorporated dependency syntactic information into deep neural networks and represented sentence dependencies by constructing DSPT.

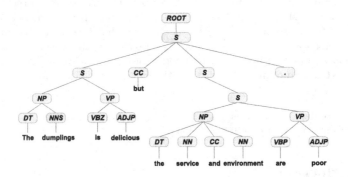

Fig. 2. Structure of the sentence phrase tree.

DSPT captures only word-to-word relationships, making it challenging to explain the complex context structure within a sentence [4,5]. Hence, as depicted in Fig. 2, the phrase tree investigates the correlation between aspects and contexts, enabling phrase-level information to reinforce short-range dependencies among words. Since previous studies have neglected the fusion of dependency and sentence phrase information, we extract short-range dependencies within sentences using phrase structure to utilize the dependency information to enhance model performance.

Meanwhile, model syntax information is often treated equally without considering syntax information asymmetry in syntax structure studies. In particular, the dense association information introduced noise and confused the relationship between aspect and target words when syntax information was automatically generated according to a syntax generator. Consequently, we introduce a pruning strategy aimed at highlighting the aspect words and leveraging the emotional distance between aspect and context words to minimize noise interference.

The contribution of our proposed SP-RGAT model is expounded upon as follows. First, it acquires syntactic information about the input text with a syntactic fusion module focusing on long- and short-distance dependencies between words. Additionally, we employ a dynamic distance metric between the aspect and context words, which serves as a control mechanism to regulate the flow of weights from the context words to the aspect words. This is accomplished through a valve mechanism that takes advantage of the dependency tree structure. As a result of these enhancements, our proposed model, SP-RGAT, demonstrates state-of-the-art performance on four benchmark datasets.

2 Models

2.1 Overview

In this section, the implementation details of the SK-ACP model are presented. As illustrated in Fig. 3, the architecture primarily comprises four components: the input layer, syntax fusion encoder, aspect-context module and output layer. For a given sentence $W = \{W_1, W_2, \cdots, W_n\}$ consisting of n words and m aspect terms $A = \{W^{a_1}, W^{a_2}, \cdots, W^{a_m}\}$. The primary objective of the SP-RGAT model is to predict sentiment polarity $y_i = \{positive, negative, neural\}$.

2.2 Input Layer

The primary purpose of the input layer is to map each word in a sentence into a high-dimensional real-valued vector space [6]. This mapping is achieved by assigning a vector $h_t \in \mathbb{R}^{d_{emb} \times 1}$ to each word, where d_{emb} represents the hidden dimension of the word vector.

In order to fine-tune the SP-RGAT model, the input word is reconstructed as $\{[CLS] + Sentence + [SEP] + Aspect + [SEP]\}$ Formally, we denote the input sequence as:

$$W^t = \{w_0^t, w_1^t, \cdots, w_n^t, w_{n+1}^t, w_{n+2}^t, \cdots, w_{n+1+m}^t, w_{n+2+m}^t\} \qquad (1)$$

where n and m stand for the lengths of the input sentence and aspect term, and w_0^t and w_{n+1}^t for "$[CLS]$" and "$[SEP]$". After the embedding layer, the feature representation of the input sequence is obtained:

$$\mathbb{E}_{BERT}^t = \{h_0^t, h_1^t, \cdots h_n^t, h_{n+1}^t, h_{n+2}^t, \cdots, h_{n+1+m}^t, h_{n+2+m}^t\} \qquad (2)$$

where $\mathbb{E}_{BERT}^t \in \mathbb{R}^{d_{emb} \times H}, H = n + 2 + m, h_1^t, \cdots h_n^t$ is the output context representation of the input word, and $h_{n+2}^t, \cdots, h_{n+1+m}^t$ is the feature representation of the aspect term.

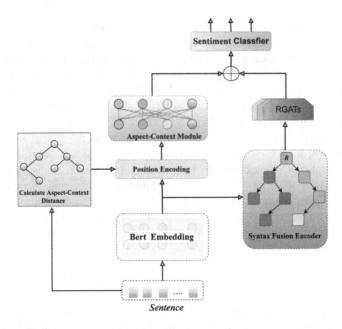

Fig. 3. Overview of the architecture of SP-RGAT.

2.3   Syntax Fusion Encoder

We propose the syntax fusion module to enhance the rich syntactic information of sentences, as the previous modules primarily focus on obtaining semantic information. Specifically, the module obtains the dependency tree (DT) and phrase tree (PT) of the sentence from the existing toolkit Stanford CoreNLP.

Phrase Dependency Graph. DT, obtained through the Stanford toolkit, is proficient in extracting long-distance dependencies between words in sentences. As shown in Fig. 1, the sentence "the battery life is also relatively excellent. ", according to Eq. 3 and previous work [7], a self-loop is added to each node.

$$DA_{i,j} = \begin{cases} 1 & w_i \ , \ w_j \ have \ direct \ \ link \ in \ DT \\ 0 & otherwise \end{cases} \tag{3}$$

In addition, the phrase tree is obtained from the Stanford toolkit. Figure 2 reveals that node "[S]" usually contains aspect words and target sentiment words under the node. Therefore, we use a top-to-bottom approach for the composition [8] and search subtrees that do not contain the node "[S]" starting from the root node. Finally, the adjacency matrix PA is constructed by Eq. 4.

$$PA_{i,j} = \begin{cases} 1 & if \ w_i \ , \ w_j \ in \ same \ \ node \ of \ last \ S \\ 0 & otherwise \end{cases} \tag{4}$$

As shown in Fig. 2, we obtain the constructed sequence of PA {The dumplings are delicious, but the service and environment are poor}. Finally, SP-RGAT omits the dependent edges in different clauses and fuses the syntactic information of the dependency and phrase graphs by Eq. 5.

$$PD_{i,j} = DA_{i,j} \oplus PA_{i,j} \tag{5}$$

Relational Graph Attention Network. As shown in Eq. 6, the graph structure is encoded using the masked self-attention mechanism in the L-layer GAT network for a given word w_i and neighboring node index $j \in N(i)$ from the PD matrix.

$$h_{att_i}^l = ||_{z=1}^{Z} \sigma \left(\sum_{j \in N(i)} \alpha_{ij}^{lz} W_V^{lz} h_j^{l-1} \right) \tag{6}$$

$$\alpha_{ij}^{lz} = \frac{exp\left(f\left(h_{att_i}^{l-1}, h_j^{l-1}\right)\right)}{\sum_{j' \in N(i)} exp\left(f\left(h_{att_i}^{l-1}, h_{j'}^{l-1}\right)\right)} \tag{7}$$

where $||$ stands for vector connectivity, the weight parameter matrix of the z-th attention head in the l-th layer is denoted as $W_V^{lz} \in \mathbb{R}^{\frac{d}{Z} \times d}$, Z is the number of attention heads, d is the feature dimension of the word vector, h_j^l is the final vector representation of the word in the lth layer, σ is the sigmoid function, α_{ij}^{lz} is the attention coefficient of node i and the domain node in the layer l attention head z.

In addition, GCN does not assign the learned weights to different domains since it cannot handle directed graphs. Meanwhile, most previous studies do not consider the directed connections of dependencies, ignoring the effect of different dependencies on neighboring nodes [9]. Therefore, RGAT introduces internode dependencies to the GAT model. It achieves this by mapping the dependencies to the vector space and subsequently updating the relationship head nodes using Eq. 8.

$$h_{rel_i}^l = ||_{r=1}^{R} \sum_{j \in N(i)} \beta_{ij}^{lr} W_V^{lr} h_j^{l-1} \tag{8}$$

$$g_{ij}^{lr} = \sigma \left(relu \left(r_{ij} w_{r1} + b_{r1} \right) w_{r2} + b_{r2} \right) \tag{9}$$

$$\beta_{ij}^{lr} = \frac{exp\left(g_{ij}^{lr}\right)}{\sum_{j=1}^{N(i)} exp\left(g_{ij}^{lr}\right)} \tag{10}$$

where $h_{rela_i}^l$ denotes the relationship head node at layer l , r_{ij} denotes the relationship vector between words w_i and w_j During the computation, the RGAT contains Z attention heads and R relation head nodes. Finally, the syntax contextual representation v^{cs} of each node is obtained by Eq. 11, which contains context and relational dependency information.

$$h_i^l = \left[h_{att_i}^l ; h_{rel_i}^l\right] \tag{11}$$

$$v^{cs} = relu\left(W_l h_i^l + b_{l+1}\right) \tag{12}$$

2.4   Aspect-Context

The fusion of syntax information enhances the sentiment association of the aspect and the target sentiment words with higher model classification accuracy. Different dependencies of sentences are modelled equally in noisy environments, where cumbersome syntax relations may confound the classification results. To reduce the effect of noise, the aspect-context module uses syntactic relative distance (SRD) and a bidirectional attention mechanism to obtain feature representations of aspect words and context.

Aspect-Context Distance. Previous methods hindered the propagation of sentiment polarity from the target word to the aspect by calculating the distance between aspect terms and the context solely based on the distance between words. In our approach, we overcome this limitation by adjusting the weights of context words using a DT (dependency tree) to control the information flow to the words surrounding the aspect term.

Generally, the sentiment of aspect terms tends to be negatively influenced by the distance between context terms. When an aspect term consists of multiple words, the SRD can be calculated as the average distance between each aspect term and the context word. In Fig. 1, for example, the SRD between the aspect term "battery life" and the target word "excellent" is determined as follows:

$$\begin{cases} SRD\,(life, excellent) = 1 \\ SRD\,(battery, excellent) = 2 \\ SRD\,(battery\ life\ ,\ excellent) = 1.5 \end{cases} \tag{13}$$

Position Encoding. To reduce the negative effects irrelevant to aspect terms, we designed a dynamic context weighting mechanism, as shown in Eq. 14, where SRD_i for the syntactic relative distance between the aspect term and the context word, N for the length of the sentence, and α for a predefined threshold value.

$$v_t^{a_i} = \begin{cases} 1 & SRD_i \leq \alpha \\ 1 - \frac{SRD_i}{N} & SRD_i > \alpha \end{cases} \tag{14}$$

Thereafter, the feature representation $V^{a_i} \in \mathbb{R}^{d_{emb} \times H}$ with contextual location information is obtained after position encoding.

$$W^{a_i} = [v_1^{a_i}, v_2^{a_i}, \cdots, v_N^{a_i}] \tag{15}$$

$$V^{a_i} = W^{a_i} \cdot \mathbb{E}_{BERT}^t = [w_1^{a_i}, w_2^{a_i}, \cdots, w_N^{a_i}] \tag{16}$$

Aspect-Context Weight. The aspect-context weight mechanism reduces the noise impact of the syntax parser through the sentiment interaction between context and aspect words. Drawing inspiration from [9], it introduces a bidirectional attention mechanism to regulate the sentiment interaction between aspect and context words. Initially, the aspect-context weighting mechanism calculates attention weights $\beta_{a_i}^t$ for each hidden word vector $h_{a_i}^t$ of the aspect words after applying a weight transformation:

$$f_{ca}\left(\bar{E}^t, h_{a_i}^t\right) = \bar{E}^t \cdot W_{ca} \cdot h_{a_i}^t \tag{17}$$

$$\beta_{a_i}^t = \frac{exp\left(f_{ca}\left(\bar{E}^t, h_{a_i}^t\right)\right)}{\sum_{t=1}^{K} exp\left(f_{ca}\left(\bar{E}^t, h_{a_i}^t\right)\right)} \tag{18}$$

where $\bar{E}^l$ denotes the average pooling of the BERT output vector $\mathbb{E}_{BERT}^t$, and W_{ca} denotes the attention matrix. After the calculation of the attention weights, a new feature representation of each aspect word is obtained:

$$\varepsilon^{a_i} = \sum_{t=1}^{K} \beta_{a_i}^t \cdot h_{a_i}^t \tag{19}$$

Additionally, to capture the contextual information of a specific aspect word, we combine the feature representation ε^{a_i} of the aspect word with the location-encoded feature representation V^{a_i}. Finally, a vector representation v^{ac} with context semantic and location information is obtained as follows:

$$f_{ac}\left(\varepsilon^{a_i}, h_{a_i}^t\right) = \varepsilon^{a_i} \cdot W_{ac} \cdot V^{a_i} \tag{20}$$

$$\rho_{a_i}^t = \frac{exp\left(f_{ac}\left(\varepsilon^{a_i}, h_{a_i}^t\right)\right)}{\sum_{t=1}^{n} exp\left(f_{ac}\left(\varepsilon^{a_i}, h_{a_i}^t\right)\right)} \tag{21}$$

$$v^{ac} = \sum_{t=1}^{n} \rho_{a_i}^t \cdot h_{a_i}^t \tag{22}$$

2.5 Output Layer

The output layer uses a fully connected classifier network that combines the output vectors from both the syntax-fusion and aspect-context modules. This fusion process generates a probability distribution for emotional polarity by applying the Softmax activation function.

$$v^{as} = v^{ac} + v^{cs} \tag{23}$$

$$Sentiment = Softmax\left(W_o \cdot v^{as} + b_o\right) \tag{24}$$

3   Experiments

3.1   Dataset

To assess the model's performance, we employed several datasets in this paper: the SemEval-2014 Laptops and Restaurant dataset [10], the Twitter dataset [11] and the MAMS dataset [12]. The MAMS dataset comprises sentences that include a minimum of two aspect words expressing varying sentiment polarities.

3.2   Implementation Details

We employ the Cross-Entropy loss function as the objective function, as depicted in Eq. 25, where c represents the number of sentiment polarity categories, $\mathbb{Y}_i$ represents the actual sentiment polarity categories, y_i represents the sentiment polarity categories predicted by the model, λ is the $L2$ regularisation parameter and Θ is the parameter set of the model.

$$Loss = \sum_{1}^{c} \mathbb{Y}_i log y_i + \lambda \sum_{\theta \in \Theta} \theta^2 \tag{25}$$

3.3   Compared Models

AEAT-LSTM [13]: proposes aspect word attention weights and combines aspect word vectors with input vectors. MemNet [14]: developed deep memory networks that can capture important parts of context words for emotion classification at the aspect level. MAN [15]: captures information about the interaction of aspect words with context. UP-CNN-BERT [16]: applies a masking mechanism to reduce noise interference. IPAN-BERT [17]: feature extraction of individual lexical words is enhanced by an attention mechanism.

GANN [18]: utilize gate truncation RNN to capture long-distance dependency information and simultaneously encode sequential information in the context, aspect terms, and sentiment clues. ASGCN-DG [19]: overcomes the problem of low performance of CNN models for encoding noncontiguous sequences. ASGCN-DT [19]: considers the parent node to be extensively influenced by its children. RGAT [20]: proposed a BERT-based graph attention network model that enhances the classification performance of ABSA by incorporating semantic label dependencies. R-GAT [9]: uses syntactic information encoding to aggregate targets by pruning operations on dependency trees. CDT [21]: propose a GCN model based on dependency trees, which utilizes Bi-LSTM to learn the feature representations of sentences. DLCF-DCA [6]: the concept of dynamic local context focus and dependency clustering is proposed to enhance the extraction of semantic features by masking or weighting the words with low semantic relevance in the context.

Table 1. Overall performance on four benchmark datasets (%)

Model	Laptops14		Restaurant		Twitter		MAMS	
	ACC	F1	ACC	F1	ACC	F1	ACC	F1
AEAT-LSTM	68.9	–	76.6	–	–	–	–	–
IAN	72.1	–	78.6	–	–	–	–	–
MemNet	72.21	-	80.95	–	–	–	–	–
MAN	78.13	73.20	84.38	71.31	76.56	72.19	–	–
UP-CNN-BERT	76.33	–	84.82	–	73.27	-	84.81	–
IPAN-BERT	79.30	76.77	86.50	77.70	77.80	76.80	–	–
GANN	72.21	–	80.09	–	72.40	–	–	–
ASGCN-DG	74.14	69.24	80.86	72.19	71.53	69.68	–	–
ASGCN-DT	75.55	71.05	80.77	72.02	72.15	70.40	-	–
CDT	77.19	72.99	82.30	74.02	74.66	73.66	-	–
R-GAT	78.21	74.88	83.30	76.08	76.15	74.88	–	–
RGAT	80.94	78.20	86.68	80.92	76.28	75.25	84.52	83.74
DLCF-DCA	81.03	78.09	86.40	80.36	–	–	–	–
Our	**81.13**	**78.23**	**87.24**	**81.22**	**77.89**	**75.34**	**85.27**	**84.89**

3.4   Main Result

Table 1 presents a comparison between SP-RGAT and the baseline models across four datasets. The analysis yields the following conclusions.

In general, the SP-RGAT model demonstrates significant improvements over the baseline models in terms of accuracy indicators and nearly all macro-F1 score metrics. This can be attributed to two main factors. The first reason is that SP-RGAT incorporates both dependency syntax trees and phrase trees. It is found that the dependency syntax tree can help the sentence identify the directed dependencies between words. At the same time, the dependency syntax tree can capture long-range dependencies between words. The second reason is that SP-RGAT fuses the constituent information of the sentences. The fusion of constituent information brings the aspect and target words closer, enabling the model to focus on local semantic interactions.

In addition, the baseline models treated the associated relational edges equally rather than differently according to word-to-word contribution. Thus, the model classification performance is disturbed by the noise of syntax information. We analyse the relative position information of sentences with a dependency syntax tree to reduce the weights with low semantic relevance and enhance the sentiment interaction between the aspect and target word with the help of a bidirectional attention mechanism.

3.5   Analysis

The ablation experiment is conducted to verify each component's performance in the proposed method. Notably, the underlying structure uses BERT as the shared context encoder that cannot be discarded. As shown in Table 2, w/o dep indicates a reduced dependency syntax tree, w/o con indicates a reduced phrase tree, w/o syn indicates the discarding of the entire syntactic fusion module, and w/o p indicates the discarding of the positional encoding module. First, without the syntax fusion module, the overall accuracy of SP-RGAT on the four datasets decreases by 1.61%, 2.55%, 2.37% and 0.82%. It demonstrates the syntax fusion module's effectiveness and confirms the rationality of incorporating syntactic information into the sentiment classification task. Second, there is no constituent information. The phrase tree captures short-distance dependencies and improves the interaction of local context information in sentences. Additionally, discarding dependency syntax information hampers the model's ability to capture word-to-word dependencies. The dependency syntax tree, on the other hand, captures long-range dependencies between words and enhances the interaction of sentiment between aspect and target words. Finally, without the position-encoding module, the overall accuracy of SP-RGAT on the four datasets decreases by 1.14%, 1.93%, 2.89% and 0.98%. It shows that equivalent modelling of dependent terms introduces noise and thus impairs the model's performance. The relative distance between aspect words and context, as measured by the dependency syntax tree, helps reduce the impact of irrelevant words and showcases the effectiveness of the aspect word-context interaction module.

Table 2. Ablation experiments. "w/o" means without (%)

Model	Laptops14		Restaurant		Twitter		MAMS	
	Acc	F1	Acc	F1	Acc	F1	Acc	F1
w/o syn	79.33	75.58	85.35	79.26	75.52	74.39	84.08	82.96
w/o con	80.35	76.02	85.90	79.71	76.13	74.72	84.22	83.81
w/o dep	80.79	76.57	86.81	80.87	76.63	74.87	84.12	83.73
w/o p	80.99	77.53	85.97	78.99	75.00	73.16	84.26	83.33
SP-RGAT	81.13	78.23	87.24	81.22	77.89	75.34	85.27	84.89

3.6   Effect of the Bi-directional Attention Mechanism

To investigate the effect of the bidirectional attention mechanism in the Aspect-Context module, we disregard the directionality of SP-RGAT, denoted as w/o Bidire. In Table 3, the performance of w/o Bidire SP-RGAT is significantly weaker than that of Bidire SP-RGAT with the directionality of attention, which illustrates the effect of the bidirectional attention mechanism. The analysis of

Table 3. Experimental effects of the bi-directional mechanism (%)

Models	Laptops14		Restaurant	
	Acc	F1	Acc	F1
w/o Bi-dire SP-RGAT	80.12	75.88	85.43	79.23
w Bi-dire SP-RGAT	81.13	78.23	87.24	81.22

the Restaurant dataset reveals a significant presence of multiaspect sentences, attributed to the effective modelling of the Aspect-Context module. By capturing the intricate interaction between aspect words and context, this approach proves beneficial in comprehending the nuanced sentiment impact across different aspects.

4 Conclusion

We present an ABSA model that incorporates syntactic and positional information, aiming to combine dependency and constituent information while reducing the impact of irrelevant words. Our approach first leverages dependency syntax and constituent information to capture word dependencies within a sentence. Next, we introduce SP-RGAT, which utilizes sentence position information to enhance the semantic relevance of target words. This approach addresses the issue of noise generated by previous syntactic modelling techniques. Our experimental results on four benchmark datasets validate the effectiveness and efficiency of SP-RGAT.

References

1. Chen, P., Sun, Z., Bing, L., Yang, W.: Recurrent attention network on memory for aspect sentiment analysis. In: Proceedings of the 2017 Conference on Empirical Methods in Natural Language Processing, pp. 452–461 (2017)
2. Zhang, K., et al.: Incorporating dynamic semantics into pre-trained language model for aspect-based sentiment analysis. arXiv preprint arXiv:2203.16369 (2022)
3. Zhang, Z., Zhou, Z., Wang, Y.: SSEGCN: syntactic and semantic enhanced graph convolutional network for aspect-based sentiment analysis. In: Proceedings of the 2022 Conference of the North American Chapter of the Association for Computational Linguistics: Human Language Technologies, pp. 4916–4925 (2022)
4. Zeng, B., Yang, H., Liu, S., Xu, M.: Learning for target-dependent sentiment based on local context-aware embedding. J. Supercomput. **78**(3), 4358–4376 (2022)
5. Feng, L., et al.: Improving span-based aspect sentiment triplet extraction with abundant syntax knowledge. Neural Process. Lett. 1–22 (2022)
6. Xu, M., Zeng, B., Yang, H., Chi, J., Chen, J., Liu, H.: Combining dynamic local context focus and dependency cluster attention for aspect-level sentiment classification. Neurocomputing **478**, 49–69 (2022)
7. Zhao, Z., Tang, M., Tang, W., Wang, C., Chen, X.: Graph convolutional network with multiple weight mechanisms for aspect-based sentiment analysis. Neurocomputing **500**, 124–134 (2022)

8. Huang, L., Sun, X., Li, S., Zhang, L., Wang, H.: Syntax-aware graph attention network for aspect-level sentiment classification. In: Proceedings of the 28th International Conference on Computational Linguistics, pp. 799–810 (2020)
9. Wang, K., Shen, W., Yang, Y., Quan, X., Wang, R.: Relational graph attention network for aspect-based sentiment analysis. arXiv preprint arXiv:2004.12362 (2020)
10. Pontiki, M., et al.: SemEval-2016 task 5: aspect based sentiment analysis. In: ProWorkshop on Semantic Evaluation (SemEval-2016), pp. 19–30. Association for Computational Linguistics (2016)
11. Dong, L., Wei, F., Tan, C., Tang, D., Zhou, M., Xu, K.: Adaptive recursive neural network for target-dependent twitter sentiment classification. In: Proceedings of the 52nd Annual Meeting of the Association for Computational Linguistics (volume 2: Short Papers), pp. 49–54 (2014)
12. Jiang, Q., Chen, L., Xu, R., Ao, X., Yang, M.: A challenge dataset and effective models for aspect-based sentiment analysis. In: Proceedings of the 2019 Conference on Empirical Methods in Natural Language Processing and the 9th International Joint Conference on Natural Language Processing (EMNLP-IJCNLP), pp. 6280–6285 (2019)
13. Wang, Y., Huang, M., Zhu, X., Zhao, L.: Attention-based LSTM for aspect-level sentiment classification. In: Proceedings of the 2016 Conference on Empirical Methods in Natural Language Processing, pp. 606–615 (2016)
14. Tang, D., Qin, B., Liu, T.: Aspect level sentiment classification with deep memory network. arXiv preprint arXiv:1605.08900 (2016)
15. Xu, Q., Zhu, L., Dai, T., Yan, C.: Aspect-based sentiment classification with multi-attention network. Neurocomputing 388, 135–143 (2020)
16. Wang, X., Li, F., Zhang, Z., Xu, G., Zhang, J., Sun, X.: A unified position-aware convolutional neural network for aspect based sentiment analysis. Neurocomputing 450, 91–103 (2021)
17. Shuang, K., Gu, M., Li, R., Loo, J., Su, S.: Interactive POS-aware network for aspect-level sentiment classification. Neurocomputing 420, 181–196 (2021)
18. Liu, N., Shen, B.: Aspect-based sentiment analysis with gated alternate neural network. Knowl.-Based Syst. 188, 105010 (2020)
19. Zhang, C., Li, Q., Song, D.: Aspect-based sentiment classification with aspect-specific graph convolutional networks. arXiv preprint arXiv:1909.03477 (2019)
20. Bai, X., Liu, P., Zhang, Y.: Investigating typed syntactic dependencies for targeted sentiment classification using graph attention neural network. IEEE/ACM Trans. Audio Speech Lang. Process. 29, 503–514 (2020)
21. Sun, K., Zhang, R., Mensah, S., Mao, Y., Liu, X.: Aspect-level sentiment analysis via convolution over dependency tree. In: Proceedings of the 2019 Conference on Empirical Methods in Natural Language Processing and the 9th International Joint Conference on Natural Language Processing (EMNLP-IJCNLP), pp. 5679–5688 (2019)

Integrating Background and General Knowledge for Dialogue Generation

Hongsong Wang[ID], Haoxian Ye[(✉)][ID], and Jiazhan Li[ID]

South China Normal University, Foshan 528225, China
850615324@qq.com

Abstract. The traditional sequence-to-sequence model generates responses that are smooth but empty in their content. Background-based dialogue is one solution that uses the context's unstructured knowledge to generate informative responses. The key point of background-based dialogue is knowledge extraction, but some conversations have poor performance in knowledge selection due to insufficient information. At the same time, to improve the satisfaction of the responses, this paper can enhance the amount of conversational knowledge while allowing the model to carry some emotional awareness by selecting external knowledge sources with emotional information. In this paper, we introduce the CEC model, which utilizes graph attention and a double-matching matrix for the selection of external and background knowledge. The generation process is conducted within each decoding step, considering the selected knowledge's content. We conduct experiments on the Holl-E dataset. According to the experimental results, our model CEC outperforms the previous model in terms of performance.

Keywords: Background Based Conversations · Dialogue Systems · Knowledge-Enhanced

1 Introduction

Conversational systems are currently a hot topic in NLP research. Studies [1] show that 80% of enterprises will be equipped with chatbots (conversational systems) by the end of 2021, and the market will grow to $9.4 billion by 2024.

A core definition of a text generation task is the capability to generate an expected output sequence using a provided input sequence, often known as a sequence-to-sequence task. Thanks to the development of deep learning [2], numerous deep learning networks have been suggested for application in dialogue systems, encompassing recurrent neural networks (RNNs), convolutional neural networks (CNNs), and transformers. These networks offer diverse approaches to handle the complexities of dialogue generation. Although there are already many models that already perform well, traditional sequence-to-sequence models do not understand discourse well and generate responses that tend to be general replies because the input text itself contains a smaller amount of knowledge in

M. Zhang et al. (Eds.): CCF NCCA 2023, CCIS 1959, pp. 127–138, 2024.
https://doi.org/10.1007/978-981-99-8764-1_10

the traditional sequence-to-sequence models, for example, the newly proposed sequence-to-sequence model [3] can dynamically capture the range of local contexts and can better extract semantic information but can only generate meaningless responses such as "I don't know" due to the lack of external knowledge. Some models introducing external knowledge [4,5] have emerged to address this problem. Some studies demonstrate that introducing external knowledge can enhance performance, e.g., Huang [6] introduced a knowledge graph that can answer 10% more responses than the original model; introducing a knowledge graph in story generation also helps to understand the storyline [7].

To address the aforementioned limitations [8], researchers have proposed background-based dialogue approaches. These methods aim to generate sensible and informative responses by utilizing a combination of background knowledge (unstructured information) and input dialogue. The objective is to produce responses that are contextually relevant and provide valuable information to enhance the conversation. Knowledge selection is one of the most critical modules in background-based dialogues, which requires identifying the appropriate knowledge from the background knowledge based on the conversation, which will directly affect the quality of the generated response.

Using appropriate external knowledge augmentation also enables model generated responses to be implicitly emotional because, like humans, machines need to rely on experience and external knowledge to express implicit emotions [9,10]. If a dialogue system has some empathy, it can generate more appropriate and fluent responses [11,12].

Background-based dialogue research is one of the classifications of external knowledge enhancement research, and the advantage of background-based dialogue over traditional non-knowledge enhancement methods is that unstructured external knowledge is used [13]. Recent studies have shown that the coverage of a single knowledge source is not sufficient [14], and the results of several studies have shown that using more knowledge sources can improve the performance of knowledge-enhanced dialogue models [14,15].

To tackle the challenges mentioned above, this paper introduces a common sense emotional context enhanced dialog model (CEC). To fully utilize all the information (session history, background knowledge, external knowledge), a double-matching approach is proposed to fuse the information for knowledge selection. First, the model encodes the conversation history and background knowledge separately and then uses double matching to obtain the relevance weights among conversation history, background, and sentiment. After knowledge selection gets the knowledge topic transformation vector and combines it with graph feature representation to generate naturally flowing and informative responses.

In this paper, we perform an experimental analysis of CEC on Holl-E [16]. The experimental results show that CEC significantly outperforms the baseline model in machine evaluation, with stronger performance in knowledge selection and the ability to generate more appropriate responses.

The summarized contributions of this paper are as follows:

(1) We propose a dialogue model for emotional knowledge enhancement (CEC). By introducing common-sense knowledge and emotional-emotional information, the information implicit in the session is taken into account when making knowledge selection, enhancing the accuracy of knowledge selection and generating more appropriate responses.

(2) We introduced external knowledge through composition and proposed a dual matching matrix to integrate conversations with knowledge from various sources to construct an affective topic guidance vector to guide response generation.

2   Model

This model aims to combine external knowledge based on background knowledge to improve the rationality of knowledge selection and generate responses that conform to backward and forward logic. Formally this paper gives the symbolic definition. Given a session $C = \{c_1, c_2, c_3, c_4, ..., c_{\|C\|}\}$, where c_n represents the nth word, similarly for unstructured background knowledge $K = \{k_1, k_2, k_3, k_4, ..., k_{\|K\|}\}$, where k_n represents the nth word. This model generates responses $= \{r_1, r_2, r_3, r_4, ..., r_{\|R\|}\}$ based on conversation and background knowledge. The overall model framework is shown in Fig. 1.

In this section, the four modules that make up the entire model are presented.

(1) Background Context Encoder

Using two independent encoders, a given history session and background knowledge are encoded, and then an aggregation operation is performed to obtain the history session vector H_C and background knowledge vector H_K.

(2) Emotional context graph and graph encoder

ConceptNet and NRC_VAD, two sentiment enhancement libraries, are used to form a sentiment context map G with session history C. Then it is input into the graph encoder to obtain the graph feature representation H_G.

(3) Knowledge Selection

Based on the double-matching matrix, the historical session H_C, graph feature representation H_G and background knowledge representation H_K are used for matching operations.

(4) Response decoder

The knowledge topic transformation vector $H^s_{GC \to k}$ and the graph feature representation H_G are stitched together to obtain the emotional topic guidance vector H^g_{GCK}, and the module performs vocabulary generation based on this vector.

The whole process can be summarized as putting the history session C and the background knowledge K into the context encoder. The session history is combined with the knowledge base to obtain the feature representation through the graph encoding layer. Then, the knowledge selection module chooses the relevant information, which then guides the response decoder in generating the final response.

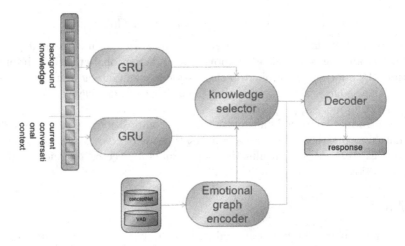

Fig. 1. The Overview of CEC

2.1　Background Context Encoder

We use two independent bidirectional GRUs to encode session history C and background knowledge K, respectively, to obtain $h_C = \{h_{c_1}, h_{c_2}, h_{c_3}, h_{c_4}, ..., h_{c_{\|C\|}}\}$ and $h_K = \{h_{k_1}, h_{k_2}, h_{k_3}, h_{k_4}, ..., h_{k_{\|K\|}}\}$.

$$h_{c_t} = BIGRU(e(c_t), h_{c_{t-1}}) \tag{1}$$

The parameters of these two GRUs are independent. We perform a highway transformation of these two vectors separately with the output of each layer of the bidirectional GRU to obtain a historical session H_C and background knowledge representation H_K for the next matching operation.

$$H_{k_t} = g_k(W_1[h_{k_t}, h_{X_{\|x\|}}] + b) + (1 - g_k)tanh(W_{n1}[h_{k_t}, h_{X_{\|x\|}}] + b) \tag{2}$$

$$g_k = \sigma(W_g[h_{k_t}, h_{X_{\|x\|}}] + b) \tag{3}$$

2.2　Emotional Context Graph and Graph Encoder

In this module, we use ConceptNet and NRC_VAD combined with Dialogue C to construct the sentiment graph G.Inspired by Li et al., we construct a series of candidate tuples $T_i = \{t_i^k = (c_i, r_k^i, x_k^i, s_k^i)\}_{k=1,2,3,...,K}$ for each non-deactivated word of the dialogue combined with the keywords in ConceptNet. The candidate tuples are filtered according to the following rules: (1) Only the tuples with confidence scores greater than 0.1 ($s_k^i > 0.1$) are retained. (2) Use NRC_VAD to calculate the sentiment intensity value ($\mu(x_i^k)$) and select the k tuples with the highest scores. We compose the composition based on candidate tuples and dialogues, and the rules are as follows: (1) Two adjacent words will point to the next word in order. (2) The selected candidate sentiment words will point to his keywords (c_i).

For the graph encoder, we need to transform each vertex of the sentiment graph G. Similar to the transformer model, our proposed model utilizes both the position embedding layer and the word embedding layer. Additionally, we incorporate the vertex state embedding to further enhance the model's performance. Therefore, the vector representation of the entire vertex consists of three embeddings:

$$v_i = E_w(v_i) + E_p(v_i) + E_v(v_i) \tag{4}$$

Then go to the multiheaded graph attention mechanism to obtain a deeper representation of each vertex.

$$\hat{v}_i = v_i + \|_{n=1}^{H} \sum_{j \in A_i} a_{ij}^n W_v^n v_j \tag{5}$$

$$a_{ij}^n = a^n(v_i, v_j) \tag{6}$$

where H represents the number of multiheads. A_i is the adjacency matrix of G, and a^n is the self-attentive module of each head. To obtain a global contextual representation, after a multiheaded graph attention layer, we use the encoding layer of the transformer for global modelling to obtain a sentiment contextual graph representation $h_g = \{\bar{v}_i\}$.

$$h_i^l = LayerNorm(\hat{v}_i^{l-1} + MHA(\hat{v}_i^{l-1})) \tag{7}$$

$$\bar{v}_i^l = LayerNorm(h_i^l + FNN(h_i^l)) \tag{8}$$

where l represents the lth layer of the coding layers, MHA represents the multiheaded attention module, and FNN represents a two-layer feedforward network with ReLU as the activation function.

2.3 Knowledge Selection

This module uses a double-matching matrix, the first of which is constructed using the potential representation of historical sessions H_C and background knowledge H_K derived in Sect. 3.1.

$$M_{kc}[i,j] = V_M tanh(W_{m_1} H_{k_i} + W_{m_2} H_{k_l}) \tag{9}$$

where V_M are the learnable vectors, and W_{m_1} and W_{m_2} are the learnable parameters. To match the sentiment map features with the background features, we first need to use a multilayer perceptron (MLP) to transform the h_g derived in Sect. 3.2 to obtain the H_G.

$$H_G = MLP(h_g) \tag{10}$$

We use a similar approach to obtain the second matching matrix M_{kg}:

$$M_{kg}[i,j] = V_{Mg} tanh(W_{mg_1} H_{k_i} + W_{mg_2} H_{g_l}) \tag{11}$$

For this dual matching matrix, we use the maximum pooling layer along the x-axis to obtain two perceptual background weight feature representations; each element in the feature represents the weight of relevance to the context, with higher weights representing greater relevance:

$$W_{C \to K} = \max_x(M_{kc}) \tag{12}$$

$$W_{G \to K} = \max_x(M_{kg}) \tag{13}$$

Finally, we combine these two perceptual contextual weight feature representations to obtain the emotional contextual perceptual weight vector $W_{CG \to K}$. Although this vector captures the relationship between the context, sentiment map and background, it only considers the distribution of relationships in the word direction. It lacks a global perspective to derive the probability distribution of knowledge selection properly. Drawing inspiration from GLKS, we adopt sliding windows for the purpose of global knowledge selection. In the knowledge selection module, we employ the "m-size unfold and sum" and "m-size unfold and attention" operations. The former operation obtains the global semantic information, and the latter operation obtains the global attention weights.

In the first operation "m-size unfold and sum", we can obtain a sliding semantic representation by the following formula:

$$W'_{G \to K} = ([W'_{G \to K}]_{0:m}, ..., [W'_{G \to K}]_{N:N+m}, ...) \tag{14}$$

$$[W'_{G \to K}]_{N:N+m} = \sum_{i=N}^{N+m} W_{CG \to K}[i] \tag{15}$$

For the second operation, we use the "m-size unfold and attention" operation for the last layer of the background knowledge representation h_k to obtain the global attention H'_K:

$$H'_K = ([h'_K]_{0:m}, ..., [h'_K]_{N:N+m}, ...) \tag{16}$$

$$[h'_K]_{N:N+m} = \sum_{i=N}^{N+m} a_i h_K[i] \tag{17}$$

$$a_i = att(h_{c_{\|C\|}}, [h_{k_m}...h_{k_{N+m}}]) \tag{18}$$

where a_i represents the attention weight of the session versus the background knowledge. Then we combine background knowledge K to generate knowledge topic transformation vectors $H^s_{CG \to k}$:

$$H^s_{CG \to k} = \sum_N P(K_N : K_{N+m}|C)[h'_K]_{N:N+m} \tag{19}$$

$$P(K_N : K_{N+m}|C) \propto \text{softmax}([W'_{CG \to K}]_{N:N+m}) \tag{20}$$

2.4   Response Decoder

During each decoding time step, the response decoder carries out a splicing operation utilizing the knowledge topic transformation vector $H^s_{GC \to k}$ and H_G in order to acquire the sentiment topic guidance vector H^g_{GCK}. Based on this vector, the response decoder obtains the probability of generating from the vocabulary and the probability of intercepting directly from the background and goes through a gate mechanism to finally decide how to generate.

First, we connect the decoded status code to $H^s_{GC \to k}$ and H_G:

$$H^g_{GCK} = [H^s_{GC \to k}, H_G, e(r_{t-1})] \tag{21}$$

where $e(r_{t-1})$ denotes the vector generated from the previous time step. Then we use the attention module to perform an attention operation on the knowledge-emotion topic vector with the background knowledge K, which will give us the background guidance vector $\bar{h}_{K_t}$. Similarly, we use the attention module to perform an attention operation with the session history C to obtain the session guidance vector $\bar{h}_{C_t}$:

$$\bar{h}_{K_t} = \sum_{i=1}^{\|K\|} a_{K_i} h_{K_i} \tag{22}$$

$$a_{K_i} = attention(H^g_{GCK_t}, h_K) \tag{23}$$

Then we join the two guidance vectors with the knowledge-emotion topic vector and use a readout layer to obtain an overall feature vector $\bar{h}_{r_t}$.

$$\bar{h}_{r_t} = \text{readout}(H^g_{GCK_t}, \bar{h}_{K_t}, \bar{h}_{C_t}) \tag{24}$$

Putting feature vectors $\bar{h}_{r_t}$ into linear layers with a softmax function to obtain the probability of generating words from the vocabulary:

$$P_v(r_t) = \text{softmax}(W_v \bar{h}_{r_t}) \tag{25}$$

For $P_k(r_t)$, we use an attention module for background knowledge to learn the intercept's start position pointer and end position pointer.

$$P_k(r_t) = \text{attention}(H^g_{GCK_t}, h_K) \tag{26}$$

Finally, we combine $P_v(r_t)$ and $P_k(r_t)$ as follows:

$$P(r_t) = gP_v(r_t) + (1-g)P_k(r_t) \tag{27}$$

3   Experiments

3.1   Implementation Details

The word embedding size is configured as 300, while the hidden layer size is set to 256. The number of vocabulary words is limited to approximately 26,000, the length of the conversation history is limited to 65, and the length of the background knowledge is limited to 256. The optimizer uses Adam, and the batch size is set to 32. The entire model was trained for 20 rounds, and the highest scores were taken for comparison in the evaluation phase.

3.2 Datasets

To ensure a more accurate representation of the model's performance, we opted for Holl-E as the benchmark for our comparative experiments. The number of samples in the datasets is shown below.

Holl-E: This is a dataset with the correct labels containing background knowledge and the correct knowledge selection labels. The dataset focuses on the movie part, two people having a conversation about the movie plot, and each response will be a change or copy of the background knowledge to reply. The background knowledge consists of four parts: movie plot, reviews, professional commentary, and fact sheets related to the movie. The experiments in this paper use two versions of Holl-E: oracle background and mixed-short background. We partition the dataset into three according to its original partitioning method, with the training set containing 34486 samples, the validation set containing 4388 samples, and the test set containing 4318 samples (Table 1).

Table 1. Dataset sizes.

Datasets	train	validation	test
Holl-E	34486	4388	4318

3.3 Evaluation Metrics

In this paper, the evaluation metrics chosen for machine evaluation are ROUGE-1, ROUGE-2, and ROUGE-L. Since dialogue responses are generated using background knowledge, previous studies have shown that these metrics are consistent with BLEU. Therefore, employing these metrics would provide a comprehensive assessment of the model's performance.

3.4 Results

The experimental results are shown in the table. Table 2 and Table 3 subtables represent the results of the oracle background and oracle mixed-short background in Holl-E.

The experimental results demonstrate that CEC outperforms the baseline model across all metrics, providing evidence that CEC can enhance knowledge selection performance and generate more appropriate responses. Compared with BiDAF (extraction-based generation method), which benefits from combining extractive and generative approaches, CEC generates more reasonable and natural responses while using background knowledge well. RefNet uses span annotations, while CEC does not need additional annotation information and can better locate the correct background knowledge location. This is because we use guidance vectors and learn two pointers to locate background knowledge in the generation process. Compared with AKGCM, which fuses knowledge graphs, and GLKS, which used to have the highest knowledge selection scores, CEC connects structured knowledge in a more rationalized way and, simultaneously, can significantly increase the performance of knowledge selection. Our advantage lies in the utilization of the double-matching matrix, which effectively fuses structured and unstructured knowledge to enhance knowledge information. This approach leads to a substantial improvement in knowledge selection performance while ensuring that empty responses are not generated. In both versions of the Holl-E dataset, we can observe that the same model in both tables (including CEC) performs better in the oracle mixed-short background version than in the oracle background. This is because the knowledge in the oracle background contains only one source, which has less information than in the oracle mixed-short background. Additionally, compared to the magnitude of the improvement of the baseline model in both datasets, we can observe that the improvement of CEC is not very significant. This may be because the knowledge richness in the dataset can already reach a standard level, and the added knowledge does not enhance it much. The above experimental analysis proves that it is essential to include additional knowledge in a session. Choosing the right way to integrate different knowledge types can improve response quality.

Table 2. Results on oracle background (256-word)

Methods	SR(%)			MR(%)		
	ROUGE-1	ROUGE-2	ROUGE-L	ROUGE-1	ROUGE-2	ROUGE-L
no background Seq2Seq	27.15	9.56	21.48	30.91	11.85	24.81
oracle background						
GTTP [16]	29.82	17.33	25.09	35.08	22.05	30.06
BiDAF [17]	39.68	31.72	35.91	46.49	40.58	42.64
CaKe [18]	42.82	30.37	37.48	48.65	36.54	43.21
RefNet [19]	42.87	30.73	37.11	49.64	38.15	43.77
GLKS [20]	43.75	31.54	38.69	50.67	39.20	44.64
CEC(ours)	44.47	32.03	39.28	50.73	39.22	45.35

3.5   Ablation Study

Since the performance of CEC is consistent across datasets, the experiments in this section are conducted in the oracle background for ablation experiments only. We will analyze three aspects: (1) w/o emo_embedding+emo_match: No sentiment matching matrix and sentiment vector. (2) w/o emo_match:No sentiment matching matrix. (3) w/o emo_embedding:No emotion vector.

The experimental results are shown in Table 4. Both the sentiment matching matrix and the sentiment vector impact the final generation, and removing

Table 3. Results on mixed-short background (256-word)

Methods	SR(%)			MR(%)		
	ROUGE-1	ROUGE-2	ROUGE-L	ROUGE-1	ROUGE-2	ROUGE-L
GTTP	30.77	18.72	25.67	36.06	23.7	
BiDAF	38.79	32.91	35.09	43.93	39.5	40.12
CaKe	41.26	29.43	36.01	45.81	34	40.79
AKGCM [21]		29.29	34.72			
PostKS [22]	27.52	9.21	21.23	31.57	12.55	25.15
SKT [23]	35.28	21.74	30.06	41.68	28.3	36.24
RefNet	41.33	31.08	36.17	47	36.5	41.72
DukeNet [24]	36.53	23.02	31.46	43.18	30.13	38.03
GLKS	44.52	33.05	39.63	50.06	38.87	45.12
MIKe [25]	37.78	25.31	32.82	44.06	31.92	38.91
CEC(ours)	44.58	33.22	39.7	50.69	39.33	45.29

either will degrade performance. Second, the performance degradation is most obvious if we remove the sentiment matching matrix (w/o emo_match) alone for knowledge selection. This demonstrates that adding additional sentiment-structured knowledge significantly improves the accuracy of knowledge selection and enhances model performance, possibly because the added knowledge is generated based on the current session and is, therefore, highly relevant and contains a more significant amount of valuable knowledge. Finally, to validate the effectiveness of the sentiment vector, we remove the sentiment vector (w/o emo_embedding) directly when combining the sentiment topic guidance vectors. The results demonstrate that adding sentiment vectors can improve the performance of the generation module, which means that sentiment vectors can provide additional sentiment information in addition to the session itself. It also improves the correctness of the selection knowledge when generating responses and making the responses more reasonable and justified.

Table 4. Ablation study

Methods	SR(%)			MR(%)		
	ROUGE-1	ROUGE-2	ROUGE-L	ROUGE-1	ROUGE-2	ROUGE-L
w/o all	43.75	31.54	38.69	50.67	39.2	44.64
w/o match	43.91	31.52	38.73	50.65	39.21	45.17
w/o embedding	44.01	31.57	38.8	50.68	39.18	45.20
CEC(ours)	44.58	33.22	39.7	50.69	39.33	45.29

4   Conclusion

In this article, we introduce external knowledge by constructing a sentiment graph, generating a sentiment vector using graph attention, and then using a matching matrix to combine the background knowledge with the sentiment vector to enhance both the precision of knowledge selection and the naturalness of response generation. The experimental results are better than all the baselines.

This paper introduces a sentiment knowledge base. Although it can improve the final response, the model does not explicitly model sentiment classification or recognition; therefore, this model can only restrict the generated responses to the session sentiment. To construct an empathic dialogue model, in the future, our work will focus on enhancing the model's capabilities in both emotion recognition and inference.

References

1. Abro, W.A., Aicher, A., Rach, N., Ultes, S., Minker, W., Qi, G.: Natural language understanding for argumentative dialogue systems in the opinion building domain. Knowl.-Based Syst. **242**, 108318 (2022)
2. Lecun, Y., Bengio, Y., Hinton, G.: Deep learning. Nature **521**(7553), 436–444 (2015)
3. Xu, M., Zeng, B., Yang, H., Chi, J., Chen, J., Liu, H.: Combining dynamic local context focus and dependency cluster attention for aspect-level sentiment classification. Neurocomputing **478**, 49–69 (2022)
4. Ghazvininejad, M., et al.: A knowledge-grounded neural conversation model. In: Proceedings of the AAAI Conference on Artificial Intelligence, vol. 32 (2018)
5. Zhong, P., Wang, D., Li, P., Zhang, C., Wang, H., Miao, C.: CARE: commonsense-aware emotional response generation with latent concepts. In: Proceedings of the AAAI Conference on Artificial Intelligence, vol. 35, pp. 14577–14585 (2021)
6. Huang, L., Wu, L., Wang, L.: Knowledge graph-augmented abstractive summarization with semantic-driven cloze reward. arXiv preprint arXiv:2005.01159 (2020)
7. Guan, J., Wang, Y., Huang, M.: Story ending generation with incremental encoding and commonsense knowledge. In: Proceedings of the AAAI Conference on Artificial Intelligence, vol. 33, pp. 6473–6480 (2019)
8. Zhou, K., Prabhumoye, S., Black, A.W.: A dataset for document grounded conversations. arXiv preprint arXiv:1809.07358 (2018)
9. Zhong, P., Wang, D., Miao, C.: Knowledge-enriched transformer for emotion detection in textual conversations. arXiv preprint arXiv:1909.10681 (2019)
10. Young, T., Cambria, E., Chaturvedi, I., Zhou, H., Biswas, S., Huang, M.: Augmenting end-to-end dialogue systems with commonsense knowledge. In: Proceedings of the AAAI Conference on Artificial Intelligence, vol. 32 (2018)
11. Liu, S., et al.: Towards emotional support dialog systems. arXiv preprint arXiv:2106.01144 (2021)
12. Wang, L., et al.: CASS: towards building a social-support chatbot for online health community. Proc. ACM Hum. Comput. Interact. **5**(CSCW1), 1–31 (2021)
13. Wu, S., Wang, M., Li, Y., Zhang, D., Wu, Z.: Improving the applicability of knowledge-enhanced dialogue generation systems by using heterogeneous knowledge from multiple sources. In: Proceedings of the Fifteenth ACM International Conference on WEB Search and Data Mining, pp. 1149–1157 (2022)
14. Wu, S., Li, Y., Wang, M., Zhang, D., Zhou, Y., Wu, Z.: More is better: enhancing open-domain dialogue generation via multi-source heterogeneous knowledge. In: Proceedings of the 2021 Conference on Empirical Methods in Natural Language Processing, pp. 2286–2300 (2021)

15. Bai, J., Yang, Z., Liang, X., Wang, W., Li, Z.: Learning to copy coherent knowledge for response generation. In: Proceedings of the AAAI Conference on Artificial Intelligence, vol. 35, pp. 12535–12543 (2021)
16. Moghe, N., Arora, S., Banerjee, S., Khapra, M.M.: Towards exploiting background knowledge for building conversation systems. arXiv preprint arXiv:1809.08205 (2018)
17. Seo, M., Kembhavi, A., Farhadi, A., Hajishirzi, H.: Bidirectional attention flow for machine comprehension. arXiv preprint arXiv:1611.01603 (2016)
18. Zhang, Y., Ren, P., de Rijke, M.: Improving background based conversation with context-aware knowledge pre-selection. arXiv preprint arXiv:1906.06685 (2019)
19. Meng, C., Ren, P., Chen, Z., Monz, C., Ma, J., de Rijke, M.: RefNet: a reference-aware network for background based conversation. In: Proceedings of the AAAI Conference on Artificial Intelligence, vol. 34, pp. 8496–8503 (2020)
20. Ren, P., Chen, Z., Monz, C., Ma, J., de Rijke, M.: Thinking globally, acting locally: distantly supervised global-to-local knowledge selection for background based conversation. In: Proceedings of the AAAI Conference on Artificial Intelligence, vol. 34, pp. 8697–8704 (2020)
21. Liu, Z., Niu, Z.Y., Wu, H., Wang, H.: Knowledge aware conversation generation with explainable reasoning over augmented graphs. arXiv preprint arXiv:1903.10245 (2019)
22. Lian, R., Xie, M., Wang, F., Peng, J., Wu, H.: Learning to select knowledge for response generation in dialog systems. arXiv preprint arXiv:1902.04911 (2019)
23. Kim, B., Ahn, J., Kim, G.: Sequential latent knowledge selection for knowledge-grounded dialogue. arXiv preprint arXiv:2002.07510 (2020)
24. Meng, C., et al.: DukeNet: a dual knowledge interaction network for knowledge-grounded conversation. In: Proceedings of the 43rd International ACM SIGIR Conference on Research and Development in Information Retrieval, pp. 1151–1160 (2020)
25. Meng, C., Ren, P., Chen, Z., Ren, Z., Xi, T., Rijke, M.D.: Initiative-aware self-supervised learning for knowledge-grounded conversations. In: Proceedings of the 44th International ACM SIGIR Conference on Research and Development in Information Retrieval, pp. 522–532 (2021)

Fine-Grained Style Control
in VITS-Based Text-to-Speech Synthesis

Zhong Huihang[1], Dengfeng Ke[1](✉), Li Ya[2], Wenhan Yao[1], and Wenqian Bao[1]

[1] Beijing Language and Culture University, Beijing, China
dengfeng.ke@blcu.edu.cn
[2] Beijing University of Posts and Telecommunications, Beijing, China
yli01@bupt.edu.cn

Abstract. In this paper, a fine-grained style controllable speech synthesis model based on VITS is presented. To achieve fine-grained emotional speech, global and local emotion features are extracted using GST and LST, respectively. A multi head cross-attention mechanism is used to align the text with emotion features, achieving prosodic control on the text side. Experiments demonstrate that the original text encoder of VITS is not capable of handling both text and emotion features simultaneously. Therefore, an emotion-text encoder is proposed, which significantly improves the ability of the prior encoder and enables fine-grained emotion speech synthesis. Results show that the system achieves the highest levels of naturalness, style conversion ability, and speech quality in synthesized speech. Audio samples are publicly available (https://lunar333.github.io).

Keywords: Text to speech synthesis · Fine-grained style control · Style conversion

1 Introduction

The purpose of speech synthesis is to synthesize speech similar to that of humans. As a classic sequence-to-sequence speech synthesis model, Tacotron2 [1] can synthesize speech similar to humans, with MOS value of up to 4.52 compared to 4.58 for human speech. However, this autoregressive model has the drawbacks of slow training speed and slow synthetic inference. The nonautoregressive text-to-speech models uses parallel network structures to accelerate the synthesis speed, such as FastSpeech [2], FastSpeech 2 [3]. However, these models require external aligners, making data preprocessing complicated. Despite these differences, all of these models use a two-stage training method, where the acoustic model is first trained to generate the Mel spectrum, followed by training the vocoder to synthesize audio from the spectrum. To solve this problem, VITS uses variational autoencoders with normalizing flows to project the liner spectrum to the latent variable z and then utilizes monotonic alignment search to align the distribution of text. This is followed by direct audio synthesis from the latent variables

M. Zhang et al. (Eds.): CCF NCCA 2023, CCIS 1959, pp. 139–147, 2024.
https://doi.org/10.1007/978-981-99-8764-1_11

through adversarial training, thereby eliminating the gap caused by two-stage training. As a result, it has become the state-of-the-art text-to-speech model.

Despite the high quality of speech synthesis, the needs of human-computer interaction and audiobook applications cannot be fully met by depending solely on natural speech. Therefore, there is a growing need to synthesize emotionally expressive speech. Global style token (GST) [5] employs a reference encoder to capture speaker style features by representing the weight of learnable coding vectors. Text-to-speech models can synthesize speech with different speaking styles conditioned on GST. However, GST can only capture a global style and cannot obtain fine-grained styles. In reality, the expression of human speech styles is essentially multi scale rather than single-scale. To address this, [6] incorporates a global-level emotion presenting module (GM), utterance-level emotion presenting module (UM), and local-level emotion presenting module (LM) is proposed. This method enhances the expressiveness of synthesized speech. However, training the GM and LM increases the complexity of the model and the time cost of training. To improve the granularity of speech synthesis, [7] proposes using emotion features with time dimensions. They also propose two methods of style control to solve the problem of the reference audio length being different from the synthesized audio length during model inference. The first method uses an autoregressive model with an appropriate design to make the time dimension of emotion features and synthesized speech the same. The second method uses attention mechanisms to align text and emotion features, allowing the model to learn the alignment between them without the need for emotion features to have the same time dimension as text. Although there have been many previous studies on emotional style control speech synthesis, they are all based on autoregressive speech synthesis models. While the autoregressive model has advantages in emotion speech synthesis, such as the ability to use historical information for emotion speech synthesis and generate the voice of different emotions through conditional probability, it also has drawbacks. The use of two-stage training, where the acoustic model is trained first and then the vocoder is trained, creates a natural gap between them, and the quality of synthesized speech is not as good as that of an end-to-end speech model (VITS), which limits its application in emotion speech synthesis.

In this paper, we propose a method based on the end-to-end speech synthesis model VITS. We were inspired by [8] and extracted global and local emotional features using GST and LST. We aligned the text and emotion features using a cross-attention mechanism to achieve prosodic control on the text end. Our experiments showed that the original text encoder's ability is insufficient to simultaneously model text and emotions. Therefore, we proposed an emotion-text encoder that significantly improves the ability of prior encoders. Our system achieves the highest levels of naturalness, style conversion ability, and speech quality in the synthesized speech. We will discuss the emotion-text encoder in Sect. 2.4.

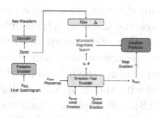
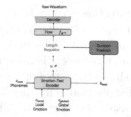

Fig. 1. FG-VITS training procedure   **Fig. 2.** FG-VITS inference procedure

2 Method

In this section, we will discuss our proposed method and its architecture. Our method differs from VITS in that we replaced VITS' text encoder with an emotion-text encoder and replaced the stochastic duration predictor with a regular duration predictor (similar to the FastSpeech duration predictor). We replaced the text encoder with an emotion-text encoder because we found that the ability of the text encoder was insufficient to simultaneously model emotions and text, resulting in low-quality synthesized speech with odd accents, pronunciation errors, and even content leakage. We used a regular duration predictor because we found that the speaking style of synthesized speech mainly comes from the reference audio, so there is no need to use a stochastic duration predictor to increase the diversity of synthesized speech. In contrast, using the stochastic duration predictor can also make it difficult for the model to converge. In the following section, we briefly review VITS and introduce our approach.

2.1 VITS

VITS is a speech synthesis model based on variational autoencoder (VAE) [9], which is mainly divided into two parts: the prior encoder and the posterior encoder. The posterior encoder with normalizing flows [10] projects the input linear spectrum to the hidden variable z. The prior encoder projects the text to a mean of μ, variance of σ distribution. Then the distribution of the spectrum is aligned with the hidden variable z using the monotonic alignment search (MAS). Finally, the adversarial learning was introduced, using a multi period discriminator (HIFI-GAN) [11] to distinguish the generated audio. This solves the gap problem caused by the previous two-stage training of acoustic models and vocoders, improves the quality of speech synthesis, and makes VITS the state-of-the-art text-to-speech model.

2.2 Training and Inference Procedures

Figure 1 shows the training procedure of the model. Initially, the emotion-text encoder maps the text and emotion to a mean of μ, variance of σ distribution.

Essentially, this process transposes text and emotional information into a latent semantic space. Similarly, a posterior encoder maps the linear spectrum into a latent variable, z. Subsequently, via normalization flow, this mapping evolves into a more complex distribution. The aim of this progression is to increase the complexity of the latent space distribution to better capture the intricacies of the audio distribution. This distribution is then aligned with the emotion-text distribution using the monotonic alignment search (MAS), the result of which trains the duration predictor. Ultimately, multi period discriminator (HIFI-GAN) [11] and adversarial learning approach, trains the latent variable z to generate audio. The role of the multi period discriminator is to evaluate the quality of the generated audio at various time scales. Adversarial learning, on the other hand, is a training methodology that enhances the quality of the audio generated by the generator through competition with the discriminator.

Figure 2 illustrates the inference procedure of the model. The emotion-text encoder initially maps the text and emotion into a distribution with a mean of μ and variance of σ. Subsequently, the duration predictor performs length regularization on this distribution. Finally, through the normalizing flows and decoder, audio is generated.

Our system uses the same loss function as VITS. During training, we use pairs of speech and text, and select a reference audio from the same emotion category. Like [8], we adopted a random truncation of emotion features with a truncation length of $[\alpha, l_{sty}]$, l_{sty} is the length of the LST. α is hyperparameter, we choose $\alpha = 15$. Random truncation is used to simulate the situation where the reference audio may be shorter than the synthesized audio during model inference, which can increase the robustness of the model.

2.3   Emotion Feature Extraction

The feature extraction module is the same as [8]. Figure 3 is the overall structure of our feature extraction network.

Wav2Vec2.0 Features. Instead of using Mel spectrum, we adopt wav2vec 2.0 [13]to extract meaningful representations from the audio. we found that using wav2vec2.0 to extract features can effectively solve the problem of high-frequency aliasing in synthesized speech.

Global Emotion Features. The extracted Wav2Vec2.0 features are passed through a network similar to GST [5] that summarizing different weights of learnable codebook vector. First, through the Linear layer with the ReLU activation function. Then the global mean is taken at the time dimension to obtain a global style query vector with a time dimension of one, and a multi head cross attention is taken with the trainable codebook (key and value) to obtain the global emotion features.

Local Emotion Features. Similarly, the extracted Wav2Vec2.0 features are processed through LSTM to obtain a fine-grained style feature. The output of each time step is used as a query vector, and a multi head cross attention is taken with the trainable codebook (key and value) to obtain an output. Finally, the output of the time dimension is passed through an average pooling with stride 6 and kernel size 10 to obtain local emotion features.

Fusion Emotion Features. Specifically, the global emotional features are extended in the time dimension to the same length as the local emotion features and added together to obtain the fusion representations.

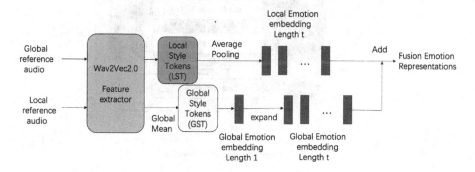

Fig. 3. Feature Extraction Module

2.4   Emotion-Text Encoder

Figure 4 in the paper shows our proposed emotion-text encoder. We found that the original text encoder of VITS did not have sufficient ability to simultaneously model both text and emotion. Therefore, we proposed an emotion-text encoder that has the ability to model both emotion and text simultaneously. The input of the emotion-text encoder includes global emotional features, local emotional features, and text. The output is a joint distribution of the mean of μ and variance of σ for both emotion and text. We changed the transformer encoder of the text encoder to create a 6-layer cross-attention block. The text representations are first processed through self-attention, normalization, projection, and residual concatenation and then used as a query. The fusion emotion features are used as Key and Value to perform a multi head cross attention calculation. The purpose is to enable the model to learn the alignment relationship between text and emotion features in different time dimensions. Similarly, the calculation results of multi head attention are normalized, projected, and residual-connected to the input of the next layer's cross attention block. A total of 6 layers of cross attention blocks are used to obtain the final output results. This process can be considered a process of emotion feature refinement learning. This refined learning process is beneficial for the model to focus on learning emotion features, ignore some information about reference audio text content, and effectively reduce the problem of content leakage.

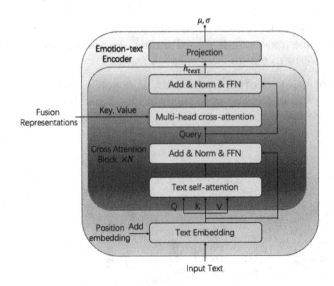

Fig. 4. Emotion-Text Encoder

3   Experiment Setup

Our experiment was conducted in a single speaker setting, and we used two datasets, the Chinese female emotion dataset DB-6 and the LJ Speech dataset [12]. The DB-6 includes seven emotions: angry, disgust, fear, happy, neutral, sad and surprise. Each emotion has 2000 audios, for a total of 14000 audios, containing 14000 different sentences. The audio sample rate is 44000 Hz, and we resample it at 16000 Hz. The LJ Speech dataset is commonly used for single-speaker TTS systems. It contains 13100 English utterances from a single female speaker with a total duration of approximately 24 h.

We used 64 GSTs and 32 LSTs and set the embedding and hidden sizes of all modules to 192, except for the FFN of the cross attention block, which was set to 1024. N=6 in the cross attention block. System training is optimized using Adam, with an initial learning rate of 2×10^{-4}. We trained 100k steps using two 3090 24 g GPUs with a batch size of 32.

3.1   Comparing Methods

We used FG-TRANSFORMER [8], GST-TE-VITS and FG-TE-VITS as the baseline, and our proposed method named FG-ETE-VITS. TE (Text Encoder) refers to using the original text encoder of VITS, while ETE (Emotion Text Encoder) refers to using our proposed emotion-text encoder. GST-TE-VITS refers to extracting a global emotion feature through GST with the input of Mel Spectrum, then through a linear layer, directly adding it to text representation as text encoder input. FG-TE-VITS refers to using fusion emotion features as input (key and value) and text representation as a query. Multi head cross attention is used to obtain a mixed representation. Then, text representation is added through a broadcast mechanism as text encoder input.

3.2 Subjective Evaluation

We initiated a subjective evaluation procedure to gauge the perceived naturalness and emotional congruency of our speech synthesis framework. For Mandarin speech, we randomly chose five sets of textual content and corresponding reference speech from our testing data, generating five synthetic audio pieces for each emotion, culminating in a total of 35 audio files. For English speech, we arbitrarily selected 30 pairs of text and matching reference speech from the test set, producing a total of 30 audio files. The reference audio and synthesized speech were not paired. We enlisted the help of 13 evaluators, none of whom had prior experience in speech synthesis, to assess the naturalness and emotional similarity or stylistic likeness of the synthesized speech. They scored on a scale of 1 to 5, with 1 signifying 'poor' for naturalness or 'not at all similar' for emotional or stylistic likeness, and 5 signifying 'excellent' or 'highly similar', respectively. Different evaluators assessed each audio file, after which we computed the mean opinion score (MOS) and a 95% confidence interval for each assessment category. The insights gleaned from this experiment shed valuable light on our speech synthesis system's capability in terms of naturalness and emotional congruence.

Table 1 presents the evaluation results of the DB-6 datasets, showing that FG-TE-VITS outperforms GST-TE-VITS, which demonstrates the effectiveness of incorporating local emotion features. Our system also outperforms FG-TRANSFORMER in terms of synthesized speech clarity, which is not surprising given that FG-TRANSFORMER is not a completely end-to-end model and has inherent limitations in the quality of synthesized speech. The synthesized speech produced by FG-TRANSFORMER contains electronic sounds, omissions, and repeated endings. However, our system achieves similar emotional similarity indicators to FG-TRANSFORMER. Finally, our system outperforms FG-TE-VITS in terms of speech clarity and emotional similarity, providing evidence for the effectiveness of our proposed emotion-text encoder.

Table 2 provides an assessment of the LJ speech datasets. Here, our suggested model demonstrates a slight edge over the baseline models. The reason for this, we believe, stems from the absence of emotional data within the LJSpeech dataset. Our novel approach, which significantly enhances the capacity to model emotion, thus leads to a modest but noteworthy improvement when dealing with the LJSpeech datasets.

3.3 Discussion on the Impact of Transformer on the Model

From a large perspective, the main reason for the performance improvement of our system is the increase in the number of transformer layers, which improves the ability of the model. From a deeper perspective, Transformer has some features that are very suitable for speech synthesis, making it easier for the model to learn emotion features. In speech synthesis, transformers easily learn some

Table 1. MOS with 95% confidence interval on DB-6

	Naturalness	Emotion similarity
GT	4.01 ± 0.05	–
GST-TE-VITS	3.12 ± 0.08	2.91 ± 0.09
FG-TE-VITS	3.09 ± 0.10	3.02 ± 0.09
FG-ETE-VITS	**3.54 ± 0.12**	**3.31 ± 0.11**
FG-TRANSFORMER	3.24 ± 0.12	3.26 ± 0.11

Table 2. MOS with 95% confidence interval on LJSpeech

	Naturalness	Style similarity
GT	4.21 ± 0.05	–
GST-TE-VITS	3.38 ± 0.10	3.09 ± 0.09
FG-TE-VITS	3.29 ± 0.10	3.12 ± 0.09
FG-ETE-VITS	**3.48 ± 0.10**	3.22 ± 0.09
FG-TRANSFORMER	3.46 ± 0.10	**3.26 ± 0.09**

repetitive regular features. In most cases, this feature has more advantages than disadvantages because it helps the model quickly capture some formant features. The disadvantage is that if it is a pure Transformer speech synthesis model, the model may still not be able to learn more fine-grained emotion in the later stages of training, resulting in monotonous and boring listening of synthesized speech. However, this problem can be solved by VITS. VITS is a variational autoencoder with normalizing flows to model complex distributions. Consequently, it forms a complementary relationship with Transformer. The transformer can first learn some repetitive regular formant features, and VITS's posterior encoder further refines the formant features, allowing the model to learn more fine-grained emotion features.

4   Conclusions

In this paper, we implement a VITS-based fine-grained style controllable speech synthesis model. Through experiments, the effectiveness of the emotional text encoder in enhancing VITS emotional speech synthesis has been fully verified. In future work, we will further explore ways to decouple content and emotional features to reduce the word error rate of the system.

References

1. Shen, J., et al.: Natural TTS synthesis by conditioning Wavenet on MEL spectrogram predictions. In: 2018 IEEE International Conference on Acoustics, Speech and Signal Processing (ICASSP), pp. 4779–4783. IEEE (2018)

2. Ren, Y., et al.: Fastspeech: fast, robust and controllable text to speech. In: Advances in Neural Information Processing Systems, vol. 32 (2019)
3. Ren, Y., et al.: FastSpeech 2: fast and high-quality end-to-end text to speech. In: International Conference on Learning Representations (2021). https://openreview.net/forum?id=piLPYqxtWuA
4. Kim, J., Kong, J., Son, J.: Conditional variational autoencoder with adversarial learning for end-to-end text-to-speech. In: International Conference on Machine Learning, pp. 5530–5540. PMLR (2021)
5. Wang, Y., et al.: Style tokens: unsupervised style modeling, control and transfer in end-to-end speech synthesis. In: International Conference on Machine Learning, pp. 5180–5189. PMLR (2018)
6. Lei, Y., Yang, S., Wang, X., Xie, L.: Msemotts: multi-scale emotion transfer, prediction, and control for emotional speech synthesis. IEEE/ACM Trans. Audio Speech Lang. Process. **30**, 853–864 (2022). IEEE
7. Lee, Y., Kim, T.: Robust and fine-grained prosody control of end-to-end speech synthesis. In: ICASSP 2019–2019 IEEE International Conference on Acoustics, Speech and Signal Processing (ICASSP), pp. 5911–5915. IEEE (2019)
8. Chen, L.-W., Rudnicky, A.: Fine-grained style control in transformer-based text-to-speech synthesis. In: ICASSP 2022–2022 IEEE International Conference on Acoustics, Speech and Signal Processing (ICASSP), pp. 7907–7911. IEEE (2022)
9. Kingma, D.P., Welling, M.: Auto-encoding variational Bayes. In: 2nd International Conference on Learning Representations, ICLR 2014, Banff, AB, Canada, 14–16 April 2014, Conference Track Proceedings. http://arxiv.org/abs/1312.6114v10
10. Rezende, D., Mohamed, S.: Variational inference with normalizing flows. In: International Conference on Machine Learning, pp. 1530–1538. PMLR (2015)
11. Kong, J., Kim, J., Bae, J.: HiFi-GAN: generative adversarial networks for efficient and high fidelity speech synthesis. In: Advances in Neural Information Processing Systems, vol. 33, pp. 17022–17033 (2020)
12. Ito, K., Johnson, L.: The LJ Speech Dataset (2017). https://keithito.com/LJ-Speech-Dataset/
13. Baevski, A., Zhou, Y., Mohamed, A., Auli, M.: Wav2vec 2.0: a framework for self-supervised learning of speech representations. In: Advances in Neural Information Processing Systems, vol. 33, pp. 12449–12460 (2020)

Text Sentiment Analysis Based on a Dynamic Pruning Capsule Network

Hankiz Yilahun, Peiliang Zhang$^{(\boxtimes)}$, Mijit Ablimit, and Askar Hamdulla

Xinjiang University, Xinjiang, China
1334195383@qq.com

Abstract. Dynamic pruning of capsules and a variable weight BIGRU model (DP-CAPS-VW-BIGRU) are proposed in this paper to address the problem of unnecessary capsule connections that cause noise and the insufficient utilization of bidirectional GRU network information. The input text is vectorized using the ERNIE pretraining model, and the convolutional layers are used to extract context information from the text. The main capsule layer uses vector output instead of the scalar output of the convolutional network to preserve instantiation parameters, and the convolutional capsule layer further extracts deeper feature information. To reduce the impact of noise caused by unnecessary capsule connections on model performance, dynamic pruning of the capsule network is proposed in this paper. At the same time, a variable weight bidirectional GRU network is proposed to improve the utilization of forward and backwards information. Experimental results show that the proposed model can effectively improve the performance of text sentiment analysis tasks.

Keywords: Capsule Network · Dynamic Pruning · Sentiment Analysis

1 Introduction

Currently, people can freely express all kinds of content and sentiment on social media every day. And Weibo has become the main internet platform for most Chinese people in their everyday life, for communicating, and obtaining various information [1]. Therefore, research on Weibo comments has become increasingly important. Based on previous research, this paper proposes a sentiment analysis model based on a dynamic pruning capsule network and variable weight bidirectional GRU. This method can reduce the problem of noise caused by unnecessary connections between capsules, and simultaneously improve the context utilization, thus effectively improveing the model performance and providing new solutions for sentiment analysis researchers.

2 Research Status

There are currently two mainstream methods for sentiment analysis: sentiment dictionaries and machine learning/deep learning. In research on emotion dictionary methods, Whissell C [2] proposed a classification method based on sentiment dictionary for the

M. Zhang et al. (Eds.): CCF NCCA 2023, CCIS 1959, pp. 148–160, 2024.
https://doi.org/10.1007/978-981-99-8764-1_12

first time. He used digit-marked sentiment words to generate sentiment dictionaries and then matched them with the corpus text to achieve sentiment classification. Li Tong et al. [3] used the concept of "center words" to solve complex information extraction tasks and evaluated important information in the text using statistical analysis. Thelwall M et al. [4] added words and phrases that appeared multiple times in social commentary texts to the sentiment dictionary and achieved sentiment classification for informal commentary texts posted on social media. Pan Minghui [5] specifically constructed two Weibo sentiment word dictionaries for her subsequent research tasks, formulated corresponding sentiment classification rules for the two dictionaries, and finally used SVM to achieve a six-class sentiment task. Saif H et al. [6] took the co-occurrence patterns of vocabulary in different contexts as factors affecting sentiment polarity determination, and updated the polarity or intensity values of sentiment words in different contexts. In 2016, Li Yuqing [7] constructed a bilingual sentiment dictionary and improved the generalization performance of the dictionary by using relative entropy and a Gaussian mixture model.

In the field of traditional machine learning research, Bo Pang et al. [8] used three machine learning methods (Naive Bayes, Maximum Entropy Classification, and Support Vector Machine) for emotion task classification, eliminating the need to be limited by emotion dictionaries and achieving more free and flexible emotion classification. Sharma A et al. [9] successfully improved the performance of SVM by integrating "weak" support vector machine classifiers using boosting algorithm classification performance. Jiang et al. [10] selected five specific topics on Twitter and used support vector machines to sentiment classify Twitter texts on a particular topic. Dragoni M et al. [11] used the overlap of possible conceptual domains to construct a universal model that can calculate the polarity of text belonging to any domain. Sentiment words were extracted from the text and then SVM models were used for sentiment classification, dividing sentiment into different categories based on weights.

In the field of deep learning, many researchers have applied deep learning technology to text sentiment analysis. Ghorbani M et al. [12] proposed an integrated structure that combines CNN and LSTM networks to accurately determine the polarity of emotions and viewpoints. Basiri M. E et al. [13] used a neural network model with an improved attention mechanism for text sentiment analysis, showing good sentiment classification performance on the Twitter dataset. Luo Fan et al. [14] combined CNN with RNN to propose the HRNN-CNN model for text sentiment analysis. The model introduced a sentence layer in the middle layer to solve the problem of difficult feature extraction when feature information is far away, and combined convolutional neural networks to achieve cross-language information extraction. Wang et al. [22] skillfully merged monolingual and bilingual information words into vectors within their document representations. They employed the innovative bilingual attention network (BAN) model to seamlessly integrate attention vectors and achieve accurate emotion classification. Tang et al. [16] proposed a model that uses CNN, LSTM, and gated recurrent neural networks to learn sentence representation for the first time, and uses Gated RNN to achieve adaptive encoding of sentence semantics. Yang et al. [17] made a groundbreaking contribution to text classification by introducing capsule networks. They developed two architectures, Capsule-A and Capsule-B, and proposed three strategies to ensure a stable dynamic routing process. These strategies effectively mitigate interference from "background" information or noise capsules that may not have been adequately trained. Kim et al. [18] proposed a static routing method to simplify the complexity of dynamic routing calculations. Ren et al. [19] proposed a composite weighted encoding method as an alternative to traditional embedding layers. They utilized a routing algorithm based on k-means clustering theory for text classification to fully explore the relationships between capsules. DONG et al. [20] proposed a capsule network model called caps-BiLSTM for sentiment analysis. This method outperformed traditional machine learning methods and deep learning models on the MR, IMDB, and SST datasets.

3   DP-CAPS-VW-BIGRU Model

The DP-CAPS-VW-BIGRU model proposed in this paper consists of a word embedding layer, a capsule network, and a VW-BIGRU network, as shown in Fig. 1. The input layer utilizes the pretrained ERNIE model provided by Baidu to obtain the vectorized representation of the text. The capsule network layer extracts local information features of the text, while the VW-BIGRU network extracts global information features. Finally, the text classification result is obtained through softmax.

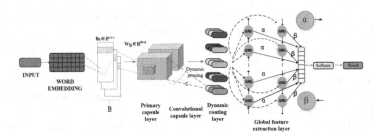

Fig. 1. DP-CAPS-VW-BIGRU Network Model Diagram

3.1   Input Layer

After performing data cleaning on the raw comment text, the cleaned text is then normalized and inputted into the pretrained ERNIE model. The text data entering the ERNIE layer are represented as $X = (X1, X2, ..., XN)$, where XN represents the Nth text.

3.2   Word Embedding Layer

ERNIE [21] is a knowledge-enhanced pretrained language model proposed by Baidu in 2019. During training, BERT uses a mask mechanism based on characters, ignoring the relationships between characters. The ERNIE model incorporates a wealth of prior semantic knowledge, enhancing the model's semantic representation capability. The specific mask mechanism is shown in Fig. 2. In this article, ERNIE is used as the word embedding layer.

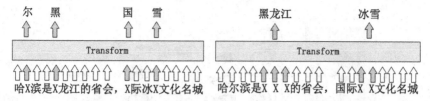

Fig. 2. Comparison of BERT and ERNIE Mask Mechanisms (Left BERT and Right ERNIE)

3.3 Capsule Network

Convolutional Layer. The convolutional layer extracts n-gram features at different positions of the ERNIE output sequence $E \in R^{L \times V}$ using convolution filters. Here, L represents the length of the text, V represents the dimension of the word embedding, and the size of the convolutional kernel $W_a \in R^{K \times V}$ represents the size of the n-gram features to be extracted. The convolutional layer has B convolutional kernels with a stride of 1. m_i^a is the i-th feature vector generated by kernel W_a at the sequence $e_{i:i+k-1}$, and the calculation formula is shown in Eq. (1).

$$m_i^a = Relu\left(e_{i:\ i+k-1} \oplus Wa + b1\right) \tag{1}$$

where, $\oplus$ represents the convolution operation, b_1 is the bias term, and M is the generated feature mapping matrix, $M = [m_1, m_2, \ldots, m_B] \in R^{(L-K+1) \times B}$ where $a \in \{1, 2, \ldots, B\}$, $m_a \in R^{(L-K+1)}$.

Primary Capsule Layer. In this network layer, the capsule network uses vector output instead of the scalar output of the convolutional network to preserve instantiation parameters. u_i is the initialized capsule vector, which is generated by sliding a filter of size $w_b \in R^{B \times b}$ over different vectors Mi, $i \in \{1, 2, \ldots, L - k + 1\}$. The calculation formula is shown in Eq. (2):

$$u_i = squash\left(M_i \otimes w_b + b2\right) \tag{2}$$

Among them, $u_i \in R^d$, d represents the capsule dimension, and the primary capsule layer has C filters that generate $u \in R^{(L-K+1) \times d}$ on each feature vector. Therefore, the number of initialized capsules generated is $(L - K + 1) \times C$. The generated capsule matrix $U = [U_1, U_2, U_3, \ldots, U_C] \in R^{(L-K+1) \times C \times d}$, where, $U_C = [u_1, u_2, u_3, \ldots, u_{(L-K+1)}] \in R^{(L-K+1) \times d}$.

Convolutional Capsule Layer. Similar to convolutional layers. Using Z transformation matrices to perform the capsule convolution operation on U, the capsule matrix $J = [J_1, J_2, J_3, \ldots, J_E] \in R^{(L-K-K1+2) \times Z \times d}$ is obtained, $J_E = [j_1, j_2, j_3, \ldots, j_{L-K-K1+2}] \in R^{(L-K-K1+2) \times d}$. Figure 3 visually displays the structure of each layer in the capsule network.

Dynamic Pruning Routing. In this paper, capsule network improvement occurs between the convolutional capsule layer and the dynamic routing layer. With increased dynamic routing iterations, certain capsule connections may weaken (coupling coefficients decrease), typically containing noise or irrelevant information to the model.

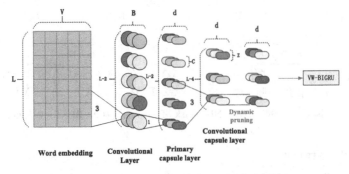

Fig. 3. DP-CAPS-VW-BIGRU Network Model Diagram

Therefore, in the last routing process of dynamic routing, this paper sets a threshold for the dynamic coupling coefficient. When the coupling coefficient is less than this threshold, the corresponding capsule is directly discarded, reducing the transmission of useless information to the parent capsule. At the same time, since different capsules represent different levels of importance, the threshold size is set as a parameter updated with the model in this paper. The dynamic pruning algorithm is shown in Table 1.

Table 1. Dynamic pruning algorithm flowchart.

DYNAMIC PRUNING ALGORITHM

Procedure ROUTING (u_j, r, t)

Initialize the coupling coefficients $b_i \leftarrow 0$
$$C_i \leftarrow softmax\ (b_i)$$
For r=1 To R do:

    for all capsule i in layer t and capsule j in t+1
$$C_{j|i} = softmax\ (b_i^r)$$
    Initialization: threshold value $\leftarrow$ 0.005

    If r=R:

        If $C_{j|i}<$threshold value:
        $C_{j|i}=0$

    Update threshold value

    For all capsule j in layer t+1:
$$s_j = \Sigma C_{j|i}u_j$$
$$v_j = squash\ (s_j)$$
    Return v_j

Where $U_j \in R^d$ represents the prediction vector, $C_{j|i}$ represents the updated coupling coefficient during the dynamic routing process, where its magnitude indicates the probability of connection between capsules, s_j represents the output of the t + 1 layer parent capsule, b_i^r represents the weight after iterative updates, and the calculation formulas are as follows:

$$b_i^r = b_i^{r-1} + a_r u_j \qquad (3)$$

$$a_r = squash\left(s_j\right) \qquad (4)$$

VW-BIGRU Layer. Traditional bidirectional GRU networks output concatenated forward and backwards extracted features with equal weights. Due to the unevenness of text features, the feature information represented by a text from backwards to forward is different from that from forward to backwards. Therefore, in this paper, a trainable weight is added to both the forward and backwards outputs of the bidirectional GRU, allowing the model to better learn different aspects of the input sequence and better capture different aspects of the sequence. Figure 4 illustrates the structure of VW-BIGRU.

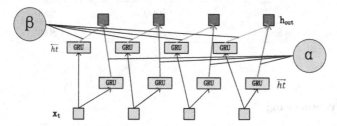

Fig. 4. VW-BIGRU Structure Diagram

In Fig. 4, α represents the weight of the forward GRU output, and β represents the weights output by the backwards GRU. In this article, these two parameters are constantly updated with the gradient, so they are called variable weight bidirectional GRU networks. The output of traditional bidirectional GRU networks is shown in Eq. (5):

$$h_{out} = \overrightarrow{h_t} + \overleftarrow{h_t} \qquad (5)$$

Variable weight bidirectional GRU network with updatable weights α, β Empowering the model with stronger ability to utilize previous and subsequent information, the output of VW-BIGRU is shown in Eq. (6):

$$h_{out} = \alpha * \overrightarrow{h_t} + \beta * \overleftarrow{h_t} \qquad (6)$$

Output layer: The forward and backwards hidden layers are spliced and sent to the full connected layer. Due to the large amount of data, to reduce the risk of "overfitting", the full connected layer introduces dropout to reduce the dimension of the data. The output layer classifier uses the softmax function for text classification and obtains text sentiment analysis results.

4 Experiment Settings

4.1 Data Set

This article selects two publicly available datasets for testing. Dataset 1 contains a total of 119988 Weibo comment texts, including 59993 texts with positive polarity (labelled 1) and 59995 texts with negative polarity (labelled 0). Dataset 2 contains two categories: universal and epidemic, each containing six emotions: happy (labelled 1), angry (labelled 0), sad (labelled 2), fearful (labelled 4), surprised (labelled 5), and emotionless (labelled 3). The sample size of each category is shown in Table 2.

Table 2. Number of categories in Dataset 2

	Train	Dev	Test
Usual	27768	2000	5000
Virus	8606	2000	3000

4.2 Data Preprocessing

Some special characters in the original text can impact the accuracy of the model. In this paper, text cleaning was performed on Dataset 1 and Dataset 2, and a portion of the cleaned text is shown in Table 3.

Table 3. Partial text after cleaning

Let us continue to develop delicious food during our break haha [hee hee] (dataset 1)	1
The girl sitting next to me started dating in October and received her certificate today (dataset 2)	5
Prevention and control of the epidemic. We always keep an eye on the latest developments together. Let us work together to prevent and control the epidemic. We must be vigilant, not underestimate, and take protective measures seriously. Let us work together. (dataset 2virus)	1

Due to the uneven distribution of some text on dataset 2. Considering the impact of uneven label distribution on the model, this article uses EDA [22] technology to expand some of the text in dataset 2. The number of texts before and after expansion is shown in Fig. 5.

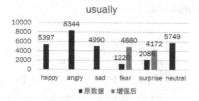
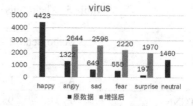

Fig. 5. Number of texts before and after data enhancement

4.3 Parameter Settings

In this experiment, the ERNIE1.0 model proposed by Baidu was used as the pretrained model. The capsule network had a filter size of 3 with 32 filters. The primary capsule layer had 32 filters with a capsule size of 16. The convolutional capsule layer had a window size of 3 with 16 filters and a size of 16. The BIGRU hidden layer had a dimension of 128, and the number of dynamic routing iterations (R) was set to 3. Additional parameters are listed in Table 4 (Table 5).

Table 4. Related model parameters

Parameter	Value
Batch size (dataset1)	25
Batch size (dataset 2)	32
Learning rate (dataset 1)	5e–5
Learning rate (dataset 2)	1e–5
Embedding Hidden size	768
dropout	0.1
Epoch	5

4.4 Evaluating Indicator

This article uses the accuracy A and F1 values on the test set as evaluation indicators, and the specific calculation formula is as follows:

$$P = \frac{T_P}{T_P + F_P} \quad R = \frac{T_P}{T_P + F_N} \tag{7}$$

$$F1 = \frac{2PR}{P + R} \quad A = \frac{T_P + T_N}{T_P + F_N + T_N + F_P} \tag{8}$$

In the above formulas, T_P represents the number of true positive cases (actual positive and predicted positive), F_P represents the number of false positive cases (actual negative but predicted positive), T_N represents the number of true negative cases (actual negative and predicted negative), and F_N represents the number of false negative cases (actual positive but predicted negative).

Table 5. The results of Various Models (%)

Model	weibo_senti_100k		smp2020			
			usual		virus	
	A	F1	A	F1	A	F1
TEXTCNN	95.41	95.39	72.12	67.33	72.59	56.48
CNN-LSTM	95.63	95.63	76.37	73.21	76.13	61.01
Capsule-A	95.54	95.54	75.83	72.35	76.29	61.32
G-Caps	96.13	96.13	76.09	72.36	76.81	61.76
Capsule-BILSTM	95.71	95.70	75.52	71.23	75.83	60.23
Capsule-VW-BIGRU	**96.44**	**96.44**	**76.86**	**73.44**	**76.53**	**61.74**
PC-Capsule-VW-BIGRU	**98.12**	**98.11**	**78.74**	**75.81**	**78.63**	**63.92**

5 Experimental Results and Discussion

5.1 Experiment 1

TEXTCNN [23]: The core idea of TextCNN is to use different-sized convolutional kernels on the input text to capture various local information.

CNN-LSTM [24]: The CNN-LSTM model initially extracts local features from the text using convolutional layers. Then, a max pooling layer is used to pool each convolutional feature into a fixed-sized vector. These vectors are then fed into an LSTM layer, which effectively handles the temporal information of the text and converts it into a fixed-sized vector representation.

Capsule A: The core of the capsule A model is a network structure composed of multiple capsule layers and fully connected layers. This model can avoid information loss caused by pooling operations in traditional convolutional neural networks.

G-Caps [25]: Yang et al. proposed a sentiment analysis model based on a unidirectional GRU and capsule feature fusion.

5.2 Experiment 2

To compare the impact of dynamic routing times on model performance in convolutional capsule layers, experiments were conducted at times 2, 3, 4, and 5. Figure 6 shows the experimental results.

5.3 Experiment 3

To verify the impact of setting thresholds on model performance in dynamic routing, experiments were conducted with threshold sizes of 0 (without improving dynamic routing), 0.01, 0.015, 0.02, 0.03, and auto (updated with the model). Figure 7 shows the experimental results.

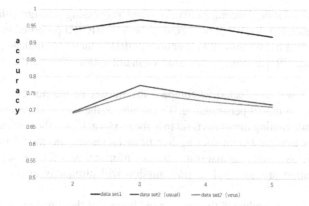

Fig. 6. Impact of Iteration Times on Model Performance

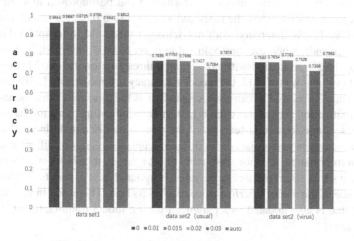

Fig. 7. Impact of Threshold on Model Performance

5.4 Result Analysis

The results of experiment 1, show that compared with TEXTCNN, Capsule-A has improved accuracy on both datasets, which demonstrates that the capsule network, using dynamic routing instead of pooling, can effectively reduce information loss. Compared with the baseline model Capsule-A, the DP-Capsule-VW-BIGRU model achieved improvements of 2.58% and 2.57% in accuracy and F1 value, respectively, on dataset 1; 2.91% and 3.46% on the "usual" category of dataset 2; and 2.34% and 2.60% on the "virus" category of dataset 2. This indicates that adding a bidirectional GRU network behind the capsule network can compensate for the capsule network's difficulty in extracting contextual information. Compared with the CNN-LSTM model, the effect of the capsule network in handling multigranularity sentiment classification tasks is significantly better than that of traditional convolutional neural networks. This also indicates that some inconspicuous feature information will be discarded by the pooling layer in traditional convolutional neural networks when processing multigranularity sentiment analysis tasks. Finally, it can be seen that the VW-BIGRU proposed in this article performs better than the traditional bidirectional GRU, which also indicates that traditional bidirectional GRU networks have insufficient utilization of forward and backwards information.

Experiment 2 was conducted to compare the impact of the number of dynamic routing iterations on model performance. The results in the figure, show that when the number of dynamic routing iterations is set to 3, the model achieves the best classification performance. As the number of routing iterations increases, the model performance decreases, which also confirms that some useless information will be generated during the dynamic routing process, and its transmission will ultimately affect the model's performance.

Experiment 3 was conducted to compare the impact of the threshold value set during dynamic routing on model classification performance. Overall, when an appropriate threshold value is set, the model's performance can be improved to some extent. Specifically, on dataset 1, when the threshold value is set to 0.02, the model's accuracy is improved by 1.52% compared with not setting a threshold (threshold value of 0); on dataset 2 (usual), when the threshold value is set to 0.01, the model's accuracy is improved by 1.52% compared with not setting a threshold; on dataset 2 (virus), when the threshold value is set to 0.015, the model's accuracy is improved by 1.30% compared with not setting a threshold. It can also be seen that as the threshold value increases, the model's classification performance tends to decrease, indicating that a too-large threshold will cause some important features of the text to be discarded, thus reducing the model's classification performance. As different capsules represent different levels of information importance, it is not reasonable to set a single threshold value for all capsules. It shows that when the threshold value is updated as a parameter during model gradient descent, the model's performance reaches its best. Therefore, in this paper, the threshold value is also updated as a parameter during model training, rather than as a hyperparameter.

6 Conclusion

In this paper, a text sentiment classification model based on capsule networks is proposed. The capsule network is used to address the problem of information loss in the pooling process of convolutional neural networks and improve the representation of detailed information. Additionally, to reduce the propagation of irrelevant information (noise) between subcapsules and parent capsules, a dynamic pruning strategy is employed during the dynamic routing process to avoid this issue. Experimental results demonstrate that the proposed model achieves good classification performance on the Weibo_senti_100k and smp2020 datasets. Future work could consider using multiple window sizes for the convolutional kernels in the capsule network layer to extract multigram syntactic information from the text.

Acknowledgements. This work was supported by the provincial and ministerial key project of the 14th Five Year Scientific Research Plan of the State Language Commission in 2022 (No. ZDI145–58) and National Social Science Fund Project (No.22XYY048).

References

1. Zhou, C., Yan, X., Yu, Z.T., Hong, X.D., Xian, Y.T.: Weibo new word recognition combining frequency characteristic and accessor variety. J. Shandong Univ. (Nat. Sci.) **50**(03), 6–10 (2015)
2. Whissell, A.C.: Objective analysis of text: II. using an emotional compass to describe the emotional tone of situation comedies. Psychol. Rep. **82**(2), 643–646 (1998)
3. Li, C., Fu, Y., Cao, Y.D.: Text sentiment classification based on phrase patterns. Comput. Sci. **04**, 132–134 (2008)
4. Thelwall, M., Buckley, K., Paltoglou, G., et al.: Sentiment strength detection in short informal text. J. Am. Soc. Inform. Sci. Technol. **61**(12), 2544–2558 (2010)
5. Pan, M.: Dictionary Based Sentiment Analysis on Chinese Weibo. Nanjing University of Aeronautics and Astronautics (2014)
6. Saif, H., He, Y., Fernandez, M., et al.: Contextual semantics for sentiment analysis of Twitter. Inf. Process. Manage. **52**(1), 5–19 (2016)
7. Li, Y., Li, X., Han, X., et al.: A bilingual dictionary based multi category emotion analysis method for weibo. J. Electr. Sci. **44**(9), 2068–2073 (2016)
8. Pang, B., Lee, L., Vaithyanathan, S.: Thumbs up? Sentiment Classification using Machine Learning Techniques. arXiv (2002)
9. Sharma, A., Dey, S.: A boosted SVM based ensemble classifier for sentiment analysis of online reviews. ACM SIGAPP Appl. Comput. Reviewed **13**(04), 43–52 (2013)
10. Jiang, H.L, Yu, M., Zhou, M., et al.: Target-dependent twitter sentiment classification. In: Proceedings of the 49th Annual Meeting of the Association for Computational Linguistics: Human Language Technologies, pp. 151–160 (2011)
11. Dragoni, M., Petrucci, G.: A fuzzy-based strategy for multidomain sentiment analysis. Informational J. Approximate Reasoning **93**(10), 59–73 (2018)
12. Ghorbani, M., Bahaghighat, M., Xin, Q., et al.: ConvLSTMConv network: a deep learning approach for sentiment analysis in cloud computing. J. Cloud Comput. Adv. Syst. Appl. **9**(1), 1–12 (2020)
13. Basiri, M.E., Nemati, S., Abdar, M., et al.: ABCDM: An attention-based bidirectional CNN-RNN deep model for sentiment analysis. Futur. Gener. Comput. Syst. **115**, 279–294 (2021)
14. Luo, F., Wang, H.: Chinese text sentiment classification using RNN and CNN hierarchical networks. J. Peking Univ. (Nat. Sci. Ed.) **54**(03), 459–465 (2018). https://doi.org/10.13209/j.0479-8023.2017.168
15. Wang, Z., Zhang, Y., Lee, S., et al.: A bilingual attention network for code-switched emotion prediction. In: Proceedings of COLING 2016, the 26th International Conference on Computational Linguistics: Technical Papers, pp. 1624–1634 (2016
16. Tang, D., Qin, B., Liu, T.: Document modelling with gated recurrent neural network for sentiment classification. In: Proceedings of the 2015 Conference on Empirical Methods in Natural Language Processing, pp. 1422–1432 (2015)
17. Yang, M., Zhao, W., Ye, J., et al.: Investigating capsule networks with dynamic routing for text classification. In: Proceedings of the 2018 Conference on Empirical Methods in Natural Language Processing, pp. 3110-3119 (2018)
18. Kim, J., Jang, J., Chois, S., et al.: Text classification using capsules. Neuro comput. **376**, 214 (2020)
19. Ren, H., Lu, H.: Compositional coding capsule network with k-means routing for text classification. Pattern Recogn. Lett. **160**, 1–8 (2022)
20. Dong, Y., Fu, Y., Wang, L., et al.: A sentiment analysis method of capsule network based on BiLSTM. IEEE access **8**, 37014–37020 (2020)

21. Sun, Y., Wang, S.H., Li, K., Wu, H.: ERNIE: enhanced representation through knowledge integration [EB/OL](2019−04−19)[2019−12−23]. https://arXiv.org/abs/1904.09223v1

22. Wei, J., Zou, K.: Eda: Easy data augmentation techniques for boosting performance on text classification tasks. arXiv preprint arXiv:1901.11196 (2019)

23. Kim, Y.: Convolutional neural networks for sentence classification. In: Proceedings of the 2014 Conference on Empirical Methods in Natural Language Processing, Doha, Qatar, pp. 1746–1751 (2014)

24. Wang, J., Yu, L.C., Lai, K.R., et al.: Dimensional sentiment analysis using a regional CNN- LSTM model. In: Proceedings of the 54th Annual Meeting of the Association For Computational Linguistics (Volume 2: Short papers), pp. 225–230 (2016)

25. Yang, Y., Sun, J., Song, G.: Text sentiment analysis based on gated recurrent unit and capsule features. J. Comput. Appl. **40**(9), 2531–2535 (2020)

Research on Ceramic E-commerce Product Review Analysis Based on Semantic Analysis

Lihua Yang[1(✉)] [iD], Xinyang Li[1], Wenye Luan[1], Jun Wang[1], and Wangren Qiu[1,2]

[1] School of Information Engineer, Jingdezhen Ceramic University, Jingdezhen, China
jdzylh@126.com
[2] China Ceramic Development Research Institute of Jingdezhen Ceramic University, Jingdezhen, China

Abstract. Emotional factors play an increasingly important role in the selection and design of ceramic products. This study used semantic analysis to analyse the emotion of ceramic product reviews. There are three main processes in this study: semantic analysis of comment text, calculation of product affective value, and linear fitting of product affective value. In the process of semantic analysis, ROSTCM6 is used to calculate the emotional polarity of the ceramic product comment text, and the emotional value can be calculated by comparison with the feature dictionary. The parameters obtained by fitting the calculated results can be used as a reference for the analysis of ceramic products. Analysing the product reviews left by consumers can not only help other consumers understand the features of the products intuitively but also urge merchants to improve the design of the products they offer, quickly grasp market trends, and make adjustments in a timely manner.

Keywords: Sentiment Analysis · E-commerce · Characteristic Sentiment Value · Ceramic Products

1 Introduction

Mobile Internet has become an indispensable part of people's lives, and shopping through networks has also been an in-depth ordinary part of people's daily lives. Due to the virtual nature of online shopping, it is difficult for users to construct an intuitive impression of goods from pictures and text descriptions [1, 2]. Therefore, consumers in the selection of goods will usually refer to the evaluation of other consumers to provide guidance for their own purchasing decisions [3].

However, with the explosion of reviews on a single product, consumers are not able to quickly extract useful information from others' reviews. At the same time, each individual is an individual, and the commodity characteristics of the indicators are not the same expectations, simply from the independent review of the results they want to obtain. In this context, it is very important to analyse the emotion of a large amount of text data [4].

© The Author(s), under exclusive license to Springer Nature Singapore Pte Ltd. 2024
M. Zhang et al. (Eds.): CCF NCCA 2023, CCIS 1959, pp. 161–167, 2024.
https://doi.org/10.1007/978-981-99-8764-1_13

By using the technology of sentiment analysis of text semantics, it can provide scientific reference results for users to select goods and help users to understand the features of goods comprehensively and quickly [5]. For the merchant, the merchant can use semantic analysis technology to understand the market demand of goods and clear the advantages and disadvantages of goods to improve the design of goods. Moreover, semantic analysis can also be used to understand the attitude of users to third-party service feedback for the selection of third-party services after reference materials [6].

2   Semantic Emotion Analysis of the Commentary Text

Based on the background of emotion analysis and the research direction of ceramics, this paper conducts emotion analysis on the comments in this field to determine the opinion information in the comments of this field and analyse the attitude and evaluation of the users towards the commodities to obtain the emotional attributes of the user to a certain feature of the product [7].

In general, the basic flow for semantic sentiment analysis is shown in Fig. 1.

Fig. 1. Basic flow of semantic analysis

First, from the e-commerce platform to crawl ceramic comment data, these data can to a certain extent reflect the consumer's emotional attitude toward goods. Because of the variety, uncertainty and complexity of real life and scientific research, the original data collected are scattered. Therefore, before you can analyse the raw data, you need to perform a data preprocessing operation. The flow of preprocessing is shown in Fig. 2.

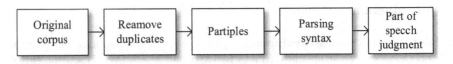

Fig. 2. Flow chart of raw corpus preprocessing

Data preprocessing needs to de-emphasize, segment, and analyse text data to turn scattered text into words that can be analysed. The general text is made up of many kinds of words, and each word has its own sense and emotion. The accumulation of the emotional polarity of the respective words constitutes the emotional value of the sentence [5].

The word segmentation operation breaks a complete sentence into individual words using spaces. For example, the string "Baby received, very beautiful, to give a friend or to their own use are very appropriate," "Will get" Baby, received, very beautiful, give a friend, or for their own use are very appropriate".

After word segmentation, we need to judge the part of speech and label the part of speech of a single word to determine the syntactic and modifying relationship between them. For example, a part-of-speech test on the previous string yields "N v U W P D A W P V N C P R v d a". The rules for part-of-speech tagging are shown in Table 1.

Table 1. Rules for part of speech tagging

Notes	Meaning	Notes	Meaning	Notes	Meaning	Notes	Meaning
b	A distinguish word	j	For short	ni	Agency number	q	Measure words
a	Adjectives	i	Idioms	nl	Noun of place	r	Pronouns
d	Adverbs	k	Followed by the ingredient	ns	Place names	u	Auxiliary words
c	Conjunction	m	Numerals	nt	Time word	v	Verbs
e	Exclamations	n	Nouns	nz	Other names	wp	punctuation
g	Morphemes	nd	Noun of position	o	Onomatopoeia	ws	String
h	Antecedent ingredient	nh	Names	p	Prepositions	x	Nonmorpheme words

After part-of-speech judgment, the emotional polarity of each word is determined according to the emotion dictionary of ROSTCM6, and the final emotional value of the whole sentence is the sum of the emotional polarity of all words. Calculate the characteristic emotional value of the commodity.

The structured data obtained from the affective analysis of the text can be used as a corpus to extract the key information according to certain rules. Usually, the "Feature, emotional word" model is used to extract feature words and evaluation words from all texts to calculate the emotional value of a feature of a commodity [8, 9]. First, segmentation of all words can obtain the high-frequency words of the whole text, and from these high-frequency words can obtain the feature words of goods. Second, the characteristic words are induced to construct the characteristic words dictionary. Finally, the affective value of the commodity can be obtained by comparing the dictionary of the feature words. Through the analysis of the emotional value of a feature, the degree of a feature of goods can be directly seen.

Build a dictionary of feature words to facilitate the collection of ceramic product features. In this study, 14 ceramic bottles were collected from Tmall, and all comments were cleaned and word-segmentation processed. Some of the results are shown in Table 2.

The statistical results were classified and combined to select six characteristics that best reflect the nature of the commodity as ceramic commodity indicators. The six features and the second-level words that belong to the same feature form the dictionary of features. The specific contents of the dictionary are shown in Table 3.

Table 2. Partial results of word frequency statistics

Words	Word frequency	Words	Word frequency	Words	Word frequency	Words	Word frequency
Vase	1014	Work	624	Damaged	264	Color	238
Satisfied	917	Atmosphere	534	Fine	261	Seller	236
Beautiful	911	Baby	474	Living Room	259	Purchase	235
Packaging	799	Logistics	451	Classy	255	Worth it	221
Roger that	770	Good reviews	304	Patterns	248	Put it on	203
Quality	739	Exquisite	274	Soon	239	Tight	199
Nice	676	Services	268	Attitude	238	Home	196

Table 3. Dictionary of characteristic words

Features	Characteristic words
Logistics	Express delivery, speed, arrival, transportation, delivery
Price	Price, value, cost-performance ratio
Appearance	Picture, color, pattern, pattern, color, color difference, color, texture, decal, glaze color
Style	Effect, grade, collocation, style, modelling, pattern, size
Function	Effect

This paper uses the dictionary of feature words to search the feature words that belong to all the comments of the product, takes the average value of the sentences that contain the feature words, and obtains the average value of a feature of the product. The higher the value is, the more positive the feedback is; the lower the value is, the more negative the feedback is.

3 Linear Fitting was Used to Fit the Emotional Value of Commodity Characteristics

After calculating the 6 features of 14 commodities, we can obtain the emotional value vector of 14 commodities by adding the sales volume of each commodity to the emotional value word. By arranging the 14 vectors vertically, a matrix of 14 * 7 is obtained, as shown in Table 4.

These 14 vectors can be viewed as 14 discrete points corresponding to 14 observations of the overall mass of ceramic bottles on the market. The discrete points in the analysis process cannot reflect the characteristics of the ceramic bottle market well, so it is

Table 4. The results of semantic analysis

	Quality	Logistics	Price	Appearance	Style	Function	Sales
Goods_01	2.045	9.889	1.486	3.166	9.468	5.884	146
Goods_02	7.935	8.949	0.373	4.665	1.161	9.250	164
Goods_03	7.094	1.165	8.900	1.375	1.346	4.036	114
Goods_04	0.758	8.922	0.871	0.940	1.498	9.380	97
Goods_05	8.707	6.340	1.872	5.391	9.331	7.398	149
Goods_06	4.171	9.478	6.674	1.370	1.583	0.660	93
Goods_07	0.333	4.323	3.103	3.377	1.179	1.437	88
Goods_08	3.886	4.322	8.597	3.515	3.654	8.664	127
Goods_09	9.068	8.890	7.267	5.020	8.318	3.224	214
Goods_10	5.195	8.845	0.551	6.745	9.551	7.628	192
Goods_11	6.074	4.961	7.375	0.181	8.343	8.805	185
Goods_12	7.099	3.143	6.943	7.397	0.839	5.052	155
Goods_13	3.912	3.400	9.043	7.215	6.105	4.70	188
Goods_14	2.927	4.944	9.201	2.470	2.0216	6.848	119

necessary to further study the impact of the ceramic bottle market characteristics on sales through the form of functions; therefore, the 14 items need to be linear fitting of the emotional value of the characteristics of processing.

The concrete process of linear fitting is to divide the 14 * 7 matrix into a 14 * 6 affective value matrix and a 14 * 1 sales vector. Using the regress function of MATLAB, the emotion value matrix can be fitted linearly with six variables, and the fitting results are shown in Table 5.

Table 5. Linear fitting results

	Quality	Logistics	Price	Appearance	Style	Function
Influence coefficient	4.28	3.15	3.96	6.7	5.04	3.16

The fitted function is:

$$f(x) = 4.28x_1 + 3.15x_2 + 3.96x_3 + 6.70x_4 + 5.04x_5 + 3.16x_6 + 16.41 \qquad (1)$$

The larger the fitted coefficient is, the greater the impact of this feature on sales [10].

The fitting function needs to be validated before processing the data. The verification method is to select a commodity from the re-e-commerce platform, analyse it according to the same processing method, and use ROSTCM6 to calculate its characteristic emotion value (7.778, 2.275, 7.315, 9.370, 2.377.3.680). The group of data is brought into the fitting function, and the fitting value is 172.22, which is close to the real value of 188. Therefore, the parameters of the fitting function can be used as reference data.

4   Conclusion

According to the result of linear fitting, the influence coefficient of quality, logistics, price, appearance, style and function on sales volume can be obtained. Table 5 shows that appearance is the most influential factor among the six factors, and quality, style, price, logistics and function are the two least influential factors among the six factors.

Further analysis of the data first shows that the impact of sales is far greater than the impact of other factors, indicating that consumers buying ceramic bottles is not only the functional value of ceramic bottles; relatively speaking, consumers are more concerned about the ornamental value of goods. Second, style has the greatest influence on sales after appearance, while "Quality", the most important indicator of practicality, is only the third, reflecting that consumers are more concerned about the ornamental value of ceramic products. The degree to which each factor affects sales can be visualized in Fig. 3.

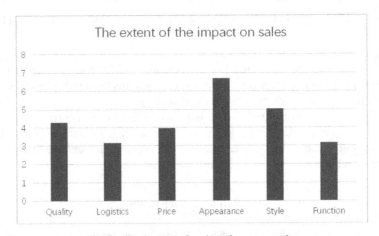

Fig. 3. The impact of various factors on sales

In summary, the following suggestions can be made: businesses should focus on the appearance of ceramic goods design, enhance the design of the commodity itself, and use a more modern, beautiful appearance style to further cater to market consumption trends. In addition, ceramic manufacturers should increase the style of ceramic products so that consumers have more choices.

Project Support. Jiangxi Provincial Education Department Science and Technology Project (GJJ201342); Jingdezhen City Science and Technology Project (20212GYZZD009–05); Innovation Project for Students at Jingdezhen University of Ceramics (202110408024); Jiangxi Social Science Planning Commission Project (2023WT03)

References

1. Chen, P.: Research Onemotion Mining of User's Viewpoint in E-Commerce Environment. Sichuan Normal University (2019)
2. Zhang, Y.: A Study on the Selection of Foreign Trade E-Commerce Products Based on Sentiment Analysis and Sales Forecast. Beijing Jiaotong University (2019)
3. Chen, Y.: Research on Sentiment Analysis of Commentary Text Based on Deep Semantic Features. Wuhan University of Science and Technology (2019)
4. Hui, S.Y.: Research on Text Sentiment Analysis Based on Deep Semantic Features. Hangzhou Dianzi University (2018)
5. Esther, Z.Y., Zhang, X., Yu, X.: Consumer preference analysis based on product review mining. Inf. Sci. **40**(01), 58–65 (2022). https://doi.org/10.13833/J.ISSN.1007-7634,2022.01.009
6. Law, H.C.: Research and Application of Recommendation Algorithm based on Semantic Analysis. North China University of Technology (2019)
7. Yang, B.: User interest evolution model based on semantic analysis. Jiangsu Bus. Rev. **04**, 22–24 (2020)
8. Montgomery. Research on User Product Reviews Based on Text Mining Technology. Hebei University of Economics and Business (2022). https://doi.org/10.27106/d.CNKI.Ghbju.2022.000290
9. Hong, K.: Winter Festival. Research on Sentiment Analysis Based On E-Commerce Product Reviews. Heilongjiang University (2022).https://doi.org/10.27123/d.CNKI.Ghlju.2022.000821
10. Nie, Q.: Analysis and research on user evaluation of ceramic e-commerce products based on semantic analysis. Mall Modernization **21**, 19–21 (2020). https://doi.org/10.14013/J.CNKI.SCXDH.2020.21.007

Research on Clarification Question Recognition and Generation in Intelligent Q&A

Juncheng Hou[1,3], Wen Du[1,2(✉)], Qing Mu[1], Kunpeng Zhang[2], and Zhidong He[2]

[1] The First Research Institute of Telecommunications Science and Technology,
Shanghai 200032, China
daviddu999@outlook.com
[2] DS Information Technology CO., LTD., Shanghai 200032, China
[3] Shanghai Research Institute of Criminal Science and Technology, Shanghai 200083, China

Abstract. Intelligent question answering systems often encounter ambiguous questions that require the generation of clarification questions to understand users' true intentions. Without clarification questions, syestems may be confused by ambiguous questions. In this paper, the generation of clarification questions is separated into three subtasks. This study focuses on the three subtasks of the clarification question identification and generation process. We propose the DeBERTA v3 + FC model for clarification question detection and entity prediction, and an improved ByT5-based model for generating diverse and comprehensible clarification questions. On the MSParS dataset, our method outperforms traditional DMN models by 11.2% and 15.17% in accuracy for clarification question detection and entity prediction tasks respectively, while the BLEU score is 4.9% higher than the traditional Seq2Seq models. The efficacy of our proposed methods is verified by their superior performance to traditional methods on all three subtasks. The results on the MSParS dataset demonstrate the effectiveness of our framework for generating clarification questions and entity predictions.

Keywords: Intelligent Question Answering Systems · Clarification Questions · Identification and Generation · Entity Prediction

1 Introduction

Questioning is a fundamental aspect of natural language human-computer interaction systems, including conversational information retrieval and conversational question answering. These systems aim to bridge the gap between users and machines [1]. In particular, clarification is a commonly used tool for knowledge-based Q&A, especially when addressing ambiguous questions [2]. For such ill-defined questions, it can be challenging to provide a satisfactory answer without first asking clarifying questions to confirm the questioner's intention. Therefore, detecting and generating clarification questions is of great practical significance and has garnered attention from academia and industry [3].

However, at the outset of the research, there was a paucity of datasets for clarifying questions, which significantly hindered progress for some scholars and research teams. Stoyanchev et al. [4] propose a method for randomly removing a phrase from a question and asking an annotator to clarify the resulting question, e.g., the question: "Do you know XXX's birthday?" However, the size of the dataset limited the method's generality and applicability. Later, Guo et al. [5] presented a more extensive synthetic dataset, QRAQ, that relies on entity/variable substitution. Li et al. [6] propose a method for creating ambiguous questions by replacing entities in the question with misspelled word parts, which is groundbreaking but leads to unnatural questions. Xu et al. [7] construct the open-domain clarification corpus CLAQUA, which supports all three primary clarification tasks. They also propose a coarse-to-fine clarification problem generation model based on Seq2Seq and Transformer models as the baseline, which significantly improves performance.

The traditional method of clarifying problem generation involves manually setting rules to address context semantic generation clarification problems. However, this method is time-consuming, labor-intensive, and difficult to apply to different fields [8]. With the rapid development of natural language processing in representation learning and text generation, deep learning-based methods have been proposed and applied to this task [9]. For example, Gao et al. [10] improve traditional Seq2Seq performance by proposing a difficulty estimator to generate clarification questions according to different difficulty levels. Similarly, Rao et al. [11] construct a model based on generative adversarial networks (GANs) that generate clarification questions by estimating potential problem validity. However, existing methods lacked consideration from the user's point of view, had OOV problems when generating clarification questions, and did not have a good understanding of ambiguous statements.

To address these shortcomings, we first present a framework for the algorithmic flow of clarification questions. Research on clarification questions can be broadly divided into three parts: clarification question detection, clarification question generation (CQG), and final entity prediction. In this paper, we examine these three parts by combining single-turn Q&A and multi-turn Q&A. We propose a DeBERTa-based model for clarification question recognition and entity prediction, significantly improving the accuracy of the current SOTA model. Additionally, we propose a clarification question generation framework based on ByT5 that accurately understands the user's intentions and clearly repeats the user's ambiguous questions, using easy-to-understand and representative language to ask the user's final intentions. This approach resolves the issue of nonhumanized and rigid clarification questions, filling the gap in the generation of a representative framework for clarifying questions.In conclusion, our approach provides an improved method for generating clarification questions that is more user-centered, accurate, and understandable, thereby enhancing communication between humans and machines.

In this paper, Sect. 2 describes the process of detecting and generating clarification questions. Section 3 introduces the improved model that incorporates clarification question detection and entity prediction. Section 4 outlines the proposed architecture for clarification question generation and its specific details. In Sect. 5, we conduct ablation experiments and comparative experiments to verify the effectiveness of the proposed model. Finally, the paper concludes with a summary of the study's findings.

2 Design of Clarification Process Framework

We first present our framework for the algorithmic flow of clarification questions, which divides the overall algorithm process into three subtasks, i.e., clarification question detection, clarification question generation, and entity prediction. These tasks are defined as Task1, Task2, and Task3, respectively, as illustrated in Fig. 1 below:

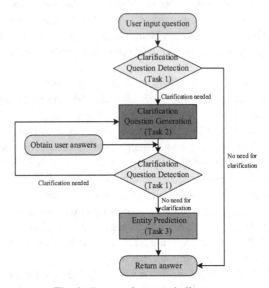

Fig. 1. Process framework diagram

2.1 Task 1: Clarification Question Detection

The detection of clarification questions is the initial and crucial step in the entire task, as it determines whether the QA system comprehends the user's intention and properly addresses it. The detection process takes into account the dialogue context and analyses the specific context of the question and the knowledge base information provided to judge whether the system needs to clarify the current question.

In this task, the input comprises the user and system's historical dialogue, from round 0 to t $< U_0, M_0, U_1, M_1, ..., U_t >$, where U_k denotes the k-th round of the user session and M_k denotes the k-th round of the system session. The output is the system's prediction of whether the current question requires clarification and can also serve as a binary text classification task. By analysing the user's question and employing previous rounds of dialogue knowledge information, reasoning can determine whether the user requires clarification of their question.

2.2 Task 2: Clarification Question Generation

If the outcome of the detection of clarification questions is true, the intelligent question answering system instigates the generation of a corresponding clarification question to seek a more precise understanding of the user's intent. The input data are the user and system's historical dialogue from round 0 to t, $< U_0, M_0, U_1, M_1, ..., U_t >$. The output generated by the system is a clarification question Q. Through the analysis of previous rounds of dialogue information, clear or ambiguous expressions that do not express the user's intention accurately are extracted, and the system formulates questions in natural language to elicit the user's true intent.

2.3 Task 3: Entity Prediction

After clarifying the user's questions, the intelligent question answering system must further evaluate and comprehend the user's answers. The input for this task is denoted by $< U_0, M_0, U_1, M_1, ..., U_t, Q, A >$, where Q represents the clarification question asked by the system, and A represents the user's corresponding answer. The model output is the entity referred to by the user in their response A. Thus, based on all relevant conversation information, the system infers the user's intention and identifies the appropriate entity.

2.4 Overall Process

The process for the clarification question algorithm involves three distinct tasks: clarification question detection, clarification question generation, and entity prediction. When users input natural language questions, the system initially determines whether their questions are ambiguous. If clarification is necessary, the system extracts relevant information from the user's query, generates a corresponding natural language clarification question, and awaits the user's response. This response is then analysed to determine whether further clarification is needed, and the process continues until the user provides a clear question that requires no further elucidation. Once a clear question is provided, the system combines the user's answer with the dialogue history to extract the central entity. If no clarification is needed, the answer is immediately returned by the system.

3 The Model of Clarification Question Detection and Entity Prediction

This paper utilizes the DeBERTa pre-training model for problem detection. Microsoft introduced the decoding-enhanced BERT with disentangled attention(DeBERTa) model in 2021 [12].

The DeBERTa model improves upon the BERT and RoBERTa [13] models through two new methods: attention decoupling and an enhanced mask decoder. The attention decoupling mechanism represents each input word using two independent vectors for content and location. Meanwhile, its attention weight between words is calculated through a decoupling matrix of their content and relative positions. Similar to BERT, DeBERTA uses MLM mask language modelling for pretraining. While distraction mechanisms account for the content and relative position of contextual words, they do not consider the absolute position of those words, which is critical for prediction in many cases.

Additionally, the enhanced mask decoder merges all transformer layers before the softmax layer to predict mask words. This allows DeBERTa to capture relative positions in all transformers and add absolute position information only when decoding mask words.

For clarification question detection, the dataset is cleaned, and the DeBERTa v3 [14] architecture segments words and extracts feature vectors. The final hidden layer state splices into a fully connected layer to obtain the label for whether it is a clarification question. The model structure diagram is shown in Fig. 2 below:

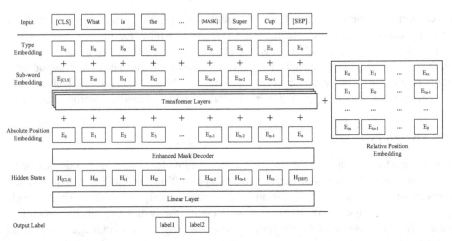

Fig. 2. Structural diagram of clarification question detection model

3.1 Disentangled Attention

In the BERT model, each word in the input layer is represented using a vector obtained by summing the word content embedding and word position embedding. This is achieved by adding Token Embedding, Segmentation Embedding, and Position Embedding. On the other hand, the DeBERTa architecture utilizes bidirectional quantity notation to embed both content and location into each word. For a word at i, the vector H_i is used to represent its content embedding, $P_{i|j}$ represents its relative position embedding relative to the word at j, the cross-attention score for words at i and j is $A_{i,j}$, and the score is calculated as follows:

$$A_{i,j} = \{H_i, P_{i|j}\} \times \{H_j, P_{j|i}\}^T$$
$$= H_i H_j^T + H_i P_{j|i}^T + P_{i|j} H_j^T + P_{i|j} P_{j|i}^T \tag{1}$$

In formula (1), it is observed that the weight of a word's attention not only depends on its content, but also has a strong correlation with its position. The weight of a word's attention can be calculated as the sum of four attentions: content-to-content, content-to-location, and position-to-content. Since location-to-location completely separates the importance of content, its reference value is very low, and the information it provides is negligible, so it will be ignored $P_{i|j} P_{j|i}^T$ in this experiment.

3.2 Enhanced Mask Decoder

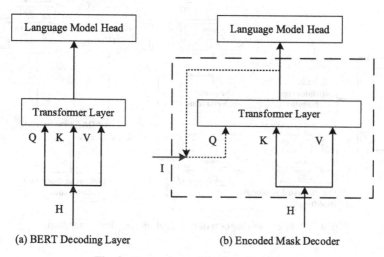

Fig. 3. Comparison of the decoding layer

The EMD (Encoded Mask Decoder) structure is shown in Fig. 3(b) above. The EMD structure has two inputs: H and I. Here, H represents the hidden state of the previous transformer layer, while input I represents any necessary information used for decoding. N represents the number of stacked layers of EMD. The output of each EMD is the input I for the next EMD, and the output of the last EMD is directly fed into the LM head. When I = H and n = 1, the encoded mask decoder layer is the same as the BERT decoder. In the model settings in this chapter, we set n = 2 to reduce the number of parameters, and the input I for the first layer is an absolute position embedding.

4 The Model of Clarification Question Generation

First, this paper intends to address this task through text summarization, that is, to summarize the QAD part of the dataset and form a restated problem description clarify_state and ques_term, which is placed at the beginning of the question; E, E_ATT, and E_DESC represent the entity name, entity attribute and entity description, respectively, and summarize them in text to obtain a descriptive overview of two entities entity_desc. However, during the experiment, we found that generating clarify_state and ques_term together affects the accuracy of the results, i.e., it enhances the generation effect of ques_term and weakens the generation effect of clarify_state.

After several poor attempts, this paper splits the overall model structure into the following three parts: Model 1 problem retelling model, Model 2 entity difference generation model, and question answering terminology module. In this paper, before passing into Model 1 and Model 2 the data need special processing, so the attribute tree module and semantic understanding module are added. Finally, the output of the two models is merged and stitched with the template to obtain the final generated clarification problem. The overall model architecture diagram is shown in Fig. 4 below:

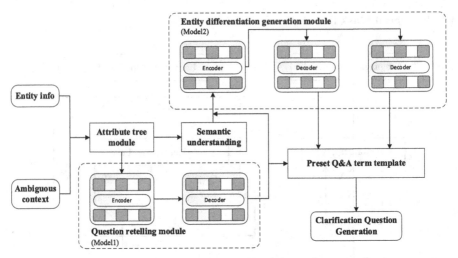

Fig. 4. Architecture diagram of clarification question generation

4.1 Attribute Tree and Semantic Understanding Module

The original JSON data take too long to train when input into the model due to their excessive length. Although the data have been cleaned of irrelevant information, the two models have different tasks that require different information. Therefore, the data preprocessing before entering Model 1 is called Module 1, which includes the attribute tree module, and the data preprocessing before entering Model 2 is called Module 2, which includes both the attribute tree module and the semantic understanding module. The specific flow chart is shown in Fig. 5 below:

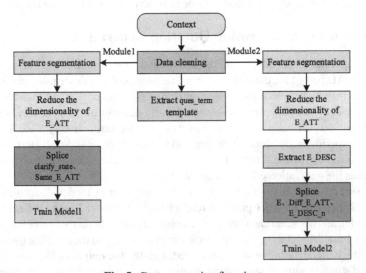

Fig. 5. Data processing flowchart

In Module 1, the cleaned text data are used for feature segmentation, and then E_ATT is reduced in dimension (specific segmentation characters in the dataset < SP >, < S > etc.), which is also the ultimate purpose of the attribute tree module. During the process of generating clarify_state, the dataset is used in several ways, including simple para-phrasing users' questions, extracting entities mentioned by users, extracting common attributes of two entities E as attributes of E, and directly replacing two entities E with the same attribute value. Therefore, the dimensionality reduction process of Module 1 is to treat the E_ATT as the attribute tree of the entity, extract the common attributes and attribute values in the two attribute trees, and record them as Same_E_ATT. The different attributes in the two entities E1 and E2 are recorded as Diff_E1_ATT and Diff_E2_ATT, while the different attribute values are discarded in Module 1 and used in Module 2. For example:

| E1_ATT : media_common.creative_work ratings.rated_entity theater.production |
| E2_ATT : media_common.creative_work award.winning_work ratings.rated_entity |
| Same_E_ATT: media_common.creative_work ratings.rated_entity |
| Diff_E1_ATT: theater.production |
| Diff_E2_ATT: award.winning_work |

After dimension reduction of attributes, it is convenient to extract synonyms or attributes from the same Same_E_ATT of two entities for replacement when generating clarify_state to enhance the diversity and generalization of model generation and facili-tate the model to learn synonyms and sentences from it. The final input of Model 1 is in the form of [clarify_state < SP > Same_E_ATT]. Example input data are as follows:

| Directors of Two Trains Running **<SP>** media_common.creative_work rat-ings.rated_entity theater.production award.winning_work me-dia_common.cataloged_instance |

In Module 2, the first is the attribute tree module. It utilizes the cleaned text for feature segmentation, and performs E_ ATT dimensionality reduction, but the dimensionality reduction process of Module 2 is different from that of Module 1. In the process of gen-erating the entity_desc of the dataset, to distinguish between two entities E, if they do not have the same name, it is easy to distinguish between the two entities. Simply list the user to know which entity E to point to. In contrast, entities usually have different attributives, which may appear in the E_ATT or E_DESC of the two entities, to distinguish entities with the same name. Therefore, in Module 2 we extract different attributes Diff_E_ATT separately, and discard the same attributes Same_E_ATT. The different attribute values Diff_E1_ATT and Diff_E2_ATT in the two entities E are retained.

Through the calculation of regular expressions, in most cases (more than half), entity_desc of different names of E uses different attribute Diff_E_ATT as attributive and uses E_DESC of the two entities to generate different descriptions. For example, when information such as year, location, occupation appears, etc., priority will be given to using them as attributives to distinguish them. Therefore, the purpose of the extraction of E_DESC is to extract useful relevant information and remove redundant information.

The semantic understanding module uses TF-IDF for the calculation of text similarity. The TF-IDF method requires calculating both Term Frequency and Inverse Document Frequency [15]. Word frequency means that the more times a word appears in the text, the more relevant it is to the text topic. Inverse text frequency means that the more times a word appears in multiple texts in the entire text collection, the worse the distinguishing ability of the word, indicating that the word has a worse ability to discriminate. When the word frequency and inverse text frequency are calculated, these two values are multiplied to obtain get the TF-IDF value of a word, and the larger the TF-IDF value of a word in the article, the more important the term is in this article.

Through TF-IDF similarity calculation, it is concluded that 96.12% of the strong correlation descriptions of entity_desc and E_DESC appear in the first 5 sentences of the E_DESC, the remaining text is either too redundant E_DESC (the longest text can reach 15680 characters), or E_DESC tends to be narrative, which may be the story line of entity E, the biography, etc. Therefore, the relevant dataset has a limited relationship with entity E regardless of the extraction, and thus has a limited overall negligible impact. The maximum length of the input in this setting is 1024. The comprehensive evaluation shows that the first four sentences of E_DESC have the best text effect, and they are recorded as E_DESC_n.

The input of Model 2 is a splicing of E, Diff_E_ATT, and E_DESC_n, and the input form is: [E1 < S > Diff_E1_ATT < S > E1_DESC_4 < TSP > E2 < S > Diff_E2_ATT < S > E2_DESC_4].Example data are as follows:

Two Trains Running <S> award.nominated_work <S> Two Trains Running is a 1991 pre-Broadway theater production of the play by August Wilson, performed at Kennedy Center. <TSP> Two Trains Running <S> <S> Two Trains Running is a 2006-2007 theater production of the play by August Wilson.

4.2 ByT5 Model

This paper uses the ByT5 model as a pre-training model for problem generation.The T5 (Text-To-Text Transfer Transformer) model is a model proposed by Google in 2020 [16], which converts all natural language processing tasks into text-to-text tasks.

T5 model compares various architectures in pre training, such as the Encoder-Decoder model, language model, and Prefix LM model, where the encoder takes in the entire input sequence and passes the result to the decoder. The representative models of this architecture are BART, MASS, etc. The language model is equivalent to using only the decoder part, and only the data information of the previous time step can be seen within the current time step, which is often used in machine translation.The representative models of this architecture are GPT2, CTRL, etc.; The third Prefix LM type is a fusion of the encoder and the decoder, one part of which can see all the data information, and the other part can only see the past information like the decoder. The representative model is UniLM. To make the model have a unified input and output mode, T5 adds a prefix before the input sequence Sequence A. The prefix format not only contains the label, but also contains the essence of the task to be solved, and the unified format of T5 input and output is shown in Fig. 6 below:

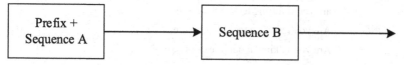

Fig. 6. The input and output diagram of T5 model

The T5 model uses the architecture of the original transformer and does not modify it on a large scale.but highlights some key aspects. The encoder and decoder are still retained, and the sublayers become subcomponents, containing the self-attention layer and the feed-forward network. Self-attention is order independent, using the matrix dot product for operations, and positional encoding is added to the embedding of words before the dot product. T5 modifies the position embedding of the original trans-former, using relative position embedding, and the position encoding is shared while re-evaluating in all layers of the model.

ByT5 is an improvement on the T5 model. In the existing model mainly based on word segmentation, an attempt is made to use a byte-based approach for segmentation, replacing the traditional SentencePiece vocabulary [17] with UTF-8 bytes to directly enter the model without any data processing and using 256 different bytes and three special tag characters for byte embedding. In addition, the improved model pretraining no longer adds 100 new ID tags for sentinels, but reuses the last 100 byte IDs and replaces the mask longer byte span with the average mask length. ByT5 makes the encoder depth three times that of the decoder, making this heavier encoder outstanding in text generation and text classification tasks.

4.3 Q&A Term Template

The development of deep learning is weakening the concept of templates, because the setting of templates is easily solidifies people's thinking and increases manpower, main-tenance and other costs. Therefore, this task adopts the idea of weak templates and extracts a fixed template by matching and calculating through regular expressions.The fixed Q&A terms that rank among the top 6 in ques_term and whose repetition exceeds 10% of the total, are used as templates for ques_term, as shown in the following table (Table 1):

5 Experiments

5.1 Dataset

This experiment is performed on the public dataset MSParS (Multi-perspective Semantic ParSing Dataset). MSParS is a large-scale dataset published by Microsoft Research Asia for open-domain multi-type semantic analysis tasks. This dataset (V2.0) contains

Table 1. Extracted Q&A Terminology Template

Q&A Template
Which one do you mean, < e > or < e >
are you referring to < e > or < e >
Are you referring to < e > or < e >
Are you talking about < e > or < e >
Do you mean < e > or < e >
are you talking about < e > or < e >

approximately 81,826 natural language problems and their corresponding structured semantic representations, covering 12 different domain problem types. It is currently the most comprehensive semantic analysis dataset in academia. MSParS is annotated based on Microsoft's Open Domain Knowledge Graph Satori. Entities, predicates and types in MSParS follow the standard form in Satori.

In this paper, experiments are performed on single-turn, multi-turn, and single + Multi datasets. The data of the experiments are shown in the following table (Table 2):

Table 2. Experimental Dataset

Class	Task	Train(piece)	Val(piece)	Test(piece)
Single-turn	Task1	10099	853	1175
	Task2	3507	431	497
	Task3	3502	431	502
Multi-turn	Task1	20462	973	828
	Task2	12173	372	384
	Task3	12173	372	384
Single + Multi	Task1	30561	1826	2003
	Task2	15680	803	384
	Task3	15675	803	384

5.2 Evaluation Indicators and Benchmark Models

In this paper, Task 1 clarification detection and Task 3 entity prediction use the accuracy P and F1 values as the performance indicators of the model. Task 2 clarification question generation uses the BLEU (Biling Evaluation Understudy) score [18] as the evaluation indicator of the model. The BLEU score was originally widely used in the field of machine translation to assess the quality of translations by comparing the similarity of machine translation output translations to the translations given in the original corpus.

At present, the BLEU score is widely used in the field of text generation and is one of the most widely used automatic evaluation indicators, which evaluates the advantages and disadvantages of the model by calculating the difference between the content generated after model training and the actual content given. It is calculated as the n-grammatical mean of n = 1 to N and the shorter output is penalized by a short penalty. Its calculation formula is shown as (2), (3).

$$BP = \begin{cases} 1, L_{sys} > L_{ref} \\ e^{(1-L_{ref}/L_{sys})}, L_{sys} \leq L_{ref} \end{cases} \tag{2}$$

$$BLEU = BP * \exp(\sum_{n=1}^{N} W_n * \log p_n) \tag{3}$$

where L_{sys} is the length of the model output, L_{ref} is the length of the reference text in the original corpus, the standard value of BLEU's N is 4, different N-gram lengths are rarely used, and W_n are positive weights of 1. p_n is the number of matching n-grams in the model output divided by the number of n-grams in the original corpus.

5.3 Experimental Environment

This chapter conducts all experiments using Torch.Due to graphics memory limitations, this chapter uses Nvidia Tesla T4 16 GB graphics cards for training and testing on Task 1 and Task 3, and Nvidia Tesla A40 48 GB graphics cards for training and testing on Task 2.The hardware settings and software environment of the experiment are shown in the following table (Table 3):

Table 3. Experimental environment configuration

Class	Specific configuration
CPU	Inter(R) Xeon(R) Platinum 8253 CPU @ 2.20GHz × 4
Internal storage	64 GB
GPU	Nvidia Tesla T4/ Nvidia Tesla A40
Python version	3.7
Torch version	1.6.0 + cu101

5.4 Results and Discussion

The Results of Clarification Question Detection. In this experiment, three pre-trained models BERT, RoBERTa, and Longformer were selected for ablation experiments.They were carried out on single-turn question answering, multi-turn question answering and single + Multi question answering datasets.Due to the limitations of the length of the results, each experiment showed the results of accuracy and F1 value. The results are shown in Tables 4 and 5:

Table 4. Ablation experiment on clarification question detection (Acc)

Model	Single-Turn(test)	Multi-Turn(test)	Single + Multi(val)	Single + Multi(test)
BERT + FC	0.791	0.819	0.829	0.803
RoBERTa + FC	0.800	0.826	0.826	0.811
Longformer + FC	0.843	0.873	0.875	0.858
DeBERTa-v3 + FC	**0.928**	**0.946**	**0.946**	**0.935**

Table 5. Ablation experiment on clarification question detection (F1)

Model	Single-Turn(test)	Multi-Turn(test)	Single + Multi(val)	Single + Multi(test)
BERT + FC	0.752	0.781	0.789	0.764
RoBERTa + FC	0.776	0.811	0.810	0.796
Longformer + FC	0.818	0.849	0.846	0.838
DeBERTa-v3 + FC	**0.915**	**0.944**	**0.939**	**0.928**

Tables 4 and 5 show that our proposed model of clarification question detection has very good performance, i.e., both the accuracy and the F1 score improve by 10% compared to the original pre-trained BERT model, and are nearly 8.23% higher than the Longformer pre-training model. In the comparison between single-turn dialogue and multi-turn dialogue, the results show that the accuracy and F1 value of multi-turn dialogue are nearly 2% higher than those of single-turn dialogue, because the user provides more information in multi-turn dialogue, which is convenient for the model to obtain more information. Meanwhile, most of the single-turn dialogue has the same name entities, and the difficulty of distinguishing between entities with the same name is much greater than that of nonsame-name entities, which is one of the reasons affecting the accuracy of the model. In addition, the F1 score is slightly lower than the accuracy score, indicating that the model has a slight category imbalance, which is also closely related to the inconsistency of the number of single-turn and multi-turn conversations.

The comparative experiment of clarification question detection selected CNN, Transformer, HAN (Hierarchical Attention Networks) [19] and DMN (Dynamic Memory Networks) [20] as comparisons. The HAN model was proposed in 2016, using a bidirectional GRU structure and considering the attention mechanism at the word and sentence level. The DMN mainly uses the triplet of < input - question - answer > as input, calculating the vector representation of all inputs and questions and training the processing of the attention mechanism with questions. The relevant facts are retrieved in the input. The memory module provides all the relevant vectors of facts to the answer module to generate answers. The results of the clarification question detection comparison experiment are as follows (Table 6):

Table 6. Comparative experiment on clarification question detection (Acc)

Model	Single-Turn(test)	Multi-Turn(test)	Single + Multi(test)
CNN	0.801	0.721	0.767
Transformer	0.822	0.704	0.773
HAN	0.809	0.822	0.815
DMN	0.840	0.798	0.823
DeBERTa-v3 + FC	**0.928**	**0.946**	**0.935**

This comparative experiment shows the powerful ability of the clarification question detection model, overwhelmingly supassing the traditional neural network model. And the pre-trained model makes DeBERTa-v3 + FC surpass the DMN model by 11.2% in accuracy and it is also the only model that can achieve more than 90% of the results. However, the recognition accuracy of the multi-turn model exceeds that of the single-turn model, while the traditional neural network models have high single-turn question answering accuracy. This indicates that our DeBERTa-v3 + FC model is different from the traditional model in extracting key information. The more information there is, the higher the recognition rate and the better the generalization ability.

The Results of Clarification Question Generation. Due to the memory limit of the graphics card, the base ByT5 is selected for the experiment. The ablation experiment in this section uses T5 (base), mT5 (base) and ByT5 (small) for experiments. The Module1 and Module2 ablation experiments are shown in Tables 7 and 8 below:

Table 7. Result generated by Module1 (BLEU)

Model	Single + Multi (val)	Single + Multi(test)
T5	0.476	0.463
mT5	0.485	0.479
ByT5-small	0.483	0.462
ByT5-base	**0.515**	**0.499**

It can be seen from the above table that the generative model based on ByT5-base shows very good performance, improved by 7.21% and 11.88%, respectively, compared to the original T5 model on the test set. When compared with the generative model based on ByT5-small, the larger pre-training model has a positive effect on the BLEU score. However, the results are often closely related to training data, and there are still differences between different data.

The clarification question generation comparison experiment adds the original Seq2Seq model and the Transformer model. The results are shown in the following table (Table 9):

Table 8. Result generated by Module2 (BLEU)

Model	Single + Multi (val)	Single + Multi(test)
T5	0.568	0.534
mT5	0.572	0.561
ByT5-small	0.592	0.606
ByT5-base	**0.619**	**0.606**

Table 9. Comparative experiment on clarification question final generation result (BLEU)

Model	Single + Multi (val)	Single + Multi(test)
Seq2Seq	0.398	0.403
Transformer	0.421	0.423
T5	0.436	0.434
mT5	0.425	0.427
ByT5-small	0.438	0.435
ByT5-base	**0.447**	**0.449**

According to the comparative experimental results table, the effectiveness of the traditional model does not differ significantly from that of the ByT5 based model, which is significantly different from the BLEU scores obtained in the Module 1 and Module 2 sections above. This is due to the addition of a question and answer terminology template when splicing into the final answer. The model generates different answers each time, resulting in a decrease in the BLEU score, but this does increase the diversity of the final generated answer, making each generated answer personalized without losing its original semantics.

In this task, the attempted model structure is evaluated, and the following three examples are selected for display (The table can be found in the appendix), including single-turn and multi-turn question answering, including both generated answers that are almost the same as the ground truth and generated answers that are different from the ground truth's sentence structure with the same semant, and it is more in line with the current context. Our goal is to find simpler and more representative answers, simplify the generation of clarification questions, and enable users to better understand the generated answers for the required clarification content.

In the examples, Example 1 is a single-turn dialogue. The answer generated based on the ByT5 model is consistent with the semantic of the ground truth, only inconsistent at the template, and can be completely used as an alternative answer. Example 2 is a multi-turn dialogue, again only inconsistent at the template, and all other anthers are the same. Example 3 is a multi-turn dialogue. When generating clarification questions, the more obvious different characteristics of the entities are extracted, so that users can understand the clarification content more clearly.

The Results of Entity Prediction. Similar to the clarification question detection, the same model was selected for ablation and comparative experiments. The results are shown in Tables 10, 11 and 12 below:

Table 10. Ablation experiment on entity prediction (Acc)

Model	Single-Turn(test)	Multi-Turn(test)	Single + Multi(val)	Single + Multi(test)
Bert + FC	0.865	0.873	0.878	0.866
RoBERTa + FC	0.870	0.878	0.886	0.875
Longformer + FC	0.979	0.974	0.983	0.976
DeBERTa v3 + FC	**0.982**	**0.997**	**0.991**	**0.989**

Table 11. Ablation experiment on entity prediction (F1)

Model	Single-Turn(test)	Multi-Turn(test)	Single + Multi(val)	Single + Multi(test)
Bert + FC	0.865	0.873	0.877	0.866
RoBERTa + FC	0.871	0.879	0.880	0.878
Longformer + FC	0.980	0.974	0.982	0.976
DeBERTa v3 + FC	**0.981**	**0.997**	**0.991**	**0.988**

Table 12. Comparative experiment on entity prediction (Acc)

Model	Single-Turn(test)	Multi-Turn(test)	Single + Multi(test)
CNN	0.801	0.721	0.784
Transformer	0.822	0.704	0.789
HAN	0.809	0.822	0.834
DMN	0.840	0.798	0.839
DeBERTa v3 + FC	**0.982**	**0.997**	**0.989**

The long-sequence model Longformer also showed very good accuracy in this training. However, again, the DeBERTa-v3-base pre-trained model + FC fine-tuned model has the best effect, reaching 0.99 +. Similarly, the accuracy rate on the test set is close to 0.99, more than 15 percentage points more than the traditional neural network model, indicating that the model has played a full role in understanding the problem and distinguishing different entities. Similarly, the model performs better in the multi-turn question answering than in single-turn question answering. The traditional model has a better effect of single-turn question answering, indicating that the proposed DeBERTa v3 + FC model has a better understanding of the context and can extract and understand the semantic information proposed by the user.

6   Conclusions and Future Work

This paper proposes a clarification question detection and generation framework, which consists of three tasks, i.e. clarification question detection, clarification question generation and entity prediction. Specifically, The DeBERTa v3 + FC model architecture is proposed for clarification question detection and entity prediction. A clarification question generation model based on ByT5 is proposed for generating clarification questions. The proposed approach greatly addresses the difficulty of poor interaction with users during the intelligent Q&A process, maximizes the understanding of the semantics of user contextual conversations, and reduces the possibility of system misunderstandings of user intentions. Experimental results show that on the MSParS public dataset, the accuracy of clarification question detection and entity prediction tasks improved by 11.2% and 15.17%, respectively, compared to traditional DMN models. The BLEU score of the clarification question generation task improved by 4.9% compared to traditional Seq2Seq models, achieving breakthroughs in all three tasks. Combined with weak templates, the generated clarification questions are personalized and more understandable to users. We will conduct further research on the generation of clarification questions to enable them to have excellent performance on issues in all fields, and improve the timeliness of the output of results (Table 13).

Funding. This research was funded by Special Fund Project for Promoting High Quality Industrial Development in Shanghai (Number: 2021-GZL-RGZN-01018) and Shanghai "Science and Technology Innovation Action Plan" Project (Number: 21DZ1201400; 22DZ1200500; 22QB1400200).

Appendix

Table 13. Examples of clarification question final generation result (Examples).

Example 1	Context	The Comet's costume designer
	Entity1	The Comet <S> media_common.creative_work media_common.cataloged_instance broadcast.content film.film ratings.rated_entity <S> The Comet is a 1996 drama film written by Claude Santelli and Suzanne Jacques-Marin and directed by Claude Santelli.
	Entity2	The Comet <S> film.film award.**nominated_work** ratings.rated_entity media_common.creative_work media_common.cataloged_instance broadcast.content <S> After witnessing the arrest of her father for publishing subversive material against the dictatorship of Porfirio Díaz, Valentina escapes taking a sack of gold coins with her in order to ...
	Our model	When you say the costume designer, are you talking about non nominated work The Comet or nominated work The Comet?
	Ground Truth	Which one do you mean, non nominated work The Comet or nominated work The Comet, when you say the dress designer?
Example 2	Context	Who follows madonna? <EOS> Tila Tequila <EOS> What was a famous quote quoted?
	Entity1	madonna <S> biology.organism award.winner award.ranked_item award.nominee award.hall_of_fame_inductee award.competitor media_common.subject tv.actor theater.actor ratings.rated_entity people.person organization.founder tv.crewmember music.producer music.musician music.lyricist music.composer music.artist me-

(continued)

Table 13. (*continued*)

dia_common.cataloged_instance internet.social_network_user
film.writer film.subject film.producer music.singer tv.writer
tv.personality film.music_contributor film.director film.actor fiction-
al_universe.person_in_fiction event.agent celebrities.celebrity broad-
cast.artist book.author <S> Madonna Louise Ciccone (/tʃɪˈkoʊni/;
Italian: [tʃikˈkoːne]) (born August 16, 1958) is an American singer,
songwriter, actress, and businesswoman. She achieved popularity by
pushing the boundaries of lyrical content in mainstream popular music
and imagery in her music videos, which became a fixture on MTV.
Madonna is known for reinventing both her music and image, and for
maintaining her autonomy within the recording industry. Music critics
have acclaimed her musical productions, which have generated some
controversy. Often referred to as the Queen of Pop, she is cited as an
influence by numerous other artists around the world.

Entity2   Tila Tequila <S> internet.social_network_user me-
dia_common.cataloged_instance music.musician people.person rat-
ings.rated_entity tv.actor award.competitor award.nominee
award.ranked_item award.winner biology.organism celebri-
ties.celebrity event.agent film.actor tv.personality music.artist <S> Tila
Tequila net worth: Tila Tequila is a Singaporean-American model and
television personality who has a net worth of $500 thousand. Tila Te-
quila Nguyen was born in Singapore in October 1981. Her family
moved to Houston, Texas when she was a year old. In high school she
started using drugs and joined a gang. Her friends gave her the nick-
name Tila Tequila due to her allergy to alcohol. As a teen she experi-
enced a drive-by shooting, and became pregnant before suffering a
miscarriage. In 2001 she moved to California. At 19 she was discovered in a shopping mall by a Playboy scout. She was Playboy's Cyber
Girl of the week in April 2002 and became the first Asian Cyber Girl
of the month. She became popular through the import racing scene and
was featured on the covers of magazines, at car shows, and in video
games. She hosted Fuse TV's Pants-Off Dance-Off. She has been featured on the cover of Stuff and Maxim UK. She was a contestant on the
NC show Identity and appeared in I Now Pronounce You Chuck and
Larry. In 2009 she was featured in the MTV reality show A Shot At
Love with Tila Tequila. The show was a bisexual-themed dating which
featured straight men and lesbian women as would-be suitors. In 2006
she was signed to the Will.I.Am music group. She has released two
solo EPs and five singles. In 2008 she released a self-help book. She
has also started her own record label called Tila Tequila Records and a
management firm called Little Miss Trendsetter Management LLC.
Tila has been romantically linked to football player Shawne Merriman
and heiress Casey Johnson. In 2011 a sex tape of Tequila was released.
In 2012 she checked into rehab, and in 2014 she announced she is

(*continued*)

Table 13. (*continued*)

	pregnant with her first child.
Our model	When you say the person's famous quote, are you referring to madonna or Tila Tequila?
Ground Truth	Are you talking about music contributor madonna or Tila Tequila when you say the person's famous quote?
Context	What is island group of Seymour Island
Entity1	Seymour Island <S> location.administrative_division geography.island geography.geographical_feature location.location travel.destination media_common.subject <S> North Seymour is a small island near to Baltra Island in the Galapagos Islands. It was formed by uplift of a submarine lava formation. The whole island is covered with low, bushy vegetation. The island is named after an English nobleman, Lord Hugh Seymour. It has an area of 1.9 square kilometres and a maximum altitude of 28 metres. This island is home to a large population of blue-footed boobies and swallow-tailed gulls. It hosts one of the largest populations of frigatebirds Fregata magnificens and a slow growing population of the Galapagos land iguana. North Seymour has a visitor trail approximately 2 kilometres in length crossing the inland of the island and exploring the rocky coast. One of the most famous birds found in the Galapagos are the Blue-footed Booby that are found on North Seymour. The stock for the captive breeding program of the Galapagos Land Iguana is descended from iguanas which Captain G. Allan Hancock translocated from nearby Baltra Island to North Seymour Island in the 1930s. This was very important because Baltra Island during World War 2 was populated by airplane base by the U.S.
Entity2	Seymour Island <S> location.location geography.island geography.geographical_feature <S> Seymour Island is an uninhabited island in the Qikiqtaaluk Region of northern Canada's territory of Nunavut. A member of the Berkeley Islands group, it is located approximately 30 mi (48 km) north of northern Bathurst Island. Between Seymour Island and Bathurst Island lies Helena Island. Penny Strait lies about 90 km (56 mi) to the east where open water polynyas occur.
Our model	Do you mean Seymour Island in the Galapagos Islands or Seymour Island in Nunavut, when you say the sequence of islands?
Ground Truth	When you say the name of the group of islands, are you talking about Seymour Island near to Baltra Island in the Galapagos Islands or Seymour Island in the Qikiqtaaluk Region of northern Canada's territory of Nunavut?

Example 3

References

1. Shin, S., Lee, K.H.: Processing knowledge graph-based complex questions through question decomposition and recomposition. Inf. Sci.f. Sci. **523**, 234–244 (2020)

2. Demetras, M.J., Post, K.N., Snow, C.E.: Feedback to first language learners: the role of repetitions and clarification questions. J. Child Lang. **13**(2), 275–292 (1986)
3. Aliannejadi, M., Zamani, H., Crestani, F., et al.: Asking clarifying questions in open-domain information-seeking conversations. In: Proceedings of the 42nd International ACM SIGIR Conference on Research and Development in Information Retrieval, pp. 475–484 (2019)
4. Stoyanchev, S., Liu, A., Hirschberg, J.: Towards natural clarification questions in dialogue systems. In: AISB Symposium on Questions, Discourse and Dialogue, pp. 20 (2014)
5. Guo, X., Klinger, T., Rosenbaum, C., et al.: Learning to query, reason, and answer questions on ambiguous texts. In: International Conference on Learning Representations (2017)
6. Li, J., Miller, A.H., Chopra, S., et al.: Dialogue learning with human-in-the-loop. arXiv preprint arXiv:1611.09823 (2016)
7. Xu, J., Wang, Y., Tang, D., et al.: Asking clarification questions in knowledge-based question answering. In: Proceedings of the 2019 Conference on Empirical Methods in Natural Language Processing and the 9th International Joint Conference on Natural Language Processing (EMNLP-IJCNLP), pp. 1618–1629 (2019)
8. Liu, B., Zhao, M., Niu, D., et al.: Learning to generate questions by learningWhat not to generate. In: The World Wide Web Conference, pp. 1106–1118 (2019)
9. Dong, L., Yang, N., Wang, W., et al.: Unified language model pre-training for natural language understanding and generation. In: Advances in Neural Information Processing Systems, vol. 32 (2019)
10. Gao, Y., Bing, L., Chen, W., et al.: Difficulty controllable generation of reading comprehension questions. arXiv preprint arXiv:1807.03586 (2018)
11. Rao, S., Daumé III, H.: Answer-based adversarial training for generating clarification questions. arXiv preprint arXiv:1904.02281 (2019)
12. He, P., Liu, X., Gao, J., et al.: DeBERTa: decoding-enhanced BERT with disentangled attention. arXiv preprint arXiv:2006.03654 (2020)
13. Liu, Y., Ott, M., Goyal, N., et al.: RoBERTa: a robustly optimized BERT pretraining approach. arXiv preprint arXiv:1907.11692 (2019)
14. He, P., Gao, J., Chen, W.: Debertav3: improving deberta using electra-style pre-training with gradient-disentangled embedding sharing. arXiv preprint arXiv:2111.09543 (2021)
15. Christian, H., Agus, M.P., Suhartono, D.: Single document automatic text summarization using term frequency-inverse document frequency (TF-IDF). ComTech Comput. Math. Eng. Appl. **7**(4), 285 (2016). https://doi.org/10.21512/comtech.v7i4.3746
16. Raffel, C., Shazeer, N., Roberts, A., et al.: Exploring the limits of transfer learning with a unified text-to-text transformer. J. Mach. Learn. Res. **21**(1), 5485–5551 (2020)
17. Xue, L., Barua, A., Constant, N., et al.: Byt5: towards a token-free future with pre-trained byte-to-byte models. Trans. Assoc. Comput. Linguist. **10**, 291–306 (2022)
18. Papineni, K., Roukos, S., Ward, T., et al.: Bleu: a method for automatic evaluation of machine translation. In: Proceedings of the 40th Annual Meeting of the Association for Computational Linguistics, pp. 311–318 (2002)
19. Yang, Z., Yang, D., Dyer, C., et al.: Hierarchical attention networks for document classification. In: Proceedings of the 2016 conference of the North American Chapter of the Association for Computational Linguistics: Human Language Technologies, pp. 1480–1489. (2016)
20. Kumar, A., Irsoy, O., Ondruska, P., et al.: Ask me anything: dynamic memory networks for natural language processing. In: International Conference on Machine Learning, pp. 1378–1387. PMLR (2016)

Dictionary-Assisted Chinese Nested Named Entity Recognition

Ye Wang, Tongtong Ding, and Lijie Li[✉]

College of Computer Science and Technology, Harbin Engineering University, Harbin, China
{wangye2020,dingtongtong,lilijie}@hrbeu.edu.cn

Abstract. Chinese Named Entity Recognition is a challenging task, made even more difficult by the presence of nested entity structures. Previous work on Nested Named Entity Recognition focused only on exploiting internal contextual information, while ignoring the use of external information. In this paper, we propose a dictionary-assisted Chinese Nested Named Entity Recognition model, called KBCNER. Our model uses the dictionary to obtain matching words, combines characters and phrases into character-phrase pairs, and integrates them into BERT. By doing so, we can extract richer semantic information from Chinese phrases than from a single character. The use of external information from the dictionary enhances the features of our model and obtains richer semantics. To avoid constraints from specific-length enumerations, we use bi-affine structures to obtain a global view of spans. We also model local interactions between spans using a Convolutional Neural Network (CNN), taking advantage of the spatial correlation between adjacent spans. Finally, we adopt the idea of contrastive learning based on R-drop to enhance the model's robustness. Experimental results demonstrate that our model achieves excellent performance on multiple datasets. By introducing external information, we improve the performance of the model, highlighting the significance of external information for Chinese Nested Named Entity Recognition.

Keywords: Chinese Nested Named Entity Recognition · Dictionary Assistance · Bi-affine Structure · Convolutional Neural Network

1 Introduction

Nested Named Entity Recognition (NNER) refers to the simultaneous recognition of multiple nested levels of named entities in text. For example, in Fig. 1 "哈尔滨医科大学附属第一医院(First Affiliated Hospital of Harbin Medical University)", it contains three entities: "哈尔滨(Harbin)" belongs to LOC entity, "哈尔滨医科大学(Harbin Medical University)" belongs to ORG entity, "哈尔滨医科大学附属第一医院(First Affiliated Hospital of Harbin Medical University)" belongs to ORG entity. They overlap each other and are nested entities. NNER has a wide range of applications in information extraction, question answering systems, natural language understanding and other fields. However, most current NNER research focuses on English corpora, while relatively few

M. Zhang et al. (Eds.): CCF NCCA 2023, CCIS 1959, pp. 189–205, 2024.
https://doi.org/10.1007/978-981-99-8764-1_15

studies on Chinese corpora. There are some notable differences between Chinese and English Nested Named Entity Recognition. First of all, the vocabulary structure of Chinese and English is different from that of English. The fundamental unit of composition in Chinese is characters, while in English, it is letters. Therefore, identifying nested named entities in Chinese needs to take into account more complex language structures and features, such as polyphonic characters, ambiguous words, word order, etc. This also makes Chinese Nested Named Entity Recognition tasks more challenging than English. Secondly, Chinese Named Entity Recognition often needs to solve ambiguity problems, because words in Chinese often have many different meanings, and contextual information and context need to be considered to determine the correct entity type. Compared to English, the task of named entity recognition in Chinese is more challenging due to the presence of more ambiguities and context dependencies. Therefore, it is more crucial to incorporate external information for Chinese Nested Named Entity Recognition than for English Nested Named Entity Recognition.

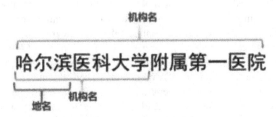

Fig. 1. Nested Entity Structure Example

Integrating external knowledge has been shown to be effective in various natural language processing tasks, such as text classification [1], semantic matching [2], text generation [3], and Named Entity Recognition [4].Among these, the dictionary- enhanced approach has demonstrated a notable improvement in Chinese Named Entity Recognition task. BERT is based on character-level granularity for Chinese and cannot capture the overall information of multi-word words, which hinders the identification of entity boundaries. Therefore, incorporating additional lexical knowledge is crucial for improving the accuracy of named entity recognition. Existing methods, such as Lattice LSTM [5] and FLAT [6], input extra vocabulary information alongside the sentence sequence into BERT and apply a specific attention mechanism to calculate them separately. However, this approach results in longer sequences, increasing computation time and memory consumption and introducing noise to the semantic representation. Recently, Liu et al. [7] proposed LEBERT, a model that integrates external dictionary information into the middle layer of BERT as an additional module, achieving promising results. In this study, we aim to apply the LEBERT dictionary-enhanced approach to Chinese Nested Named Entity Recognition to improve its performance.

In the field of Nested Named Entity Recognition, span enumeration is one of the prevailing approaches. Sohrab and Miwa et al. [8] have proposed a method of exhaustively enumerating all possible spans up to a specified length by connecting the output of start and end position LSTMs, which is then used to calculate the score for each span. To overcome the limitation of length in predicting entities, a bi-affine based structural model is employed. By constructing the token-token table in parallel, the bi-affine decoder generates a global view of the sentence, including vector representations of all possible spans, thus improving efficiency. This approach has been demonstrated as effective in various works, such as Dozat and Manning (2017) [9] and Yu et al. (2020) [10]. In recent advances in Nested Named Entity Recognition research, Hang Yan et al. [11] treated the feature matrix as a view and utilized CNNs to model the spatial relationships between adjacent spans in the scoring matrix, which resulted in significant improvements in the task performance.

To improve the performance of Chinese Nested Named Entity Recognition, this paper proposes a dictionary-assisted method to capture richer semantics. The model constructs character-word pairs by using matching phrases obtained from a wiki dictionary and integrates them into the middle layer of BERT, fully utilizing its representational capacity. Chinese phrases contain richer semantic information than single characters, and introducing dictionary information enhances the feature richness. The model uses a bi-affine structure to obtain a global view of the span, avoiding the limitation of specific length enumeration. Additionally, the local interaction between spans is modeled using a Convolutional Neural Network (CNN) to capture spatial correlation between adjacent spans. Finally, the model's robustness is enhanced using the R-drop based contrastive learning approach. The model in this chapter aims to optimize the characteristics of the Chinese language, improve the accuracy and efficiency of Chinese Nested Named Entity Recognition.

The main contributions of this work are as follows:

1) Proposing a simple and effective model for Chinese nested named entity recognition, aimed at improving the accuracy and efficiency of the task.
2) Considering that phrases can provide richer semantics and better handle Chinese nested entity structures, integrating dictionary information into BERT to achieve deep lexical knowledge fusion. Applying the idea of contrastive learning based on R-drop to enhance the robustness and generalization ability of the model, while reducing overfitting.
3) Evaluating and validating the proposed method on both Chinese flat and nested datasets, and comparing it with baseline models, achieving the best results.

2 Related Work

Currently, methods for Nested Named Entity Recognition can be classified into four main categories: 1) Improved sequence labeling framework: through the design of a trade-off scheme, the sequence labeling task is capable of handling nested named entities; 2) Hypergraph-based methods: by utilizing a hypergraph structure, nested structures can be effectively addressed; 3) Parsing tree-based methods: similar to Constituency Parsing tree structures, they are used in nested named entity recognition; 4) Span-based methods: candidate spans are first exhaustively enumerated, and then assigned a corresponding category.

2.1 Improved Sequence Labeling Framework

Traditional sequence labeling methods, such as Hidden Markov Models and Conditional Random Fields, are usually inadequate for dealing with nested named entities. However, the improved sequence labeling method can handle nested named entities by introducing additional features and constraints. In 2018, Ju et al. [13] proposed a dynamic stacking plane NER method, which treats each plane NER as a single-layer sequence labeling, to extract entities from the inside to the outside. However, this approach is prone to error propagation. To model multiple named entity labels, Strakova et al. [14] proposed a linearized encoding scheme that combines all categories that may co-occur in pairs to generate new labels (e.g., combining B-Location with B-Organization to construct a new label B-Loc | Org). Shibuya et al. [15] provided a sub-optimal path solution that treats the label sequence of nested entities as the second-best path within the span of their parent entities, extracting entities from outside to inside. To identify nested named entities from bottom to top, Li et al. [16] proposed a Chinese NER model based on a self-attention aggregation mechanism, which connects a series of sub-models of multi-layer sequence labeling. Wang et al. [17] designed a pyramid framework to recognize nested entities. The improved sequence labeling method is straightforward and convenient to use, but it is not sufficiently accurate for modeling the nesting relationship.

2.2 Hypergraph-Based Approaches

A hypergraph is a graphical structure in which a node can be associated with multiple edges, and it can be used to model the nested structure of a sentence where each entity is a node and the nested relationship between entities is an edge. Hypergraph-based methods aim to better capture dependencies between entities by using hypergraphs. These methods typically transform the reasoning problem on hypergraphs into an integer linear programming problem. Lu et al. [18] proposed a joint entity extraction and classification model for nested NER that can effectively capture nested entities with infinite lengths. Katiyar et al. [19] extracted a hypergraph representation from an RNN and trained the model using greedy search. Wang et al. [20] proposed a piecewise hypergraph representation that avoids structural ambiguity. Luo et al. [21] proposed a bipartite planar graph structure that uses a planar NER module for the outermost entity and a graph module for all entities located in the inner layer to perform two-way information interaction between layers. Although hypergraph-based methods can explicitly capture nested entities, they require skillful hypergraph design to handle complex reasoning problems and may result in long running times.

2.3 Parsing Tree-Based Methods

Parsing tree-based methods use a tree-based algorithm to analyze the relationship between nested entities, similar to the constituency parsing tree structure used in syntactic analysis. A parsing tree is constructed in a bottom-up or top-down manner, and different features can be used for classification. In 2009, Finkel et al. [22] proposed converting a sentence into a constituency tree, with each entity corresponding to a phrase in the tree and a root node connecting the entire sentence. Fu et al. [23] proposed regarding nested NER as the constituency resolution of the tree using local observations, with the entity spans of all markers as the nodes observed in the constituency tree, and other spans as potential nodes. Lou et al. [24] improved the method proposed by Fu by using a two-stage strategy and head-aware loss, which effectively utilized the effective information of entity heads. Yang et al. [25] proposed a new pointer network for the bottom-up analysis of nested NER and constituency resolution. Parsing tree-based methods can accurately capture nested relationships, but require more computing resources.

2.4 Span-Based Methods

Span-based methods are among the most widely used approaches for nested NER. These methods involve enumerating all potential spans in a sentence and classifying each one. While some approaches exhaustively list all possible spans, such as Sohrab et al.'s method [25], this is computationally intensive. Other approaches, like Lin et al.'s [26], first locate an anchor word and then match the entire span for classification, but this approach only works for specific structures. Xia et al. [27] proposed a multi- granularity NER method that includes a detector for entity locations and a classifier for entity types. The boundary-aware model proposed by Zheng et al. [28] uses sequence labeling to determine span boundaries before classification. Yu et al. [29] applied the bi-affine model to nested NER, pinpointing spans and scoring each one using start and end markers. Xu et al. [30] proposed a supervised multi-head self- attention mechanism, where each head identifies a category and uses a boundary detection module as an auxiliary task. Finally, Shen et al. [31] developed a two-stage method that generates candidate spans by filtering and boundary regression of seed spans before marking the corresponding category.

3 Model

This paper proposes a KBCNNER model. As shown in Fig. 2, the model is divided into three parts: the first part is the dictionary information introduction module, which integrates the matched character-word pairs information into the BERT intermediate layer; the second part is the bi-affine decoder layer, which obtains the global view of the sentence; and the third part is the Convolutional Neural Network (CNN) layer, which models the relationship between adjacent spans using CNN.

3.1 Import Dictionary Information

Define the input as a Chinese sentence, $S = \{c_1, c_2, ..., c_n\}$, where n represents the number of characters in the sentence. Next, two parts of the operation are performed on the input sentence S at the same time, one part is to use the BERT embedding layer to extract the vector representation of each character, and get $E = \{e_1, e_2, ..., e_n\}$, and then input E into the Transformer encoder for the following calculation:

$$G = LN(H^{l-1} + MHAttn(H^{l-1})) \tag{1}$$

$$H^l = LN(G + FFN(G)) \tag{2}$$

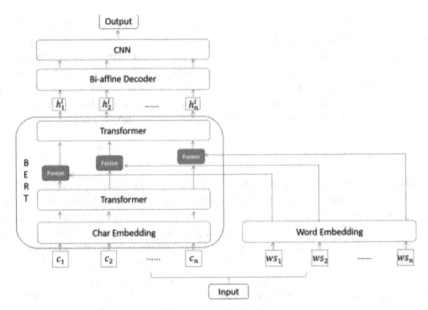

Fig. 2. KBCNNER model diagram

where $H^l = \{h_1^l, h_n^l, \ldots, h_n^l\}$, represents the output of the first layer of Transformer.

LN is a normalization operation, MHAttn is a multi-head attention mechanism, and FFN is a two-layer feedforward neural network using Relu as the activation function.

In the other part, the sentence S is matched with the dictionary D to construct character-word pairs, where the dictionary D is prepared in advance, as shown in Fig. 3. The specific method is as follows: First, build a dictionary tree Trie based on the dictionary D, then we iterate through all possible character subsequences in the input sentence and match them against the Trie tree, resulting in a list of potential words. For example, the sentence "中国人民" can be matched to "中国", " 中国人", "国人", "人民". For

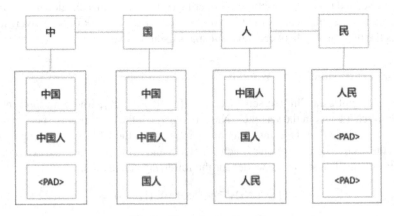

Fig. 3. Character-words pair

each matched word, assign the characters it contains. For example, the matched word "中国" is assigned to the characters "中" and "国". We pair each character with the matching word to form a character-word pair $s_{CW} = \{(c_1, ws_1), \ldots (c_i, ws_i), (c_n, ws_n)\}$ where c_i denotes the i−th character in the sentence and wsi denotes matched words assigned to ci.

Next, use the Fusion module in Fig. 4 to inject vocabulary information into BERT, and the input of Fusion is a character−word pair (h_i^c, x_i^{ws}), where h_i^c is a character vector, the output of a certain transformer layer in BERT, and $x_i^{ws} = \{x_{i1}^w, x_{i2}^w, \ldots x_{im}^w\}$ is a set of word embeddings to the i-th character, where m is the number of words. The j-th word in x_i^{ws} is represented as following: $x_{ij}^w = e^w(w_{ij})$, where e^w is a pre-trained word embedding lookup table and w_{ij} is the j-th word in wsi. Align word representations and word representation dimensions using nonlinear changes:

$$v_{ij}^w = w_2(\tanh(w_1 x_{ij}^w + b_1)) + b_2 \tag{3}$$

where $w_1 \in R^{d_c * d_w}$, $w_1 \in R^{d_c * d_c}$, and b_1 and b_2 are scaler bias. d_c and d_w denote the dimension of word embedding and the hidden size of BERT respectively.

To pick out the most relevant words from all matched words, we introduce a character-to-word attention mechanism. We denote all v_{wij} assingned to i-th character as $v_i − (v_{i1}^w, v_{i2}^w, \ldots v_{im}^w)$. The relevance of each word can be calculated as:

$$a_i = \mathrm{softmax}(h_i^c w_{attn} v_i^1) \tag{4}$$

where wattn is the weight matrix of billinear attention. Consequently, we can get the weighted sum of all words by:

$$z_i^w = \sigma_{j=1}^m a_{ij} v_{ij}^w \tag{5}$$

Finally, the weighted lexcion information is injected into the character vector by:

$$\tilde{h}_i = h_{ic} + z_i^w \tag{6}$$

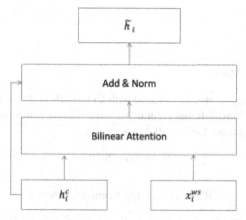

Fig. 4. Structure of Fusion. Enter a character vector and paired word features. By bilinear attention on characters and words, the lexical features are weighted into a vector. This vector is added to the character-level vectors, followed by layer normalization.

Input the fused vector into the remaining Transformer layer for calculation, and finally get $H^l = \{h_1^l, h_2^l, \dots h_n^l\}$.

3.2 Bi-affine Decoder

The obtained vector representation of each character is input into the bi-affine decoder and mapped to a scoring matrix R of L × L × k, as shown in Fig. 5. L is the sentence length, k ∈ {1,...,|k|}, is the type of entity, |k| is the number of entity types. Specifically, each span (i, j) can be expressed as a tuple (i, j, k). i, j are the start, end index of entity. After BERT encoding, The embedding of the token at the position i, j are h_i, h_j, where h_i, $h_j \in R^d$, d is the hidden size of embedding. We compute the score for a span(i, j):

$$f(i, j) = h_i^T U h_j + w([h_i; h_j]) + b \tag{7}$$

where U is a d × k × d tensor, W is a 2d × k matrix and b is the bias.

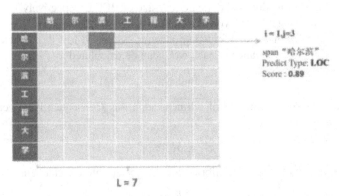

Fig. 5. Scoring matrix R, the element of each position of the square matrix is a k- dimensional vector, which is used to represent the distribution of named entity categories of the text segment corresponding to the position.

3.3 CNN on Score Matrix

Understand the scoring matrix as a picture with k channels and L × L length and width, and further use the Convolutional Neural Network (CNN) commonly used in the field of computer vision to model this spatial connection:

$$R' = Conv2d(R) \tag{8}$$

$$R'' = Gelu(LayerNorm(R' + R)) \tag{9}$$

where Conv2d is 2DCNN, the convolution kernel performs a sliding window operation in two-dimensional space. LayerNorm is layer normalization, which performs normalization operations in the feature layer, and Gelu is the activation function. Since the

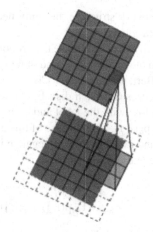

Fig. 6. CNN

number of tokens in the sentence is different, their R have different shapes. In order to ensure the same result when processing R in batches, 2DCNN has no bias and fills R with 0, as shown in Fig. 6.

We use a perceptron to get the prediction logits as follows:

$$P = \text{Sigmoid}(w_0(R' + R'') + b) \tag{10}$$

where $w_0 \in R^{|k| \times d}$, $b \in R^{|k|}$, $P \in R^{L \times L \times |k|}$.

3.4 Loss Function

(1) (1) The loss function of the model itself we use the binary cross entropy to calculate the loss as:

$$\mathcal{L}_{BCE} = -\sigma_{0 \leq i,j < L} Y_{ij} \log(P_{ij}) \tag{11}$$

where Yij is ground truth entity, Pij is the predicted probability.

The tag for the score matrix is symmetric, namely, the tag in the (i,j)-th entry is the same as in the (j-i)-th. When inference, we calculate scores in the upper triangle part as:

$$\widehat{P}_{ij} = (p_{ij} + p_{ji})/2 \tag{12}$$

where $i \leq j$. Then we only use this upper triangle score to get the final prediction.

(2) Contrastive learning based on R-drop

In order to enhance the robustness and generalization ability of the model and reduce the occurrence of overfitting, this paper adopts the idea of contrastive learning based on R-drop. During the training process, because dropout randomly discards some hidden units, the same sentence is input into the model twice to get two different vector representations, but they have the same label. This data augmentation method does not require any modifications to the neural network structure, but only needs to add a KL bifurcation loss function, so no noise is introduced.

For the construction of positive examples, use the dropout data enhancement method to input a sample sentence into the model twice, and obtain two probability distributions p(i, j), p^+ (i, j) through the Bert, Bi-affine and CNN modules. In order to construct negative examples, this paper uses Gaussian distribution to initialize M distribution of K × L × L and calculates the loss with the label and then selects the N with the largest loss ass, the negative example $p_{\bar{n}}(i, j)$. The purpose of this is to introduce noise, increase the robustness of the model, and avoid too much negative impact on the training of the model. The loss of contrastive learning is expressed as

$$\mathcal{L}_{\mathrm{KL}} = \frac{K_L p(i, j) p^+(i, j)}{\sigma_{n=0} KL, p(i, j), p_{\bar{n}}(i, j)} \tag{13}$$

The purpose is to minimize the kl divergence of positive examples and maximize the kl divergence of negative examples to optimize the training effect of the model.

(3) Final Loss Function

The final loss function is expressed as

$$\mathcal{L} = \mathcal{L}_{\mathrm{BCE}} + \mathcal{L}_{\mathrm{KL}} \tag{14}$$

3.5 Entity Decoding

First discard all fragments with a predicted probability lower than 0.5, then sort the spans from high to low according to the predicted probability, and then select the fragment with the highest current predicted probability in turn, if it does not conflict with the previously decoded named entity, then the The fragment is decoded into a new named entity, otherwise it is discarded. By doing this iteratively, all non- conflicting named entities of the input sequence predicted by the model are obtained.

4   Experimental Analysis

4.1   Dataset

We conduct experiments on both the Chinese nested NER dataset and the flat NER dataset. Among them, the Chinese nested NER dataset selects "人民日报" and the Chinese medical dataset CMeEE, and the Chinese flat NER dataset selects Weibo and Resume.

The "人民日报" dataset belongs to the news field and contains three entity types, namely, person names, place names, and organization names. The number of nested entities accounts for about 12.81% of the total number of entities. The CMeEE dataset is called Chinese Medical Entity Extraction dataset. It contains nine types of medical entities such as common pediatric diseases, body parts, clinical manifestations, and medical procedures. Nesting is allowed in the "clinical manifestations" entity category, and other eight types of entities are allowed within this entity. The Weibo dataset is generated by filtering and filtering the historical data of Sina Weibo from November 2013 to December 2014, including 1890 Weibo messages. The entity category of this dataset is divided into four categories: people, organizations, addresses and geopolitical entities. The Resume data set is generated by screening and manual labeling based on the summary data of resumes of senior managers of listed companies on Sina Finance and Economics. The data set contains 1027 resume summaries, and the entity annotations are divided into 8 categories including name, nationality, place of origin, race, major, degree, institution, and job title. The statistics of the above datasets are shown in Table 1.

Table 1. The statistics of the datasets

Dataset	Train	Dev	Test
《人民日报》	15.3K	1.9K	2. 1K
CMeEE	15K	5K	5K
Weibo	1.4K	0.27K	0.27K
Resume	3.8K	0.46K	0.48K

4.2 Experimental Settings

The BERT-base-chinese pre-training model with 12 hidden layers, outputting 768-dimensional tensors, 12 self-attention heads, and a total of 110M parameters is used in this study. The model is pre-trained on Simplified and Traditional Chinese texts. The 200-dimensional pretrained word embeddings of Song et al. [32] are used, which are trained on news and webpage texts using a directional tab model. Dictionary D is trained on texts such as Wikipedia and Baidu Baike. The Adam optimizer with a learning rate of 2e−5 is used for model optimization during training. The maximum epoch on all datasets is 30, and the maximum input length is 150. The character-word pair information between the 1st and 2nd Transformers in BERT is fused, and BERT and pretrained word embeddings are fine-tuned during training. The CNN convolution kernel is set to 3. An entity is considered correct when both the predicted class and the predicted span are exactly correct. Evaluation metrics used in this study include Precision (P), Recall (R), and F-score (F1). The hyperparameter settings are summarized in Table 2.

4.3 Analysis of Results

Baselines:

LSTM-Crf [33]: The LSTM-CRF model is a traditional sequence labeling model composed of two parts. First, the LSTM (Long Short-Term Memory) neural network maps each input element to a high-dimensional vector space by learning the contextual information in the input sequence. The LSTM network can handle variable-length sequences and update the parameters.

Table 2. The hyper-parameter in this paper

Parameter	Value
Optimiser	Adam
BERT leaning rate	2e−5
Epoch	30
Max seqence length	150
Lexcion add layer	1
CNN kernel size	3

BERT-Crf [34]: The BERT-CRF model is a sequence labeling model based on a pre-trained Transformer model. It first uses the pre-trained BERT model to encode the input sequence to obtain context-aware word embeddings. These embeddings capture rich semantic information of the input sequence and are fed to the CRF layer for label prediction. Compared with traditional models such as LSTM-CRF, BERT-CRF can better capture rich semantic information and dependency relationships between labels.

LEBERT-Crf [8]: LEBERT-CRF model is a sequence labeling model that integrates external lexical knowledge directly into the BERT layer. Specifically, it integrates external lexical knowledge into the BERT layer through the vocabulary adapter module, and uses a linear transformation layer to fuse external knowledge with internal embeddings. Then, the CRF layer is used for label decoding. The advantage of the LEBERT-CRF model is that it can directly integrate external knowledge into the model, thereby improving its performance.

To assess the efficacy of the model proposed in this study, we compared its experimental outcomes against those of the baseline model across four datasets. The comparative findings are presented in Tables 3 and 4.

Table 3. Nested dataset comparison experiment results

Models	《人民日报》			CMeEE		
	P	R	F1	P	R	F1
LSTM-Crf	86.02	81.37	83.63	50.20	44.20	47.00
BERT-Crf	92.26	90.58	91.41	56.90	56.00	56.45
LEBERT-Crf	92.51	93.49	93.00	58.26	56.47	57.35
Ours	96.08	96.13	96. 11	64.98	65.46	65.22

According to the results in Table 3, on the Chinese nested dataset "人民日报", both the BERT-CRF and LEBERT-CRF models outperformed the LSTM-CRF in terms of precision, recall, and F1-score. The proposed method in this paper achieved higher precision, recall, and F1-score (96.08%, 96. 13%, and 96. 11%, respectively) than the corresponding values of the other three models. Specifically, compared with the LEBERT-CRF model, our proposed method showed improvements of 3.57%, 2.64%, and 3. 11%, indicating better performance in the task on this dataset. On the nested dataset CMeEE, our proposed method achieved better performance in precision, recall, and F1-score than the other three models. Compared with the F1- score values of the LSTM-CRF, BERT-CRF, and LEBERT-CRF models (47.00%, 56.45%, and 57.35%, respectively), the proposed method achieved an F1-score of 65.22%, representing relative improvements of 18.22%, 8.77%, and 7.87%, respectively. These results demonstrate that our proposed method achieves better performance and usability than the other three models on this dataset.

Table 4. Flat dataset comparison experiment results

Models	Weibo			Resume		
	P	R	F1	P	R	F1
LSTM-Crf	53.04	62.25	58.79	94.81	94.11	94.46
BERT-Crf	57. 14	66.67	59.92	95.37	94.84	95. 11
LEBERT-Crf	70.94	67.02	70.50	95.75	95.10	95.42
Ours	70.84	73.87	72.32	96.96	96.35	96.65

According to the results in Table 4, the proposed method in this paper achieves significant improvement in precision, recall, and F1 score on the flat data set Weibo compared to the LSTM-CRF model and BERT-CRF model. Specifically, compared to the LSTM-CRF model, the proposed method improves precision, recall, and F1 score by 17.80, 11.62, and 13.53% points, respectively. Compared to the BERT- CRF model, the proposed method improves precision, recall, and F1 score by 13.70, 7.20, and 12.40% points, respectively. Compared to the LEBERT-CRF model, the proposed method has similar precision but significantly higher recall and F1 score, improving by 6.85 and 1.82% points, respectively. These results demonstrate that the proposed method outperforms the other three models in terms of performance, indicating its superior classification ability and generalization performance on this data set.

On the flat data set Resume, the proposed method also exhibits excellent performance with higher precision (96.96%), recall (96.35%), and F1 score (96.65%) than the other three models. Specifically, compared to the LSTM-CRF model, the proposed method improves precision, recall, and F1 score by 1.15, 2.24, and 1.19% points, respectively. Compared to the BERT-CRF model, the proposed method improves precision, recall, and F1 score by 1.59, 1.51, and 1.54% points, respectively. Compared to the LEBERT-CRF model, the proposed method improves precision, recall, and F1 score by 1.21, 1.25, and 1.23% points, respectively. Therefore, the proposed method exhibits significantly superior performance on the flat data set Resume compared to the other three models.

5 Ablation Study

To verify the effectiveness of our proposed method in Chinese nested named entity recognition, we chose to conduct ablation experiments on the Chinese nested datasets "人民日报" and CMeEE. We further chose to delete some components and conducted three experiments: 1) Our complete model, using dictionary assistance, incorporates character-word pair information into BERT, and uses bi-affine structure encoding to obtain a 3D feature matrix. At the same time, the feature matrix is regarded as an image, and the local interaction between spans is modeled by using the convolutional neural network (CNN), and the spatial correlation between adjacent spans is fully utilized, and finally all non-conflicting features of the predicted input sequence are obtained. Named entity. 2) Remove the CNN module, skip formulas (6)–(7), and directly obtain the predicted entity after bi-affine structure decoding. 3) Remove the dictionary auxiliary module, skip formulas (3)–(5), and refer to the use of character information. 4) Remove the contrastive learning module, skip formulas (13) The comparison between our full model(14), and only use binary cross-entropy to calculate the loss function. The experimental results are shown in Table 5.

Table 5. The comparison between our full model and ablated models

Models	《人民日报》			CMeEE		
	P	R	F1	P	R	F1
Ours	96.08	96.13	96.11	64.98	65.46	65.22
Ours(w/o CNN)	94.71	94.08	95.09	63.25	71.43	62.50
Ours(w/o KB)	92.35	91.87	92.56	63.25	54.20	58.38
Ours(w/o contrast)	95.75	95.10	95.42	65.58	62.73	64. 12

On the nested data set "人民日报", the performance of the model decreased slightly after removing the CNN module, with precision, recall, and F1 score decreasing by 1.37%, 2.05%, and 1.02%, respectively. Removing the dictionary- assisted module had a greater impact on the model's performance, with precision, recall, and F1 score decreasing by 3.73%, 4.26%, and 3.55%, respectively. The removal of the contrastive learning module had a relatively small impact on the model's performance, with precision, recall, and F1 score decreasing by 0.33%, 0.03%, and 0.69%, respectively. On the nested data set CMeEE, the F1 score of this approach (65.22%) was higher than that of the other three experiments, with the experiment that removed the dictionary-assisted module achieving the lowest F1 score. When the CNN module was removed, the F1 score decreased by 2.72, indicating that the CNN module has certain advantages in modeling local interactions between spans on this dataset. Additionally, the dictionary-assisted module in this approach had a significant effect on Chinese nested named entity recognition, with a significant decrease in F1 score after its removal. The effect of the contrastive learning module was relatively stable, and its removal also led to a slight decrease in F1 score, which indicates that the module can enhance the model's robustness and generalization ability while reducing overfitting. Overall, the various components in this approach contributed to the model's performance to varying degrees.

6 Conclusion

In this paper, we propose KBCNER, a dictionary-assisted Chinese Nested Named entity Recognition model. The matching words are obtained through the dictionary, and the character-phrase pairs are formed and integrated into BERT. The semantic information contained in Chinese phrases is richer than that of a single character, and the dictionary information enhancement feature is introduced to obtain richer semantics. Using the bi-affine structure, get a global view of the span. At the same time, the feature matrix is regarded as an image, and the local interaction between spans is modeled by using a Convolutional Neural Network (CNN), which improves the recognition accuracy of nested entities. Finally, the idea of contrastive learning based on R-drop is adopted to enhance the robustness of the model. In the experimental part, the model is compared with the Chinese nested NER dataset ("人民日报", CMeEE) and the flat NER dataset (Weibo, Resume). At the same time, we conduct ablation experiments to analyze in detail the influence of the main components of the model on its performance. The model has achieved better performance than the baseline model on all data sets, indicating that the model has strong adaptability and versatility in different fields and different data sets.

Acknowledgment. This work was supported by the National Key R&D Program of China under Grant No. 2020YFB1710200.

References

1. Yao, H., Wu, Y., Al-Shedivat, M., et al.: Knowledge-aware meta-learning for low- resource text classification. arXiv preprint arXiv:2109.04707 (2021)
2. Chen, M.Y., Jiang, H., Yang, Y.: Context enhanced short text matching using clickthrough data. arXiv preprint arXiv:2203.01849 (2022)
3. Yu, W., Zhu, C., Li, Z., et al.: A survey of knowledge-enhanced text generation. ACM Comput. Surv. **54**(11s), 1–38 (2022)
4. Wang, X., Shen, Y., Cai, J., et al.: Damo-NLP at semeval-2022 task 11: A knowledge-based system for multilingual named entity recognition. arXiv preprint arXiv:2203.00545 (2022)
5. Zhang, Y., Yang, J.: Chinese NER using lattice LSTM. arXiv preprint arXiv:1805.02023 (2018)
6. Li, X., Yan, H., Qiu, X., et al.: FLAT: Chinese NER using flat-lattice transformer. arXiv preprint arXiv:2004.11795 (2020)
7. Liu, W., Fu, X., Zhang, Y., et al.: Lexicon enhanced Chinese sequence labeling using BERT adapter. arXiv preprint arXiv:2105.07148 (2021)
8. Sohrab, M.G., Miwa, M.: Deep exhaustive model for nested named entity recognition. In: Proceedings of the 2018 Conference on Empirical Methods in Natural Language Processing, Brussels, Belgium, pp. 2843–2849. Association for Computational Linguistics (2018)

9. Timothy Dozat and Christopher Manning. 2017. Deep biaffifine attention for neural dependency parsing. In: Proceedings of 5th International Conference on Learning Representations (ICLR)

10. Yu, J., Bohnet, B., Poesio, M.: Named entity recognition as dependency parsing. In: Proceedings of the 58th Annual Meeting of the as Sociation for Computational Linguistics, ACL 2020, Online, July 5–10, 2020, pp. 6470–6476. Association for Computational Linguistics (2020)

11. Yan, H., Sun, Y., Li, X., et al.: An embarrassingly easy but strong baseline for nested named entity recognition. arXiv preprint arXiv:2208.04534 (2022)

12. Wu, L., Li, J., Wang, Y., et al.: R-drop: regularized dropout for neural networks. Adv. Neural. Inf. Process. Syst. **34**, 10890–10905 (2021)

13. Ju, M., Miwa, M., Ananiadou, S.: A neural layered model for nested named entity recognition. In: Proceedings of the 2018 Conference of the North American Chapter of the Association for Computational Linguistics: Human Language Technologies, vol. 1 (Long Papers), pp. 1446–1459 (2018)

14. Straková, J., Straka, M., Hajič, J.: Neural architectures for nested NER through linearization. arXiv preprint arXiv:1908.06926 (2019)

15. Shibuya, T., Hovy, E.: Nested named entity recognition via second-best sequence learning and decoding. Trans. Assoc. Comput. Linguist. **8**, 605–620 (2020)

16. Li, H., Xu, H., Qian, L., et al.: Multi-layer joint learning of Chinese nested named entity recognition based on self-attention mechanism. In: CCF International Conference on Natural Language Processing and Chinese Computing. Springer, Cham (2020) 144–155

17. Wang, J., Shou, L., Chen, K., et al.: Pyramid: a layered model for nested named entity recognition. In: Proceedings of the 58th Annual Meeting of the Association for Computational Linguistics, pp. 5918–5928 (2020)

18. Lu, W., Roth, D.: Joint mention extraction and classification with mention hypergraphs. In: Proceedings of the 2015 Conference on Empirical Methods in Natural Language Processing, pp. 857–867 (2015)

19. Katiyar, A., Cardie, C.: Nested named entity recognition revisited. In: Proceedings of the 2018 Conference of the North American Chapter of the Association for Computational Linguistics: Human Language Technologies, 1 (2018)

20. Wang, B., Lu, W.: Neural segmental hypergraphs for overlapping mention recognition. arXiv preprint arXiv:1810.01817 (2018)

21. Luo, Y., Zhao, H.: Bipartite flat-graph network for nested named entity recognition. arXiv preprint arXiv:2005.00436 (2020)

22. Finkel, J.R., Manning, C.D.: Nested named entity recognition. In: Proceedings of the 2009 Conference on Empirical Methods in Natural Language Processing, pp. 141–150 (2009)

23. Fu, Y., Tan, C., Chen, M., et al.: Nested named entity recognition with partially-observed treecrfs. In: Proceedings of the AAAI Conference on Artificial Intelligence **35**(14), 12839–12847 (2021)

24. Lou, C., Yang, S., Tu, K.: Nested named entity recognition as latent lexicalized constituency parsing[J]. arXiv preprint arXiv:2203.04665 (2022)

25. Yang, S., Tu, K.: Bottom-up constituency parsing and nested named entity recognition with pointer networks. arXiv preprint arXiv:2110.05419 (2021)

26. Lin, H., Lu, Y., Han, X., et al.: Sequence-to-nuggets: nested entity mention detection via anchor-region networks. arXiv preprint arXiv:1906.03783 (2019)

27. Xia, C., Zhang, C., Yang, T., et al.: Multi-grained named entity recognition. arXiv preprint arXiv:1906.08449 (2019)

28. Zheng, C., Cai, Y., Xu, J., et al.: A boundary-aware neural model for nested named entity recognition. In: Proceedings of the 2019 Conference on Empirical Methods in Natural Language Processing and the 9th International Joint Conference on Natural Language Processing (EMNLP-IJCNLP). Association for Computational Linguistics (2019)
29. Yu, J., Bohnet, B., Poesio, M.: Named entity recognition as dependency parsing. arXiv preprint arXiv:2005.07150 (2020)
30. Xu, Y., Huang, H., Feng, C., et al.: A supervised multi-head self-attention network for nested named entity recognition. In: Proceedings of the AAAI Conference on Artificial Intelligence, vol. 35, no. 16, pp. 14185–14193 (2021)
31. Shen, Y., Ma, X., Tan, Z., et al.: Locate and label: a two-stage identifier for nested named entity recognition. arXiv preprint arXiv:2105.06804 (2021)
32. Song, Y., Shi, S., Li, J., Zhang, H.: Directional skip-gram: Explicitly distinguishing left and right context for word embeddings. In: Proceedings of the 2018 Conference of the North American Chapter of the Association for Computational Linguistics: Human Language Technologies, vol. 2 (Short Papers), pp. 175–180, New Orleans, Louisiana. Association for Computational Linguistics (2018)
33. Huang, Z., Xu, W., Yu, K.: Bidirectional LSTM-CRF models for sequence tagging. arXiv preprint arXiv:1508.01991 (2015)
34. Li, X., Zhang, H., Zhou, X.H.: Chinese clinical named entity recognition with variant neural structures based on Bert methods. J. Biomed. Inform. **107**, 103422 (2020)

Cce-SpERT: A Span-Based Pre-trained Transformer Model for Chinese Civil Engineering Information Joint Extraction

Lei Zhu[1,2] , Bing Chao[1(✉)], Tong Zhang[1], Qin Zhao[1], Mingsong Yang[1], and Rui Jiao[1]

[1] Xi'an University of Technology, Xi'an 710048, China
`2211221074@stu.xaut.edu.cn`
[2] State Key Laboratory of Rail Transit Engineering Information (FSDI), Xi'an 710048, China

Abstract. In this paper, we apply a word encoding averaging approach to Transformer incorporating embedded codes of domain lexicons, and propose a Span-based joint information extraction model Cce-SpERT for Chinese civil engineering information specifications. In the proposed model, we study the multi-domain specialized vocabulary in the domain of Chinese civil engineering, and build a specific domain vocabulary embedding approach based on the word encoding average mechanism. With the aid of domain adaptive and task adaptive pre-trainings, we combine BERT and Transformer to generate a Span-based Transformer model Cce-SpERT for extraction of the entity and inter-entity relation at one-time. The experimental results demonstrate the potential of our model on pre-training, negative sampling, Span-based joint extraction, domain word embedding, and relative position embedding, and show that our model achieves an excellent result of joint information extraction on the regulatory text of Chinese civil engineering.

Keywords: Chinese natural language processing · BERT · SpERT · word embedding · relative position encoding

1 Introduction

In recent years, a large number of Transformer-based [1] models have been proposed and achieved excellent performance on NLP tasks, such as BERT [2], GPT [3], and RoBERTa [4]. Most existing models utilize the Transformer-based self-attention mechanism, which can effectively mine the association relationship between context and tokens and generate the code with embedding "attention" in accordance with the quantification of the relationship. This embedding approach can be more sensitive to obtaining semantic and syntactic information from contexts.

With the pre-training of a massive open domain corpus, these models can more efficiently acquire a large amount of world knowledge, and their embedding and representation with world knowledge can be easily transferred to different downstream transduction tasks by using specifically designed schemes. Thus, existing models employ

M. Zhang et al. (Eds.): CCF NCCA 2023, CCIS 1959, pp. 206–220, 2024.
https://doi.org/10.1007/978-981-99-8764-1_16

the pre-training of massive open domain corpora and a small amount of supervised target corpora to quickly implement downstream NLP tasks with high performance, including natural language understanding (NLU) [5], natural language generation (NLG) [6], named entity recognition (NER) [7], relation extraction (RE) [8], natural language question and answer (QA) [9], etc.

In this paper, we investigate the regulatory text of Chinese civil engineering and propose a pre-training Transformer-based language model to solve the problem of joint entity and relation extraction. Specifically, given a set of the predefined entity and relation categories of Chinese civil engineering information, a sentence selected from regulatory text is input, and our goal is to extract all triplets < Entity1, RelationType, Entity2 >, which contains the identification of all entities of the sentence.

Table 1. An example of joint information extraction.

Chinese civil engineering specification	Entity1	RelationType	Entity2
Traction substations should be equipped with stray current monitoring and drainage facilities, and should be based on the monitoring of stray currents to decide whether to put the drainage facilities into use (牵引变电所应设置杂散电流监测及排流设施, 应根据杂散电流的监测情况决定是否将排流设施投入使用.)	Traction substations (牵引变电所)	Arrange (设置)	Stray current monitoring (杂散电流监测)
	Traction substations (牵引变电所)	Arrange (设置)	Drainage facilities (排流设施)

Table 1 shows that the joint information extracted result contains two triplets when given a sentence from the regulatory text of Chinese civil engineering. Usually, the information extraction problem comprises two subtasks: *i*) NER and *ii*) RE. These two subtasks are separately solved by traditional methods without regard to their correlation [10]. Since the recognition of entity categories significantly affects the extraction of inter-entity relations, more recent neural networks simultaneously handle these two sub-tasks and achieve better results by fully exploiting the information between entities and relations [11]. In the regulatory text of Chinese civil engineering, for instance, "Traction substations" is recognized as an entity of "Building", and "Stray current monitoring" is recognized as an entity of "ConstructionElements". Thus, their relation of "Arrange" can be quickly extracted, benefiting from the results of entity recognition and their structural relationship.

Inspired by the above, we propose a Span-based pre-trained Transformer model for joint information extraction of Chinese civil engineering information specifications. The core module of our model is BERT and Transformer, and an extraction scheme based on a Span-based labeling mechanism is presented to substitute the traditional BIO/BILOU labels. The Span-based labeling mechanism uses all subsequences in sentences as candidate entities, and the size of candidate subsequences is customizable according to the different subsequence criteria [12]. Based on the advantages of Span-based entity extraction, the candidate subsequences are input into the entity classifier to recognize the entity category for each subsequence, even including labeled "non-entities" span for undefined subsequences. A relation classifier classifies the labeled sequences with predefined relation categories, and the final triplet is extracted.

In our model, all the overlapping entities can be classified, which avoids some of the misclassifications of overlapping entities, such as "Subway(地铁)" and "Subway station(地铁车站)" by the traditional BIO label. Thus, we call the proposed model the "Chinese civil engineering Span-based Entity and Relation Transformer model" (Cce-SpERT), and the main contributions of this paper are listed as follows.

(1) We present a specific domain vocabulary encoding approach based on a word average encoding mechanism for multi-domain vocabularies.
(2) We propose a novel Span-based joint model for joint information extraction. For the named entity recognition task, we also present a specially constructed relative position embedding matrix for positional encoding. Meanwhile, we incorporate Lattice [13] into the Span-based joint information extraction model for the first time.

2 Data

This section introduces the datasets in our work, the classification criteria of entities and relations for Chinese civil engineering information, and some data enhancement approaches to processing dataset establishment.

2.1 Datasets

Table 2. Datasets in our experiments.

Text Corpuses	Count
Pre-training texts of Chinese civil engineering information	800K
Information extraction text of open domain	50K
Information extraction text of civil engineering information	3K

As shown in Table 2, we utilize three datasets in our experiments: *i*) pre-training text of Chinese civil engineering information, *ii*) open domain joint information extraction text and *iii*) joint information extraction text of Chinese civil engineering information specifications.

The pre-training text contains 800K items of unlabeled unsupervised sentences, and it is adjusted to the upper and lower-based sentence format in accordance with the training rules of BERT. The open domain information extraction text contains 50K labeled data sorted from the open-source dataset [14], labeled the entity span category and span boundary. The third dataset contains 3K items of NER&RE joint extraction data of Chinese civil engineering information, which is manually labeled and established for training processing. It annotates the possible entities in the corpus and the relations between entities, which is finally converted to the text in "JSON" format. The entity boundary and entity category are labeled with the position index and category index.

2.2 The Categories of Entities and Relations

The classification criteria of entities in our datasets are based on "Standard for Classification and Coding of Construction Engineering Design Information Models" [15] and "ISO 12006–2 International Standard" [16]. These criteria mainly address the structure, components, and attributes of building information models. The classification and coding of the system promote the processing of information standardization, particularly speeding up the development of building information modeling (BIM). Based on these criteria, we merge the entity's categories and generate six categories. Table 3 shows the final classification criteria of entities.

Table 3. The entity categories.

Index	Entity Categories	Instances
1	Building	Station building
2	ConstructionElements	Stray current monitoring
3	Activity	Maintenance
4	ProperNouns	Strength requirements of subway subgrade engineering
5	OrganizationalRole	Engineer
6	Others	The actual situation

For the relation categories, there are too many classification criteria of relations in the original standard, which may reduce the accuracy of entity recognition, and too many categories of relations can further affect the accuracy of relation extraction based on entities. To evaluate our model, we study the classification criteria of Semeval-Task8 [17] and merge the related categories of Chinese civil engineering information. In our study, we finally generate the eight categories of relations and build triples < Entity1, RelationType, Entity2 > from structured data. Table 4 shows the final classification criteria of relations.

3 Model

Figure 1 shows the framework of our model, which includes three parts: *i*) preprocessing module, *ii*) Transformer module, and *iii*) classification module. The preprocessing module is mainly to handle the current batch data, which is inputted into the model. The preprocessing includes lattice word querying, index encoding of Chinese characters and words, and word representation embedding with domain adaptive pretraining (DAPT) and task adaptive pretraining (TAPT) by BERT.

Table 4. The relation categories.

Index	Relation Categories	Description
1	Arrange	Configuration relationship
2	Set	Containment relationship
3	Use	Use/adoption relationship
4	Satisfy	Limited satisfaction relationship
5	With	Function relationship
6	Location	Physical/abstract location relationship
7	Modification_Limit	Modified relationship
8	Others	Others

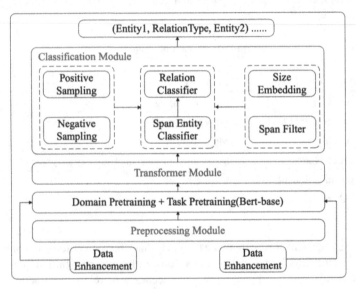

Fig. 1. Framework of the Cce-SpERT model.

The Transformer module is the core module of our model to calculate the attention between words. It includes multiple neural network modules, such as a self-attention layer, residual connection layer, feedforward neural network layer, and linear mapping layer. After calculating the attention, our model can effectively obtain the potential connection between the word and the lattice words, which is convenient for the subsequent model to classify the entity and relations.

The classification module includes an entity classifier and a relationship classifier. The entity classifier mainly classifies multiple words or spans to generate entity categories. The relation classifier mainly performs relation extraction between multiple spans to obtain their relation category. Moreover, we also employ an additional span length size-embedding approach to recognize the span boundary. The approaches or mechanisms used in our model are described as follows.

3.1 Preprocessing Module

In the preprocessing module, our model uses the original version of BERT as the initial embedding and conducts pre-trainings on the large-scale corpora to acquire the related knowledge, which includes two corpora: the 800K unsupervised corpus of Chinese civil engineering information, and the 50K open domain span-NER corpus. Similar to BERT, the domain pre-training utilizes the same masked language model (MLM) to predict the covered target word by covering and replacing the single word with a specific probability.

The TAPT corpora are collected from NER data of Internet news and adjusted to the format of multiple span tags. The goal of the TAPT is to determine the boundary of the span entity and the category of each entity. Note that these open domain corpora contain the labeled entities and unlabeled relations between entity pairs since the manual labeling of relations in the open domain dataset will greatly increase the workload of NER and RE tasks. Thus, the secondary adaptive pre-trainings is only performed on the single task of Span-based NER.

The preprocessing module of our model also utilizes some other encoding schemes, such as lattice encoding and relative position encoding, which are described as follows.

Lattice Encoding. At the current stage, the vocabulary is established by the preprocessing module, and the input token sequence is compared with the instances of the vocabulary class to generate multiple lexicons [13]. That is, some potential words are composed of single-character tokens. Similar to FLAT, the lexicon is converted to a flat-lattice, which is a collection of a series of spans. The head and tail position indexes are also recorded separately, which indicate the start and end positions of the word lexicon. When a word is composed of a single Chinese character, its start and end positions are the same index. Since the additional position encoding does not change the encoding of the original lexicon, the original features of the input sequence are maintained, which guarantees the stability of our model.

Relative Position Encoding. In FLAT, the entity is composed of different spans. Thus the length of each entity's token is different from the other. Due to the difference in length, "relative position embedding" is more important than "absolute position embedding" for the NER task. Therefore, our model preprocessing embeds each span's relative position.

In fact, there are three different relationships between different spans: intersection, inclusion, and separation. For example, the relationship between the two spans "Subway(地铁)" and "Subway station(地铁车站)" is the intersection. To solve the multi-entity overlapping, we employ the same relative position embedding method Transformer-xl [18]. With relative position embedding, the relation between two spans is clearly represented, and the distance information between spans is also effectively encoded.

3.2 Transformer Module

To fully learn the associated information, our model utilizes the self-attention mechanism in the Transformer module, which is defined as follows.

$$A_{i,j}^* = W_q^T E_{sp_i}^T E_{sp_i} W_{k,E} + W_q^T E_{sp_i}^T R_{ij} W_{k,R} + u^T E_{sp_i}^T W_{k,E} + v^T R_{ij} W_{k,R} \qquad (1)$$

where all W represents the weight matrix, u and v are also learnable parameters. The final output is the embedding tensor incorporating the relative position information of the span.

After the input sentence is handled by the preprocessing module and the Transformer module, its code is generated, and the attention information between words is embedded. Then, it is input into the subsequent entity and relation classifiers for joint information extraction.

3.3 Classification Module

After the Transformer module, all the words and contextual embedding representations of the entire sequence can be obtained, and then these embedding representations are input into this classification module to perform entity and relation classification tasks.

As shown in Fig. 1, the embedding representation first performs the entity classification based on the span label based on the entity classifier. The input vector comprises the embedding representation, contextual embedding representation, and size-embedding embedding representation of all words in a span. The output code is a representation vector with the same dimension as the single word's token. Then, the classification of the relation between the two candidate entities pair is performed using a negative sampling mechanism. The main approaches in the classification module are described as follows.

Span Classifier. For the NER task, the span classifier is the key classifier of our model. It is based on a fully connected neural network, and the original input sequence is divided into some single tokens. Assume $sp_n = (e_i, e_{i+1}, ..., e_j)$ is a single span and input into the span classifier, composed of multiple word candidate tokens, and ε is a pre-defined collection of multiple entity categories. The goal of the span classifier is to map a span into the set of $\varepsilon \cup \{none\}$, where "none" represents the "non-entity" category.

The input of the entity classifier consists of three parts. The first part is the span embedding composed of multiple single-word tokens, mapped into the same Tensor dimension as the single-word token through max-pooling. The second part is context embedding. The third part is the size-embedding of an entity. To enhance the recognition ability of span boundary, we specifically construct a training parameter matrix of size-embedding and splice it with span embedding to perform span classification.

A span is represented as the splicing operation of tensors, and it can be defined as follows.

$$e(sp_n) = A_{i,j}^* \circ c \qquad (2)$$

where $e(sp_n)$ represents the encoding of the n-th span, $A_{i,j}^*$ represents the span embedding from i to j, and c represents the contextual global embedding of the sequence, which is generated from the "[cls]" token.

Size Embedding. After span classification, the constructed embedding matrix with dynamics span size is spliced using the size-embedding approach. The size-embedding is established by an especially linear network *nn. Linear*, whose parameters are customizable by training, and its input is the size of the boundary of each span. The output is a mapping of the same tensor size and dimension as e. It is finally expressed as w_n. The span tensor can be defined as follows.

$$e(sp_n) = A_{i,j}^* \circ c \circ w_n \tag{3}$$

To employ the span mechanism for the NER task, the splicing of the global vector c may be fully exploited in the context of the current sentence and the correlation between span tags. For example, given two spans of "Subway tunnel (地铁隧道)" and " Subway tunnel (铁隧) (The subsequence of the first span, not an Entity)", if the correlation between the previous span and the context of the sequence is higher, it should be classified as an entity. Otherwise, the last span should not be classified as an entity. Essentially, this approach is very similar to Transformer's self-attention mechanism.

Different from the traditional BIO labeling methods, a single token of our model can be classified as multiple entities with different boundaries. In traditional labeling approaches, a single token has only one corresponding entity category, and it does not need to recognize the entity boundary. Benefiting from CRF [19], the unique classification result of a single token can be directly obtained. In our model, we first recognize span boundaries in the input sequence and then classify the entity category. The boundary size vector should be customizable by training, and the span is finally classified by Softmax according to the entity category set $\varepsilon \cup \{none\}$. The classification result can be calculated with the following equation.

$$y^s = softmax(W^s e(sp_n) + b^s) \tag{4}$$

where y^s is the final span classification result, W^s is the classifier weight matrix, and b^s is the bias value.

Relation Classifier. After span classification with an entity category, spans are added to the set of candidate entity pairs, which can be denoted as $\{sp_1, sp_2, ..., sp_n\}$. Then, the relation between each pair of entities is exhausted, which is denoted as a candidate entity pair (sp_j, sp_k). The relation of the candidate entity pair is classified with the relation classifier according to the pre-defined relation category set $R \cup \{none\}$, where "none" represents the "non-relation" category.

In summary, the embedding representation of the relation between two entities is defined as follows.

$$rela_{\rightarrow}^{j,k} = e(sp_j) \circ c(e(sp_j), e(sp_k)) \circ e(sp_k) \circ c \tag{5}$$

$$rela_{\leftarrow}^{j,k} = e(sp_j) \circ c(e(sp_j), e(sp_k)) \circ e(sp_k) \circ c \tag{6}$$

$$y_{\rightarrow/\leftarrow}^r = \sigma(W^r \cdot rela_{\rightarrow/\leftarrow}^{j,k} + b^r) \tag{7}$$

Among the above equations, the relations are divided into forward and backwards relationships. The final embedding representation contains three parts: *i*) entity embedding, *ii*) token embedding between entities, and *iii*) entire contextual embedding. All embeddings can participate in the calculation of the weight matrix W and are activated by the activation function. Since there may exist many relations in the inference processing, our model sets a threshold α, and the relation is directly discarded when its calculated result is less than α, which can reduce the time of relations inference processing.

Negative Sampling. In addition, we also utilize a negative sampling mechanism to improve the overall efficiency of the model. In training datasets, the limited scale of labeled entities may result in insufficient training on span classification, especially for "none-entity" spans. Therefore, a negative sampling mechanism is essential. Specifically, the training samples of labeled entities are first collected to a set S^{true}, and then the negative sample data classified as "none-entity" are generated, which is denoted as $S^{negative} \in \{none\}$. Training on negative samples, our model fully learns the features of the span, which are uncorrelated to the global context information of the input sentence, and these uncorrelated spans are classified as "non-entity".

Meanwhile, our model also generates a large number of negative relation samples, which is labeled as "non-relation" for supplement training of the relation classifier, and it is denoted as $R^{negative} \in \{none\}$.

4 Experimental Results

4.1 Pre-training

The datasets of our model include three datasets: *i*) the unsupervised dataset of Chinese civil engineering information; *ii*) the task pre-training open domain dataset; and *iii*) the NER&RE joint information extraction training dataset of Chinese civil engineering information. Since the traditional CNN [20], and LSTM [21] infrastructure models cannot effectively solve the overlapping entity problem in the NER task, we choose "BERT$_{base}$ + EntityClassifier + RelationClassifier" as the baseline in our experiments. Based on the original BERT, we conduct DAPT and TAPT, respectively, which are described as follows [22].

Domain Adaptive Pre-training (DAPT). We use a large-scale unlabeled corpus of Chinese civil engineering information for DAPT. The reason is that the corpus of the original BERT is mainly concentrated on the domains of English news and encyclopedias, but the domain vocabulary of Chinese civil engineering information is multi-domain specialized dictionaries and different from that of English news and encyclopedias. The original BERT cannot make the model fully learn the hidden features of Chinese civil engineering information, and thus the secondary domain adaptive pre-training is essential for joint information extraction. The processing of the DAPT runs on GTX2080TI and in our experiments, and its duration reaches two weeks.

Task Adaptive Pre-training (TAPT). The TAPT of our model is mainly designed for the span-NER task. In our model, the Transformer module followed by the pre-training has a large number of parameters, and its initialization usually uses a random scheme, which may decrease the inference ability of the optimal solution of the downstream task. Therefore, it is necessary to perform the TAPT on the Transformer module to acquire the best initialization parameter. For the TAPT, our model conducts pre-training on 50K items of the open domain span-NER dataset. The boundary rule of span classification is learned and embedded into the hidden vectors.

4.2   Training Parameters

Table 5 shows the relevant parameters in our experiments, which proved to have good performance.

Table 5. The training parameters.

Parameters	Abbreviation	Value
TrainBatchSize	train_batch_size	2
Negative sampling entity size	neg_entity_count	50
Negative relationship size	neg_relation_count	50
Epochs Size	epochs	50
Learning Rate	lr	5.00E-5
Learning Rate Warmup	lr_warmup	0.1
WeightDecay	weieght_decay	0.01
Maximum gradient clipping Size	max_grad_norm	1
Relational filtering threshold	rel_filter_threshold	0.4
Entity size embedding	size_embedding	50
Neurons drop probability	prop_drop	0.1
MaxSpanSize	max_span_size	12
MaxSpanPairsCount	max_pairs	1000

4.3   Training Result of NER with Different Parameters

For the NER task, our model tests the efficiency of different negative sample sizes. Table 6 shows the results of negative sampling with different sizes from 0 to 100. With increasing negative sample size, the F1-score increases, which improves the performance to 48.45%. The results show that negative sampling is useful, and the negative sampling mechanism can achieve a significant improvement in the NER task. However, when the size of the negative samples increases from 50 to 100, the improvement in the F1-score is very slight. Thus, we set the size of negative sampling to 50 in our experiments.

Table 6. NER results of different negative sample parameters.

Model	Neg_entity_relation	Precision	Recall	F1
Cce-SpERT	0 epoch50	33.19	17.66	23.05
	25 epoch50	51.80	33.94	40.74
	50 epoch50	**55.24**	**44.33**	**48.45**
	75 epoch50	56.02	43.09	47.76
	100 epoch50	55.80	43.87	48.29

4.4 NER Results

The BERT and RoBERTa models are mainly used in a scheme with span labels for classification, and they are selected to evaluate the performance. In our experiments, the BERT, RoBERTa models and our secondary pre-training models are used as initial embeddings, combined with the Transformer module integrated with the relative position embeddings. The results of these different models in the NER task are shown in Table 7.

Table 7. The result of NER task.

Model	Epoch	Precision	Recall	F1
BERT + SpERT	50	36.31	30.73	33.29
RoBERTa + SpERT	50	39.89	32.57	35.86
RoBERTa + SpERT + relaPOS	50	55.02	41.12	46.46
Cce-SpERT	**50**	**55.24**	**44.33**	**48.45**

As shown in Table 7, RoBERTa is pretrained on Chinse corpora. Thus its F1 value is more than that of BERT. Relative position embedding is used to describe the distances between entities, which may contain contextual semantical information and Chinese syntax information. The NER result of RoBERTa + SpERT + relaPOS is better than that of RoBERTa. Since Cce-SpERT is integrated into DAPT, TAPT and relative position embedding, its F1 value is best in our experiments.

4.5 RE Result

Table 8 shows the performance of relation extraction on different models with entity categories. Similar to the NER results, the RoBERTa + SpERT + relaPOS is better than RoBERTa and BERT, and Cce-SpERT performs the best, which finally achieves the best F1 value of 60.90.

4.6 Knowledge Graph

After the entity-relationship extraction step, we finally build triples < Entity1, RelationType, Entity2 > from structured data, such as < Traction substations, Arrange,

Table 8. The result of RE task.

Model	Recall (micro)	F1 (micro)	Recall (macro)	F1 (macro)
BERT + SpERT	34.86	51.70	44.70	56.00
RoBERTa + SpERT	33.94	50.68	43.89	54.92
RoBERTa + SpERT + relaPOS	34.40	51.19	45.60	57.03
Cce-SpERT	**37.61**	**54.67**	**49.34**	**60.90**

Stray current monitoring >. Then, insert all triples into the Neo4j database with the Cypher statement. The final constructed rail transportation knowledge graph is partially visualized as shown in Fig. 2.

The Cypher query language is a declarative query language for the Neo4j database, and Cypher is also known as CQL. Cypher language is equivalent to Sql for relational databases, and its most important feature is the flexibility to add, delete and query any node or relationship in the graph. Then, based on the Cypher language, some simple associative network analysis is performed for knowledge graphs in the Chinese civil engineering domain.

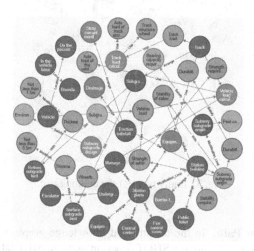

Fig. 2. Partial knowledge graph.

Create Entity Nodes. Before adding nodes, the Cypher statement needs to query whether there are duplicate nodes in the database, and if there are, add new relationships or new attributes based on the entity node, if not, as shown in the following example: CREATE (n:Building{name:'Traction substations'}) RETURN n;. Among them, CREATE is a creation grammar, which is used to create entity and relationship attributes. The label of the node is the building entity type in the entity classification, and the name represents the name of the node. After RETURN, the new node created will be returned.

Update Nodes relationships. Adding a node relationship is similar to creating an entity node, also using the CREATE statement. In this paper, the process of creating relationships is divided into creating relationships directly in the process of entity creation and creating relationships under existing entities. For example: Match (a: Building), (b: ConstructionElements) where a.name = 'Traction substations' AND b.name = ' Stray current monitoring' create (a)-[r: Arrange]- > (b) return; Among them, the MATCH statement is first matched to two entity nodes named Traction substation and Stray current monitoring, and then the relationship is set as 'Arrange'.

Query Entity Nodes. Querying entity nodes requires a MATCH statement to match. Whether it is before creating a node, creating a relationship, or updating an attribute, you can use MATCH to match whether there is a node with the same name of the same type to avoid duplicate creation of entity nodes. As shown in the following example: MATCH p = (n:Building) RETURN n LIMIT 25, representing the query entity type Building nodes, Building entity nodes under LIMIT 25 show the results as shown in Fig. 3.

Fig. 3. Entity types of the building part.

Query the Shortest Path. In the constructed knowledge graph of the Chinese civil engineering domain, we can use the SHOT function in the neo4j database to perform the shortest path query between two entities. For example, we used MATCH p = shortest-path((:Building{name: "Track"})-[*..6]-(:ProperNouns{name: "Not less than 0.5m"})) RETURN p, this Cypher statement indicates that we query the shortest path between two entities of not more than six, the shortest path between node Track of entity type Building and node not less than 0.5m of entity type ProperNouns, the query result is shown in Fig. 4.

As shown in Fig. 4, we performed the shortest path query between two entities, and we can obtain the relational path information between two entities. The thickness of the

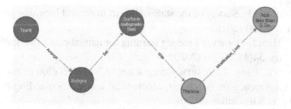

Fig. 4. Shortest path graph between entities.

surface roadbed bed on the track should be not less than 0.5m. The obtained knowledge map of the Chinese civil engineering domain can be used in areas such as QA and automated compliance checking (ACC) [23].

5   Conclusions

In this paper, we propose a joint information extraction model called Cce-SpERT based on the BERT and Span-based Transformer. Our model utilizes the word encoding average approach to integrate the embedding of the domain dictionary and combine the embedding of additional information, such as lattice embedding and relative position embedding, to improve the efficiency of NER and RE tasks on the specifications of Chinese civil engineering information. Moreover, DAPT and TAPT are also applied to enhance the inference ability of our model on a specific domain. The experimental results show that our model outperforms the variant models of BERT and RoBERT. In the future, we will find and embed other high-quality, valuable and structured information, such as graphs, to improve the performance of joint information extraction.

Acknowledgements. The research presented in this paper is supported in part by the National Key R&D Program of China (2022YFB2602203), the National Natural Science Foundation of China (grant: 61602374, 51878556), and the State Key Laboratory of Rail Transit Engineering Informatization (FSDI) of China (grant: SKLKZ19–05).

References

1. Vaswani, A., Shazeer, N., Parmar, N.: Attention is all you need. In: 31st Conference on Neural Information Processing Systems (NIPS 2017), pp.1–11. Neural Information Processing Systems Foundation, Long Beach, CA, USA (2017)
2. Devlin, J., Chang, M.W., Lee, K., et al.: BERT: pre-training of deep bidirectional transformers for language understanding. arXiv preprint arXiv:1810.04805 (2018)
3. Radford, A., Narasimhan, K., Salimans, T.: Improving language understanding by generative pre-training. Technical report, OpenAI (2018)
4. Liu, Y., Ott, M., Goyal, N., et al.: RoBERTa: a robustly optimized BERT pretraining approach. arXiv preprint arXiv:1907.11692 (2019)
5. Bender, E.M., Koller, A.: Climbing towards NLU: on meaning, form, and understanding in the age of data. In: Proceedings of the 58th Annual Meeting of the Association for Computational Linguistics, pp. 5185–5198. Association for Computational Linguistics, Online (2020)

6. Gatt, A., Krahmer, E.J.: Survey of the state of the art in natural language generation. J. Artif. Intell. Res. **61**, 75–170 (2018)
7. Li, J., Sun, A., Han, J.: A survey on deep learning for named entity recognition. IEEE Trans. Knowl. Data Eng. **34**(1), 50–70 (2020)
8. Zhang, X., Dai, Y., Jiang, T.: A survey deep learning based relation extraction. In: 2020 4th International Conference on Electrical, Mechanical and Computer Engineering (ICEMCE 2020), pp. 19–21. IOP, Online (2020)
9. Zhang, R., Wang, Y., Mao, Y.: Question answering in knowledge bases: a verification assisted model with iterative training. ACM Trans. Inf. Syst. **37**(4), 1–26 (2019)
10. Zeng, D., Liu, K., Lai, S.: Relation classification via convolutional deep neural network. In: Proceedings of COLING 2014, 25th International Conference on Computational Linguistics: Technical Papers, pp. 2335–2344. COLING, Dublin, Ireland (2014)
11. Bekoulis, G., Deleu, J., Demeester, T.: Joint entity recognition and relation extraction as a multi-head selection problem. Expert Syst. Appl. **114**, 34–45 (2018)
12. Eberts, M., Ulges, A.: Span-based joint entity and relation extraction with transformer pre-training. arXiv preprint arXiv:1909.07755 (2019)
13. Li, X., Yan, H., Qiu, X., et al.: FLAT: Chinese NER using flat-lattice transformer. arXiv preprint arXiv:2004.11795 (2020)
14. Xu, L., Dong, Q., Liao, Y., et al.: CLUENER2020: fine-grained named entity recognition dataset and benchmark for Chinese. arXiv preprint arXiv:2001.04351 (2020)
15. GB/T 51269–2017: Classification and coding standards for building information models-building standards (2017)
16. BS ISO 12006–2:2015: Building construction-Organization of information about construction works (2015)
17. Hendrickx, I., Kim, S.N., Kozareva, Z., et al.: Semeval-2010 task 8: multi-way classification of semantic relations between pairs of nominals. arXiv preprint arXiv:1911.10422 (2019)
18. Dai, Z., Yang, Z., Yang, Y., et al.: Transformer-xl: attentive language models beyond a fixed-length context. arXiv preprint arXiv:1901.02860 (2019)
19. Zheng, S., Jayasumana, S., Romera-Paredes, B.: Conditional random fields as recurrent neural networks. In: Proceedings of the IEEE International Conference on Computer Vision, pp. 1529–1537. IEEE, Chile (2015)
20. Gui, T., Ma, R., Zhang, Q.: CNN-based Chinese NER with Lexicon rethinking. In: Proceedings of the Twenty-Eighth International Joint Conference on Artificial Intelligence, pp. 4982–4988. Morgan Kaufmann, Macao (2019)
21. Yu, Y., Si, X., Hu, C.: A review of recurrent neural networks: LSTM cells and network architectures. Neural Comput. **31**(7), 1235–1270 (2019)
22. Gururangan, S., Marasović, A., Swayamdipta, S., et al.: Don't stop pretraining: adapt language models to domains and tasks. arXiv preprint arXiv:2004.10964 (2020)
23. Beach, T.H., Hippolyte, J.L., Rezgui, Y.: Towards the adoption of automated regulatory compliance checking in the built environment. Autom. Constr. **118**, 103285 (2020)

A BMRC Algorithm Based on Knowledge Enhancement and Case Regularization for Aspect Emotion Triplet Extraction

Wei Cheng(✉) , Ye Liu , and Yimeng Yin

Hebei University of Economics and Business, Shijiazhuang, HeBei, China
chengwei2021@stu.heuet.edu.cn

Abstract. Aspect Emotion Triplet Extraction (ASTE) is a vital branch in the field of NLP that strives to identify triads consisting of aspect words, opinion words, and emotional polarity from sentences. Each triplet contains three elements, namely, aspect words, opinion words and their emotional polarity. How to effectively extract attribute and opinion words and detect the connection between them is extremely important. Early work often focused on only one of these tasks and could not extract triples simultaneously in the same framework. Recently, researchers proposed using the bidirectional machine reading comprehension model (BMRC) to obtain triples of aspects, opinions, and emotions in the same framework. However, the existing BMRC model ignored professional domain knowledge, and the equal treatment training ignored the special contribution of individual instances in sentences to sentences. To this end, this paper proposes a BMRC with knowledge enhancement, which integrates the knowledge of specialized fields into the model, strengthens the connection between specific fields and open fields, increases instance regularization, and pays attention to the contribution of individual instances to sentences. Our experiments on several benchmark data sets have shown that our model has reached the most advanced performance.

Keywords: Triplet extraction · Machine Reading Comprehension · Emotional analysis

1 Introduction

Fine-grained emotion analysis is an important branch of NLP. According to the existing fine-grained emotion analysis model, it aims to mine more detailed opinions and emotions in specific aspects. It includes many tasks: aspect terms (ATE) [4,10,13], viewpoint identification terms (OTE) [7,14,20], aspect-based sentiment analysis (ASA) [3,4,23], aspect - opinion extraction (AOE) [1,28], etc. Nevertheless, the existing research generally deals with these tasks separately. It is not possible to extract the triple information of sentence, opinion and emotion

Supported by Hebei Provincial Department of Education Fund.

on the same platform. To completely solve this problem, Peng [13] proposed aspect emotion triple extraction (ATSE), which enables the model to carry out the triplet extraction of scheme opinions within the same framework.

Although these studies have made substantial headway in the extraction of emotional triplets, they still face many great challenges. First, in the BMRC model, we use the training model obtained from the large-scale open domain corpus, which is the general representation of knowledge, making the extraction and realization of emotional triplets in the professional field not good. Second, in the training phase of BMRC model in the past, training examples are often treated equally, and the special contribution of individual examples to sentences is rarely noticed. For example, the "not" in "this food is not delicious" is covered up, and the message of the broken sentence becomes opposite to the original sentence, resulting in the reduction of the accuracy and robustness of the model.

In response to the former problems, we propose a BMRC method based on knowledge enhancement and instance regularization. This task is transformed into a machine reading comprehension model. Through bidirectional complex queries, we can find the triple information of aspects, opinions and emotions of sentences. Different from the general BMRC model, in the pretraining stage, we used data sets that emphasize specific areas and integrated the knowledge map into the model so that the model can be equipped with some professional domain knowledge, strengthen the connection between specific areas and open areas, and diminish the differences between the pretraining model and the downstream task fine-tuning. In addition, we have added an automatic noise coder to the model to recover the damaged marks and calculate the difference between the damaged sentence and the original sentence to provide a clear regular signal to better focus on the contribution of individual instances to the sentence. The key points of our contributions are listed below:

- The BMRC model incorporates a knowledge map to equip itself with domain-specific expertise, thus fortifying the linkage between particular domains and the broader open domain.
- An automatic denoising encoder is added to the model to improve the model's capacity to center on the contribution of individual instances to sentences and improve the robustness and prediction accuracy of the model.
- Through many experiments on standard data sets, our model has achieved optimal results.

2 Related Work

2.1 Fine Grained Emotional Analysis

Traditional affective analysis tasks are text-level affective analysis tasks, sentence-level affective analysis tasks, and aspect-level affective analysis tasks. Among them, aspect-level affective analysis tasks are aspect-oriented or entity-oriented more fine-grained affective analysis tasks, mainly including aspect-class affective analysis (ACSA), opinion term extraction (AOE), aspect-specific sentiment recognition (ASR). These studies are mainly aimed at the fixed level, and some tasks are extracted separately, ignoring the dependency between different aspects. In an effort to explore the dependency between different tasks, some scholars are committed to coupling different subtasks and proposing effective models. For example, Wang et al. [20] proposed a multilayer attention-based deep learning model for extracting aspect and opinion terms, and [22] proposed a grid marking scheme (GTS), which extracts the emotional polarity of terms through a grid marking task to form opinions. Chen et al. [2] proposed a dual-channel recursive network to extract aspects and opinions. However, these methods cannot extract aspects, feelings and opinions within the same framework. To solve this problem, Peng [13] and others took the lead in transforming ASTE into a machine reading comprehension problem, using a two-stage framework to extract aspects, opinions, and emotions. Liu et al. [17] proposed a robust BMRC method to carry out ASTE tasks. Although these studies have made substantial progress, these methods do not fully consider prior knowledge and only obtain the general representation of knowledge, which makes some differences between the pretraining model and the fine-tuning of downstream tasks, making the extraction and realization of emotional triplets in professional fields not good. At the same time, the individual instances' contribution to sentences is inadequate during model training.

2.2 Machine Reading Comprehension

Machine reading comprehension (MRC) aims to retrieve the target question in a designated corpus and find the corresponding answer. Over the last few years, many scholars have conducted studies on MRC so that it can better capture the required information from massive information. These MRC models fully learn the corpus and the semantic information of the problem and learn the interaction between the problem and the corpus through various models. For example, viswanatha et al. [18] used LSTM-based memory networks for encoding queries to solve long-distance dependency problems, while Yu et al. [26] also employed various self-attention mechanisms to fully obtain semantic associations between problems and dependencies.The introduction of the pretrained language model BERT has greatly promoted the development of MRC. By training with large-scale pretrained samples, it can better capture deeper semantic features and improve the performance of MRC models.

Over the last few years, MRC has shown a high application trend in many NLP tasks, such as Li [9] and Zhao [29], utilizing the advantages of MRC in semantic understanding and context inference for entity extraction and entity relationship extraction. Similarly, utilizing the advantages of MRC in semantic understanding and contextual inference, we naturally integrate ABSA tasks with machine reading comprehension, enabling a more accurate construction of the relationship between opinions and emotions.

3 Methodology

Problem Formulation

Given a sentence $S = \{x_1, x_2, \ldots x_n\}$, where n denotes the word count. In the ASTE task, its goal is to identify the triad collection of aspects, opinions and emotions $T = \{(a_i, o_i, s_i)\}_{i=1}^{|T|}$, where a_i, o_i and s_i represent the ith aspect, opinion and emotion in the sentence,respectively, as shown in Fig. 1.

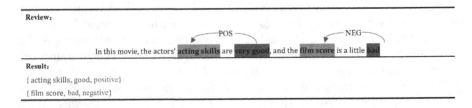

Fig. 1. The illustration of ASTE task

3.1 BMRC

BMRC performs unrestricted and restrictive queries based on the context and outputs the answers required by the model. Because each triad of ASTE tasks is activated by one aspector opinion, we construct a bidirectional reading comprehension model, carry out unrestricted queries in one direction, extract the corresponding aspect or opinion, carry out restricted queries in two directions, extract the corresponding aspect of each aspect or opinion-opinion pair, and finally classify the emotion of the corresponding opinion of each aspect through a separate emotion classifier to obtain the final aspect-opinion-emotion triple answer. In addition, we improved the model through BERT in the BMRC model. By integrating the knowledge map into the model, we can equip the model with some professional domain knowledge, strengthen the connection between specific domains and open domains, and make the model have richer semantic expression. In the stage of model building, we can restore the damaged mark by adding an automatic denoising encoder and evaluate the distinction between the damaged sentence and the original sentence. To provide clear regular signals, we can model the signals clearly provided by the example contribution and enhance the confidence of model prediction.

Nonrestrictive Query: We query the collection of aspects or opinions contained in the context in one direction (forward or backwards). We extract the collection of aspects $A = \{a_1, a_2, \ldots, a_n\}$ by designing the query "What aspects"; here, n denotes the quantity of aspect words extracted, a represents the nth aspect word in the sentence, and we extract the collection of opinions $O = \{o_1, o_2, \ldots, o_n\}$ by designing the query "What options", where n represents the number of opinion words extracted, and on represents the nth opinion word in the sentence.

For Restricted Queries: We extract the corresponding opinions or aspects according to the aspects or opinions extracted from nonrestricted queries in one direction (forward or backwards). For example, we extract the corresponding opinions according to the aspects by designing the restricted query "What opinions give the aspect?" $O = \{o_1, o_2, \ldots, o_n\}$, we design the restricted query "What aspect gives the opinions" to extract the corresponding opinions $A = \{a_1, a_2, \ldots, a_n\}$ according to the aspects.

Emotion classification: After determining the aspect - opinion contained in the context through restricted query, we design an emotion classifier to classify the emotion corresponding to the aspect, and finally construct a triplet based on the queried aspect, opinion, and emotion. The whole process is shown in Fig. 2.

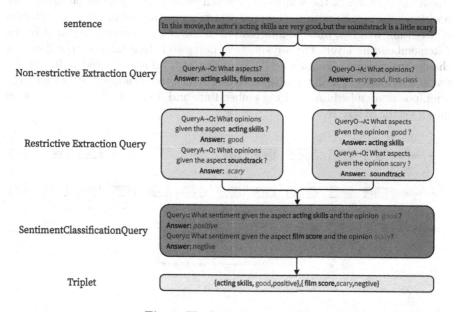

Fig. 2. The BMRC framework

Coding Layer of Knowledge Map Fusion

Given a sentence $S = \{x_1, x_2 \ldots x_n\}$, which contains n tokens, add special tags [CLS: classifier] and [SEP: separator], and give a restrictive query or nonrestrictive query $Q = \{q_1, q_2 \ldots q_n\}$, and combine the specially marked sentences and query statements to obtain $X = \{[CLS], q_1, q_2 \ldots q_n, [SEP], x_1, x_2 \ldots x_n\}$. The coding layer uses BERT to input X as the most input to obtain the context representation of each token. However, the original BERT only obtains general language features from the open domain without considering the specific domain knowledge, which makes the obtained features deviate from the meaning of the sentence, producing knowledge noise and ultimately affecting the accuracy of the answer prediction.

To alleviate knowledge noise, we incorporate domain knowledge through a knowledge map into our model. This helps establish a stronger link between specific and general domains, significantly reduces knowledge noise, and enhances the model's interpretability. Moreover, the use of a knowledge map can reduce the pretraining cost of the model. As shown in Fig. 3, the coding layer of the original sentence fusion knowledge map consists of four layers, namely, the sentence layer, subembedding layer, position embedding layer and mark embedding layer. We first transform the sentence using a knowledge map to make it a sentence tree rich in knowledge. In addition, to preserve the correct word order of the sentence and contain professional domain information, we use MASK to shield the branches of the sentence tree when embedding the position so that the position is consistent with the original sentence position during the computation of attention weights, but the information of the sentence tree is restored in the token embedding layer. The advantage of doing so is that the sentence does not change its original structure while acquiring rich knowledge and reducing the risk of knowledge. Finally, the generated sentence tree is added with subembedding, position embedding and tag embedding, and finally, each tag is converted into a vector of size H.

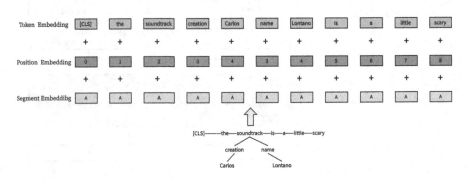

Fig. 3. The coding layer structure of knowledge map

Instance Regularization

Although many discriminative language pretraining models (BERT) have made remarkable achievements in NLP, these language pretraining models often adopt the strategy of shielding language (MLM) and achieve noise reduction and denoising by inserting, deleting, replacing and replacing the tags in sentences through tags (such as masks) [8,19,24]. However, during the training phase, these strategies treat each instance equally. We did not notice the special contribution of some specific examples to sentences. For example, after the "not" in the sentence "this movie is not good" is shielded, the sentence will have the opposite meaning. Therefore, we added instance regularization in the pretraining stage of the BMRC model and computed the discrepancy between the damaged sentence and the original sentence to obtain a clear regularization signal to improve the robustness of the model. As shown in Fig. 4, we first input the original sequence W, the destroyed sentence sequence W2, and the predicted sequence P into the encoder, and then obtain the corresponding hidden states H, $\widehat{H}$, $\widetilde{H}$ by learning different weights. Then, we calculate the distribution difference between the damaged sentence and the original sentence and between the predicted sentence and the original sentence through formula (1) and formula (2). Generally, l_1 and l_2 The larger the size, the higher the mismatch between the damaged sentence sequence, the predicted sentence sequence and the original sentence sequence, which makes the model more significantly update those "more difficult" training examples. KL is the Kullback-Leibler divergence. Finally, we use formula (3) as the loss function, where l_3 is the loss of the MLM model after denoising.

$$l_1 = d_{KL}(h, \hat{h}) \tag{1}$$

$$l_2 = d_{KL}\tilde{h}, \hat{h}\big) \tag{2}$$

$$l_{total} = l_1 + l_2 + l_3 \tag{3}$$

Fig. 4. The coding layer structure of knowledge map

4 Model Algorithm

First, input the given sentence x, and then input the pretrained knowledge graph-based model encoder to obtain the word vector $\{w1, w2 \ldots wn\}$. Then, perform a non restrictive query to obtain the matching aspect and opinion for the given problem, and then perform a restrictive query to extract aspect-opinion pairs. Finally, a sentiment classifier is used to determine the emotional polarity of the matching opinion for the aspect. The entire process will be iterated multiple times until the specified number of training rounds is reached. The specific implementation algorithm is shown in Algorithm 1.

Input: Training set $\left\{\left(x^{(n)}, y^{(n)}\right)\right\}_{n=1}^{N}$ maximum number of iterations N_2

for *each i in* 1 *to* N_2 **do**

    Obtain the set of aspects and opinions contained in each sentence through unrestricted queries T;

    while t *in* T **do**

        Obtain the aspect of each sentence through unrestricted queries - opinion pairs; Emotions corresponding to opinions in terms of calculation; Obtaining $\hat{y}_z = (a, o, s)$

    end

end

Output: T=(a, o, s)

Algorithm 1: BMRC algorithms

5   Experiment

Data Sets

To validate the efficacy of the BMRC based on knowledge enhancement and case regularization, we will conduct experiments on four benchmark data sets extracted from the SemEval [15] shared task.

Baselines

- TWSP [13] is a model that divides triplet extraction into two stages. The model first extracts the attributes and views of sentences by constructing a classifier, then calculates the emotional polarity of the views through a multilayer perceptron, and pairs them with the results of the first stage to form a triplet.
- OTE-MTL [27] is an aspect-level emotion analysis model based on a multi-task learning framework. This model first detects the relationship between attributes, opinions and emotions in sentences through LSTM in the prediction phase and then performs reverse traversal of tags to finally achieve the task of triple group extraction.
- DGEIAN [16] is an aspect-based opinion mining model based on graph-enhanced interactive attention mechanism networks. This model learns more grammatical and semantic dependencies from sentences by designing an interactive attention mechanism and then generates the final triplet through GTS.

Experimental Settings

During the experiment, we used a computer equipped with an Intel(R) Xeon(R) Platinum 8358P CPU and NVIDIA GeForce RTX 3090 graphics card and developed the model using the PyTorch framework. Through a copious number of experiments, we optimized various hyperparameters of the model to obtain the best effect. The specific software and hardware environment is shown in Table 1. See Table 2 for specific hyperparameter settings.

Table 1. Experimental Environment Information

Experimental environment	Specific information
operating system	Ubuntu 18.04.5
memory	80 GB
CPU	Intel(R) Xeon(R) Platinum 8358P CPU
GPU	NVIDIA GeForce RTX 3090 (24 GB)
CUDA Version	11.1
development language	Python 3.8
deep learning framework	Pytorch 1.8.1

Table 2. Parameter Setting

parameter name	Value
batch size	8
learning rate	1e−3
epochs	200
regularization coefficient	1e−5
hidden size	769
beta	1
inference beta	0.9
dropout rate	0.5
weight gate	0.3
optimization function	Adam

Evaluation Metrics

This article uses accuracy, recall rate, and F1 score as evaluation indicators. These indicators are mainly based on the mixed calculation of indicators in the confusion matrix, where TP denotes the count of positive samples successfully predicted, FP denotes the count of service samples that failed to predict, FN denotes the count of positive samples that failed to predict, and TN denotes the count of negative samples successfully predicted. According to the confusion matrix, the accuracy rates P, R, and F1 can be calculated. The calculation formulas are shown in (4)–(6):

$$P = \frac{TP}{TP + FP} \tag{4}$$

$$R = \frac{TP}{TP + FN} \tag{5}$$

$$F1 = \frac{2 \times P \times R}{P + R} \tag{6}$$

6   Results

The results of our experiments on four benchmark data sets are shown in Table 3. According to the results, our model achieves optimal results on all four benchmark data sets, which indicates that our improvement further improves BMRC's performance in processing ASTE tasks. On the four benchmark data sets of ASTE-Data, the F1 score of our model is 0.85, 2.71, 5.81 and 0.76 higher than the most advanced BMRC at present. This shows that the effect of our improvement is very significant.

Table 3. Experiments on benchmark data sets

model	14-Res			14-Lap			15-res			16-res		
	P	R	F1	P	R	F1	P	R	F1	P	R	F1
TWSP	42.19	51.98	46.57	40.41	47.25	44.13	40.98	54.69	46.85	46.77	62.98	53.67
OTE-MTL	67.97	60.32	63.92	58.47	43.67	50.00	58.35	51.43	54.67	64.77	61.29	62.98
DGEIAN	71.55	69.14	70.32	57.39	53.88	55.58	63.78	51.87	57.21	68.60	66.24	67.40
Ours	74.31	76.95	75.60	68.00	62.24	64.99	70.91	72.73	71.81	74.01	78.27	76.08

7   Ablation Experiments

First, the model is tested without improving the benchmark data set. The model is based on the representation of BMRC, and then the model introduced into the knowledge map and the example regularization method are gradually superimposed for ablation experiments, and the following questions are answered:

- How much improvement can the introduction of knowledge graphs and instantiation regularization bring?
- After introducing knowledge graph and instantiation regularization, in which aspect do we mention the effectiveness?

Table 4. Results of ablation experiment

Evaluation	Model	14-Res				14-Lap				15-res				16-res			
		A	O	A-O	A-O-S	A	O	A-O	A-O-S	A	O	A-O	A-O-S	A	O	A-O	A-O-S
Precision	BMRC	81.41	84.35	77.22	73.84	83.65	81.74	76.49	66.66	78.55	80.06	70.81	66.96	81.21	80.35	76.50	71.14
	+KG	84.90	86.70	78.11	73.96	86.61	83.70	76.98	67.14	81.44	82.21	71.46	67.53	83.88	84.06	77.14	72.05
	+IR	82.13	84.52	78.79	74.19	84.01	82.44	77.61	67.46	79.93	81.52	72.19	68.23	82.11	81.88	77.75	72.41
	+KG+IR	85.55	87.21	79.38	74.31	87.90	85.44	78.11	68.00	82.82	83.67	72.63	70.91	85.83	85.82	78.16	74.01
Recall	BMRC	82.53	84.41	78.08	75.98	78.71	77.90	68.65	58.36	77.76	80.18	70.52	66.37	87.29	85.54	82.33	76.34
	+KG	86.78	87.01	78.67	76.33	80.06	78.79	70.10	61.21	79.85	81.89	71.78	68.89	88.82	88.63	82.94	76.44
	+IR	83.66	86.02	79.44	76.60	79.12	78.00	70.99	61.53	78.19	81.22	72.86	70.11	88.01	86.55	83.45	76.95
	+KG+IR	87.91	88.82	80.00	76.95	81.90	80.32	71.51	62.24	80.14	82.96	73.23	72.73	90.06	90.53	84.08	78.27
F1	BMRC	81.97	84.37	77.64	74.89	81.10	79.77	72.36	62.23	78.15	80.12	70.66	66.66	84.14	82.86	79.31	73.65
	+KG	85.83	86.85	78.39	75.38	83.21	81.17	73.38	64.04	80.64	82.05	71.62	68.20	86.28	86.28	79.93	74.18
	+IR	82.89	85.26	79.11	75.37	81.49	80.16	74.15	64.36	79.05	81.37	72.52	69.16	84.96	84.15	80.50	74.61
	+KG+IR	86.71	88.00	79.68	75.61	84.79	82.8	74.66	64.99	81.46	83.31	72.93	71.81	87.89	88.11	81.01	76.08

Experimental Design: Knowledge Augmentation Ablation Experiment Based on Knowledge Graph: Only the original BMRC model was used for the emotion triplet extraction task and compared with the complete BMRC model with knowledge augmentation. At the same time, experiments were repeated on four data sets: 14-Res, 14-Lap, 15-Res, and 16-Res. The prediction accuracy of the model's aspect extraction, opinion extraction, aspect-opinion pair extraction, and aspect-opinion-sentiment triplet extraction on each data set was recorded, and the impact of knowledge augmentation on model prediction accuracy and generalization was analysed.

Case Regularization Ablation Experiment: Only the original BMRC model is used for the emotion triplet extraction task and compared with the BMRC model added with case regularization. At the same time, experiments are repeated on four data sets, 14-Res, 14-Lap, 15-Res, and 16-Res, and the prediction accuracy of the model with respect to extraction, opinion extraction, aspect-opinion pair extraction, aspect-opinion emotion triplet extraction and other tasks on each data set is recorded. The influence of example regularization on the prediction accuracy and generalization of the model is analysed.

Joint Ablation Experiment of Knowledge Enhancement and Instance Regularization Based on Knowledge Graph: Only the original BMRC model is used for the emotion triple extraction task and compared with the complete experiment of introducing the joint ablation experiment of knowledge enhancement and instance regularization. At the same time, experiments are repeated on four data sets, namely, 14-Res, 14-Lap, 15-Res, and 16-Res, and the model's aspect extraction, opinion extraction, and aspect-opinion pair extraction on each data set are recorded. The prediction accuracy rate of aspect-opinion-sentiment triple extraction is analysed, and the impact of instance regularization on the prediction accuracy and generalization of the model is analysed.

Experimental Results: From Table 4, it can be perceived that the BMRC model that separately introduces knowledge enhancement based on knowledge graph and instance regularization has obvious improvement in aspect extraction, opinion extraction, aspect-opinion extraction, and aspect-opinion-sentiment triplet extraction tasks, but the BMRC model that only introduces knowledge enhancement based on knowledge graph has better effect in aspect extraction than the BMRC model that only introduces instance regularization, The BMRC model with knowledge enhancement based on knowledge graph is 2.14% and 1.38% higher than the BMRC model with instance regularization in aspect extraction, and the BMRC model with instance regularization only is 0.79% higher in aspect-opinion pair than the BMRC model with knowledge enhancement based on knowledge graph only, which suggests that knowledge enhancement based on knowledge graphs primarily impacts the aspect extraction and opinion extraction of BMRC in the nonrestricted query phase, while instance regularization primarily impacts the performance of restrictive phase aspect-opinion pair extraction. In addition, we can also see from Table 4 that the F1 value of the BMRC model combined with knowledge enhancement based on knowledge map and instance regularization in various tasks is higher than that of the BMRC model that separately introduces knowledge enhancement based on knowledge map and instance regularization, which indicates that knowledge enhancement and instance regularization can complement each other and improve the performance of the model.

8   Conclusion

Based on the BMRC algorithm, this paper improves the triple extraction task of aspect emotion so that the model can effectively extract the triple of aspect, opinion and emotion in the context. With the aim of addressing the current challenges of the emotion triplet extraction task based on BMRC, we added a knowledge map, instance regularization and other measures to improve it. This method can effectively deal with complex ASTE tasks. Furthermore, our model's effectiveness has been demonstrated through a multitude of ablation experiments.

References

1. Chakraborty, M., Kulkarni, A., Li, Q.: Open-domain aspect-opinion co-mining with double-layer span extraction. In: Proceedings of the 28th ACM SIGKDD Conference on Knowledge Discovery and Data Mining, pp. 66–75 (2022)
2. Chen, S., Liu, J., Wang, Y., Zhang, W., Chi, Z.: Synchronous double-channel recurrent network for aspect-opinion pair extraction. In: Proceedings of the 58th Annual Meeting of the Association for Computational Linguistics, pp. 6515–6524 (2020)
3. Chen, S., Wang, Y., Liu, J., Wang, Y.: Bidirectional machine reading comprehension for aspect sentiment triplet extraction. In: Proceedings of the AAAI Conference on Artificial Intelligence, vol. 35, pp. 12666–12674 (2021)
4. Dehong, M., Li, S., Zhang, X., Wang, H.: Interactive attention networks for aspect-level sentiment classification. arXiv preprint arXiv:1709.00893 (2017)
5. Devlin, J., Chang, M.W., Lee, K., Toutanova, K.: Bert: pre-training of deep bidirectional transformers for language understanding. arXiv preprint arXiv:1810.04805 (2018)
6. Jiang, Q., Chen, L., Xu, R., Ao, X., Yang, M.: A challenge dataset and effective models for aspect-based sentiment analysis. In: Proceedings of the 2019 Conference on Empirical Methods in Natural Language Processing and the 9th International Joint Conference on Natural Language Processing (EMNLP-IJCNLP), pp. 6280–6285 (2019)
7. Karaoğlan, K.M., Fındık, O.: Extended rule-based opinion target extraction with a novel text pre-processing method and ensemble learning. Appl. Soft Comput. **118**, 108524 (2022)
8. Lewis, M., et al.: Bart: denoising sequence-to-sequence pre-training for natural language generation, translation, and comprehension. arXiv preprint arXiv:1910.13461 (2019)
9. Li, X., Feng, J., Meng, Y., Han, Q., Wu, F., Li, J.: A unified MRC framework for named entity recognition. arXiv preprint arXiv:1910.11476 (2019)
10. Liu, K., Xu, L., Zhao, J.: Opinion target extraction using word-based translation model. In: Proceedings of the 2012 Joint Conference on Empirical Methods in Natural Language Processing and Computational Natural Language Learning, pp. 1346–1356 (2012)
11. Liu, P., Joty, S., Meng, H.: Fine-grained opinion mining with recurrent neural networks and word embeddings. In: Proceedings of the 2015 Conference on Empirical Methods in Natural Language Processing, pp. 1433–1443 (2015)
12. Mao, Y., Shen, Y., Yu, C., Cai, L.: A joint training dual-MRC framework for aspect based sentiment analysis. In: Proceedings of the AAAI Conference on Artificial Intelligence, vol. 35, pp. 13543–13551 (2021)
13. Peng, H., Xu, L., Bing, L., Huang, F., Lu, W., Si, L.: Knowing what, how and why: a near complete solution for aspect-based sentiment analysis. In: Proceedings of the AAAI Conference on Artificial Intelligence, vol. 34, pp. 8600–8607 (2020)
14. Pereg, O., Korat, D., Wasserblat, M.: Syntactically aware cross-domain aspect and opinion terms extraction. In: Proceedings of the 28th International Conference on Computational Linguistics, pp. 1772–1777 (2020)
15. Pontiki, M., et al.: Semeval-2016 task 5: aspect based sentiment analysis. In: ProWorkshop on Semantic Evaluation (SemEval-2016), pp. 19–30. Association for Computational Linguistics (2016)
16. Shi, L., Han, D., Han, J., Qiao, B., Wu, G.: Dependency graph enhanced interactive attention network for aspect sentiment triplet extraction. Neurocomputing **507**, 315–324 (2022)

17. Shu, L., Li, K., Li, Z.: A robustly optimized BMRC for aspect sentiment triplet extraction. In: Proceedings of the 2022 Conference of the North American Chapter of the Association for Computational Linguistics: Human Language Technologies, pp. 272–278 (2022)

18. Viswanathan, S., Anand Kumar, M., Soman, K.P.: A sequence-based machine comprehension modeling using LSTM and GRU. In: Sridhar, V., Padma, M.C., Rao, K.A.R. (eds.) Emerging Research in Electronics, Computer Science and Technology. LNEE, vol. 545, pp. 47–55. Springer, Singapore (2019). https://doi.org/10.1007/978-981-13-5802-9_5

19. Wang, W., et al.: Structbert: incorporating language structures into pre-training for deep language understanding. arXiv preprint arXiv:1908.04577 (2019)

20. Wang, W., Pan, S.J., Dahlmeier, D., Xiao, X.: Coupled multi-layer attentions for co-extraction of aspect and opinion terms. In: Proceedings of the AAAI Conference on Artificial Intelligence, vol. 31 (2017)

21. Wu, S., Fei, H., Ren, Y., Ji, D., Li, J.: Learn from syntax: improving pair-wise aspect and opinion terms extractionwith rich syntactic knowledge. arXiv preprint arXiv:2105.02520 (2021)

22. Wu, Z., Ying, C., Zhao, F., Fan, Z., Dai, X., Xia, R.: Grid tagging scheme for aspect-oriented fine-grained opinion extraction. arXiv preprint arXiv:2010.04640 (2020)

23. Xu, L., Li, H., Lu, W., Bing, L.: Position-aware tagging for aspect sentiment triplet extraction. arXiv preprint arXiv:2010.02609 (2020)

24. Xu, Y., Zhao, H.: Dialogue-oriented pre-training. arXiv preprint arXiv:2106.00420 (2021)

25. Yan, H., Dai, J., Qiu, X., Zhang, Z., et al.: A unified generative framework for aspect-based sentiment analysis. arXiv preprint arXiv:2106.04300 (2021)

26. Yu, A.W., et al.: QANet: combining local convolution with global self-attention for reading comprehension. arXiv preprint arXiv:1804.09541 (2018)

27. Zhang, C., Li, Q., Song, D., Wang, B.: A multi-task learning framework for opinion triplet extraction. arXiv preprint arXiv:2010.01512 (2020)

28. Zhao, H., Huang, L., Zhang, R., Lu, Q., Xue, H.: SpanMLT: a span-based multi-task learning framework for pair-wise aspect and opinion terms extraction. In: Proceedings of the 58th annual meeting of the association for computational linguistics, pp. 3239–3248 (2020)

29. Zhao, T., Yan, Z., Cao, Y., Li, Z.: Asking effective and diverse questions: a machine reading comprehension based framework for joint entity-relation extraction. In: Proceedings of the Twenty-Ninth International Conference on International Joint Conferences on Artificial Intelligence, pp. 3948–3954 (2021)

A Method for Extracting Clinical Diagnosis and Treatment Knowledge for Traditional Chinese Medicine Literature

Kehan Zhen, Dan Xie, and Yu Peng[✉]

College of Information Engineering, Hubei University of Chinese Medicine, Wuhan 430065, China

{dinaxie,pengyu}@hbtcm.edu.cn

Abstract. To realize automatic extraction of rich clinical diagnosis and treatment knowledge from traditional Chinese medicine (TCM) literature, a method using information extraction technology to achieve automatic acquisition of clinical diagnosis and treatment knowledge in TCM is proposed. First, the entity types of TCM clinical diagnosis and treatment were defined, and the corpus base of TCM diagnosis and treatment was constructed. Then, the literature sample set was labelled based on the corpus, several commonly used information extraction models were selected to train the sample set, and the most appropriate models and training parameters were selected to extract clinical diagnosis and treatment knowledge. Finally, a case study of breast cancer was carried out, and the implementation scheme of diagnosis and treatment knowledge extraction based on the literature is described in detail. The experimental results show that the UIE model has the best information extraction effect, and its F1 value is 89.69%. Data mining was carried out on the extracted diagnosis and treatment knowledge, and it was found that the basic principles of drug use were qi and blood circulation and liver and spleen strengthening, and the main drugs were tonifying deficiency and clearing heat. This method provides an effective technical route for the automatic acquisition of TCM clinical diagnosis and treatment knowledge, which can help clinical researchers quickly and accurately obtain diagnosis and treatment knowledge in the literature and has practical value for TCM clinical research.

Keywords: information extraction · TCM literature · rules of diagnosis and treatment

1 Introduction

As an important part of traditional Chinese culture, traditional Chinese medicine (TCM) has a profound historical accumulation and contains a wealth of diagnostic and therapeutic knowledge. In the process of inheritance and development of TCM culture, literature, as an important carrier, has recorded a large amount of valuable medical knowledge and wisdom [1]. Mining the knowledge contained in massive literature based on data mining has become a new scientific research method in the era of big data. Discovering the

© The Author(s), under exclusive license to Springer Nature Singapore Pte Ltd. 2024
M. Zhang et al. (Eds.): CCF NCCA 2023, CCIS 1959, pp. 235–244, 2024.
https://doi.org/10.1007/978-981-99-8764-1_18

knowledge contained in these documents can not only deepen the knowledge of the origin of TCM and its theoretical system but also explore latent therapeutic ideas and methods and apply them to today's clinical practice. However, most of this knowledge exists in unstructured text, and its information is often difficult to obtain and understand quickly and accurately [2]. Therefore, using information extraction techniques to semantically analyse and extract information from TCM literature and transform it into structured data that can be processed by modern computers can greatly improve the utilization of information and research efficiency and provide more valuable data to support TCM research and application [3].

As the influence of TCM continues to grow worldwide, the exploration and utilization of the knowledge contained in TCM literature has attracted increasing attention. Currently, scholars in related fields are deeply exploring the valuable information contained in TCM literature to provide theoretical support and scientific guidance for the modernization and internationalization of traditional medicine. Lu Yongmei [4] et al. designed a deep learning-based sequence annotator for identifying text fragments describing clinical experiences in ancient documents. Gao Su [2] et al. used a joint event extraction model to achieve the initial extraction of sentence-level events from TCM literature. Ma Jie [5] et al. mined the implicit knowledge in TCM medical cases based on the CART algorithm to explore the relationship between the disease and each attribute of the patient's symptoms. In this study, we proposed and established a systematic and rigorous automated knowledge mining process for Chinese medical literature and used the information extraction model to automatically extract the medical knowledge in Chinese medical literature under the guidance of the process. The feasibility and effectiveness of the process in clinical practice were verified.

The main contributions of this paper are as follows:

(1) An automatic extraction method of TCM literature diagnosis and treatment knowledge was proposed, and an empirical study was carried out with breast cancer as an example, which has strong practical significance.
(2) The knowledge base constructed is based on national and industry standards, including "Classification and codes of diseases and patterns of TCM" and "Pharmacopoeia of the People's Republic of China" (2020), as well as classic professional textbooks, such as "Chinese Medicinal Formulas" and "Chinese Materia Medica", with strong authority.

2   Method

2.1   Technical Process

To realize the automatic extraction of treatment knowledge in TCM literature and mining its treatment laws, a standardized process is constructed in this study (see Fig. 1). First, a corpus base of TCM diagnosis and treatment is constructed. Then, TCM-specific literature is retrieved from the literature database, screened and saved. Some texts are manually annotated with the knowledge base, and the annotated sample set is used for model training. The trained model is selected for information. The extracted entities are aligned, and the data are analysed.

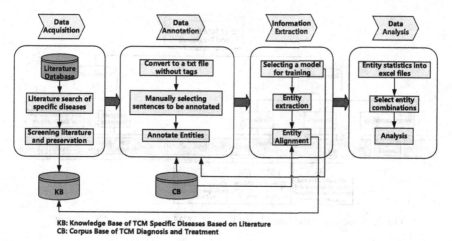

Fig. 1. Overall flow chart of extracting clinical diagnosis and treatment knowledge from the TCM literature.

2.2 Research Objects

The literature data were obtained from Chinese and English databases such as the China National Knowledge Internet (CNKI), China Online Journals (WANFANG DATA), China Science and Technology Journal Database (VIP database), PubMed and Web of Science. Taking the CNKI database as an example, the literature search formula was as follows:

$$SU = Disease\,name\,AND\,(SU = TCM\,OR\,SU = Chinese\,medicine) \qquad (1)$$

The search years were from 2010 to 2022, and the literature was screened according to the inclusion and exclusion criteria, read in full and then screened again, and saved in HTML format.

2.3 Knowledge Base of TCM Diagnosis and Treatment

The knowledge base of TCM diagnosis and treatment includes the corpus base of TCM diagnosis and treatment and the knowledge base of TCM-specific diseases based on the literature (see Fig. 2). The construction of the corpus base of TCM diagnosis and treatment refers to a series of authoritative materials, such as "Classification and codes of diseases and patterns of traditional Chinese medicine" [6], "Pharmacopoeia of the People's Republic of China" (2020 Edition) [7], "Chinese Medicinal Formulas" [8] and "Chinese Materia Medica" [9], as well as the content provisions and requirements of policies and regulations. The knowledge base of TCM-specific diseases based on the literature mainly contains literature-related information, including the literature title, abstract, author, key words, publication name, publication time, original text and annotated text of the literature.

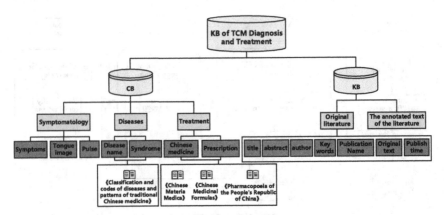

Fig. 2. Structure of the Knowledge Base of TCM Diagnosis and Treatment.

2.4 Information Extraction Models

In the current field of information extraction, there are a variety of models to choose from. Here, we introduce UIE, BERT, BiLSTM-CRF and BERT-BiLSTM-CRF, which are widely used at present. UIE [10] is a unified modelling model jointly published by the Chinese Academy of Sciences and Baidu in ACL 2022, which realizes tasks such as entity extraction, relationship extraction, event extraction, and emotion analysis and enables good migration and generalization ability among different tasks. BERT[11] is a bidirectional encoder representation based on Transformer proposed by Google AI Research Institute, which aims to pretrain deep bidirectional representation based on left and right contexts of all layers and more fully describe character-level, word-level, sentence level and even intersentence relationship characteristics. BiLSTM-CRF [12] was proposed by Baidu Research Institute in 2015 to conduct text annotation by using LSTM, a two-way long short-term memory network, and CRF, a conditional random field. BERT-BiLSTM-CRF [13] applies the language pretraining model BERT to Chinese entity recognition. It takes the pretraining results as the input of the downstream task BiLSTM-CRF, which not only reduces the workload of the downstream task but also obtains better results.

2.5 Data Analysis Methods

The extracted entities are subjected to entity alignment methods such as synonym replacement and incorrect value deletion, and then the data are analysed. The data analysis methods used were: (1) Frequency statistics were performed using Excel to discover the distribution between commonly used Chinese medicines, prescriptions and different evidence and symptoms in order to grasp the basic statistical characteristics of the data and grasp the overall distribution pattern of the data; (2) Association rule analysis was performed using the Apriori algorithm in IBM SPSS Modeller 18.0 to discover the drug-evidence, drug-symptom, prescription-evidence, prescription-symptom, and the association relationships between evidence-syndromes can help reveal the potential connections and characteristic factors contained in the healing process of various diseases in TCM clinics [14]; (3) Cluster analysis using systematic clustering in IBM SPSS Statistic 25.0 to aggregate valuable homogeneous elements for a more intuitive understanding of their common characteristics [15].

3 Experiment

Following the technical process set in Sect. 2.1, an empirical study was conducted with breast cancer as an example, and the experiment was divided into four steps: data acquisition, data annotation, information extraction and data analysis.

3.1 Data Acquisition

The literature related to the treatment of breast cancer by Chinese medicine was retrieved from the CNKI database, and the search period was from January 2010 to December 2022. A total of 3689 related studies were retrieved, and 2104 were finally included after screening.

Inclusion criteria: (1) The prescription is clear and contains specific TCM components; (2) Treatment is mainly based on traditional Chinese medicine, supplemented by radiotherapy, chemotherapy and other adjuvant therapies; (3) Summary of the experience of famous old Chinese medicine in diagnosis and treatment of diseases; (4) The patient's disease is clearly diagnosed; (5) Adopt the universal diagnostic and treatment evaluation standards recognized by international and domestic counterparts.

Exclusion criteria: (1) The main treatments were acupuncture and moxibustion, traditional Chinese medicine emotional nursing literature; (2) The research objects were animal and cell literature; (3) Recurring literature.

3.2 Data Annotation

The annotated data came from the literature on diseases treated by traditional Chinese medicine (diseases in 11 directions). Sentences in the text of some studies were randomly selected to form a sample set with 500 data points in total and then annotated using text annotation and the open-source annotation system doccano. Based on TCM theory and clinical practice, seven types of entity labels were established based on the text content in the literature, including Chinese medicine, prescription, tongue image, pulse, syndrome, symptom and disease name. Examples of annotations are shown in Fig. 3. The upper part is text annotation, and the lower part is doccano annotation.

3.3 Information Extraction

The BiLSTM-CRF, BERT-BiLSTM-CRF and UIE models were selected for information extraction, and the labelled sample set was used to train the models. The modified model parameters included learning-rate, batch-size and epoch. The value of the learning rate ranges from 0.0001–0.1, the batch size ranges from 2–64, the number of epochs ranges from 1–100, the precision, recall and F1 score are taken as the evaluation indexes of the model, and the model with the best training results is selected for extraction. The

Original text	After annotation
The dialectic of breast cancer is positive deficiency and toxic burning syndrome. Manifestations include palpitations, insomnia, purple and yellow tongue coating, weak pulse.The treatment is to give Liuwei Dihuang Wan and Sijunzi Tang. With the disease: heat poison sheng add phragmitis rhizoma, winter melon kernel; Add astragali radix for those who are weak and spiritless.	The dialectic of {disease: breast cancer} is {syndrome: positive deficiency and toxic burning syndrome}. Manifestations include {symptom: palpitations}, {symptom: insomnia}, {tongue image: purple and yellow tongue coating}, {pulse: weak pulse}.The treatment is to give {prescription: Liuwei Dihuang Wan} and {prescription: Sijunzi Tang}. With the disease: heat poison sheng add {Chinese medicine: phragmitis rhizoma}, {Chinese medicine: winter melon kernel}; Add {Chinese medicine: astragali radix} for those who are {symptom: weak} and {symptom: spiritless}. The dialectic of breast cancer is positive deficiency and toxic burning syndrome. Manifestations include ·disease name ·syndrome palpitations, insomnia, purple and yellow tongue coating, weak pulse.The treatment is to give Liuwei Dihuang ·symptom ·symptom·tongue image ·pulse ·prescription Wan and Sijunzi Tang. With the disease: heat poison sheng add phragmitis rhizoma, winter melon kernel; Add ·prescription ·Chinese medi... ·Chinese medi... astragali radix for those who are weak and spiritless. ·Chinese medi... ·symptom·symptom

Fig. 3. Annotation example.

results are shown in Table 1. The training effect of the UIE model is relatively good. The precision is 91.78%, the recall is 87.70%, and the F1 score is 89.69%. At this time, the learning rate of the model is 0.0001, the epoch is 100, and the batch size is 16. The trained UIE model was used for entity recognition of 7 types of entities in the TCM literature. An example of the entity recognition results is shown in Fig. 4.

Table 1. Training results of the BiLSTM-CRF, BERT-BiLSTM-CRF, and UIE models.

Model	Precision	Recall	F1 score
BiLSTM-CRF	79.41	67.50	72.97
BERT-BiLSTM-CRF	88.37	90.48	89.41
UIE	91.78	87.70	**89.69**

In the clinical treatment of 54 patients with breast cancer, Radix bupleurum keel Oyster soup was mainly used as the base prescription (including radix bupleurum, ginseng, glycyrrhiza, Radix pinellia, Radix scutellariae, raw keel and raw oyster, etc.) to soothe liver and regulate qi, and to support anticancer. If the liver qi cross the stomach into liver and stomach disharmony, add Sijunzi soup to strengthen the spleen and stomach effect, if nausea and vomiting, add tangerine peel, bamboo ru to reduce retinitis. Qi and blood deficiency with Siwu decoction to supplement Qi and blood; Qi and blood deficiency deficiency for a long time to damage Yin has heat into Syndrome of Yin deficiency and fire flourishing plus trichosanthin powder, dendrobium to nourish Yin Sheng Jin, plus peony bark to clear heat.

Fig. 4. Example of entity recognition results using the UIE model.

3.4 Data Analysis

Frequency Statistics

Formulary Statistics

The prescriptions that appeared 1% (21 times) or more of the total literature were counted. Fifty-nine prescriptions were counted, and the top 5 prescriptions were ranked by their frequency of occurrence, namely, Free Wanderer Powder, Rhinoceros

Bezoar Pill, Bupleurum Liver-Coursing Power, Harmonious Yang Decoction, and Four Gentlemen Decoction.

Statistics of Chinese Medicines

Chinese herbal medicines with frequencies of 1% or more of the total literature were counted, and the statistics revealed that there were 308 eligible Chinese herbal medicines with a total frequency of 58271 times. The 20 drugs with the highest frequency were listed in descending order, namely, astragalus, poria, tangkuei, ovate atractylodes, bupleurum, white peony, codonopsis, licorice, hedyotis, zedoary, bearded scutellaria, tangerine peel, shancigu, cooked rehmannia, ligusticum, curcuma, epimedium, lycium, dioscorea, and coix.

In this study, 308 Chinese herbal medicines were analysed for four qi, and the results showed that cold (33.77%) and warm (33.44%) were predominant; the five flavours were analysed, and the results showed that sweet (32.57%) was the most prevalent, as shown in Fig. 5; the top three categories of meridians were liver (21.12%), spleen (15.67%), and lung (14.61%), as shown in Fig. 6.

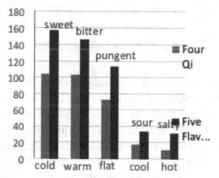

Fig. 5. Histogram of the Distribution of Four Qi and Five Flavours.

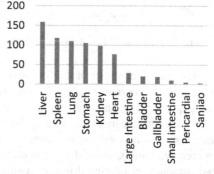

Fig. 6. Histogram of Meridian Distribution.

Association Rule Analysis

The support degree was set to 20%, the confidence degree was set to 80%, the maximum number of previous terms was set to 1 and gradually increased until no new frequent term set was generated, and the association rules were analysed for the top 20 high-frequency Chinese medicines. The association rules were extracted from the pairs and groups of Chinese medicines, among which the highest confidence level was poria-ovate atractylodes (81.752%) for 3 pairs of pairs, 89.565% for poria-white peony-ovate atractylodes (89.565%) for 10 groups of 3 groups, and 90.625% for poria-white peony-tangkuei-ovate atractylodes (90.625%) for 10 groups of 4. The network diagram of association rules is shown in Fig. 7.

Clustering Analysis

Using Pearson's correlation coefficient in systematic clustering, the top 20 Chinese medicines in terms of frequency were clustered and analysed to generate a tree cluster diagram (see Fig. 8). The diagram shows the homogeneity among Chinese medicines, and the shorter the distance corresponding to the horizontal axis, the higher the homogeneity. The Chinese medicines with distances not exceeding 22 were grouped into one category, and five groups of Chinese medicine clustering combinations were obtained by screening.

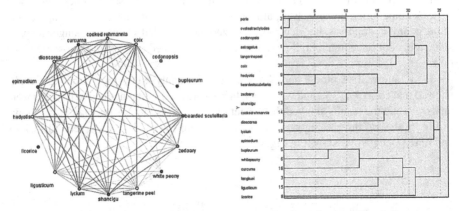

Fig. 7. Association rule network diagram.   **Fig. 8.** Tree clustering diagram.

The statistical results of the formulas show that the top 5 formulas with the highest frequency of occurrence have effects related to several categories: reconciliation, regulating qi, tonifying, and treating carbuncles and abscesses. According to the statistics of traditional Chinese medicine, among the top 20 drugs with the highest frequency of use, the main ones are tonifying deficiency drugs, followed by promoting blood circulation and resolving blood stasis drugs and clearing heat drugs, along with the use of diuretic and dampness regulating drugs, qi regulating drugs, and surface relieving drugs. The results of association rule analysis show that the confidence level of the combination of poria and ovate atractylodes is the highest, and they can be traced back to the "Shennong Materia Medica Classic". This medicine has the effect of strengthening the spleen and dispelling dampness [16]. The results of cluster analysis showed that the main drugs of traditional Chinese medicine for breast cancer were soothing the liver, promoting qi, relieving depression, clearing away heat and detoxification.

4   Conclusion

This study establishes a method for mining treatment laws from TCM literature based on an information extraction model, and this method contains several steps, such as data acquisition, data annotation, information extraction, and data analysis. Data acquisition is the foundation of the whole process, which requires collecting a large amount of TCM literature data. Data annotation and information extraction are also important. Establishing an accurate information extraction model can better extract and analyse the disease information in the TCM literature, which also needs to overcome problems such as entity recognition accuracy. In terms of mining methodology, this study uses a variety of data mining techniques, including association rule analysis and clustering analysis. Through these techniques, the treatment rules in the Chinese medical literature can be better mined.

The information extraction model-based mining method can help TCM clinicians formulate treatment plans and optimize prescriptions more scientifically and rationally. At the same time, this method can also be applied to the promotion of TCM modernization and the research and development of new drugs in TCM. The present study is mainly based on the analysis and mining of existing TCM literature, which inevitably has limitations such as language and cultural background and needs to be validated and revised in the context of actual TCM clinical practice. In addition, as the number of TCM studies is huge and covers a wide range of fields, how to classify and filter them is also a problem that needs to be considered in the follow-up of this study.

Acknowledgements. This research is supported by the Hubei Provincial Administration of Traditional Chinese Medicine (Grant No. ZY2023M072).

References

1. Guangyao, W., Haixia, Y., Xinghua, W., et al.: Approaches and methods of basic theory research of traditional Chinese medicine. Chin. J. Tradition. Chin. Med. **38**(02), 691–694 (2023)
2. Gao, S., Tao, H., Yanzhao, J., et al.: Sentence level joint event Extraction of TCM literature. Inf. Eng. **7**(05), 15–29 (2021)
3. Cheng, W., Lei, X., Yingyi, Q., et al.: Exploration of multilevel information extraction method for Chinese electronic medical records. China Digit. Med. **15**(06), 29–31 (2020)
4. Yongmei, L., Lingmei, B., Li, C., Zhonghua, Y., Tingting, Z., Ying, Y.: Clinical experience extraction of ancient Chinese medicine literature based on deep learning. J. Sichuan Univ. (Nat. Sci. Edn.) **59**(02), 109–116 (2022). (in Chinese)
5. Jie, M., Hongchen, L., Mo, H., et al.: Medical tacit knowledge mining based on CART algorithm: a case study of traditional Chinese medicine. Inf. Sci. **39**(06), 84–91 (2010)
6. State Administration for Market Regulation, Standardization Administration. Classification and codes of diseases and patterns of traditional Chinese medicine: GB/T15657–2021 (2021)
7. National Pharmacopoeia Commission of the People's Republic of China. Pharmacopoeia of the People's Republic of China. Beijing: China Medical Science and Technology Press (2020)
8. Ji, L.: Chinese Medicinal Formulas. China Publication of Traditional Chinese Medicine, Beijing (2016)
9. Gansheng, Z.: Chinese Materia Medica. China Traditional Chinese Medicine Press, Beijing (2016)
10. Lu, Y., Liu, Q., Dai, D., et al.: Unified structure generation for universal information extraction (2022)
11. Devlin, J., Chang, M.W., Lee, K., et al.: BERT: pretraining of deep bidirectional transformers for language understanding (2018)
12. Huang, Z., Xu, W., Yu, K.: Bidirectional LSTM-CRF models for sequence tagging (2015)
13. Du, Z., Tang, D., Xie, D.: Automatic extraction of clinical symptoms in traditional Chinese medicine for electronic medical records. BIBM, pp. 3784–3790 (2021)
14. Wenli, X., Jun, L., Shusong, M., et al.: Study on the knowledge association of traditional Chinese medicine symptom knowledge base. J. Med. Inf. **44**(02), 35–41 (2023)

15. Xiangjun, Q., Xinrong, C., Jiahao, M.: Analysis of prescription pattern of TCM treatment of colorectal cancer based on data mining. Chin. J. Traditional Chin. Med. **46**(15), 4016–4022 (2021)

16. Cui, Y., Mi, J., Feng, Y., et al.: Effect and mechanism of Huangqi Sijunzi Decoction on breast cancer fatigue: based on 94 cases randomized controlled trial and network pharmacology. J. Southern Med. Univ. **42**(05), 649–657 (2020)

Application and Optimization of Centroid Algorithm in Indoor Positioning

Yutang Wang[✉]

Anhui Institute of Information Technology, Wuhu City, Anhui, China
Ytwang30@iflytek.com

Abstract. Indoor mobile positioning is widely used in shopping malls, energy saving in buildings, medical care and emergency rescue. Range-free algorithms typically use the connectivity of a wireless sensor network system to estimate the location of target nodes, typically through Dv-hop, the prime method, approximate point-in-triangulation test, or APIT for short. -free algorithms can be obtained by changing the distribution density of reference nodes or by changing the blind node communication radius to obtain higher accuracy. Due to constraints such as complex indoor environments, current indoor positioning methods are often less accurate and more expensive. To address these issues, this paper improves on the traditional center-of-mass algorithm by using a six-point center-of-mass algorithm for indoor positioning to further improve the accuracy of the indoor positioning algorithm. To this end, the following work is accomplished in this paper: 1. introduced the algorithms currently used for indoor positioning and their shortcomings, laying the theoretical foundation for the improved approach proposed in the following paper. 2. introduced the basic working principle of the center-of-mass algorithm and proposed an improved system using the six-point center-of-mass algorithm. 3. established the best possible model through experiments, then input test data and evaluated it based on expert judgement. The experimental results show that the model proposed in this study has excellent accuracy in indoor wireless positioning.

Keywords: Indoor positioning · Wireless positioning · Multi technology integration · Multi-source information · The centre-of-mass algorithm

1 Introduction

Outdoor wireless positioning technology is a mature technology that has been integrated into all aspects of human life. For example, the global navigation satellite system (GNSS) provides accurate geographic positioning in outdoor scenarios. Global navigation satellite system (GNSS) can provide accurate geographical location, speed and other information in outdoor scenarios. In outdoor scenarios, for example, GNSS provides accurate information on geographical location, speed of traffic and other information, which makes people's daily lives much more convenient. However, in indoor conditions, GNSS cannot be used due to the obstruction of buildings. However, in indoor conditions, GNSS cannot provide accurate positioning and stable location information due to the obstruction of buildings.

M. Zhang et al. (Eds.): CCF NCCA 2023, CCIS 1959, pp. 245–255, 2024.
https://doi.org/10.1007/978-981-99-8764-1_19

According to research, people spend on average only 10%–20% of their time out-doors, and most of their time is spent indoors. The demand for wireless positioning is increasing. The demand for indoor positioning of industrial IoT devices, personnel positioning and various types of robots has led to further research into indoor position-ing technologies.There are currently two main types of indoor positioning algorithms: 1) range-based algorithms and 2) range-free algorithms. The measurement techniques commonly used in range-base based algorithms are received signal strength indicator (RSSI), time difference of arrival (TDOA), time of arrival (TOA). (TOA), angle of arrival (AOA), etc. Distance-based algorithms are very accurate and can reach centimeter-level accuracy with small errors in sensor acquisition data. The algorithms that do not require distance measurement usually use the connectivity of the wireless sensor net-work system to The typical algorithms are Dv-hop, prime algorithm, and distance-based algorithm.The typical algorithms are the Dv-hop, the prime algorithm, the approximate point-in-triangulation test (APIT), the Range-free based algorithms can be used to obtain higher accuracy by changing the reference node distribution density or changing the blind node communication radius The algorithm is based on the range-free. To address the problems affecting the accuracy of the center-of-mass algorithm, Huang et al. et al. pro-posed to classify the path loss coefficients and use the Euclidean distance to determine the actual RSSI value to select the corresponding path loss category. Triguero, D et al. [1] used the k-nearest neighbor algorithm to solve the problem. W. Luo et al. [2] proposed an improved center-of-mass localization algorithm when the reference nodes are not uni-formly distributed. The larger the communication radius, the smaller the error. X. Feng et al. [3] pointed out that that one or more reference nodes can be added on top of the three reference nodes. The intersection of the two intersection points of the intersecting circles can then be used to solve for the blind node coordinates. The coordinates of the blind nodes can be solved by adding one or more reference nodes to the three reference nodes.

The traditional centroid location algorithm is a very simple and practical location algorithm, which is based on network connectivity. The basic principle of this algorithm is as follows: multiple reference nodes are arranged around the blind node in advance. Every certain time, the reference node will broadcast its ID and position coordinates to the neighbor node. After receiving the reference node ID and position coordinates sent by the blind node, the blind node will find several reference nodes with the highest signal intensity. Usually, there are 3–8 reference nodes, and the 3–8 nodes with the strongest signal intensity are the reference nodes closest to the blind nodes. It can be approximately considered that the blind nodes are located at the centroid of the polygon surrounded by these reference nodes. Therefore, the geometric centroid of the polygon surrounded by these reference nodes can be used as the position coordinates of the blind nodes. The traditional centroid algorithm is very low complexity, easy to implement, and the cost is small, besides the shortage of positioning accuracy is too low, in order to improve the positioning accuracy, it is necessary to improve the layout density of the reference node, that is, to increase the cost of hardware, and the reference node should be distributed as evenly as possible. In fact, the ultimate purpose of the high-density and uniform layout of reference nodes is to minimize the polygon used for the final determination of the centroid of blind nodes. The smaller the polygon area is, the more accurate the position coordinates of blind nodes will be obtained by the determination of their centroid. Because the traditional centroid algorithm either has low positioning accuracy or high hardware cost, it has great limitations in application.

To address the shortcomings of the traditional centre-of-mass algorithm, this paper proposes an improved six-point centre-of-mass algorithm based on it [4]. The BP neural network model has already been studied to fit the traditional distance loss model, which takes the received signal strength RSSI as input and the corresponding distance d as output, avoiding the need to find the parameters A and n in the signal propagation model. Once the distance d is obtained, the three nearest reference nodes to the node to be located are also obtained, and the six-point centre-of-mass algorithm proposed in this paper uses these three reference nodes as The six-point centre-of-mass algorithm proposed in this paper makes a circle with the measured distance of the blind node from these three reference nodes as the centre of the circle, and the six intersection points of these three circles as the radius of the circle. The polygon formed by the six intersections of these three circles is used as the new polygon for the position estimation of the blind node, and the centre of mass of this hexagon is used as the centre of mass for the position estimation of the blind node. Compared with the traditional center-of-mass localization algorithm, this improves the localization accuracy without increasing the hardware overhead and has a very high level of accuracy. Improves the localisation accuracy and has a very high practical value.

2   Method

2.1   Signal Transmission Model

The theoretical model commonly used in wireless signal transmission is the fading model [5].

$$p(d) = p(d_0) - 10n \lg\left(\frac{d}{d_0}\right) + X \tag{1}$$

where: d is the distance from the blind node to the reference node; p(d) denotes the signal strength received by the blind node when the distance from the reference node is d; p(d0) denotes the signal strength received by the blind node when the distance from the reference node is d0, where d0 is the reference distance; n is the path loss factor, the value changes with the complexity of the environment, generally the more obstacles, the larger the value of n, the normal range is from 2 to 6; X is a Gaussian random variable obeying normal distribution, the unit is dBm.

Simplified models are generally used in practical engineering applications,

$$p(d) = p(d_0) - 10n lg\left(\frac{d}{d_0}\right) \tag{2}$$

To simplify the calculation process, d0 is generally taken to be 1m and let p(d) be the received signal strength estimate, p(d0) = A. Thus we have

$$I_{RSS} = A - 10n lg(d) \tag{3}$$

A is the value of the signal strength received by the blind node when it is 1m away from the reference node.

2.2 Principle of the Center-of-Mass Algorithm

The basic principle of the center-of-mass algorithm is that a blind node detects a reference node that is connected to it. The basic principle of the placentric algorithm is that a blind node detects a reference node that is connected to it and estimates its own position based on the position information provided by the reference node. The process is as follows: the reference node periodically sends its position information around, and the blind node estimates its position based on the position information received from the different reference nodes. When the number of reference nodes received by the blind node or the signal strength reaches a certain threshold value, the blind node records the coordinates of the position of the reference nodes that meet the certain threshold value and uses the centre of mass of the polygon formed by these reference nodes as the self The blind node records the coordinates of the position of the reference node that meets a certain threshold, and uses the centre of mass of the polygon formed by these reference nodes as its own position, as shown in Fig. 1.

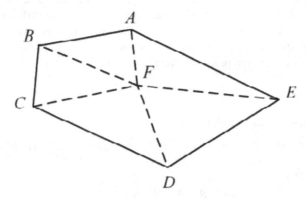

Fig. 1. Schematic diagram of the centre-of-mass positioning principle.

Suppose the blind node F (x, y) receives five reference node coordinates A to E, corresponding to the coordinate values (xi, yi), i = 1, 2, 3, 4, 5. Then the estimated coordinates of the blind node F is:

$$F(x, y) = \left(\frac{1}{5} \sum_{i=1}^{5} x_i, \frac{1}{5} \sum_{i=1}^{5} y_i \right) \tag{4}$$

2.3 The Proposed Six-Point Centre-of-Mass Algorithm

In an ideal case, [6] the blind node is at the intersection of three circles with the three reference nodes as the center of the circle and the distance between the blind node and the three reference nodes as the radius. Therefore, the intersection of the three circles can be calculated by calculating the distance between the blind node and the three reference nodes, and then the position coordinates of the blind node can be obtained [7]. However, in practice, due to the existence of errors, the three circles generally do not intersect at a point, but at an area. The position relationship between the typical three reference nodes and blind nodes is shown in Fig. 2 below:

$$F(x,y) = \left(\frac{1}{5} \sum_{i=1}^{5} x_i, \frac{1}{5} \sum_{i=1}^{5} y_i \right)$$

(4)

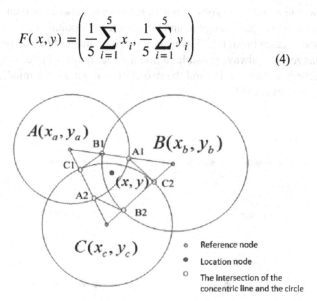

Fig. 2. Position Relation between Reference Nodes and Blind Node.

The traditional center-of-mass localization algorithm is to find the three reference nodes closest to the blind nodes [8] (i.e., the three nodes with the strongest RSSI sent to the blind nodes). (i.e., the three nodes with the strongest RSSI sent to the blind node), such as the three ABC points shown in Fig. 4-1, and then directly find the center of mass of these three reference nodes as the location estimate of the blind node. The center of mass of these three reference nodes is used as the position estimation of the blind node, but this method has too much error. In this paper, the traditional three-point In this paper, the traditional three-point center-of-mass algorithm is improved to a more accurate six-point center-of-mass algorithm, in which the received signal strength RSSI is firstly input to the trained The output is the distance d between the corresponding reference node and the blind node. The location of the blind node is on the circle with the reference node as the center and the distance d as the radius. The BP neural network is used to obtain three such distances, we can get three such circles, and the actual blind node is inside the polygon surrounded by these three circles. The actual blind nodes are inside the polygon formed by these three circles. Then we find the intersection of the three circles and the intersection of the two circles with the circle, a total of six points, and find the center of mass of these six points. The center of mass of these six points is used as the location estimate of the blind node [9].

According to the relationship between the reference nodes and the blind nodes in Fig. 2, the traditional center-of-mass algorithm is to find the center of mass of the three reference nodes ABC in Fig. 2, but the algorithm in this paper is to find the center of mass of the hexagon enclosed by the six yellow points A1, B1, C1, A2, B2, C2 in Fig. 2, so that the position of the localized nodes is precisely limited to the inside of the smaller hexagon, and the localization is more accurate. The six points of the six-point center of mass algorithm can be obtained from the position relationship between the two circles in Fig. 3 below. There are four types of position relations between two circles (tangent is divided into inner and outer tangent, and the intersection points are considered to be coincident, for one case) From Fig. 3, we can see that no matter how the position of the two circles changes, it is always possible to find the four points of intersection between the line connecting the two circles and the two circles, if we are the middle two points of these four points of intersection.

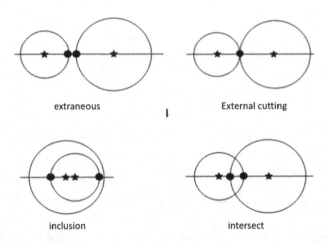

Fig. 3. Position Relation between Two Circles.

How to find the coordinates of these six points is the key to the six-point center of mass algorithm, [10] as shown in Fig. 4-1, for example. Let the signal strengths of the blind nodes received by the three reference nodes $A(x_A, y_A)$, $B(x_B, y_B)$, $C(x_C, y_C)$ are RA, RB, RC and input these three received signal strengths into the trained BP neural network to obtain the corresponding distance, , and The corresponding distances, , and RC d dB, d, so that three circles can be obtained.

$$Circle\, A : (x - x_A)^2 + (y - y_A)^2 = d_A^2 \tag{5}$$

$$Circle\, B : (x - x_B)^2 + (y - y_B)^2 = d_B^2 \tag{6}$$

$$Circle\, C : (x - x_C)^2 + (y - y_C)^2 = d_C^2 \tag{7}$$

Three straight lines:

$$LINE\, AB : \frac{y - y_A}{x - x_A} = \frac{y_A - y_B}{x_A - x_B} \tag{8}$$

$$LINE\ AC : \frac{y - y_A}{x - x_A} = \frac{y_A - y_C}{x_A - x_C} \tag{9}$$

$$LINE\ BC : \frac{y - y_B}{x - x_B} = \frac{y_B - y_C}{x_B - x_C} \tag{10}$$

First find the intersection of the line AB and the circle A. Combine (5) and (8) and solve the equations to obtain the solution as in Eqs. (10) and (11).

$$x = x_A \pm \frac{|(x_B - x_A) \times d_A|}{\sqrt{(x_B - x_A)^2 - (y_B - y_A)^2}} \tag{11}$$

$$y = y_A \pm \frac{|(y_B - y_A) \times d_A|}{\sqrt{(x_B - x_A)^2 - (y_B - y_A)^2}} \tag{12}$$

Two point can be made:

$$\left(x_A + \frac{|(x_B-x_A)\times d_A|}{\sqrt{(x_B-x_A)^2-(y_B-y_A)^2}}, y_A + \frac{|(y_B-y_A)\times d_A|}{\sqrt{(x_B-x_A)^2-(y_B-y_A)^2}} \right) \text{ and }$$

$$\left(x_A - \frac{|(x_B - x_A) \times d_A|}{\sqrt{(x_B - x_A)^2 - (y_B - y_A)^2}}, y_A - \frac{|(y_B - y_A) \times d_A|}{\sqrt{(x_B - x_A)^2 - (y_B - y_A)^2}} \right)$$

Similarly the solution to the two intersections of the line AB with the circle B can be solved by combining Eqs. (6) and (8) as in Eqs. (13) and (14).

$$x = x_B \pm \frac{|(x_B - x_A) \times d_B|}{\sqrt{(x_B - x_A)^2 - (y_B - y_A)^2}} \tag{13}$$

$$y = y_B \pm \frac{|(y_B - y_A) \times d_B|}{\sqrt{(x_B - x_A)^2 - (y_B - y_A)^2}} \tag{14}$$

Two point can be made:

$$\left(x_B + \frac{|(x_B-x_A)\times d_B|}{\sqrt{(x_B-x_A)^2-(y_B-y_A)^2}}, y_B + \frac{|(y_B-y_A)\times d_B|}{\sqrt{(x_B-x_A)^2-(y_B-y_A)^2}} \right) \text{ and }$$

$$\left(x_B - \frac{|(x_B-x_A)\times d_B|}{\sqrt{(x_B-x_A)^2-(y_B-y_A)^2}}, y_B - \frac{|(y_B-y_A)\times d_B|}{\sqrt{(x_B-x_A)^2-(y_B-y_A)^2}} \right)$$

The four points are ordered from smallest to largest (or from largest to smallest) by X-coordinate (or Y-coordinate), and then the two points corresponding to the X-coordinate (or Y-coordinate) of the middle size are the two points A1 and, and the coordinate values of the remaining four points can be obtained, assuming that the six intersections of the circle in Fig. 2 are:

$$A_1(x_{A1}, y_{A1}), A_2(x_{A2}, y_{A2}), B_1(x_{B1}, y_{B1}), B_2(x_{B2}, y_{B2}),$$
$$C_1(x_{C1}, y_{C1}), C_2(x_{C2}, y_{C2})$$

Then the loci of the blind node (x, y) can be estimated as shown in Eqs. (15) and (16) below.

$$x = \frac{(x_{A1} + x_{A2} + x_{B1} + x_{B2} + x_{C1} + x_{C2})}{6} \tag{15}$$

$$y = \frac{(y_{A1} + y_{A2} + y_{B1} + y_{B2} + y_{C1} + y_{C2})}{6} \tag{16}$$

This gives the coordinates of the estimated position of the blind node as:

$$\left(\frac{(x_{A1} + x_{A2} + x_{B1} + x_{B2} + x_{C1} + x_{C2})}{6}, \frac{(y_{A1} + y_{A2} + y_{B1} + y_{B2} + y_{C1} + y_{C2})}{6} \right)$$

3 Experiment Result

The blind nodes are randomly generated and to reduce the impact of this factor on the algorithm. To reduce the impact of this factor on the algorithm [11], 20 blind nodes were first generated randomly in a 130 m × 100 m area. The blind nodes were detected at a fixed distance (10 m to 70 m, with 5 m intervals, for a total of 13 different detection distances), and the detection distance was fixed by varying the distribution density of the reference nodes. The simulations were carried out with varying the distribution density of the reference nodes, and the results of each group were averaged to obtain Fig. 4.

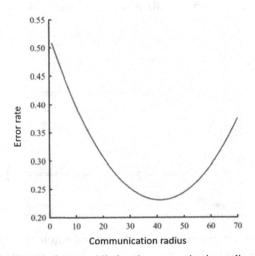

Fig. 4. The relationship between blind node communication radius and error rate.

As can be seen in Fig. 4, the error rate decreases and then increases with the communication radius. The simulation results fit a quadratic curve with a positioning error rate of approximately 0.2308 at the lowest point, which corresponds to a communication radius of 41 m, i.e. the optimum communication radius. On this basis, this point corresponds to a good positioning accuracy and the cost required under this condition is relatively low. The method used to achieve the optimum communication radius therefore gives a balance between cost and positioning error rate, which is the practical significance of finding the optimum communication radius.

A fixed monitoring area of $100 * 100$ m^2 is simulated, and the radius of communication or the number of anchor nodes is varied to see how the improved center-of-mass localization algorithm changes with the change of index. (1) When the total number of nodes is 100, simulations are performed for beacon nodes 8, 14 and 20 respectively. The average error is 8.16 when the communication radius is a certain value and the beacon node n = 8, which is 1.56 and 2.26 higher than that of the beacon node 14 and 20, respectively, indicating that the localization error is smaller when the number of anchor nodes is higher and increases when the communication radius increases. (2) The total number of nodes is 100, and the simulation is carried out for the communication radius of 10 m, 30 m and 50 m respectively. The number of anchor nodes increases, and the error decreases and levels off. When the communication radius is 10 m, the average positioning error is 9.6 m, which is higher than the communication radius of 30 m and 50 m. The larger the radius, the higher the positioning accuracy depends on the increase in the number of anchor nodes.

The results of the Matlab simulation based on the six-point center of mass method are shown in Fig. 5. It can be seen that when the distance between the reference nodes is relatively close, its average error rate decreases significantly with increasing distance, and the error increases when the distance increases gradually.

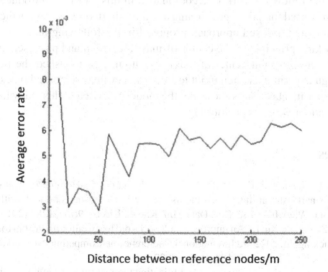

Fig. 5. Effect of varying distance on the mean error rate.

In addition, the traditional center-of-mass method and the improved algorithm are compared together, as shown in Fig. 6. It can be seen that both algorithms stabilise as the total number of beacon nodes increases to a certain value, due to the saturation of the system as the number of beacon nodes increases.

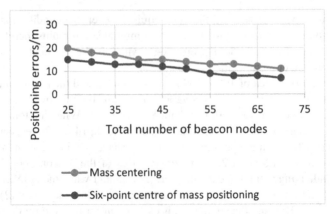

Fig. 6. Comparison of the traditional centre-of-mass method with the improved method.

Although the trends are roughly the same, the six-point placentric positioning algorithm achieves a significantly lower positioning error than the traditional placentric algorithm, proving that the proposed improved algorithm is indeed feasible.

4 Conclusion

To this end, the following work is accomplished in this paper: 1. introduced the algorithms currently used for indoor positioning and their shortcomings, laying the theoretical foundation for the improved approach proposed in the following paper. 2. introduced the basic working principle of the center-of-mass algorithm and proposed an improved system using the six-point center-of-mass algorithm. 3. established the best possible model through experiments, then input test data and evaluated it based on expert judgement. The experimental results show that the model proposed in this study has excellent accuracy in indoor wireless positioning.

References

1. Triguero, I., García-Gil, D., Maillo, J., Luengo, J., García, S., Herrera, F.: Transforming big data into smart data: an insight on the use of the k-nearest neighbors algorithm to obtain quality data. Wiley Interdisc. Rev. Data Min. Knowl. Discov. **9**(2), e1289 (2019)
2. Luo, W., Zhang, L., Xu, L.: An improved multi-centroid localization algorithm for WiFi signal source tracking. In: 2022 3rd International Conference on Computing, Networks and Internet of Things (CNIOT), pp. 100–104. IEEE (2022)
3. Feng, X., Ren, D., He, X., Ouyang, M.: Mitigating thermal runaway of lithium-ion batteries. Joule **4**(4), 743–770 (2020)
4. Strozzi, A., Mantovani, S., Barbieri, S.G., Baldini, A.: Two analytical structural models of the connecting rod cap. Proc. Inst. Mech. Eng. Part C J. Mech. Eng. Sci. 09544062221143251 (2023)
5. Trigui, I., Ajib, W., Zhu, W.-P.: A comprehensive study of reconfigurable intelligent surfaces in generalized fading. arXiv preprint arXiv:2004.02922 (2020)

6. Nowak, K., Zarnecki, A.F.: Optimising top-quark threshold scan at CLIC using genetic algorithm. arXiv preprint arXiv:2103.00522 (2021)
7. Chung, W.-Y.: Enhanced RSSI-based real-time user location tracking system for indoor and outdoor environments. In: 2007 International Conference on Convergence Information Technology (ICCIT 2007), pp. 1213–1218. IEEE (2007)
8. Lee, Y.H., Medioni, G.: RGB-D camera based wearable navigation system for the visually impaired. Comput. Vis. Image Underst. **149**, 3–20 (2016)
9. Bachrach, J., Taylor, C.: Localization in sensor networks. In: Handbook of Sensor Networks: Algorithms and Architectures, pp. 277–310 (2005)
10. Huang, Q., Deng, Z., Liu, L.: A fast prediction method for the target reachable zone of boosting gliding vehicle based on database. Appl. Sci. **13**(3), 1848 (2023)
11. Li, X., Xu, L., Wang, H., Song, J., Yang, S.X.: A differential evolution-based routing algorithm for environmental monitoring wireless sensor networks. Sensors **10**(6), 5425–5442 (2010)

MEAHO: Membrane Evolutionary Algorithm for Hyperparameter Optimization of Deep Convolutional Neural Networks

Jie Mu, Jiaxin Hou, and Ying Wan[✉]

School of Big Data and Software Engineering, Chongqing University, Chongqing 400044, China
wanying516@qq.com

Abstract. Membrane algorithm has been used to solve many optimization problems since it was put forward. These methods used the membrane algorithm as a container for other algorithms to solve many problems, such as, traveling salesman problem, the knapsack problem and so on. In this paper, from the angle of membrane algorithm, the solution of hyperparameter optimization problem by membrane algorithm is explored, with the hyperparameter space divided by lattice method, which transformed into membrane structure subsequently. For the evolution of membrane, the entropy reduction principle is proposed. Compared with other membrane algorithms, this paper solves the optimization problem from the membrane algorithm itself, designs the corresponding algorithm for the membrane structure, and obtains the experimental results through CNN experiment.

Keywords: Hyperparameter optimization · Deep Convolutional Neural Networks · Membrane Evolutionary Algorithm

1 Introduction

Inspired by the structure and evolutionary function of the biological cells, membrane computing was proposed in 2000 by Paun [1]. Initially, the early work aimed to design basic computing operators and construct membrane computing systems for computing problems at the theoretical level. Various membrane computing systems are also called membrane systems or P systems [1–5]. As a fast-growing branch of natural computing, membrane computing has been applied for a variety of fields, including NP-complete problems, parallel and distributed algorithms, graphics, linguistics and economy. It has been constructed for solving a large range of problems, for example, knapsack problem [25, 26], maximum clique problem [27], Minimum Vertex Cover Problem [28] and so on.

Benefitted from the evolutionary mechanism of biological cells, under the framework of membrane computing, the computing models perform in a parallel, and distributed way to calculate. Because the execution of the rules in membrane computing is random and parallel, which enables it to solve complex problems such as Nphard problems [36], membrane algorithm usually uses the membrane as a container to solve the optimization

M. Zhang et al. (Eds.): CCF NCCA 2023, CCIS 1959, pp. 256–272, 2024.
https://doi.org/10.1007/978-981-99-8764-1_20

problem, and different algorithms are run in each cell to solve the problem, which can be done in a parallel and distributed method. In particular, the membrane system is based on a hierarchy structure in which a single or different algorithm can interact to solve a problem. In [15], an adaptive membrane algorithm combining the hierarchical structure and local search was proposed to solve the travelling salesman problem. The structure of membrane algorithm has a good tolerance to different algorithms, so it can solve the optimization problem well. In [37], Guo et al. combined heuristic algorithm and cell-like P system, proposing a membrane evolutionary algorithm for solving TSP. Membrane algorithm can be used as the basic structure to build the corresponding algorithm to solve the corresponding optimization problems and has certain effectiveness.

As another branch of natural computing, evolutionary computation searches an optimal solution along an evolutionary route. Evolutionary computing can be used to solve optimization problems in multi-dimensional space. In [29], the Genetic algorithm (GA) is used to compute the decentralized control parameters to achieve an optimum operating point in automatic generation control (AGC), this is a problem of finding the optimal value in multi-dimensional space. Delgarm et al. prosed a mono- and multi-objective particle swarm optimization (MOPSO) algorithm to solve multi-objective optimization of building energy performance [30]. Zhu et al. used particle swarm optimization to solve the non-linear constrained portfolio optimization problem with multi-objective functions [31]. These methods use evolutionary algorithm to explore the solution of multi- dimensional space, and prove the effectiveness of evolutionary algorithm for high dimensional space optimization.

With the burst-development of deep learning, hyperparameter optimization of deep models has been becoming a barrier for practical application of deep leaning techniques [33], because deep models are very sensitive to the setting of their hyperparameters [17]. While non-experts have a hard time finding a good setting of hyperparameter parameters, automatic parameter optimization can produce hyperparameter settings that are similar to those of experts [8]. However, the computational cost of fitting large DNNs is very high, and the time overhead of automatic hyperparameter optimization prevents its widespread adoption. Moreover, the advantages and disadvantages of hyperparameter optimization require in-depth investigations through experiments.

In this work, we construct a membrane evolutionary algorithm to optimize hyperparameter setting for deep convolutional neural networks. This is the first time that a membrane system is used to solve the complex problem of hyperparameter optimization of deep neural network models. Unlike other methods that only use membranes as containers to hold other algorithms to solve optimization problems, we use the structure of membrane system itself to solve optimization problems and design corresponding evolution rules. Because the optimization space of hyperparameter optimization for deep neural network is a high dimension issue, so we construct the corresponding structure to solve this problem, and use hierarchical structure to present it. The optimization space is represented in the form of cell membrane, which is divided into a grid, and then the specific hyperparameter value is taken as the median value in each grid. In addition to the fitness evaluation of membrane evolution rules, we also evaluated the expected effect of each super parameter, which is the in-fluence of the hyperparameter on the fitness. Then, for membrane fusion we use the entropy principle for evolution. If the binding of two dividing cells can produce an entropy increase, then these two cells are worthy of binding, and the definition of entropy increase mainly depends on the expected effect of the hyperparameter. Through constant iteration, a group of better results of hyperparameter optimization are obtained.

The contributions of this paper can be summarized into the following three points:

- The structure of the membrane algorithm as the model of the evolutionary algorithm rather than having the membrane structure include other optimization algorithms.
- The membrane algorithm is used to design the hyperparameter optimization algorithm for the first time.
- The entropy theory is applied to the optimization model to increase the robustness of the model.

The other part of this paper is organized as follows. In Sect. 2, some related works about membrane algorithms and the hyperparameter optimization are introduced. Then, MEA is introduced in Sect. 3, including its operators and algorithm framework. Base on MEA, MEAHO is designed to solve the hyperparameter optimization in Sect. 4. Section 5 gives the experiment results on large real-world data set. As for Sect. 6, some problems in this paper are discussed. Finally, overall conclusions are given in Sect. 7.

2 Membrane Evolutionary Algorithm Framework for Hyperparameter Optimization

In order to handle the Hyperparameter optimization problem for deep convolutional neural network, in this section we propose a cell-like P system with a membrane evolutionary algorithm based on the nested structure of biological cells with its evolutionary rules. Here, we first introduce the hyperparameter optimization problem for deep convolution neural network. Additionally, the pro-posed membrane system is formally defined. Further, a membrane evolutionary algorithm is proposed in the membrane system. Finally, the proposed membrane system and membrane evolutionary algorithm are applied to hyperparameter optimization of deep convolutional neural network.

2.1 Hyperparameter Optimization Problem for Deep Convolutional Neural Networks

A set of hyperparameters should be configured before training, such as number of layers (depth), number of neural cells for each layer (width), learning rate, drop-out rate, size of mini bath. However, the influence of the model structure based on the results is far greater than that of other hyperparameters, so this paper focuses on the optimization of the hyperparameters of the model structure. The main hyperparameters considered in this work are listed as follows:

1) Number of layers (depth): the number of layers of convolution layer and full connection layer.
2) Number of neural cells for each layer (width): W_{ci} is number of neural cells for i th layer of convolution layer, W_{fj} is number of neural cells for j-th layer of convolution layer.

2.2 Definition of P System

At first, the proposed P system is formally defined as follows:

$$\Pi = (O, H, \mu, \omega_1, \ldots, \omega_n, R_1, \ldots, R_n, i_0) \tag{1}$$

where,

1) O is the limited alphabet. Each symbol represents one kind of objects in the system Π;
2) μ is the membrane structure with n membranes, labeled by $1, 2, \ldots, n$;
3) $\omega_i(1 \leq i \leq n)$ is multisets of objects present in the membrane i;
4) $R_i(1 \leq i \leq n)$ is the finite set of evolution rules in the membrane i;
5) i_0 is the label of the output membrane and it reserves the final result.

2.3 Space Exploration

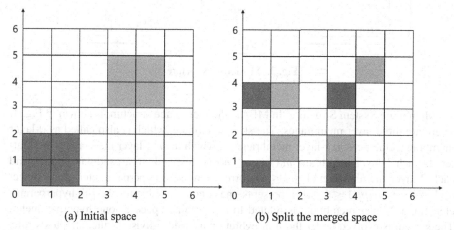

(a) Initial space   (b) Split the merged space

Fig. 1. (a) represents the initial space selected, and (b) represents the space involved after splitting and fusion.

For super parameter optimization, it all takes a point to determine a point. This article through the use of membrane structure for super parameter optimization of the algorithm, and then expands the concept of a super parameter points to the space concept, namely from a select of a point in space to represent the effect of the whole space, which can be strengthened for the exploration ability of whole space, Fig. 1 shows the split algorithm combined the membranes of the space, this paper designed by membrane algorithm is divided evenly divided, namely each dimension evenly divided, and then split up and other cells are combined, the formation of new cells, new cell contains space isn't completely close to, through this merger, can increase the whole space exploration ability. As shown in Fig. 1(b), when cells are fused in two far apart Spaces, the space in the middle part will be explored. By uniformly taking points, the whole space can be explored and a global optimal solution can be obtained.

2.4 Membrane Evolutionary Algorithm Framework (MEAF)

Inspired from the biological membrane structure and evolution process, we first construct an algorithm frame-work for hyperparameter optimization in this section. In this framework, the proposed membrane system has two layer membranes and four evolutionary rules.

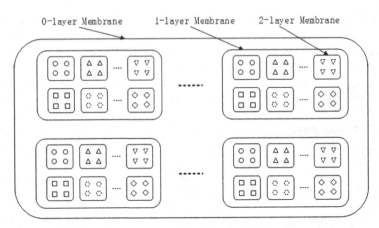

Fig. 2. Membrane structure

Membrane System Structure: In MEAF, the membrane structure is shown in Fig. 1. There are three-layer membranes. The skin membrane, which is also called as 0-layer membrane, embraces m 1-layer membranes in which the n 2-layer membranes are scattered. Each 1-layer membrane $m_i(1 \leq i \leq m)$ corresponds to a candidate model, and each 2-layer membrane $p_j(1 \leq j \leq n)$ corresponds to a hyperparameter. Each object $o_t(1 \leq t \leq v)$ in $p_j(1 \leq j \leq n)$ represents one candidate value for the j-th hyperparameter. So, a 2-layer membrane is related to a searching space of one hyperparameter. The system is evolved under the four evolutionary rules: division rule, apoptosis rule, replication rule and fusion rule, which are described as follows.

Initialization rule: Uniform values from each dimension according to uniform sampling, and then use these values as starting points.

Division rule: A biological system grows by cell division. The proposed membrane system evolves by the di-vision rule from one generation to the next generation. Each inner membrane is divided into two new 1-layer membranes. The objects of each original 1-layer mem-brane are wrapped up by one of the two new membranes in terms of the entropy decrease rule which is explained later.

Apoptosis rule: A biological system is improved and removes the inner garbage by cell apoptosis. In the pro-posed membrane system, 1-layer membranes with the lower fitness values.

Selection rule: A biological system obtains a better adaptability to the environment by selection. The 1-layer membranes with the higher fitness values are selected to evolve further.

Replication rule: self-replication.

Fusion rule: Two new 1-layer membranes are fused into a 1-layer membrane with four objects.

The membrane system is evolved under the four rules and the proposed membrane evolutionary algorithm framework is summarized in Algorithm 1.

Algorithm 1
Input: The initial membrane system
Output: The evolved membrane system
Step 1: The initial membrane structure is constructed. The initial 50candidated parameter settings are evaluated.   Step 2: The division rule is applied.   Step 3: The fusion rule is applied.   Step 4: The selection rules is applied.   Step 5: The selection rule is applied.   Step 6: Go to Step 1.

Figure 2 illustrates the initial membrane structure of MEAF, which includes the three-layer membranes. There is a 0-layer membrane, m 1-layer membranes which are related to models, and n 2-layer membranes which are related to the m hyperparameters considered. The m 1-layer membranes are labeled from 1 to m, which constitute the population of MEAF and are denoted as $\mathbb{M} = \{M_1, \ldots, M_m\}$, where m is the size of the population. $\forall M_i \in \mathbb{M}$ is one of the individuals in the population. The v objects in P_i are denoted as $O_i = \{o_{i1}, \ldots, o_{iv}\}$. One object o_{it_i} from M_i is one value in the feasible range of the i th hyperparameter. And a combination of n objects $\{o_{1t_1}, o_{2t_2}, \ldots, o_{pt_v}\}$ from the m 1-layer membranes $\{M_1, M_2, \ldots, M_m\}$ constitute a feasible solution for the hyperparameter optimization problem. The population is evolved iteratively in parallel under the membrane evolutionary algorithm framework. In the evolution process, the definition of individual's fitness (1-layer membrane fitness) will be various in terms of the considered problems. In this work, we consider the hyperparameter optimization of convolutional neural networks, so an individual's fitness is calculated according to the performance of the convolutional neural network.

The four operators can be used alone or in combination for a specific problem. For example, the selection operator can be combined with the cytolysis operator to form a complex operator. In Sect. 4, we implement a specific membrane evolutionary algorithm for hyperparameter optimization (MEAHO) under the MEAF framework.

3   Hyperparameter Optimization Based on Membrane Evolutionary Algorithm (MEAHO)

In this section, we propose a membrane evolution algorithm to solve hyperparameter optimization problem for deep convolutional neural networks, which is named MEAHO (membrane evolution algorithm for hyperparameter optimization problem).

Definitions and Notation: In MEAHO, the membrane structure is shown in Fig. 2. In this work, we consider the seven hyperparameters in this work, so $n = 7$ here. For each hyperparameter, its value range is equally divided into v segments. The v objects for the hyperparameter P_j are generated through selecting the medium value of each segment. So for each neural network model, there are v^m hyperparameter configurations, in which the setting with the lowest MSR measure is called the best object combination and denoted as O_{best}. So, each individual (1-layer membrane) generates v^m possible neural network models for each generation. Next, we define the fitness of individual in this work.

Definition 1: Fitness. The fitness $fit(M_i)$ of the individual M_i is defined as follows,

$$fit(M_i) = 1 - MSR(M_i, O_{best}) \tag{2}$$

where $MSR(M_i, O_{best})$ represents the MSR performance of the model M_i with its current best hyperparameter combination O_{best}.

MEAHO Algorithm: In this work, we construct a three-layer convolution neural network and consider seven hyperparameters, such as the width of the first convolutional layer w_1, the width of the second convolutional layer w_2, the width of the third convolutional layer w_3, the width of the fully-connected layer w_4, the learning rate w_5, the size of minibatch w_6 and the ratio for dropout w_7. In this work, $m = 7$ and $v = 4$. Here, for each generation, there are 4^7 candidate hyperparameter configurations in the membrane system. This section introduces the algorithm of MEAHO for solving the HO problem. MEAHO solves the HO problem by iteratively performing division, fusion, cytolysis, and selection operations.

At the start of each iteration, the size of the population maintains to be n, and the size of the hyperparameter division segments is v. In each generation, we first need to evaluate the fitness of the n individuals. To find the globally best model of the individual M_i we need to evaluate the all 4^7 CNN models. However, it is impractical for the time cost. Here, for each model membrane, s hyperparameter configurations are selected from the v^m. The selected configurations are respected to be most representative with the limited size s. In this work, $s = 50$. So for each model membrane, 50 CNN models from the 4^7 model set are evaluated and the performance of the best model is used to compute the fitness of the model membrane according to Eq. (2).

In order to evaluate the quality of each inner membrane, we need to define its fitness. For each hyperparameter combination, the performance of the CNN model is evaluated. Here, we select MSE as the evaluation metric. The lower the MSE value is, the higher the fitness is. The membrane with larger fitness value is more adaptive to the environment.

The natural selection strategy is uniform random sampling on the hyperparameter grid. In this work, we adopt the uniform design method which is constructed for biochemical test strategy design. The uniform design method ensures the selected points distribute on the hyperparameter grid as uniformly as possible. To illustrate the performance of uniform design sampling on the hyperparameter grid. Here, we give an example considering three hyperparameters with four-segment division for each hyperparameter value range. In Fig. 1, 50 random selected points distribute uniformly on the 3-Dim hyperparameter grid. Here, 50 selected points correspond to 50 CNN models with different hyperparameter configurations in each individual.

After the selected CNN models are evaluated for each model membrane, the fitness of individuals can be computed. In each model membrane, the best fitness from those of the 50 evaluated CNN models are selected as the fitness of the considered model membrane. So the fitness values of all the model membranes can be sorted. Then the population starts to evolve toward the biologically benefited direction. At first, in terms of the selection rule, the top α model membranes are selected and copied, where $0 < \alpha < 1$. The bottom α model membranes are selected and deleted in terms of the cytolysis rule. For the left middle $1 - 2\alpha$ model membranes, each model membrane splits into two new membranes which are called as temporary model membranes in terms of the division rule. With model membranes splitting, each hyperparameter membrane are divided into two temporary hyperparameter membranes. Meanwhile, the four value objects in each hyperparameter are grouped into two clusters according to a specific biological rule. Here, we select the entropy decrease rule to conduct the clustering procedure of the four value objects. In nature systems, a biological system is generally evolving to the entropy decrease direction. The entropy decreasing is the intrinsic rule in biological systems, which is also applied in the node division for the decision tree algorithm. The proposed MEAHO membrane system imitates this rule, and the inner membrane is divided according to the entropy decrease rule.

The entropy is used to describe the degree of distribution. Here, we define as follows.

Definition: Entropy: The degree of chaos of a system itself, in this paper entropy mainly refers to the effect value that can be achieved by cells of the membrane system.

Entropy Decrease Principle: The basic principle of the development of the world is the increase of entropy. As the living body is an open system, it can absorb nutrients from the outside world, so its growth and evolution direction are toward the direction of entropy reduction, which is a more orderly direction of organisms. Meanwhile, keeping various molecular species separated in individual compartments is another entropy reducing process [35].

In this paper, it is believed that the increase of hyperparameter effect represents the decrease of entropy, that is the combination of hyperparameter with good effect is an operation of entropy reduction, which can make the whole membrane system more stable. For the evaluation of the hyperparameter effect, we use the hyperparameter combination under the current state of the membrane system and the corresponding fitness to carry out the fitting.

$$\sigma(\ddagger) = \frac{1}{1+e^{-w^T x}} \tag{3}$$

Logical regression is the main fitting method, as shown in 3. In 3, Z represents the fitness gained which is a value, and the x represents the combination of hyperparametric. For the prediction of hyperparameter effect, the prediction is mainly based on the way of division. A possible fitness for each hyperparameter can then be obtained to achieve a fusion based on entropy decrement.

In the specific algorithm, after the membrane division, Logistic regression is performed based on the current hyperparameter combination of each cell and the corresponding fitness, and then the possible fitness can be predicted for the divided interval of each cell. The cells were then fused based on the predicted values. Based on the principle of entropy reduction, cells that can achieve better fitness can fuse with each other to achieve a more stable state. According to this rule, continuous division and fusion can be carried out to continuously reduce entropy and avoid the entropy increase caused by ablation of cells. One round of the evolution has been completed and then the next generation evolution is started. The iterative evolution process stops until an end condition to be satisfied, for example, a specific iteration number and a specific fitness. This iterative process follows the principle of entropy reduction to iterate so as to get better results.

Algorithm 2 Membrane Evolutionary Algorithm for Hyperparameter Optimization (MEAHO)
Input: The initial membrane system, population size PS, the maximum runtime MRT, α.
Output: a hyperparameter combination

(1) Initialization
The initial membrane structure is constructed.
The initial 50 candidate parameter settings are evaluated.
repeat
(2) Evolve membranes in parallel: selection(P);
cytolysis(P);
division(P);
fusion(P);
until elapsed time >= MRT;
(3) return best;

4 Experimental Results

To demonstrate the effectiveness of MEAHO, this section compares the experimental results of MEAHO with random search, genetic algorithm and PSO.

4.1 Data Sets

We used three data sets, which are MNIST,CIFFAR10,and a kind of traffic data which from the PEMS(the public accessible Caltrans Performance Measurement System).MNIST data sets is a very classic data sets in the field of machine learning, consisting of 60,000 training samples and 10,000 test samples, each of which is a grayscale handwritten digital image with 28*28 pixels.CIFFAR10 data sets is a kind of RGB color plates include 10 categories: airplanes, cars, birds, cats, deer, dogs, frogs, horses, boats, and trucks. The image size is 32*32, and there are 50,000 training and 10,000 test images in the data set. Traffic data stets is from the PeMS dataset. We select 26 sensors from the data. So we evaluate all the compared methods under these data sets.

4.2 Evaluation Metrics and Baselines

In this paper, the Mean Average Percentage Error (MAPE) is used as evaluation metric of traffic data sets, which is defined as follow:

$$MAPE = \frac{1}{N}\sum_{I=1}^{N} \frac{|\widehat{y}_i - y_i|}{y_i} \tag{4}$$

where N is the number of all samples, and $\widehat{y}_i$ is the prediction value, and y_i is the true value. The classification accuracy is used as evaluation metric of MNIST data sets and CIFFAR10 data sets. Our proposed model is compared with the following methods:

- Random Search (RS): Within a certain interval, randomly generate points and then compare the objective function, keep the points with better results, and finally get the results through multiple iterations.
- Particle Swarm Optimization (PSO): PSO is an evolutionary computing technique derived from the study of predatory behavior of birds. The basic idea of particle swarm optimization algorithm is to find the optimal solution through the cooperation and information sharing among individuals in the group [10].
- Genetic Algorithm (GA): Genetic algorithm is a computational model that simulates the natural selection and genetic mechanism of Darwinian biological evolution. It is a method to search for the optimal solution by simulating the natural evolution process. [11].

4.3 Setting of Experimental Parameters

This experiment mainly uses three data sets, MNIST, CIFFAR10 and Traffic data set. The number of iterations of MBU for these three data sets is 50. In the experiment of MNIST data set, there are 2500 sets of super parameters in each iteration, and the number of the first layer membrane is 50, and the number of the second layer membrane is 50. The first layer is divided into 4, and the second layer is divided into 10. In the experiment of Transport data set, there are 2500 sets of super parameters in each iteration, and the number of the first layer membrane is 50, and the number of the second layer membrane is 50. The first layer is divided into 3, and the second layer is divided into 6. In the experiment of CIFFAR10 data set, there are 500 sets of super parameters in each iteration, and the number of the first layer membrane is 10, and the number of the second layer membrane is 50. The first layer is divided into 5, and the second layer is divided into 8.

4.4 Results and Analysis

The comparison of the performance of our model with the three comparison methods is shown in Table 1, and the experimental results of Mnist, ciffar10 and traffic data are given respectively. Based on the consideration of training time, training is divided into coarse training and fine training. The number of iterations of coarse training is less, while the number of iterations of fine training is increased on the basis of coarse training. The number of iterations increased by different contrast methods is uniform. Coarse training is the training method used in the model. After the optimization results are obtained, the results of intensive training are obtained. As you can see from I, compared with other methods, our method can get a better result in coarse training, and the effectiveness of the optimization result is proved by the use of fine training.

The model using MNIST data set has 5 parameters that need to be trained, and each iteration has 2500 sets of parameters. The model using CIFFAR10 data set has 7 parameters that need to be trained, and each iteration has 500 sets of parameters. The model using Transport data set has 4 parameters that need to be trained and each iteration

Table 1. Result of contrast.

Methods	mnist		ciffar10		traffic data	
	Coarse training	Fine training	Coarse training	Fine training	Coarse training	Fine training
RS	0.853	0.989	0.511	0.785	0.651	0.143
GA	0.917	0.988	0.523	0.811	0.651	0.141
PSO	0.926	0.993	0.522	0.813	0.646	0.137
MBU (ours)	0.927	0.994	0.524	0.813	0.649	0.138

has 2500 sets of parameters. The experimental results are divided into coarse training with less iteration times and intensive training with retraining on the basis of rough training. The results of coarse training and fine training are shown in Figs. 3 a, 4 a and 5 a. We can see coarse training can better reflect the results of intensive training. Therefore, when looking for better parameter values, it is reasonable to use coarse training to calculate the fitness. Coarse training can better reflect the results of fine training, and because the number of iterations is less, the results can be obtained faster and the running time of the algorithm can be reduced. Parameters with week coarse training results have been greatly improved after intensive training, but will not interfere with the overall results.

Random search is superior to grid search, Random search takes less time than grid search, while more parameter values can be tried. So this paper uses random search as the baseline model, The heuristic rules of bio-logical evolution can help to optimize the optimal path and find the optimal solution more quickly in the high-dimensional space. The heuristic method can get a better result than the random method, the results of GA and PSO are better than random search.

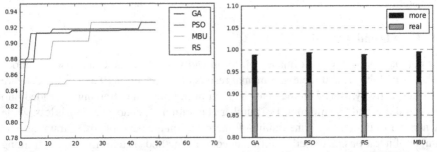

(a) Results of contrast under MNIST dataset   (b) Iteration curve under MNIST dataset

Fig. 3. For MNIST data set, coarse training was firstly used for parameter tuning, and then intensive training was used to verify the effect of parameters. (a) represents the results of contrast under MNIST dataset, and (b) represents the iteration curve under MNIST dataset.

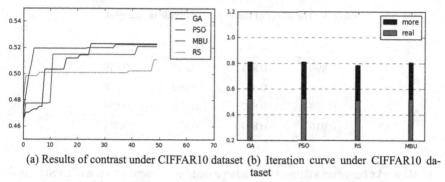

(a) Results of contrast under CIFFAR10 dataset (b) Iteration curve under CIFFAR10 dataset

Fig. 4. For CIFFAR10 data set, coarse training was firstly used for parameter tuning, and then intensive training was used to verify the effect of parameters. (a) represents the results of contrast under CIFFAR10 dataset, and (b) represents the iteration curve under CIFFAR10 dataset.

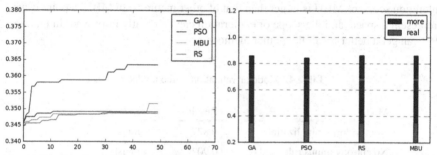

(a) Results of contrast under transport dataset (b) Iteration curve under transport dataset

Fig. 5. For transport data set, coarse training was firstly used for parameter tuning, and then intensive training was used to verify the effect of parameters. (a) represents the results of contrast under transport dataset, and (b) represents the iteration curve under transport dataset.

Table 2. The effect of the number of membranes on the result

	8	16	32	64
8	0.821	0.857	0.824	0.811
16	0.826	0.826	0.861	0.892
32	0.817	0.833	0.916	0.861
64	0.858	0.875	0.894	0.913

Compared with the genetic algorithm, MBU adds the guidance of evolution. The evaluation of each parameter can make the optimization result move forward in a beneficial direction, while the evolutionary rule of genetic algorithm is a kind of weak guidance and contains more random factors. It can be seen from the results of I that the effect of the method in this paper is better than that of genetic algorithm.

Table 3. The effect of the degree of divide on the result

	4	6	8	10
4	0.890	0.891	0.882	0.879
6	0.900	0.901	0.890	0.856
8	0.899	0.887	0.848	0.856
10	0.916	0.891	0.895	0.881

MBU works better on a dataset with a large number of parameters, while PSO works better on a dataset with a small parameter space. The iterative curves of the three data sets are shown in Fig. 3 b, 4 b and 5 b. MBU can be steadily promoted, but the initial speed of promotion is not as good as that of PSO, because MBU's consideration of blocks can increase the search range, but also reduce the search speed. At the same time, the space exploration scope of MBU is larger than that of other methods. In MBU, a point is used to represent a space, and the scope of exploration can be greatly improved. In this way, MBU can get a better result than other methods.

Table 4. Modular validation of the model

Model	Result	Dataset
Non-uniform initialization	0.877	mnist
No entropy minus rule	0.902	mnist
Complete model	0.927	mnist

Therefore, the method proposed in this paper can solve the problem of hyper-parameter optimization well, and the effectiveness of this method is proved by experiments.

4.5 Self-contrast Experiment

In this section, we will compare the effects of the size of fine granularity and the number of membrane of the model on the experimental results. Fine granularity and number of membrane are defined as follows:

Definition 1 Fine granularity: Fine granularity refers to the number of points an interval is divided into, such as the interval [0,128]. When the fine granularity is 4, the interval is evenly divided into 4 parts.

Definition 2 Number of membrane: randomly select an interval for each parameter to form the first film, and then randomly select the second film based on the first membrane. For example, when the fine granularity size of the first layer of membrane is 4, an interval is selected by one parameter to form the membrane, and the second layer of membrane is divided by the fine particle size of 10 on this interval, and then an interval is selected. Then, parameter values are randomly selected from this range.

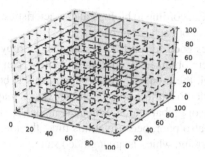

Fig. 6. Membrane space

Table 2 shows the influence of the number of mem-branes on the results. This experiment uses the accuracy of completing the classification task by using CNN as evaluation index, and MNIST is used in the data set. The fine granularity default parameter is [4, 10], which is an empirical value, and 20 iterations. It can be seen that the results do not increase completely according to the in-crease in the number of films. The value on the diagonal line increases first and then decreases. When the number of the first layer of membrane is fixed, with the number of the second layer of membrane increasing, the result shows a trend of increasing first and decreasing. When the number of the second layer of membrane is fixed, with the increase of the number of the second layer, the results also show a trend of increasing at first and then decreasing. When the number of the first layer of membrane is 32 and the number of the second layer of membrane is 32, the optimal value is obtained. As you can see, the number of mem-branes is not completely relevant to the result.

In order to study the influence of fine granularity on the experimental results, fine granularity was used as a parameter to conduct the experiment, and Table 3 was obtained. The accuracy of the classification task realized by CNN was used as the evaluation index, and MNIST was used for the data set. The parameter of membrane number is 32*32 according to the results in Table 2, and the number of iterations is 20. When the size of fine granularity of the first layer is fixed, the result increases gradually with the increase of the fine particle size of the second layer. When the size of fine granularity of the second layer is fixed, the result decreases gradually with the increase of the first layer, and the optimal value is obtained when the first layer is divided into 4 and the second layer is divided into 10. It can be seen that the fine granularity of the first layer is negatively correlated with the result, while the fine granularity of the second layer is positively correlated with the result. The first layer represents the value range of parameters, while the second layer is the refinement of the space of the first layer. The first layer could narrow the search area. The higher the level of refinement of second layer, the better.

4.6   Structural Validation

There are several important parts in our model, and this section discusses the validity of these Settings. The first is the selection of the initial point. This paper uses the uniform sampling method to select the initial point, and thinks that the global search can be carried out by this way. As for the guidance of cell division and merger, entropy minus rule is designed as a guide according to biological characteristics, and logistic regression is used to predict the effect of each set of parameters.

Experiments were designed for uniform values and entropy subtraction rules, and the results in Table 4 were obtained, according to Table 4, can know when initialized randomly take the model, the model of effect is poor, this is because the selection of initial point is effect model to explore space, random values may lead to a value into a local, from which to state of global search. When the model does not follow the entropy minus rule, the effect is also poor, because at this time, the model adopts the mode of random splitting and merging, which is an unguided state.

5   Discussion

In this section, we will discuss some of the issues in this article.

5.1   Membrane Algorithm for Space Exploration

The space explored by the membrane algorithm is a grid. Figure 6 shows the structure of MEAHO in 3-dimensions space. This algorithm explores the space in the form of a grid. A point in the grid is used to reflect the effect of the whole space, which can expand the scope of exploration and is similar to exploring the entire optimized space. This method can search a larger space than the point search. Although there are important discoveries revealed by these studies, there are also limitations. First, the size of the membrane is an important parameter. The size of the membrane greatly affects the results and is an empirical parameter. Second, the selection of initial points should be able to represent the information of the whole space. In this paper, uniform sampling is used to select the initial points. However, the uniform use of a single dimension is insufficient, and multiple dimensions should be considered simultaneously to conduct a uniform sampling. Meanwhile, how to choose a uniform point that can represent the whole space is also at issue.

5.2   Evaluation of Hyperparameter Effect

In this paper, we evaluated the expected influence of the hyperparameters on the results to combine the hyperparameters that might lead to better results, so as to conduct cell division and fusion. In this paper, the evaluations of the different hyperparameters are independent from each other, which increases independence, but also loses a way to obtain more information. The hyperparameters of different dimensions may be coupled, and therefore the interaction between different hyperparameters should be taken into account.

At the same time, the evaluation method should improve the memory. The past situation can be used as a reference for the current state, and the current approach only evaluates the parameters based on the current results. You can set up an experience pool to save past hyperparameter cases to guide the current situation.

5.3 Mechanism of Membrane Evolution

The evolution mechanism of the membrane proposed in this paper is a form of 50/50 division of the hyperparametric space. When the degree of division is greater than 2, part of the space cannot be changed. In order to solve this problem, it is necessary to refine the splitting size of the membrane, conduct the corresponding splitting process according to the degree of membrane division, and then complete the fusion of the membrane on this basis. This can better increase the ability of space exploration.

References

1. Păun, G.: Computing with membranes. J. Comput. Syst. Sci. **61**(1), 108–143 (2000)
2. Martín-Vide, C., Păun, G., Pazos, J., Rodríguez-Patón, A.: Tissue P systems. Theor. Comput. Sci. **296**(2), 295–326 (2003)
3. Alsalibi, B. et al. A comprehensive survey on the recent variants and applications of membrane-inspired evolutionary algorithms. Archives of Computational Methods in Engineering: 1–17 (2022) https://doi.org/10.1007/s11831-021-09693-5
4. Pan, L., Wu, T., Su, Y., Vasilakos, A.V.: Cell-like spikingneural P systems with request rules. IEEE Trans. Nanobiosci. **16**(6), 513–522 (2017)
5. Peng, H., et al.: Spiking neural P systems with multiple channels. Neural Netw. **95**, 66–71 (2017)
6. Young, G O. Synthetic structure of industrial plastics, in Plastics, 2nd ed., vol. 3, J. Peters, Ed. New York, NY, USA: McGraw-Hill, pp. 15–64. (1964)
7. Chen, W K. Linear Networks and Systems. Belmont, CA, USA:Wadsworth, pp. 123–135 (1993)
8. Bergstra, J., et al. Algorithms for hyper-parameter optimization .In: 25th Annual Conference on Neural Information Processing Systems (NIPS 2011), vol. 24. Neural Information Processing Systems Foundation (2011)
9. LeCun, Y., Bengio, Y., Hinton, G.: Deep learning. nature **521**(7553), 436–444 (2015)
10. Kennedy, J., Eberhart, R. Particle swarm optimization. In: Proceedings of ICNN'95-International Conference on Neural Networks. Vol. 4. IEEE. (1995)
11. Whitley, D.: A genetic algorithm tutorial. Stat. Comput. **4**(2), 65–85 (1994)
12. Bergstra, J., Bengio, Y. Random search for hyper-parameter optimization. J. Mach. Learn. Res. 13.2 (2012)
13. David, Omid E., Greental, I. Genetic algorithms for evolving deep neural networks. In: Proceedings of the Companion Publication of the 2014 Annual Conference on Genetic and Evolutionary Computation. (2014)
14. Hutter, F., Hoos, H H., Leyton-Brown, K. Sequential model-based optimization for general algorithm configuration. In: International Conference on Learning And Intelligent Optimization. Springer, Berlin, Heidelberg. (2011)
15. Juanjuan, H.E., Jianhua, X.I.A.O., Zehui, S.H.A.O.: An adaptive membrane algorithm for solving combinatorial optimization problems. Acta Math. Sci. **34**(5), 1377–1394 (2014)
16. Lorenzo, P R., et al. Particle swarm optimization for hyper-parameter selection in deep neural networks. In: Proceedings of The Genetic and Evolutionary Computation Conference. (2017)
17. Montavon, G., Orr, G.B., Müller, K.-R. (eds.): Neural Networks: Tricks of the Trade: Second Edition. Springer Berlin Heidelberg, Berlin, Heidelberg (2012). https://doi.org/10.1007/978-3-642-35289-8
18. Nishida, Taishin Y. Membrane algorithms. International Workshop on Membrane Computing. Springer, Berlin, Heidelberg. (2005). https://doi.org/10.1007/11603047_4

19. Shahriari, B., Swersky, K., Wang, Z., Adams, R.P., de Freitas, N.: Taking the human out of the loop: a review of bayesian optimization. Proc. IEEE **104**(1), 148–175 (2016). https://doi.org/10.1109/JPROC.2015.2494218

20. Xiao, J., Huang, Y., Cheng, Z., He, J., Niu, Y.: A hybrid membrane evolutionary algorithm for solving constrained optimization problems. Optik **125**(2), 897–902 (2014). https://doi.org/10.1016/j.ijleo.2013.08.032

21. Zhang, G.-X., Gheorghe, M., Chao-Zhong, W.: A quantum-inspired evolutionary algorithm based on P systems for knapsack problem. Fund. Inform. **87**(1), 93–116 (2008)

22. Zhang, G., et al. A Novel Membrane Algorithm Based on Particle Swarm Optimization for Solving Broadcasting Problems. J. UCS 18.13: 1821–1841. (2012)

23. Zhang, G., Cheng, J., Gheorghe, M., Meng, Q.: A hybrid approach based on differential evolution and tissue membrane systems for solving constrained manufacturing parameter optimization problems. Appl. Soft Comput. **13**(3), 1528–1542 (2013). https://doi.org/10.1016/j.asoc.2012.05.032

24. Zhang, Gexiang, et al. A population-membrane-systeminspired evolutionary algorithm for distribution network reconfiguration. Chinese J. Electron. 23.3: 437–441. (2014)

25. Pan, L., Martin-Vide, C.: Solving multidimensional 0–1 knapsack problem by P systems with input and active membranes. J. Parallel and Distrib. Comput. **65**(12), 1578–1584 (2005)

26. Pérez-Jiménez, Mario J., and Agustin Riscos-Núnez. A lineartime solution to the knapsack problem using P systems with active membranes. In: International workshop on membrane computing. Springer, Berlin, Heidelberg. (2003)

27. Attacking NP-complete problems: Liu, Xiangrong, et al. The power of time-free tissue P systems. Neurocomputing **159**, 151–156 (2015)

28. Guo, P., Quan, C., Chen, H.: MEAMVC: A membrane evolutionary algorithm for solving minimum vertex cover problem. IEEE Access **7**, 60774–60784 (2019)

29. Golpira, H., Bevrani, H.: Application of GA optimization for automatic generation control design in an interconnected power system. Energy Convers. Manage. **52**(5), 2247–2255 (2011)

30. Delgarm, N., et al.: Multi-objective optimization of the building energy performance: a simulation-based approach by means of particle swarm optimization (PSO). Appl. Energy **170**, 293–303 (2016)

31. Zhu, H., Wang, Yi., Wang, K., Chen, Y.: Particle swarm optimization (PSO) for the constrained portfolio optimization problem. Expert Syst. Appl. **38**(8), 10161–10169 (2011). https://doi.org/10.1016/j.eswa.2011.02.075

32. Leporati, Alberto, and Pagani, D. A membrane algorithm for the min storage problem. In: International Workshop on Membrane Computing. Springer, Berlin, Heidelberg. (2006)

33. Bischl, B., Binder, M., Lang, M., et al.: Hyperparameter optimization: Foundations, algorithms, best practices, and open challenges. Wiley Interdisc. Rev.: Data Min. Knowl. Discovery **13**(2), e1484 (2023)

34. Pelikan, Martin, David E. Goldberg, Erick Cantú-Paz. BOA: The bayesian optimization algorithm. In: Proceedings of The Genetic and Evolutionary Computation Conference GECCO-99. Vol. 1. (1999)

35. Davies, P.C.W., Rieper, E., Tuszynski, J.A.: Self-organization and entropy reduction in a living cell. Biosystems **111**(1), 1–10 (2013). https://doi.org/10.1016/j.biosystems.2012.10.005

36. G. Päun, Computing with membranes: attacking NP-complete problems, in Unconventional Models Computer. London, U.K.: Springer, pp. 94–115. (2001)

37. Guo, P., Hou, M., Ye, L.: MEATSP: a membrane evolutionary algorithm for solving TSP. IEEE Access **8**, 199081–199096 (2020). https://doi.org/10.1109/ACCESS.2020.3035058

Automatic Detection and Inspection Robot of All-Weather Urban Comprehensive Corridor Based on Voiceprint Detection

Wei Ding$^{(\boxtimes)}$ and Ruining Hu

Anhui Institute of Information Enginee, Wuhu 241000, China
1428150543@qq.com

Abstract. Aiming at the fire safety hazards of urban comprehensive corridors, an all-weather urban comprehensive corridor automatic detection and inspection robot is designed, and voiceprint recognition technology and computer vision technology are combined to realize the full coverage and all-weather automatic detection of urban comprehensive corridors. The robot can independently plan the route and realize the identification and positioning of the fire escape, thereby realizing the real-time detection of the fire escape. The experimental results show that the robot can not only detect the fire passage but also carry out real-time early warning and positioning of the fire passage. Through the application of voiceprint recognition technology, the all-weather automatic detection of urban comprehensive corridors is realized. At the same time, through the application of image recognition technology and computer vision technology, the robot can independently plan the route and realize the real-time detection of fire escape.

Keywords: urban integrated corridor · Automatic detection · Voiceprint recognition · robot

1 Introduction

With the continuous acceleration of urbanization, the fire hazard of urban comprehensive corridors is gradually increasing. Although the detection technology for fire exits has been developed for many years, it also brings certain difficulties to the detection of fire exits because urban integrated corridors often appear at the intersection of different functional areas.[1] At the same time, because urban integrated corridors usually use a large amount of energy-intensive equipment, this also leads to easy fire accidents in urban integrated corridors.

Traditionally, fire escapes have been detected using cameras to monitor them and transmit video and images in real time. Due to the large number of cables and communication cables in the urban comprehensive corridor and the existence of complex environments such as interlacing, it is difficult to achieve fire escape detection targets using camera monitoring. For the real-time detection of fire escapes, [2] the main method currently used is to combine image recognition technology and computer vision technology to achieve real-time detection of fire escapes. On this basis, domestic scholars

M. Zhang et al. (Eds.): CCF NCCA 2023, CCIS 1959, pp. 273–281, 2024.
https://doi.org/10.1007/978-981-99-8764-1_21

put forward a new urban comprehensive corridor automatic detection technology, that is, real-time detection technology for fire passages, which mainly uses voiceprint recognition technology to convert sound signals into electrical signals and complete real-time detection of fire passages [3]. The method first uses voiceprint recognition technology to classify and identify various sounds in the urban comprehensive corridor and then collects, sorts and different kinds of sounds through robots to realize real-time detection of fire escapes [4]. However, due to the difficulty of sound classification and recognition in this method, there are also certain restrictions on the collection range of sound in this method. Therefore, by the characteristics of sound in urban comprehensive corridors, this paper designs an all-weather urban comprehensive corridor automatic detection robot based on voiceprint recognition technology and computer vision technology. The robot is designed to autonomously plan paths and enable real-time detection of fire escapes, thus providing a solution for fire safety issues in urban integrated corridors [5].

2 Inspection Robot System Design

The robot system consists of 1 main control unit, 2 motor modules, 1 voiceprint recognition module, 1 path planning module and 2 actuators. Among them, the main control unit and the motor module interact with the host computer through wireless data communication. The robot can realize the automatic detection of the fire passage through voice control of the camera lens and can independently plan the robot's travel route in the fire passage and identify and locate the fire escape in real time [6]. In addition, the robot can warn of the fire escape according to the shape of the fire passage and can also locate the fire passage according to the location of the fire passage to realize real-time detection of the fire escape. At the same time, the robot can update and identify the route in real time according to information such as fire passages, fire emergency plans, and historical fire records to realize the automatic detection of urban comprehensive corridors around the clock [7].

The system sends data to the upper computer program through the wireless module during normal operation, and the upper computer then transmits the data to the STM32 lower computer. The lower computer transmits a signal to drive the motor to start, and the lower computer program accepts a feedback signal to realize the adjustment of the walking speed so that the robot can walk in the urban comprehensive corridor (as shown in Fig. 1).

The sensor equipped with the robot uses a high-definition infrared thermal imager and a visible light camera to achieve real-time detection of temperature and brightness. High-precision sensors are used to construct a three-dimensional model of the environment within the detection range of the robot, real-time calculation of spatial coordinates and motion attitude parameters through the environmental model, and real-time trajectory tracking, trajectory planning and obstacle avoidance functions on the three-dimensional map [8]. When an abnormal situation is found, the abnormal facility can be located and identified through the camera screen and voice, and the result can be fed back to the background command center. When abnormal conditions occur, video replay, panoramic linkage, manual confirmation and other operations can be performed. The robot is equipped with a set of data processing terminals based on voiceprint recognition

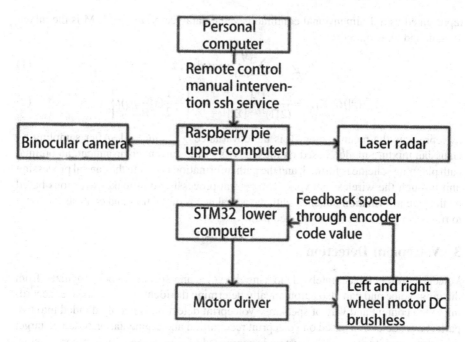

Fig. 1. Detecting the robot hardware system

technology, collects the sound in the environment through the microphone, and then uses the voiceprint recognition algorithm to process the collected sound signals to determine different sound sources [9]. Then, the sound signal heard is sent out through the speaker, and the voiceprint signal is collected through the microphone for processing. Finally, the processed voiceprint signal is sent to the host computer for judgment to realize the voiceprint recognition and early warning of the fire channel. At the same time, according to the length of the passage to be detected and the position information, the positioning of the fire escape is realized.

Path planning is one of the most important technologies to realize the autonomous walking of the robot. The path planning module includes three main parts of environment perception, obstacle perception and autonomous path planning, in which the environment perception module is responsible for collecting surrounding environmental information during the robot's travel, including sound, temperature and humidity, and processing this information after sending the information to the central processing unit through the wireless network [10]. The obstacle awareness module is responsible for sending the location and shape of obstacles to the central processing unit via the wireless network. The autonomous path planning module is the core module to realize robot path planning.

The path planning module obtains all speech samples in the current environment through the voiceprint recognition module, uses the Gaussian hybrid model method to perform speech classification recognition, and then obtains the speech samples in the current environment [11]. A Gaussian mixture model is a parametric probability density model expressed as a weighted sum of the density of Gaussian components. x is represented as a d-dimensional continuous value data vector, ω_i i = 1, M is the mixed weight, and its formula is:

$$P(x|\lambda) = \sum_{i=1}^{M} \omega_i g(x|\mu_i, \Sigma_i) \tag{1}$$

$$g(x|\mu_i, \Sigma_i) = \frac{1}{(2\Pi)^{D/2}|\Sigma_i|^{1/2}} exp\left\{-\frac{1}{2}(x - \mu_i)'\right\} \tag{2}$$

μ_i represents the mean vector Σ_i is the covariance $\sum_{i=1}^{M} \omega_i = 1$. After sampling by Gaussian mixture model, based on the analysis of the current environment, an optimal path planning scheme is formed, and the path information is sent to the central processing unit through the wireless network. The central processing unit makes decisions based on the path information obtained with the actual needs of the user and controls the robot to run according to a certain planned path.

3 Voiceprint Detection

Voiceprint refers to accurately identifying the voice and speaker to be recognized from the input voice and can also automatically determine the identity of the speaker according to the content and way of speaking. Voiceprint detection is mainly divided into two parts: target detection based on voiceprint recognition and segmentation based on target semantics, and its recognition system is composed of sound acquisition, preprocessing, feature extraction module and other modules, through the preprocessing, feature extraction and pattern classification of the collected voice signal, to realize the judgment of whether there is a specific person identity in the voice signal, and its system framework is shown in Fig. 2.

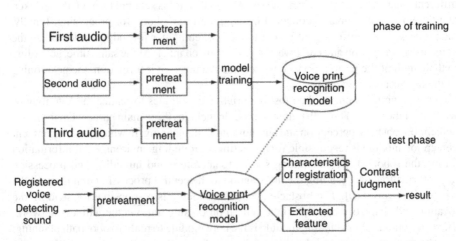

Fig. 2. Frame of voiceprint recognition system for inspection robot

This software uses to give full play to the system performance but also conducive to code modification and improvement, this software system is mainly divided into sound acquisition, main thread, registration and recognition overall process is shown in Fig. 3.

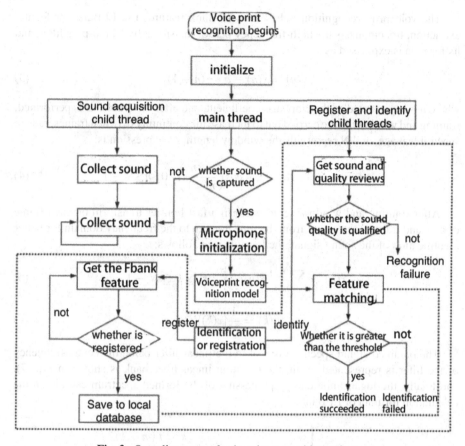

Fig. 3. Overall process of voiceprint recognition software

The technology has good robustness to various environments and background noise and can be effectively identified even in strong noise environments. Voiceprint recognition is a speech recognition method based on deep learning, computer vision, acoustics and other related technologies, which also has good performance in large noise environments. Voiceprint recognition technology can not only realize the determination of human identity but also realize the determination of people and objects and can distinguish between target objects and background sounds.

4 Key Technology of Voiceprint Recognition

The quality of the voiceprint recognition software system mainly depends on the voiceprint recognition algorithm, which refers to the application of speech recognition technology to process speech in a specific environment so that it can reflect the identity of the speaker. Similar to fingerprint recognition algorithms, voiceprint recognition algorithms are biotechnology that uses acoustic features for identity identification.

The voiceprint recognition is based on LFBank features use LFBank for feature extraction, firs emphasis the high-frequency part of the signal by a high-pass filter, and its formula is expressed as:

$$y(n) = x(n) - a * x(n - 1) \tag{3}$$

where a is represented as the emphasis coefficient, and after the emphasis is performed, framing and windowing are carried out to increase the continuity between frames, reduce spectral leakage, and N represents the window length, its expression is:

$$\omega(n, a) = (1 - a) - a * cos\left(\frac{2\pi n}{n - 1}\right), \quad 0 \leq n \leq N - 1 \tag{4}$$

After framing and windowing, to perform a fast Fourier transform on each frame of data and transfer the signal from the time domain to the frequency domain for better identification of the sound signal, the formula is as follows:

$$x(k) = \sum_{n=0}^{N-1} x(n)e^{\frac{-j2\pi k}{N}}, 0 \leq k \leq N - 1 \tag{5}$$

$$p(k) = \frac{1}{N}|x(k)|^2 \tag{6}$$

The obtained signal spectrum is sent to the linear filter bank, the center frequency of the filter is represented by m, the resulting linear filter bank is shown in Eq. (7), and finally, the logarithmic energy processing of the formed spectrum can obtain the calculation formula of LFBank:

$$L_m(k) = \begin{cases} 0 & k < f(m-1) \\ \frac{k-f(m-1)}{f(m)-f(m-1)}, f(m-1) \leq k \leq f(m) \\ \frac{f(m+1)-k}{f(m+1)-f(m)}, f(m) & < k \leq f(m+1) \\ 0 & k > f(m+1) \end{cases} \tag{7}$$

$$S_L(m) = \ln\left(\sum_{k=0}^{N-1} |X(k)|^2 L_m(k)\right), 0 \leq m \leq M \tag{8}$$

Since the working environment of the robot is dynamically changing, it is impossible to move according to the preset route every time, and the loss function is required to reduce the error rate, which combines the classification loss function based on the interval and the prototype cosine loss function based on small samples:

$$L = L_{AMS} + L_{CP} \tag{9}$$

$$L_{AMS} = -\frac{1}{N} \sum_{n=1}^{N} log \frac{e^{S_{n,n}}}{\sum_{j=1}^{N} e^{S_{n,j}}} \tag{10}$$

$$L_{CP} = -\frac{1}{N} \sum_{n=1}^{N} log \frac{e^{s(cos\theta_{y_i} - m)}}{e^{s(cos\theta_{y_i} - m)} + \sum_{j \neq y_i} e^{scos\theta_j}} \tag{11}$$

The loss function clearly encourages the spacing of voiceprint classes to increase, and in the voiceprint feature, the metric space can be optimized by finding prototypes close to the target sample, the distance between the same kind can be reduced, and the loss function can effectively deal with the sample attribution problem and improve the robustness of the model.

5 Experimental Report

In this project, the functional test of the robot is carried out through experiments to verify the practicability of its system and the advanced algorithm of its algorithm. In this experiment, a highly sensitive PanasonicWM-62A acoustic sensor was used to acquire signals, and its parameters are shown in Table 1.

Table 1. Physical parameters of sensors

parameter	Parameter value
sensitivity	−45 ± 4 dB(0 dB = 1 V/Pa,1 kHz)
Signal-to-noise ratio(S/N)	> 58 dB
impedance	< 2.2k Ω
Detection frequency range	20 ~ 16000 Hz

In order to verify the effectiveness of the algorithm proposed in this paper, a robot platform is built in the laboratory, and the proposed algorithm is experimentally verified. In the experiment, a camera and a microphone were used to collect voiceprint images of the fire scene and fire escape, respectively, and saved as a database. By filtering and threshold segmentation of the images in the database, the voiceprint images of the fire passage and fire escape are obtained. A simulated environment was set up in the laboratory, and three fire escapes were set up accuracy of the voiceprint recognition effect in different pipeline environments was explored using a variety of environments and voiceprint recognition as independent variables, and the percentages in Table 2 the accuracy a total of 540 experiments.

Table 2 that the recognition rate reaches more than 90% under the effect of slight noise in the pipeline, and the robot can effectively detect the fire passage and fire passage and can also warn the fire passage after identifying it.

Table 2. Effects of voiceprint recognition system in various environments

environment	Time		
	3s	6s	10s
Silence in the pipe (approx. 25 dB)	95.0%	99.2%	99.5%
Slight noise in the pipe (approx. 15 dB)	90.5%	95.2%	97.2%
Large noise in the pipeline (approx. 0 dB)	80.8%	88.2%	92.1%

6   Conclusion

Aiming at the fire safety hazards of urban comprehensive corridors, this paper proposes an all-weather urban comprehensive corridor automatic detection and inspection robot, which has the following advantages:

(1) All-weather detection: Due to the characteristics of fixed position of sound sources when the robot extracts sound signals proposed in this paper, the robot can detect urban comprehensive corridors around the clock.

(2) Real-time early warning: when abnormal situations such as fire are detected, the robot can carry out real-time early warning and positioning of the fire escape;

(3) Autonomous route planning: The robot can autonomously plan the route and detect the fire escape in real time.

References

1. CUI Lin,WANG Zhiyue. Research on voiceprint recognition based on LFBank and FBank hybrid features. Comput. Sci.2022,49(S2):621–625
2. GUO Xin,LUO Chengfang,DENG Aiwen. Design and implementation of voiceprint recognition system in open scene based on deep learning [J] J Nanjing Univ. Inform. Sci. Technol. (Natural Science Edition) 2021, 13(05):526–532.DOI:https://doi.org/10.13878/j.cnki.jnuist. 2021.05.003
3. Cheung S Y, Pravin v. Traffic surveillance by wireless sensor networks: final report[R].University of California,Berkeley,Jan.2007
4. LIN Linghui,ZHANG Yongfu,ZHANG Xinyue,ZHANG Fangwei,XIA Mingqian. Design of security system based on voiceprint recognition [J].Inf. Communication, 2020(06):112–114
5. Sun, Z., Bebis, G., Miller, R.: On-road vehicle detection: a review. IEEE Trans. Pattern Anal. Mach. Intell. **28**(5), 694–711 (2006). https://doi.org/10.1109/TPAMI.2006.104
6. ZHANG Yujie,ZHANG Zan. Application of DenseNet in voiceprint recognition [J].Computer Engineering and Science,2022,44(01), pp .132–137
7. Limin, L.I.U., Jiwu, J.I.N.G.: Rapidly developing biometric identification standard specification in China [J]. China Inform. Secur. 2, 68–72 (2019)
8. Reynolds, D.A., Rose, R.C.: Robust text-independent speaker identification using Gaussian mixture speaker models [J]. IEEE Trans. Speech Audio Process.S **3**(1), 72–83 (1995)
9. Desplanques B, Thienpondt J, Demuynck K. ECAPATDNN: emphasized channel attention, propagation and aggregation in TDNN Based Speaker Verification [J] . arXiv e-print, 2020, arXiv: 2005, p. 07143

10. Nagrani A, Chung J S, Zisserman A. VoxCeleb: a largescale speaker identification dataset[C] ‖ Interspeech.In: ISCA: ISCA, 2017. DOI: 10. 21437/interspeech., pp.2017–950 (2017)
11. Kye S M, Kwon Y, Chung J S. Cross attentive pooling for speaker verification [C] ‖2021 IEEE Spoken Language Technology Workshop (SLT) . January 19 - 22, 2021, Shenzhen, China. IEEE, 2021: 294-300

Author Index

Printed in the United States
by Baker & Taylor Publisher Services